The Life *and* Artistry *of* Maria Olenina-d'Alheim

THE

Life *and* Artistry

OF

Maria
Olenina-d'Alheim

ALEXANDER TUMANOV

Translated *by* Christopher Barnes

The University of Alberta Press

Published by
The University of Alberta Press
Ring House 2
Edmonton, Alberta, Canada T6G 2E1

Copyright © The University of Alberta Press 2000
ISBN 0–88864–328–4

Canadian Cataloguing in Publication Data

Tumanov, Alexander, 1930–
  The life and artistry of Maria Olenina-d'Alheim

  Translation of: "Ona i muzyka, i slovo—"
  Includes some text in Russian.
  ISBN 0–88864–328–4

  1. Olenina-d'Al'geim, M. A. (Mar'i'a Alekseevna), 1869–1970. 2.
Mezzo-sopranos—Russia—Biography. I. Title.
ML420.O455T9213 2000   782.42168'092   C00–910038–5

Printed on acid-free paper. ∞
Printed and bound in Canada by Friesens, Altona, Manitoba.

The University of Alberta Press gratefully acknowledges the support received for its publishing program
from The Canada Council for the Arts. In addition, we also gratefully acknowledge the financial support
of the Government of Canada through the Book Publishing Industry Development Program for our
publishing activities.

Photograph and Illustration Credits

University of Alberta Archives, Accession No. 89–136—
pp. xv, 53, 56–57, 65–67, 75, 87, 146, 161, 166–67, 168, 171, 178–79, 192, 213.

Courtesy of the Glinka State Museum of Musical Culture, Moscow—
pp. 5, 19, 26, 37, 45, 91, 95, 112, 135, 151, 163, 199, 207.

Courtesy of Muzyka Publishers, Moscow—
pp. 23, 29, 30, 31, 32, 33, 101, 113, 114, 187 (from *M.P. Musorgski* (1989)), 191, 278 (from *M.P. Musorgski*
(1989)), 287.

Private archive of Alexander Tumanov—
pp. 153, 154–57, 159 (Photograph by Vitali Reif), 208–9, 211, 235.

Sovetskaya muzyka 7 (1964)—p. 40.

Deutsche Fotothek, Dresden, from Horst Seeger, *Musiklexikon* (Leipzig: Veb Deuscher Verlag fur Musik,
1966)—p. 116.

Courtesy of Bibliothèque Musicale, Gustave Mahler—pp. 252–55.

To Alla Tumanova,

my first reader, critic, and friend

Contents

Abbreviations

AAO   A.A. Olenin, Reminiscences and letters (GMMC, fond 39, no. 127). See also his "Moi vospominaniya o Balakireve," in *M.A. Balakirev, Vospominaniya i pis'ma* (Leningrad, 1962).

BN   Bibliothèque Nationale, Paris.

BMGM   Bibliothèque Musicale Gustav Mahler, Paris.

BNB   M.A. Olenina-d'Alheim, Autobiographical materials (Black Notebook), Manuscript (GMMC, fond 39, no. 4607).

DC   Transcript of taped interviews with Doda Conrad, Blois, 11 December 1991, Manuscript (University of Alberta Archives, Accession No. 89–200).

DP   *Dom pesni* (monthly magazine of the House of Song), issues 1–14, February 1910-January 1911 (University of Alberta Archives, Accession No. 89–200–13).

GMMC   The Glinka State Central Museum of Musical Culture, Moscow.

KRAVT M.A. Olenina-d'Alheim, "Kratkaya avtobiografiya" (Short biography), Manuscript, March-April 1946 (in GMMC, fond 256, no. 4971).

NV Andrei Bely, *Nachalo veka* (Chicago, 1966).

SV M.A. Olenina-d'Alheim, "Snovidenie i vospominaniya" (Dream and Recollections), Manuscript (University of Alberta Archives, Accession No. 89–200–1).

UAA University of Alberta Archives.

ZM M.A. Olenina-d'Alheim, *Zavety Musorgskogo* (*The Mussorgsky Legacy*), trans. from French by V.I. Grechaninova (Moscow: Muzyka i zhizn', 1910). Originally published in French as Marie Olénine d'Alheim, *Le Legs de Moussorgski* (Paris: Eugène Rey, 1908).

Acknowledgements

This book is based largely on materials that I received in 1963–64 from Maria Olenina-d'Alheim herself, and which are now kept in the University of Alberta Archives. It also makes use of archival documents kindly placed at my disposal by the Glinka State Central Museum of Musical Culture in Moscow, thanks to the efforts of the Museum's Deputy Director I.A. Medvedeva and museum staff members, I. Palazhchenko and K.S. Balasanyan. I was also able to carry out work in the Saltykov-Shchedrin State National Library in St. Petersburg, the Bibliothèque Nationale in Paris (with thanks to P. Vidal, head of the Music Section), and the Bibliothèque Musicale Gustav Mahler, Paris, where I was kindly assisted by Mme Blavette. In addition I was able to consult archives made available to me by the International Fund of Nadya and Lily Boulanger, Paris; by Vadim Kozovoi, curator of the archive of Pyotr Petrovich Suvchinsky (Pierre Souvchinsky); and by J.C. Honneger, curator of the Claire Croiza archive in Geneva. My meetings, interviews and correspondence with Doda Conrad, Madeleine Milhaud, Arbie Orenstein, were of invaluable assistance, as also were the reminiscences of Natalya Sergeyevna and Olga Sergeyevna Solovyova, the nieces of Maria Olenina.

My researches into the life and work of Maria Olenina-d'Alheim would also have been impossible without the help of my students, friends and colleagues who collaborated closely with me at various stages. I recall with special gratitude the contribution of students, graduates and assistants at the Slavic Department of the University of Alberta, Andrew Rodomar, Marta Gibson, Barbara Brown, Patricia Andrews and Oona Schreiner, who helped shoulder many of my initial problems, when the sheer amount of material collected seemed insuperable. Priceless assistance was provided by Igor Evgenyevich Reif, my representative at the Moscow "Muzyka" publishing house, who not only supervised production of the Russian edition but earlier also performed amost impossible feats in helping me gather materials for this volume. Bella Chernis, my faithful liaison assistant, shortened the thousands of miles separating Russia and Canada by carrying out a multitude of requests during the period when I was collecting material from the Glinka Museum in Moscow. I also owe an immense debt of gratitude to Pavel Gerasimovich Lisitsian who invested much time and effort to ensure the success of this vital stage of the operation.

Of invaluable assistance to me, too, were the critical observations and advice of Professor Efim Etkind, who read my original Russian manuscript with the eye of both an interested reader and scrupulous editor. I am also deeply grateful to my colleagues, Professor Nikolai Žekulin of the University of Calgary, Professor Caryl Emerson from Princeton, and Professor Christopher Barnes of the University of Toronto, for their critical reading of the manuscript and helpful advice. I also wish to thank Vladimir Tumanov for assistance with work on the French texts from various sources in Moscow, Paris and Geneva. Invaluable too was the support of my first professional reader in Russia, *Novyi mir* editor N.M. Dolotova. My deep gratitude goes to Mary Mahoney-Robson, the editor at the University of Alberta Press, and Brenda Burgess, the designer, for their most thoughtful and sensitive work on my book.

The English-language edition of this book was made possible thanks to generous financial support from Dr. Natalka Horeczko, which I hereby gratefully acknowledge.

Preface

The history of culture, like history in general, frequently contains blank spots and missing links when an outstanding personality or an important phenomenon seems to be erased from people's memory. At such moments surprised questions are often raised: How did an historic event take place, and who helped bring it about? How was it, for instance, that the music of Mussorgsky acquired its first real audience in France rather than in Russia? How did it then become an essential part of the repertoire in Russia? How did Mussorgsky's music reach western audiences in the first place? And how did western music-lovers come to regard the name of Mussorgsky as a byword for "Russianness," no less than the names of Tolstoy and Dostoevsky in literature?

There is no single clear-cut answer to such questions, and it does not rest simply with the activity of one single person. The establishment of Mussorgsky's name in Russia and the West is still a subject of interest for music scholars and historians. It came about thanks to the efforts of many people—musicians and composers, and public figures with an interest in music. But first and foremost, it was due to the efforts of musical performers. And because of the ephemeral and fleeting nature of their activity, especially in the pregramophone era, these performers in particular have been obscured by the "blank spots" in musical history. This is where forgotten names occur. And among them, there is one in particular that is known—and even then sometimes only by hearsay—only to Mussorgsky specialists, a name virtually unknown to the general music-loving public, and one that does not always figure even in published histories of Russian music. The name is that of Maria Alexeyevna Olenina-d'Alheim (in Russian transcription: d'Al'geim).

Nevertheless, in her time Maria Olenina was a front-ranking figure in the world of Russian and French song—what in Russian is termed "vocal chamber performance," the equivalent of the Lied or chanson. Her artistry was bound up with significant musical and social developments in Russia and France at the turn of the nineteenth and twentieth centuries, and it had a marked effect on the fate of Mussorgsky's music both in Russia and abroad. As a contemporary of the so-called "Mighty Handful" (*Moguchaya kuchka*) and their campaign for a national Russian school of music, and as a powerful advocate of the vocal compositions by members of that movement, Olenina's career as performer and musical public figure was a long and brilliant one. Her activities in Russia and abroad had a great impact on her contemporaries and to this day their influence is felt in the traditions of vocal performance. In 1908 she set up a musical society called "Dom pesni" (the House of Song, known in France as "La Maison du Lied") that was designed to assist in propagating the vocal music of Mussorgsky. Through its promotion of lectures, concerts, conferences, publications and international competitions, the House of Song became an unique institution with a reputation extending far beyond the bounds of Russia. The activities of Olenina-d'Alheim and her husband, music critic and writer Pierre d'Alheim, in Paris, Brussels, London and other cultural centres influenced the overall musical climate of Europe. Every publication by the House of Song carried an epigraph with Mussorgsky's own rallying call: "K novym beregam!" (Onward towards new shores!) And these words extended beyond the House of Song. The whole of Maria Olenina-d'Alheim's own life and artistry was directed towards new and distant shores of future musical development.

As a pupil of Alexandra Molas and Yulia Platonova (who sang the role of Marina Mniszech's role in the première of Mussorgsky's *Boris Godunov*), Olenina made a significant mark on Russian classical song performance. She was one of the first Russian singers to regard the poetic text itself as a vital source of vocal interpretation. As one of the Petersburg critics observed, Olenina had the ability to "tell the song," uniting words and music in an art of vocal declamation. The result of this was to reveal a new artistic truth, which became the main criterion and touchstone of her remarkable work. Olenina-d'Alheim was one of the first Russian performers to reveal the artistic possibilities of Russian song, not just to a Russian audience but to a European audience. She was the first Russian singer to lay the foundations of the genre of "vocal chamber performance," and can be regarded as having been the first performer of Russian Lieder—the first "chamber singer."

Despite this, not only was Olenina's voice never recorded on disc, but her very name is practically unknown—both to the general public and even to the scholarly community—and her artistry has been almost forgotten. There are only a few items in various periodicals, including a short article about her life, printed in the journal *Sovetskaya muzyka* (Soviet Music) in 1960. To this day, not a single book has thrown light on any aspect of Olenina's work—especially her role in introducing the nineteenth-century Russian vocal repertoire to a European public.

Maria Olenina-d'Alheim has long deserved to have a book written about her: her achievement illuminates an obscure, but very interesting and important, aspect of the history of Russian, French and western musical culture. This immediately became clear to me when I first met her in Moscow in 1963. As a correspondent for the journal *Sovetskaya muzyka*, I was assigned to write an article about the singer who had returned to Russia after living abroad for almost fifty years. But any attempt to hold a normal interview with her failed utterly: while she had full possession of her faculties, her memory was so fragmentary that there was no way of getting a coherent story out of her. At the same time, when talking about individual works of music, the freshness and originality of her remarks—and of her memory— were astounding. She remembered literally every note, every word, and every rest in Mussorgsky's entire vocal repertoire. She also recalled her meetings with Lev Tolstoy, Balakirev, Stasov, Tchaikovsky, Alfred Cortot, Darius Milhaud, Maurice Ravel, and Claude Debussy, to name just a few. How was I to find my way into the world of this singer, who for so many decades had been a living representative of the vocal school of the Mighty Handful? How could one reproduce her manner of performance that had never been recorded? How was one to reconstruct her artistic technique? My task was not an easy one, and there was not much time left: Maria Olenina was 94 years old.

Then I found a solution: What if one were to bring a few young singers to her and perform some of Mussorgsky's repertoire? These master classes recorded on tape might serve as a reflection of Olenina's own artistry. After a first meeting, with singer Galina Pisarenko and pianist Vera Shubina taking part, it became evident that in my hands I had some fascinating and unique material. Although by that time Olenina could no longer sing herself, she could express her ideas clearly and replaced actual singing by a peculiar form of expressive speech, or recitative. The material we collected in this way was a revelation: it indicated an obvious direct correlation between the speech phrase, as pronounced by Olenina, and the musical phrase set down by the composer. This was a rich source of material for studying the relationship between text and music. Soon after that I published an article, "U sovremennitsy Stasova" (With a Contemporary of Stasov) in *Sovetskaya muzyka*, no. 7 (1964) that dealt with Olenina's interpretation of Mussorgsky's cycle *The Nursery*. Although this publication did not do proper justice to the wealth of ideas in Olenina's own performances, it was an attempt to demonstrate her profound understanding of the artistic imagery of Mussorgsky's *Nursery*, in a way that came as close as possible to the composer's own conception of it.

Subsequently, further master classes with Olenina-d'Alheim were recorded on tape. My own dealings with her proved extremely interesting, and eventually we became sufficiently close for her to present me with a series of her archival documents and other materials. Among them was the manuscript of her reminiscences, entitled "Snovidenie i vospominaniya" (Dream and Recollections). It was her wish that some of these documents be published, and she believed I might be able to help in this.

While still living in the Soviet Union, I contemplated writing a book about Maria Olenina-d'Alheim, but circumstances conspired against this. Then, unfortunately, our meetings came to an end. Subsequently, for personal and other reasons, I was prevented from pursuing my plan. It was only much later, when I was in the West and working in the Slavic Department of the University of Alberta in Canada, that I returned to the idea of writing a book about Olenina.

I wanted not only to publish as much as possible of the singer's own memoirs, which are written with a lively talent, but also, as it were, to bring Olenina herself back to life. In this account of her life which lasted 101 years, beginning just eight years after Russia's serfs were emancipated in 1861 and running on into the late 1960s, I have tried to allow Olenina's own voice to speak as much as possible, with her own unique tone and accent.

For this reason I abandoned the idea of writing a conventional life story and conceived the idea of a *documentary* biography. In it the story of Olenina's life and work would be recounted not by some chronicler, but by Olenina herself, her friends, critics, members of her public, opponents and supporters. The book as a whole would speak with the voice of her time. While still considering this book and planning a trip to Moscow, Leningrad and Paris in search of material, I was once sitting at home in Edmonton when I decided after many years to listen again to the tape-recording of Olenina's master classes. And it was there in the quiet of that room, in distant Canada, thousands of miles away from Russia and France where Maria Olenina spent her life, that I heard her voice again and realised that my main task should be to allow it to sound once more at full strength.

In this book there is therefore relatively little text written by myself. I have used my own writings mostly in order to make a connected story out of the various memoirs, letters, diaries, reviews and other records of Olenina's life and art. Eighty percent of the archival documents quoted in the book are published in English for the first time. It is my hope that amidst this material readers will hear the voice of Olenina and of those who lived and worked with her, and that as they turn the final page they will indeed be able to say: "So that's how it all came about…"

Maria Olenina-d'Alheim, c. 1900s. From her book *Le Legs de Moussorgski* (Paris: Eugène Rey, 1908).

She is the music and the word,

And thus the unbroken linkage

Of everything that is alive.

Osip Mandelstam

CHILDHOOD AND YOUTH

Russia — *1869-1893*

Childhood in Istomino

 aria Alexeyevna Olenina was the younger daughter of a Russian noble family. She was born in central Russia, on the family estate of Istomino, near the town of Kasimov[1] in Ryazan Province. There were two families of Olenin in Russia, both going back to the sixteenth century. Maria's family belonged to a line that figured in genealogical books of the provinces of Voronezh, Ryazan, Tver, and Tula, and at the turn of the eighteenth and nineteenth centuries the most celebrated member of this line was one Alexei Nikolayevich Olenin, great-grandfather of the future singer. The roots of their family were deeply embedded in Russian cultural history, and Maria's "Kratkaya avtobiografiya" (Short Autobiography) of 1946 recorded several of her family's connections.

Olenina-d'Alheim:
My great grandfather Alexei Nikolayevich Olenin[2] was first president of the [Russian] Academy of Fine Arts. [...] His father, Nikolai Yakovlevich, was married to Princess Volkonskaya, an aunt of the Decembrist Volkonsky. Alexei Nikolayevich had three sons and two

daughters: Nikolai, Pyotr, Alexei, Varvara and Anna; the last-named was celebrated in verse by Alexander Pushkin who fell under her spell. Anna Alexeyevna was my godmother. (KRAVT, 1.)

Pushkin's poem "Sing not, beauty, in my presence" ("Ne poi, krasavitsa, pri mne…") was dedicated to Anna Olenina, the god-mother of Maria, who herself had a lovely singing voice and took lessons from the composer Glinka. The Olenin household became a sort of cultural centre in St. Petersburg, where Glinka's latest songs and romances were first performed, and Pushkin too recited his verses there. (It was in the Olenins' house that he first met Anna Petrovna Kern,[3] to whom the poem "One wonderous moment I recall" ("Ya pomnyu chudnoye mgnovenye") was addressed.) As Olenina recalled, "Alexei Nikolayevich gathered around him every writer, artist, poet, and also Granddad Krylov[4] as we called him when we were children —that is, not Krylov himself, but his bust which used to stand in father's study." (SV, 10.)

Olenina-d'Alheim:
Nikolai, the eldest [son of Alexei Nikolayevich Olenin], was killed at the battle of Borodino, and Pyotr was rescued by their servant just at the moment when they were lowering him into the tomb [believing he too had been killed]. Pyotr Alexeyevich was then aged just sixteen. My father [Alexei Petrovich] was the eldest son of Pyotr Alexeyevich, and he married my mother, Varvara Alexandrovna Bakunina. Our family consisted of a foster son, Alexander [Sasha] Stepanov, two sons, Pyotr [Petya] and Alexander [Sasha], and two daughters, Varvara [Varya] and Maria. Maria—that's me.[5] (KRAVT, 1.)

Maria Olenina's mother, Varvara Alexandrovna, was the daughter of the Governor General of Tver, and according to his granddaughter, "Alexander Nikolayevich Bakunin was apparently a second cousin of the well-known revolutionary and anarchist Mikhail Bakunin." (SV, 11.)

The family estate of the Olenins had the Tatar name of Salaur and lay not far from the village of Kopnovo. It should rightfully have been inherited by Maria Olenina's father, who was the eldest son of the family. But for some reason Alexei Olenin did not take possession of his inheritance, and Salaur passed to the youngest brother Nikolai. Maria Olenina's parents in fact lived on her mother's fairly ample dowry, although it soon became apparent that the estate was not being run as it should, money was being lent out to many people indiscriminately but was rarely returned, and the artistic fantasies of her father, who was an amateur artist and sculptor, cost the family dear.

Olenina-d'Alheim:
It was quite obvious that under such management, even if the fortune provided by grandfather had been twice as large, it was bound to get frittered away very quickly. I remember my nurse saying, "There goes your mother repairing other people's roofs when her own roof is leaking." The whole story ended tragically. (SV, 13.)

By the time Maria came into the world, her parents lived on the estate of Istomino, which her father had bought back in 1860. It was there that Maria was born. Almost from birth, she evidently suffered from extremely poor eyesight, although, as she later claimed, her weak vision had the effect of sharpening her hearing and promoted her early musical development.

Olenina-d'Alheim:
Regarding my own appearance on this earth. It took place in the fall, at the end of September—on the 19th September [1869, or the 1st October by modern dating] to be precise, just when the woodcock were flying. My mother and father had been out hunting until about five in the evening—obviously I had not cramped mother's style. But then, after dinner, she brought into the world such a tiny frail creature, no longer than half a yard, that everyone versed in such matters—the midwife chief among them—decided that the little creature in question would never live to see the morning. So God's newborn servant was laid out on the couch in front of the blazing hearth, and to everyone's amazement I actually survived till next morning. But my eyes were closed up by a terrible inflammation, and they remained that way for two whole months. That is why my eyesight stopped developing, and it stayed that way for the rest of my life. As I see it, all this affected my character, and forced me to

live mainly within myself, and it concentrated my impressions of the outside world on my hearing. They told me that I began singing even before I started speaking; probably I just imitated the birds.

This was also to affect the development of my memory, which was amazing particularly where music was concerned, and the texts of the songs that I used to include in my programmes. There was a countless profusion of them. Yet I have to admit that in all other matters my memory often let me down. Even now I cannot recall everything about my life. Memories only come back little by little, and not everything is as clear to me as the things that I used to sing. (SV, 49–50.)

The Istomino estate lay in a picturesque setting on the bank of the river Oka. It was a typical estate for an average genteel family such as the Olenins. Maria's parents had bought it from one Prince Maksutov after observing it from a boat as they sailed along the Oka from Salaur to Kasimov. Her father was particularly taken by the lofty tower on the house. For all his fantasies, Alexei Olenin had a definite artistic gift: he was a good graphic artist and sculptor, and after buying Istomino he immediately set about rebuilding it. The spacious house had more than twelve rooms, but had been badly neglected. Olenin transformed it into a villa in the Italian style, with balconies, caryatids and a splendid garden. As often in the families of landed gentry, the Olenin children grew up in close proximity to nature and the life of the peasantry, and peasant songs and customs were familiar to them from early childhood.

Olenina-d'Alheim:
My dearest memories of all are bound up with our meadowland. Each summer we went to the mow. How splendid that was. I remember once towards evening I dug myself a nest in a large haycock. I covered myself over with a big scarf and listened to the concert of night birds and the futile shrilling of mosquitoes over my roof. It sounded like violin pizzicato. And there was splendid bathing in the small but deep lakes on our meadowland. (SV, 7.)

In the area in front of the house there was a very large garden set out in broad half-moon shape. It was bordered by linden trees and lilac and acacia bushes. As you entered it there were two balsam

The Olenin family estate of Istomino in the Ryazan Province.
This view of the back of the house from the backyard was
taken probably before or during WWI.

poplars, and in one of them was a birdhouse. In the centre of the
garden was a big flowerbed where white hyacinths grew in spring,
my favourite flowers. On the northern side was a large flower garden which was tended especially by our mother. It was bordered by
various trees: rowan, acacia and cherry, and there were two ledges
on the slope down to the river. On the actual path down there was a
very tall weeping birch.

The village a kilometer away from Istomino was Chernyshovo.
And when the peasant population from there came at Whitsuntide
along the road to the Oka to throw garlands, the young folk always
stopped by this weeping birch, and they would weave more garlands from its long branches. It was an amazing procession: first
came the lads, and after them the little girls, then the young men
and girls, and then came the fathers and mothers followed by the
old men and women, and all of them decked with wreaths of birch.
Arriving at the river, they stood with their backs to the water and
threw their wreaths back over their heads. I think there was some

sort of tradition or belief connected with this. Of course, everyone was dressed in their best festive clothing, and with a predominance of red. (SV, 20.)

As a child Maria heard a lot of stories and legends linked with the history of the Murom forests and the tradition of outlaws and runaways. As she later recalled, even the local names bore this out. Dobrynin Island was named after Dobrynya Nikitich who, according to legend, hurled his ax from there, right across the Oka, to Alyosha Popovich. The names of villages and settlements also recalled the age of the outlaws: Slyozovo was where people shed tears (*slyozy*); Istomino was a place of torment (*tomit'*); and the name Telebukino suggested infliction of a type of ordeal by water (*buchit'*). The atmosphere of such tales and peasant customs also formed an integral part of the land-owners' lives as well, and the life of the Olenin family was always marked by various elements of creativity and fancy.

Olenina-d'Alheim:
Our family had eight members: father, mother, and an aunt [Ekaterina Bakunina] who always lived with us; how and why she came to join her sister's family I don't know; and there were five children: Sasha Stepanov, our mother's foster son, Petya, the eldest Olenin, Sasha, Varya and myself. Sasha Stepanov was already studying in Moscow at the Polytechnic College; he was about three years older than Petya. (SV, 21.)
My brothers and I were very close as children, and later on we always remembered our mother's wish that we should remain friends and never let serious quarrels arise. Our brother Sasha sometimes played with us and our dolls, but only when we used them as characters in some magical fairy tale. I remember he once dressed himself in a robe made of newspapers and pretended to say mass; Varya and I had to play the deacon and his assistant. I know about my brothers' childhood from stories. Their upbringing followed the English model....
Sasha was a very kindly brother and he shared everything with Petya. Once he was on a boat with mother and another passenger took a liking to him and gave him a candy. "What about Petya?"

Sasha asked, and of course he was given a candy for his brother too. Petya was very kind as well, but a regular tease, and Varya was the one to suffer most from this. She became irritated, flushed and wept whenever Petya teased her. He was evidently not averse to fighting too, judging by the fact that the peasant boys who came to play with him once complained to our mother that "Petya keeps fighting."—"Then just you give him some of his own medicine!" mother told them.

When Sasha was sent off at the age of about fourteen to Kurland[6] to see the famous Professor Pabst,[7] in his desk they found several pieces of gingerbread, chocolate and candy—he had hidden all these things "for Mama" but then forgotten to give her them. From the age of three he sat for hours under the grand piano, listening to Aunt Katya play exercises and sonatas (she was a good pianist and also had a pleasant singing voice). After that it was not long before Sasha could climb up on the stool and play his own music.

Our brothers had two English governesses. Both boys spoke English splendidly. Petya could translate Shelley and Byron "à livre ouvert,"[8] and when he came back from Kurland Sasha knew German as well. By the age of nine he was composing and at that time adored Mendelssohn whose portrait hung above the piano. He played all the compositions of his favourite in arrangements for four hands with his aunt Katya. Our father listened with admiration. But once after Sasha had spent the winter in Moscow, where he got to know the Mighty Handful, he and his aunt played Mussorgsky's *Night on Bald Mountain* (*Noch' na Lysoi gore*),[9] and father plugged his ears and ran out of the room!!

Using coloured pencils Varya constantly drew pictures illustrating the story of a numerous family we had invented, or sometimes the life of mermaids. I always collaborated in this, but only by following her own drawing—I could not draw myself. Most of all I loved to sing, and I knew a great many songs and immediately memorised everything I heard. In the evenings we often gathered round the piano and sang in chorus. Father too sometimes joined in these choruses. (SV, 22–23.)

My sister had a very jolly personality. She was a prankster, but also particularly kind and obliging with everyone. Grandmother christened her "our kindly heart" and loved her greatly, and to the end of her days Varya was always her favourite. I think that it was Varya's self-effacing kindness that prevented her from becoming a great artist, but she was really very talented. As a child she was a real eccentric. If she ever hurt herself or got angry with Petya and ran to her nurse weeping and saw that nurse was resting, she would tiptoe away again and came back to play with me. But a couple of hours later, when she heard nurse get up, Varya would dash back to her with tearful complaints and expect to be consoled. (SV, 25.)

I knew some songs which I think were in fashion then, by Gurilyov[10] and others [...] and the aria "Close by the city of Slavyansk" ("Blizko goroda Slavyanska").[11] My aunt also taught me a few French songs, or to put it more exactly, she sang them to me [...] When I was small, I used to get Varyusha the nurse to sing me various songs, and most of all I liked the one with words by Pushkin that went: "A maiden walked in places desolate / Through the ill-weather of an autumn eve, / And in her trembling hands she carried / The fruits of an unhappy love." And at the point where the maiden "bent low and laid / The child at a stranger's door," I always began to weep. Although I was ashamed and hid my head under Varyusha's apron, I could not stop crying. "Come on, stop crying. Stop it, or else I shall never sing you that song again," she said. "No, Vayuta," I said (I couldn't pronounce the letter "r"). "Sing it again from the beginning, please." Finally she agreed and sang the song again, and again at the same place I burst into bitter tears. And whenever I wept after hurting myself or got annoyed at something, even after the pain or sorrow had subsided I still carried on weeping in order to listen to the echoing sound of my own voice.

At the age of about eight, I used to sit on a rowan bough that bent and swayed in the wind, and in a low voice and with great feeling I would sing, "I am consumed by anguish, and a leaden weight has settled deep within my heart." Of course, I did not realise then that this was the Russian version of Margarita's song from *Faust*. Evidently I had a particular liking for everything tragic and sorrowful. And my repertoire was a fairly broad one.

I was also very fond of fairy tales, and when I was still quite small and awoke at night, I would wake up my poor aunt and get her to tell me about the Tsar Saltan. And whenever she confused things in her sleepiness, I would pester her: "Aunty, you're getting it wrong!" And I also loved tales of magic and preferred them to any novels. I was especially fond of "The Water Nymph" by Hans Andersen. Mama also used to get the children's magazine *Igrushechka* [The Little Plaything][12] for us. Of course we read it, but we were far more amused by the stories of our own imagination, and [instead of reading the magazine] I soon went back to my own singing. I used to sit up at the piano with Lermontov's verse on the stand and, making sure to use the right-hand sustaining pedal, I would accompany myself and sing about the Empress Tamara perched on her black crag. (SV, 23–25.)

Just as in fairy tales, two kindly fairies hovered over my cradle. Their names were Pushkin and Lermontov. From an early age I knew Pushkin's "Autumn Eve" ("Pod vecher osen'yu") and Lermontov's "Down the blue river a mermaid there swam" ("Rusalka plyla po reke goluboi"). The first of these used to reduce me to tears, and the second I used to sing to music by my brother Sasha. (BNB, 138.)

Grandmother and other visitors used to come to us for Christmas. Sasha Stepanov would bring all sorts of presents and decorations for the Christmas tree. My brother Sasha used to arrange concerts on feast days, and we would also take part in them. Varya had a high soprano voice, but a very poor ear. Nevertheless, I do remember she once sang a song by Mendelssohn quite well—one of his folk settings; and I also sang. In addition I sang a poem by Petya, set to music by Sasha, about a gorgeous mermaid, and also Desdemona's prayer from Rossini's *Otello*. I sang it in Italian, with great expressiveness, so they said, although I was only about six years old. I also often sang country songs and tried to sing them in the way the peasant-women did—one often heard them singing, especially in summer. You could hear them singing from far off, and it always seemed as if the countryside itself was singing. The voices in our area were not at all harsh, but deep and sonorous.

Whenever aunt Tatyana Bakunina came, we put on various tableaux and merry playlets from our children's repertoire. The whole family was involved, of course: someone was the producer, someone did the costumes, and I clearly recall that I had some jolly part to play [and] walked freely up and down the stage and felt not the slightest fear. When aunt Tatyana put on the scene of "Sleeping Beauty," I had the leading role, and Varya played the handsome Prince. (SV, 23–26.)

The girls in the Olenin family grew up according to the rules of "free education," which meant that schools, tutors or governesses were dispensed with. The few governesses that did appear in the house never stayed for long, and the children acquired their knowledge from books selected by their parents. Much attention was devoted to developing their natural talents. And certainly each child showed his or her individual character. As a boy, Pyotr was passionately fond of chemistry and even corresponded with the celebrated French astronomer Camille Flammarion;[13] later he became a writer and was known under the name of Olenin-Volgar. Varya wanted to become an artist; Sasha wrote music from his earliest years and dreamed of becoming a composer; and Maria thought of herself only as a singer. All these artistic ambitions flourished as a result of the general atmosphere in the Olenin household. And while not promoting the acquisition of any systematic knowledge, this atmosphere certainly stimulated young imaginations and awakened natural abilities. The children's proper education only started later, when the family removed to Moscow. However, it was in early childhood that Maria first came to life emotionally, and in this world of emotion she was later able to forget everything else and devote herself wholeheartedly to the words and music of the works that she performed.

Olenina-d'Alheim:
The actual atmosphere of my childhood, which was so bright and free, is something I recall with such clarity and affection. There was one very good side to our liberal education, and that was our total unawareness of the practical importance of money. We never thought about money or knew the value of it. I am convinced that a total belief in the omnipotence of money is a poison, a dangerous poison that can affect human reason. This conviction of mine eventually turned into a revulsion against money, and it arose in me a long time ago. I was about five, I think, when I once ran along

the corridor and saw an old beggar standing in our hall who had come to ask for charity. I rushed back to my room. I had a money-box there, which I knew contained a few small coins I had been given, and I ran to fetch them. But when I opened the money-box, all I found there was one shiny silver rouble. Intending to give me a pleasant surprise, someone had swapped my small change for this one wonderful rouble! I suddenly felt loath to part with it. My infant heart could not bear such an awful conflict, and I burst into tears. Then someone hurried to comfort me, and they told me that the little old man had been given both money and bread. But they could not console me, and I felt suffocated by a dull sense of shame. (SV, 28.)

Even in early childhood Maria showed a remarkable, almost fanatical desire to become a singer, which sometimes struck those around her as abnormal.

Olenina-d'Alheim:
I was—and still am of course—a sort of maniac [*yurodivaya*] with a constant *idée fixe* about my future career. For a long time I dreamed of it. When I was still a little girl I used to write on the trunks of birch trees: "I want to be a singer, like young Lavrovskaya."[14] We had a photograph of her in the role of the princess in Dargomyzhsky's *Rusalka* (The Water Nymph). But of course I thought only about singing and not about the stage or the opera. I had an all-consuming desire to be a singer. Such a desire surely has to rule the entire being of anyone striving to fulfil it—all scholars, poets and artists, particularly musicians, and even more so composers, live under the yoke of this obstinate desire. There is good reason why such people are regarded as being not quite normal. (SV, 48.)

Moscow and First Musical Impressions

In the year 1880, the Olenin family removed to Moscow, where Alexei Petrovich had been appointed director of the Stroganov Institute of Painting and Sculpture.[15] It was now time to think about the children's education, although as yet they had no wish to give up Istomino completely. At the age of eleven Maria for the first time left the home where she was born.

Olenina-d'Alheim:

It was the end of 1880, in late November. After the first snowfall, our entire family left for Ryazan, and from there we travelled to Moscow by train. Nothing in the world would persuade me to leave without Varyusha my nurse, and I wept so bitterly that mama decided to take her with us to Moscow for a week. The first thing I learned about the civilised world, and the first thing that astonished me was the train—not the one we were travelling in, but another one that rushed to meet us. For some reason I imagined I would see it somewhere in the distance, as one did with steamers, and when it suddenly thundered past outside our window I was completely baffled.

We stayed the entire winter in a wing of uncle Nikolai Bakunin's house in Staro-Pimenovsky Lane. We arrived in the evening and after dinner the whole family sat and drank tea in the large dining room…. [In the Bakunin family] there were four children—Kolya, Sonya, Anna, and Misha. That evening everyone apart from Kolya was there. Towards nine o'clock Kolya and his friend came into the dining room, but I did not see them and never looked at them. I only heard aunt Anna introduce them to my parents. But then, when Kolya went round everyone as they sat there and came to me, something happened which I never expected and quite failed to understand. I was seized by a strange feeling. This was how a sensation of first love was born in me as an eleven-year-old girl. But it was a first love that failed.

I must confess that it never had any influence on my character and did not alter my resolve to become a singer and not just a mere amateur. Although even later on I was very much in love with that cousin of mine, and we even decided to marry, I twice postponed taking any action, and the second time—for such a long interval that the whole venture came to an end of its own accord. But why go on about my plans to get married? The same thing also happened with my second suitor, and I turned him down as well.

[On the third occasion, however] I did not refuse. But that was something quite different; here I had no actual suitor as such. Pyotr d'Alheim was himself a writer and artiste, and a very talented one at that. In joining my own fate to his, I never left the road I had been following and I did not have to give up my own career. Quite the contrary, Pyotr helped to confirm me in it and to make me realize my own true calling as a performing artist. When he was about sixteen years of age he himself recorded in his notes: "Être artiste, cela seul donne une véritable valeur à la vie." [To be an artist is the only thing that gives life true value.] (SV, 37–38.)

We lived in Moscow only in winter of course, and in early June we returned to Istomino. My brothers went on to study: Petya at Fidler's Modern School, and Sasha at the Conservatoire. Varya and myself were placed by Mama with the Princesses Meshchersky, who ran something like a high school. We were admitted without any entrance examination, which was a bad thing and meant that I, for instance, was ahead of the other pupils in some subjects, but behind in others.

What then happened in our family I don't quite know. Probably mother had many worries and a great deal of sadness, which might explain why she was so careless about our education, even though she loved us with all her heart. Immediately when studies began in the second winter, I refused to go to the Meshcherskys' boarding school since I believed I was simply wasting my time there. Mama raised no objection to this, although I was only thirteen at the time —which all goes to show how lax our upbringing was.

I never arrived at school on time, and after prayers I always heard other pupils whispering that Olenina was late again. Actually I never did learn the words of the prayer they said before lessons. It was all done in such an arid, official manner and was quite unlike any real prayer. I remember when I was a child, Varyusha used to make me recite "Our Father" and the prayer to the Virgin. Each morning I had to whisper these two prayers while kneeling in front of an armchair by the window. And I use to rattle off those prayers in a *prestissimo* whisper, as it were. I never understood a single word. […]

When I refused to go to school, Mama made no attempt to force me. Instead she simply called in a final-year university student, and he taught me various subjects in a free and easy manner. And whenever he went on about something that didn't interest me, I listened absent-mindedly and simply gazed out and admired the dark-blue twilight. (SV, 38.)

From the very first winter Sonya Bakunina and I became friends. She was fourteen and attended the First Moscow High School; under the influence of her cousin Leonid Kuznetsov she already held progressive ideas and was of course perpetually arguing with her mother. My friendship with Sonya was a close one. We spent almost all our spare time together, and for about three years she came to spend the summer holidays with us at Istomino. (SV, 39.)

By the following winter (in 1881), we were already living in the Stroganov Institute of Painting and Sculpture where father had had been appointed Director. The Institute stood on Strastnaya Square, right opposite the convent where we used to go for Easter mass. The house was a historic one. Griboyedov set the whole action of his play "Woe from Wit" ("Gore ot uma")[16] there. The Director's apartment occupied the whole of the second and top floor. Probably its entire furnishing was seen to by our father in the summer before we removed there, and of course it was done with immense taste: the study and living room were beautifully furnished. The living room was very large, with a white cupola in the centre of the ceiling, supported by four columns which were also white. The walls were of light turquoise. The benches and stools were covered with a patterned brocade matching the colour of the walls. And on both sides, under an overhang, there were couches, mother's writing desk and the grand piano. Each year, we used to give a ball on the 4th of December, which was the nameday of both mother and Varya. (SV, 44–45.)

I forgot to say something about my "first performance." It took place the day after we removed to Moscow, in November of 1880. Uncle Nikolai sat his sister Katya down at the piano. He evidently loved singing although he had a husky voice and a poor ear. He made Aunt Katya accompany him, although what he sang I cannot recall— maybe Schubert's "Serenade." When he had finished, my aunt called on me to show how I could sing. I had brought Dargomyzhsky's[17] song "I will tell not a soul" ("Ne skazhu nikomu") with me. After I had sung it, our uncle exclaimed: "And how does such a puny little creature manage to produce a voice like that?"—I was extremely small and slightly built. And that was how my first début in Moscow took place. My second one was also in November, [but that was] in 1901. (SV, 47.)

The first opera I heard was *La Traviata*. The singer was an Italian woman called Saggini. She died very young. I listened to— or rather heard—only her. My ear was unaccustomed and did not really take in all the rest.... After that [came] Gounod's *Faust, Les Huguenots* by Meyerbeer, Verdi's *Aida*, and Mozart's *Don Giovanni* —all in the course of three years. In addition there was *La somnambula* [by Bellini], *Lakmé* [by Delibes], and *Mignon* [by Thomas]. All four of these featured Marie van Zandt,[18] a singer who had a wonderful, special timbre to her voice. Among Russian operas I heard [Glinka's] *A Life for the Tsar* (*Zhizn' za tsarya*),[19] as it was then called, [Dargomyzhsky's] *Rusalka* with a marvellous singer called Pavlovskaya,[20] and finally [Rimsky-Korsakov's] *The Snow Maiden* (*Snegurochka*), in its original orchestration. (SV, 50–51.)

In [1884?], if I'm not mistaken, our father handed in his resignation, since his former school friend Bazilevsky had offered him a post as director of his fishing industry in Astrakhan. The family reaped no benefit from the change. We continued gently going to ruin as before, and if father did have any more money, his personal expenses probably increased as well. The removal to Istomino alone must have cost a great deal. (SV, 51–52.)

In Olenina's tales and reminiscences the subject of the family's financial ruin is often repeated. She always blamed their father for it, and for the fact that this prevented the Olenin children from fully developing their talents. But even if the accusation was true, there was a certain irony to it, since it was obviously from their father Alexei that the children inherited their creative talents and ambitions.

Olenina-d'Alheim:
We all stayed in Moscow at the Stroganov Institute for four years. Whenever I think about that period and wonder why father gave

up the post, it strikes me that he cannot have been sufficiently serious as a school director. Probably in the Ministry [of Education] they had hoped the grandson of Alexei Nikolayevich Olenin would be as talented as his grandfather, but experience proved this was not the case. [...] He was what they called a "jouisseur" [i.e., a fast liver and *bon vivant*], and of course he took advantage of his stay in Moscow and at one time [appeared] in the company of the Consul General of France [...], although the latter was much younger —about thirty—and he naturally lived it up for all he was worth. (BNB, 177.)

However, there was another, perhaps positive, side to the Olenins' departure from Moscow: not long afterwards various changes took place in Maria Olenina's life that affected the whole of her subsequent fate.

Olenina-d'Alheim:
When Varya turned sixteen, she became engaged to a Conservatoire friend of Sasha's called Sergei Nilus. He was a good pianist and had a lovely baritone voice, and of course I often spent time at the piano with him.... A year after our return to Istomino, Varya broke up with Nilus and he left to go off to Optina Pustyn, as I think it was called. It was he who [later] started the movement and disturbance over the Elders of Zion.[21] In the winter after Varya broke her engagement, I stayed with Aunt Katya at Istomino until the end of January. But in February [1887] I was in St. Petersburg, at Tavrida, and taking singing lessons. The end of May also saw the arrival of father and Sasha, who was anxious to continue his musical education under one of the "Mighty Handful."[22] (SV, 51–52.)

St. Petersburg, First Singing Lessons and Meeting with the Mighty Handful

The Olenins' removal to St. Petersburg (in May 1887 according to some sources) was an event of immense importance in Maria Olenina's life. It was here that she became familiar with the music and activities of the Mighty Handful, and this led to personal links with members of the group, most notably with Balakirev[23] and Stasov.[24]

In St. Petersburg Olenina also came to hear plenty about her French relatives the d'Alheims. Relations between the Olenin and d'Alheim families originated on her father's side. His mother's eldest sister had married an immigrant from France, the Baron de Limosin d'Alheim, and Olenina's father and uncle Ivan d'Alheim were therefore cousins.

Olenina-d'Alheim:

The surname of Uncle Ivan's family was not d'Alheim but de Limosin, but under Emperor Paul I, who was such a fervent Germanophile, the Baron gave up his French name and contented himself with the name of their castle in Lorraine called Alheim. His children who remained in Russia were called simply Dalheim [Dal'geim], written as one word, although they retained their baronial title. The eldest, Ivan, returned to the land of his French ancestors. He was a very talented artist. When he was only twenty, he won a prize for a picture he exhibited and was able to travel abroad, which he did. Slightly earlier, before his departure, he had got married and he set out on his travels with [his wife] and little daughter.

After spending two years in Dresden, Uncle Ivan made his way to France, bought a small house in Burgundy, in Laroche, and soon afterwards established friendly relations with the famous Barbizon[25] group of artists. They all visited his home, and Millet[26] painted a white horse on a white wall there. (Unfortunately, when Uncle's family broke up, this picture could not be transported, and the great artist's work was therefore lost when they had to sell the villa.) Much later, Uncle Ivan was friendly with [Léon] Gambetta[27] and all his entourage, and he also knew Clemenceau[28] although he disliked him.

(SV, 14–15.)

This same Uncle Ivan d'Alheim also had a son who Maria Olenina had known about ever since she was a child. Their distant, half-French half-Russian cousin lived in Paris, which was where the family eventually moved, and for the Olenin children he was a personality shrouded in mystery. The cousin's name was Pierre d'Alheim—or "Pyotr" in its

Russian rendering—and he was Maria Olenina's future husband. However, their actual meeting only took place much later.

Meanwhile, in 1887, Olenina's life centred on the singing lessons that she began taking with Yulia Platonova.[29] Platonova had studied the part of Marina Mniszech under Mussorgsky himself, and *Boris Godunov* had been staged on her initiative in the year 1874. Not only was Platonova a famous singer, but she was also a champion of works written by composers of the New Russian Musical School. Olenina's brother Alexander has left a description of this episode.

Alexander Olenin:
On this visit I had two concerns: the first was to arrange for my own studies; and the second, almost more important, was to fix up my sister Maria's singing lessons. [...] Since early childhood she had shown uncommon musical ability. She had such an ear that I only needed to play through a song once or twice for her to know it and be able to sing it. [...] She had an amazingly true and pleasant voice. And she immediately picked up not only the melody but also the character of whatever she was performing.

I recall the following incident from my early childhood. Sometimes a large company would come out to the country to visit us. My older brother, who later became the well-known playwright and journalist Olenin-Volgar and who was always a good organiser, used to put on a concert on these occasions. Posters were painted, tickets were distributed among the guests at 10 or 15 kopecks, chairs were set out in rows in the hall, and the concert would begin. I used to play, my sister would sing, and the public who had been hauled away from their card-games and conversations would graciously applaud. After the concert was over, the takings from the concert were usually divided up in the nursery, and my brother always tended to allot himself a larger portion, based on the fact that he was the organiser. Often this would lead to shouting and ended up with the brothers punching one another.

In this way my sister and I grew up together and also developed musically. For me her talent was a real treasure. She performed pieces by myself and by other composers I revered at that time, i.e., the Mighty Handful. I obviously dreamed of her becoming a

Maria Olenina in 1887.

second Purgold-Molas,[30] who was the most famous performer of music by the "Handful."

When my sister came to St. Petersburg, she already had a wide repertoire, although she had not yet studied singing anywhere, and there was a boldness, passion and talent about everything she performed. Since on returning to St. Petersburg I regarded myself almost like a Prodigal Son (I had not only deserted Balakirev but had not even written to him) [i.e., after their father's transfer to Astrakhan and the family's return to Istomino], I did not know how to approach him again and for that reason initially concerned myself more with my sister's affairs than with my own.

I did not know who was then regarded as the best singing teacher in St. Petersburg, and I never strove to find out. I thought the best must be the one who recognised Balakirev and Mussorgsky —that was all. With this in mind I insisted that my sister begin studying with Platonova. [...] My parents and even my sister in a sense allowed me the deciding vote on this, and so the three of us set off to see her—my sister, myself, and our Aunt Ek[aterina] Al[exandrovna] who lived with us. [...] We took a lot of vocal music with us. We rang the bell, and were received very warmly. On hearing we had arrived from the country, Platonova tried to jolly my sister up. But this was quite unnecessary: it never occurred to my sister to be at all bashful.

"Well, sing us something! You can do that, can't you?" Platonova finally turned to my sister. I prompted her in a whisper, and she began with César Cui's[31] "Tormented with Sorrow" ("Istomlennaya gorem"). I looked at Platonova. She was utterly astonished. "Where, and how do you come to know that? And how you sang it! Let's hear something else!" Then my sister sang Mussorgsky's "The Mischief" ("Ozornik"), something else by Balakirev, and something by Rimsky-Korsakov. By now Platonova was quite beside herself with surprise and delight. She rushed to embrace my sister (and did almost the same with me and my aunt) and kept on repeating: "Just imagine it! Here all this is unrecognised and rejected. And there, out in the wilds, there are talents ripening that are even familiar with it." Then she hastily showed us portraits of Mussorgsky and others, all of them signed, and the piano score of *Boris* that the composer had given her. It took her a long long time to calm down from her joyful excitement.

It was immediately decided that my sister would begin studying with her, and she would not hear of any payment. Alas, however, poor Platonova was in for a sad disappointment. Only a few days later the Mighty Handful supreme council, so to speak, in the persons of Balakirev, Stasov and others, decided that my sister should study not with Platonova, who was a superb operatic performer, but with Alexandra Nikolayevna Purgold-Molas, the sister of Rimsky-Korsakov's wife Nadezhda. She was a splendid Lieder singer and an exquisite performer of works by the group, starting with Dargomyzhsky, whose pupil she had been. My sister was in fact preparing for a concert-hall rather than an operatic career, and her voice and the nature of her talent all pointed strongly in that direction. For the composers in the group the appearance of such an artiste was a genuine discovery: with the exception of Molas nobody performed their chamber music at that time. Much to Platonova's credit, it must be said that like any true artist who served her art rather than herself, she gave this decision her total approval. However, I am jumping slightly ahead of my story. (AAO, 21–25.)

Alexander Olenin's account of his sister's study with Platonova slightly diverges from what Olenina herself wrote. According to her, their lessons went on for some time and were then curtailed at her own initiative. The important thing, though, is not the duration but the actual fact of her study under Platonova. It was with her that she began working on Mussorgsky. From the very outset, however, Olenina sought out and followed her own path. She was quite particular, for instance, about the works she sang, and her tastes drew her well away from the standard repertoire that was popular in society drawing-rooms of the time. Even at that early stage she was quite able to swim against the current. As she admitted, she did not have an easy character.

Olenina-d'Alheim:
I had a will of my own…. When I was working with Platonova in St. Petersburg I was already drawn towards Mussorgsky. Once at the house of Countess Grabbe I was singing gypsy songs and duets with

Muravyov. He was like a gypsy himself and played the guitar well. We were a great success, and the Countess and my father decided among themselves that I should leave Platonova and go to study with His Imperial Highness' [court] soloist, in order later to replace her. When father told me of their plan back at home, the answer he immediately got was: "I am a bird that goes in for free flight, and I'm not prepared to go even into a gilded cage." And I remained a free-flyer all my life, and I refused to sign a contract with the Director of the Paris Opéra Comique because I was told that once I signed it I would be obliged to learn all the roles the directors offered me, even if I regarded the actual opera as not worthwhile. (SV, 46.)

Doubtless Platonova's stories of Mussorgsky and the general atmosphere of reverence for him made a deep impression on Olenina. She also sensed her own special affinity for his music, and a sense of organic kinship with Mussorgsky appears to have been something that was inborn. Later on Olenina attempted to fathom the nature of this.

Olenina-d'Alheim:
I had never been in the local town [of Spassk] before. Not far from it was the estate of Mussorgsky's brother. While spending the summer there, he [Mussorgsky] wrote the first act of [his opera] *The Marriage* (*Zhenit'ba*).[32] Instinctively I can imagine him at that landing-stage —he feels so familiar to me, even though I never set eyes on him. I was just eleven years old when the whole of our family moved to Moscow, and in March of that same year Mussorgsky had died at the Nikolayevsky Military Hospital in St. Petersburg.

It was that same March when Alexander II was killed, and that was all people talked about in Moscow—not myself, of course, but everyone around me. At that time for some reason I had a strange, unpleasant feeling in the big city, and after a second winter there I simply could not stand it any more and persuaded my father to take me back to Istomino—for some reason he was going there at the time. I had such an urge to welcome the early spring in the countryside and to see my nanny, my dear Varyusha.

At that point we had never even heard of Mussorgsky. But later on, when I got to know his work, I was immediately gripped by it.

Modest Mussorgsky. Portrait by Ilya Repin, March 1881.

Why? Perhaps because he was a campaigner for the truth, he himself desired it and he conveyed it in his own works.... Also, he was the only one to express the soul of the Russian nation with such power, and that too was something I held dear. (sv, 6–7.)

Platonova was enthusiastic about her new pupil and talked a lot about her. The name of Maria Olenina thus began to figure in conversation with members of the Handful, and it was good fortune that brought the young singer to the home of Balakirev. Many people witnessed that fateful meeting, and Vladimir Stasov left a written record.

Vladimir Stasov:
In winter of 1887 there was once a musical gathering at Balakirev's in honour of Tchaikovsky, who had come to spend some time in St. Petersburg. The conversation was lively and animated. And most of the talk was about what Yulia Platonova, the former Russian opera prima donna who was sincerely admired and appreciated by the entire musical company, had recently been telling her closest friends —namely that among her many pupils a new and talented girl called Maria Olenina had appeared, who had just arrived from the provinces. Platonova talked about this pupil of hers with great enthusiasm, and referred to her not just as a remarkable talent, but as a "phenomenon"—so great was her apparent musical ability and artistic sensibility, and such was her ability to grasp immediately the true character and every nuance of drama and expressivity. Those present were highly interested in Platonova's opinion and her verdict.

At that time Balakirev had been visited by Olenina's father— Alexei Petrovich Olenin, who was known to none of those present except the host. At our request Maria Olenina came that evening to join our company along with her father, and she sang songs and compositions by all the leading new Russian composers. And what Platonova said turned out to be true. All of Balakirev's guests found her pupil to have an unusual natural gift, most of all in her declamation and dramatic expressiveness, and of a sort that struck all the Russian composers present. Everyone was enraptured and simply besought Olenina to continue her studies and her development.
(*Novosti i birzhevaya gazeta*, 17 (30) January 1902)

Apart from Balakirev and Tchaikovsky, that evening was attended by almost all the Mighty Handful: Rimsky-Korsakov, Glazunov,[33] Lyadov,[34] Dyutsh,[35] Shcherbachev,[36] and all the Stasovs. Olenina was later to collaborate with several of them, and included their works in her programmes. Her friendship with Balakirev lasted many years. It is perhaps ironical, though, that she was destined never to meet the one member of the Mighty Handful who played the greatest role of all in her life and artistry—Modest Mussorgsky.

Olenina's first meeting and acquaintance with the Handful—no less than their own encounter with her—are described variously by her brother and herself.

Alexander Olenin:
Some five or six days later I decided to send our father to [Balakirev] to reconnoitre. It was evening time and we were all sitting at Tavrida, when he set off. I waited excitedly to hear what transpired. About an hour passed, when suddenly there was a ring: father was back. We heard his voice down in the hall: "Sasha, Marusya! Quick! Get ready to go and see Balakirev!" What was this? Why? What had happened? He was surrounded and deluged with questions. This is what had happened: when father rang the bell at Balakirev's and entered the hall and told Adrian [the butler] his name and asked to be announced, the latter looked at father with some surprise. Meanwhile someone in the drawing-room next door suddenly called out his name in a loud voice.

There was a very large company gathered in the drawing room as father entered, and he had no time even to introduce himself to Balakirev before the latter stepped forward and greeted him: "Tell me, please, aren't you the father of that phenomenal girl Olenina who was at Platonova's a few days ago, and who they do nothing but talk about in our circle?" Hearing this was the case, Balakirev continued: "Where is she? Is she here?" Then he suddenly added: "Perhaps you're also the father of that talented young man who left me and disappeared without trace a couple of years ago? Is he here as well? And wasn't he there with his sister at Platonova's?" Father confirmed all this too and added that I could not bring myself to appear again because of my sense of guilt. "What nonsense," Balakirev went on. "You know what? Do us all a big favour: bring both of them here right now, immediately." A bearded gentleman (Stasov) and various others repeated the request. So here was father, coming to collect us. Quickly we got ready and dashed off.

It should be said that the gathering at Balakirev's was in honour of Tchaikovsky, who I believe was leaving for abroad. When we

Maria and her brother, composer Alexander Olenin, c. 1900.

arrived at Balakirev's, my sister immediately became the centre of attention. She was quizzed and people joked with her, and she answered back boldly and jauntily, as if she was in perfectly ordinary company and not at a gathering of all Russia's finest musical forces. [...] They made her sing there and then, and her singing aroused general delight. Part of which, of course, was due to the fact that at that time it was somehow a strange and novel thing to hear all these items (works by the Handful) sung by a girl from the back-woods of Ryazan, when nobody in the capital cities was performing them. She was accompanied by Balakirev and myself. Stasov was especially frenzied in his enthusiasm and kept repeating: "Splendid! Wonderful!"

It was decided there and then that my sister should study under Molas, and it was Stasov again who undertook to fix up the whole business, and also square things with Platonova. While my sister was actually singing, Balakirev quietly asked her whether she could sing something by Tchaikovsky. Alas, my sister sang only one piece by him—"So soon forgotten" ("Zabyt' tak skoro")—and she had not even brought the music for this with her. And it was fortunate that things turned out as they did. [...]

Then the company sat down to supper. My sister was seated between Balakirev and Stasov. The latter still kept on roaring, "Maria Alexeyevna, you are our one and only hope!" [...] I was seated between Tchaikovsky and Dyutsh, I seem to recall. [...] Tchaikovsky was inattentive and not very talkative. It was apparent that he was not at home in this circle. The company dispersed at a late hour and in very elevated mood. The next few days we spent in a sort of daze. [...] I remember a luncheon at the Molas's, where again Stasov, the R[imsky]-Korsakovs and many others were present; another evening at their home, a dinner, and again an evening at Balakirev's, etc. Finally everything settled into a routine, and we began our proper studies, my sister with Molas, and myself—on the advice of Balakirev—with Conservatoire professor A.A. Petrov.[37] (AAO, 25–27.)

Both Alexander and Maria Olenina recalled the same details of their visit to Balakirev, especially its initial phase. Thereafter, however, their accounts diverge quite radically.

Olenina-d'Alheim:

That evening was my actual début in Petersburg and my first acquaintance with the members of the Mighty Handful. They were all in attendance, apart of course from Mussorgsky and Borodin who had died that winter. Balakirev greeted us very cordially.

"Won't you perhaps sing something for us?"

"With great pleasure," I answered, and walked over to the grand piano. Sasha sat down to accompany me—he himself was neither alive nor dead, and was so agitated at having landed among all the composers he adored. I could see no one clearly and I didn't look at anyone. I sang Tchaikovsky's song "So soon forgotten." When I had finished, there was an exclamation from Stasov: "Ugh, how vile!" He did not bother himself with good manners in respect to anyone or anything, and was always plain-spoken with praise or blame. At his exclamation everyone rocked with laughter, even the actual composer of the song. I very much loved the melody and freshness of his songs, but was always embarrassed by their texts. Tchaikovsky was somehow very careless about his choice of poems to set, and I paid special attention to the words and attached great meaning to them.

I sang a few more songs by Tchaikovsky, Rimsky, and Cui, and one by Borodin.[38] Then our host called us to supper. I was the only lady in the company, and Balakirev sat me down next to him on his right hand. [Evidently] this was a great honour for such a young singer. But that young singer was me [and] as I already described myself, I was a crazy young thing [*yurodivaya*] [and had no sense of any honour]. (AAO, 53–54.)

Stasov's bluntness and lack of ceremony were legendary, and there is no particular reason to doubt the incident described by Olenina. A quite different matter, though, was Tchaikovsky's reaction. It is known how complex and contorted his relations were with members of the Mighty Handful. Would he have treated Stasov's words so lightly? After all, they reflected Stasov's attitude to anyone who was not a campaigner for the New Russian school, and especially his view of Tchaikovsky's music. Alexander Olenin's memoirs give a quite different account of that evening. According to him, Olenina sang "So soon forgotten" not at Balakirev's farewell gathering for Tchaikovsky, as she described, but on a subsequent occasion, several days later.

The Mighty Handful.
Mily Balakirev.

Alexander Olenin:
About three days later, she chanced to sing this item [*Zabyt' tak skoro*] among others at the home of the Molas family. Stasov was sitting two rooms away. Hardly had she finished when he came rushing out in his usual frenetic state and exclaimed loudly "How vile! How utterly vile!" He did not actually know this song by Tchaikovsky at all. What would have happened if my sister had sung it at Balakirev's, and if Stasov had slated it in the presence of its author? That would have created a real scandal! [But Stasov] kept thundering, "Maria Alexeyevna, you are our one hope!" (VP, 26.)

Much later, in 1906, Balakirev wrote about the same event in reply to a letter from Stasov. But he made no mention at all of his outrageous opinion of Tchaikovsky's song. (In his own letter, Stasov had evidently forgotten about Tchaikovsky's presence and now confused him with Chekhov of all people.) All of which drew an amusing jibe

The Mighty Handful.
Vladimir Stasov.

from Balakirev. The interesting thing, however, was that more than twenty years later the most memorable aspect of that evening for Balakirev was Maria Olenina's first appearance at his house.

Mily Balakirev:
You ask me to remind you of that evening at my home when we were all gathered and reading Chekhov! Evidently your memory is letting you down this time, because nobody read me even a line of Chekhov, and to this day I myself have never read a single work by that (reportedly) mediocre author. In fact I only heard of his existence after his death when all the newspapers started jangling on, praising works by him that were absolutely unheard of during his lifetime.

Perhaps you are confusing it with that evening when all my musical friends of the time were here, including Tchaikovsky as well, and when the Olenins (Maria Alexeyevna and her father and brother) looked in briefly for the first time. (M.A. Balakirev, letter of 27 January 1906 to V.V. Stasov, in M.A. Balakirev and V.V. Stasov, *Perepiska*, 2 vols. (Moscow, 1971), Vol. 2, 242.)

That memorable evening at Balakirev's decided the fate of Maria Olenina for many years ahead—indeed for the rest of her life. As she

The Mighty Handful.
Nikolai Rimsky-Korsakov.

recounts, her studies with Platonova continued, as also did her meetings and contacts with the Mighty Handful, especially Balakirev and Stasov. Her voice developed well, although she never had any remarkable timbre or power. At an early stage, she set greatest store on artistic expressivity and conveying the text of the song. As for her repertoire, during her vocal training in Petersburg, it consisted basically of music by the Mighty Handful, with Mussorgsky of course in first place.

Olenina-d'Alheim:
Soon after the evening at Balakirev's, we left for Istomino. I know that he spoke with Sasha and introduced him to his pupil Petrov, [who] if I'm not mistaken, was a professor at the Conservatoire. On returning to Petersburg in the fall, I continued working with Platonova, but not for very long—about a couple of months, because she immediately scared me when she told me that by spring she would give me the part of the Snow Maiden to learn. But I knew that role was for a high soprano, whereas I felt that I had a mezzo-soprano voice, and a fairly low one at that. Nevertheless, I could quite easily and effortlessly get up to the lyric soprano range. Also I believed that although high voices are very pleasant to listen to,

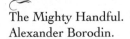

The Mighty Handful.
Alexander Borodin.

unlike a mezzo they are insufficiently adapted to expressive singing, and the latter was the only thing I set real store by. I was afraid that my lady professor had evidently wrongly identified my voice type and might ruin it for me. I began missing the occasional lesson and complained of headaches, and it was only when the holidays came that I told her the doctor had forbidden me to sing: I did not want directly to offend her. (SV, 54–55.)

It was around the time of the Christmas holidays when Vladimir Stasov heard about this and hauled me along to see Alexandra Molas. [At my audition with her] apart from a vocalise and an aria from Rossini's *Otello* (Desdemona's aria), Molas also gave me duets by Mendelssohn (I had already sung Desdemona's prayer before), and nothing by any of the Handful, or maybe just one song by Cui, "Tormented by sorrow". (BNB, 37.)

Alexandra Molas agreed to work with me, and when my aunt and I were leaving and going down the stairs, Stasov called out from up above, "We have expectations of you! Do you hear? We have expectations!" Seemingly, even by that time he and others foresaw that as a performer I would be to their liking. And when I sang Mussorgsky in St. Petersburg in 1902, the whole Stasov family

The Mighty Handful.
César Cui.

were so delighted with my performance that the old ladies had tears in their eyes as they kissed my hands and my dress, and I did not know how to calm them. But I felt that I had been proved right since I was praised and thanked so much by people who knew Mussorgsky and remembered what he wanted of his performers and how he himself performed his songs. It might now seem like blowing my own trumpet, but at the time when this [episode] might have been of benefit to me, I never breathed a word about it to anyone, and I left all the Stasov family's ecstasies to mingle in with all the rest. (SV, 54–55.)

Lessons with Alexandra Molas, visits to the Petersburg opera, dealings with musicians and, of course, the music of the Mighty Handful, made up the substance of Olenina's life in St. Petersburg. In his memoirs, Alexander Olenin emphasised the atmosphere prevailing at the Molas's evenings: "It was a special circle of people. On Sundays Rimsky-Korsakov and his wife, the Blumenfelds,[39] the Shcherbachevs, and many others gathered there. But it was Stasov who dominated those evenings, filling the rooms with his loud voice." (GMMC, fond 39, no. 127, 49.) Some impressions were specially vivid. In Olenina's memoirs we read how once at the house of some acquaintances she heard Doctor Ilyinsky,[40] a great friend of Mussorgsky's, sing "The Forgotten One" ["Zabytyi"] (the composer's own original name for this "Ballade"). "And his performance struck me," Olenina recalled, "and it went deep into my heart." (SV, 57.) Indeed, the world of Mussorgsky increasingly occupied her imagination.

Olenina-d'Alheim:
Of course, I was very happy, yet I still think that we only experience perfect happiness and joy when we can tell ourselves that we have performed the task we set ourselves without a single blemish. Then our soul rejoices, and it rejoices with a joy beyond all compare. I could often tell myself that I was honestly performing my task: after all, I also ascribed a special meaning to the words, just as Mussorgsky himself wished and sought for. Maybe that was why I earned special appreciation for my performance from Claude Debussy [in the *Revue blanche*]. He wrote that it bordered on the miraculous. And the music critic Pierre Lalo[41] gave such an assessment that modesty forbids one to speak of it. [I am actually none too modest], not at all. I have simply never done anything with the mere aim of winning praise or some reward, and I am sure that any such thoughts would inevitably reflect on the quality of a performance.

Apart from what I have said already, even as a child I was embarrassed by the promises in the Gospels of some reward for the good works that we have done. I could not help thinking that the very quality of some good deed performed with the idea of reward is already devalued thereby. Later I realised from another phrase in the Gospel about the Kingdom of God—that "the Kingdom of God is within thee"—that one may wish for such a reward. The work of anyone who creates anything, who loves his creation, and who seeks and wants it to be perfect, is based on the desire for such a reward. And so I know that the highest reward of all is born within the secret recesses of our hearts, where the Kingdom of God is also to be found.

I read the critique [by Lalo] only in the year 1929. [In *Le Temps*, 18 April 1901] He described his impression as follows: "The voice, intonation, diction, expression—all this is so naturally, so faithfully and truly, so deeply felt; they are so fused with the music, they harmonise so profoundly, that one seems to hear not the voice of the artiste, but the music itself." I am certain that a performance of that sort is achievable by anyone on the sole condition that they totally renounce their own personality and place their strength, physical and spiritual, at the disposal of the composer. We then achieve a sort of secret union with the author, and all his thoughts and desires then become our own. This is not at all a difficult task, but it is such a merry and joyful one! (SV, 55–57.)

In 1893 the life of the Olenin family was darkened by the illness of their mother. It turned out she had not long to live. The children, now grown up, had gone their various ways, and the family was fairly close to ruin. That same year their Uncle Ivan d'Alheim came to Istomino, and it was then that Maria and Varya Olenina renounced their portion of Istomino in favour of the brothers: "after all, they needed some work qualification, and both of them were already married." (SV, 72.) The fate of the Olenin children did not turn out as their parents wished however.

Olenina-d'Alheim:
Our father was always proud that his children had great artistic ability. Only neither he, nor our mother, who was totally dependent on him and never contradicted him, were capable of allowing these abilities to develop. And the reason? It was not the desire, but the money that they lacked. They squandered a great deal while we were still children, and at the time when it was needed for our work, money was short.

When Petya should have been finishing his general education and going to university (he had outstanding potential talent as a writer), and when Sasha [i.e., Alexander] should have been continuing his musical education, our father gave up his job in Moscow and dragged them off to Astrakhan, where he had been invited by a friend to run his fishing business. Yet why should such young men go off to Astrakhan? And from the time of that foolish expedition everything began to go awry.

I know from mother's letters how distressed she was by all this, and even now I cannot recall that whole crazy business without getting upset. I also know that the very difficult life of Alexander and his family in Moscow after the revolution stood him in good stead: he created many splendid compositions that he would never have done running the estate at Istomino. He was always fond of ordinary folk (he even wanted to have himself classified as a peasant), and he respected the peasants and was always drawn towards them. I know that he also brought his young wife to peasant recreational gatherings. And how many ancient songs he noted down from the men and women who actually sang them!

And again, no matter how Uncle d'Alheim helped her with advice —he was a fine artist—Varya too was unable to fully develop her talent. She was constantly forced to break off her work—sometimes for her brothers and their families, sometimes for our father.

I was the only one to realise the full measure of my natural talent. And that was because Aunt Katya arranged for a loan against her pension, in order to give me the chance to have singing lessons first in [St.] Petersburg, and then in Paris. And I thought only of my singing and stubbornly forged ahead to develop it. My aunt helped me, but in fact only reluctantly, because she gave her own money to run the estate here. I, however, achieved my aim, and I put my heart and soul into my work. (SV, 74.)

Olenina did her utmost to press on and complete her professional training. So that when Uncle d'Alheim invited her sister Varya to Paris to study painting under his supervision, Maria decided to go with her. According to Olenina, by that time she had been studying with Alexandra Molas for two years. And although these studies were satisfying, the young singer now wanted to expand her horizons and try her strength in some new setting.

Olenina-d'Alheim:
I wanted to achieve the final result [in my singing] as soon as possible, in order to enable us to bring our mother to join us in Paris. She had always dreamed so much of going to the south and tried to get to Paris. But probably she was thinking of Nice, where she had been so happy during her engagement and where she had actually got married.

In the fall [of 1893] when I returned to St. Petersburg [from Istomino], I told Alexandra Molas of my decision. She was very sad

Maria Olenina, before leaving for Paris in 1893.

to lose her favourite pupil and wept, and so did I. A year prior to that Sasha had had a son, and Balakirev was the child's godfather. He was already very fond of my brother and counseled him not to seek for profit from his art, but to provide for his family by some other means. This was how our plans worked out eventually. My sister decided not to leave for France immediately—in spring, that is—but in the fall instead. She wanted to spend the whole summer with mother, realising how difficult it was for her parting with us. I meanwhile set off on my travels with Aunt Katya and Uncle Ivan.

We settled in the 9th arrondissement of Paris, on rue Dupeire, not far from the studio that our uncle had rented. Very soon after that I made the acquaintance of Pyotr. (sv, 57.)

II

THE BEGINNING
OF A CAREER

Paris — 1893-1901

The Start of Life in Paris — Meeting and Union with Pyotr d'Alheim

hen talking about her family, Olenina often mentioned an Uncle Dmitry who at one time had threatened his aunt and heir, Tatyana Balavinskaya, that he would leave his entire fortune not to her but to the grandson of a sister surnamed d'Alheim. "He knew this French relative in Paris from visits to his niece... [and] told him lots of stories about Russian huntsmen, and the grandson listened to them enthralled." (SV, 40.) This twelve-year-old boy was Pyotr (or Pierre) d'Alheim.

Later, when Pyotr d'Alheim grew up and came to Russia as the correspondent for a French newspaper, he was supposed to visit all his parents' relatives. Unfortunately we do not know whether he met and got to know his second cousin Maria at that time. In her memoirs she writes only of their having met in Paris. Be that as it may, soon after her arrival in Paris, the two cousins turned out to have a great deal in common. Pyotr was extremely interested in Russian culture and especially Russian music, and he strongly sympathised with his cousin's musical ambitions. There was also something of the Pygmalion about him, and his enthusiasm for the young singer's talent quickly developed into a powerful amorous feeling. And although the young couple could not wed formally, since Pyotr was not legally free to marry, Olenina became his *de facto* wife. At that time she was aged twenty-four. Soon afterwards the couple had a daughter called Marianna, whose life was to be a tragically short one.

Olenina-d'Alheim:

When I joined my fate to that of Pyotr, I had no thought of marriage, and Pyotr was not at that time divorced from his wife although they already lived apart. We were married only in 1898. Pyotr's father-in-law Murat was strongly in favour, and was much disturbed by our illegal cohabitation. Apart from which, it became more convenient to be man and wife for the sake of our subsequent work together. Pyotr's wife readily agreed to a divorce, and he of course took the blame upon himself. However, as I realised, all this official procedure was not at all to his taste and I felt very sorry for him. [Later] Pyotr's wife was present at his talks on Mussorgsky, and I think that she liked me. Subsequently she also remained on good terms with me.

[Pyotr and I] did not have a real wedding in the Orthodox religious sense. We simply received a blessing from the mayor of the 12th arrondissement of Paris. In Russia our marriage was invalid of course, and my father in Russia and mother in Paris both wanted us to be married in church. There were various negotiations, representations to the Synod, etc. We had no wish to oppose this, although it was all the same to us. But things turned out quite differently. It emerged that the Synod demanded a considerable sum in order to recognise our civil marriage, and Pyotr asked me what I thought of the whole business and whether I was in agreement to pay the Synod. I told him frankly that I regarded such an expense as utterly excessive; we needed money for our project and we could very well do without a church marriage, and I was not agitating at all for my position to be legalised in Russia. At that time we had just returned from Brussels, where the Mussorgsky *conférences* had gone brilliantly. This is just one more illustration of how I utterly ignored life's accepted rules and regulations. (SV, 57–58.)

But if one could get away with ignoring the rules in France, in Russia it was essential for Pyotr and Maria d'Alheim to prove that they were in fact man and wife. Later on, when they resided for a long period in Moscow and St. Petersburg, they needed a marriage certificate. This was issued on the 15 November 1911 by the Consul General of France in Moscow, and it stated that "the litterateur Baron Pierre d'Alheim, resident in Moscow, born in La Roche sur Yonne, was married to the French subject Maria Olenina, as confirmed by an entry in the 73rd dossier, under No. 4326." (GMMC, fond 256, no. 4954.)

The union of Maria and Pyotr d'Alheim was not just a marriage however. It was a link between the plan and its realisation, between an artistic conception and its embodiment. And in this both participants took over ideas and actions from one another. There is no doubt that Pyotr d'Alheim had an immense influence on his wife. At the same time however, she remained an outstanding creative personality in her own right, and it was she who infected her husband with an enthusiasm for Mussorgsky's music that ultimately became a lifelong common cause. Maria Olenina always emphasised that this could never have been achieved without Pyotr, and after his death in 1922 when she was left alone, she was unable to continue the work that had started out with their first *conférences* on Mussorgsky. Olenina writes of her husband with great warmth, and her recollections are often full of pain for this talented man who she believed had never fully realised himself. She in fact intended writing a complete biography of him, but never did so. Such details as she did recount were what she had heard from Pyotr himself and from his mother.

Pyotr d'Alheim — The Making of a Pygmalion

Olenina-d'Alheim:
Pyotr d'Alheim was the manager-in-chief of all our activities, and certainly nothing would have happened without him. He was half-Russian. His grandfather married the sister of my grandmother Olenina. [...] I should add briefly that the Barons de Limousin d'Alheim received their title from Charles V, and their extensive

estates in Lorraine and the main [location] where they had their château was, and still is, called Alheim [...]. Pyotr's father, Uncle Ivan—he was the eldest—returned to the land of his French ancestors. He settled in La Roche in Burgundy, bought a tiny estate, and very soon joined up with the well-known Barbizon group of artists. [...] The d'Alheim family already had a daughter [Magdalina] aged about five, and shortly afterwards a son called Pyotr was born (on 8 December 1862).

The child's first impression of life around him was a branch of white lilac blossom by the window of the room where his cot stood. When he grew older, his great friend was [...] a Pyrenean hound, and little Pierre rode around the village on his back. [...] Thus the years passed, and then something dreadful happened between Pierre's parents. The younger sister of Tatyana d'Alheim, who had long been in love with her brother-in-law [Pierre's father], began trying to entice him to move to Paris. She had the idea of becoming an artist, and gradually she drew Ivan away from his wife and children. Eventually there was a divorce, and Pyotr's mother was left alone with the children in La Roche. The village population were very sympathetic and helped her as much as they could. Ten years after her divorce, she married [Casimir] Murat. Fairly soon after the divorce she moved to Paris, and her mother's sister, surnamed Poltoratskaya, came from Russia to join her. The mother and children settled in Paris on the rue Monge. [...] Beneath the windows of the d'Alheims' apartment there was a cab-drivers' depot; the lanterns on their cabs were of different colours, and young Pierre used to stand at the window and admire them [...]. In spring they began taking walks in the Jardin du Luxembourg and there met and became friendly with the Jewish family of Cornelli. The children, Anna and Robert, began visiting, and their mother who strictly observed the rules of the synagogue, stayed at home on Saturdays but invited Pierre and Magdalina d'Alheim to visit them and even sometimes had them stay overnight, tucking all four of them up in a big wide bed.

When Pierre was almost eight years old, just before the start of the Franco-Prussian War [in 1870], Tatyana d'Alheim sent the children with their Aunt Poltoratskaya to London to stay with a good friend of hers, a Russian singer [Nevedomskaya] who at that time was famous under the name of "The Northern Star."[1] Madame Nevedomskaya immediately sat little Pierre down at the piano, and fairly soon he could play some Mozart variations very well. She told him he would be a second Beethoven. She was joking of course, but the idea took root in the mind of this fledgling musician, and ordinary folk kept stopping by the open window to listen to his playing [...].

Nevedomskaya often took Pierre to concerts. There he once heard a symphony called "The War" conducted by Colonne,[2] who was at that time unknown in France. Half the musicians were dressed in French Army uniform, and the other half in Prussian uniform; two singers famous at the time represented France (Teresa) and Prussia (a German woman whose name Pierre did not remember). During the interval several musicians walked around the hall, some of them playing French, and others Prussian marches. Little Pierre did not like this at all. Even then he was all in favour of the Republic [...].

After the war was over, Tatyana d'Alheim came to collect the children, and together with their aunt they returned to Paris. Pyotr told me how glad he was when he saw the flags of the Republic flying at the stations between Le Havre and Paris.

Soon after their return he had to forget his dreams of a musical career. His long hair fell beneath the scissors, and the virtuoso was sent off to study at the Lycée Condorcet.[3] There, at the age of about twelve, he already began putting out a literary-political journal and campaigning for Gambetta. By that time his mother was married to Murat, and the d'Alheim children had a brother and sister called Serge and Jeanne [...]. The d'Alheim children, like their mother, were of the Orthodox faith and were friends with the sons of a priest, Father Prilezhayev, who had recently been transferred from Nice to Paris. It was he who married my parents back in 1860 [...]. I am writing about my husband in such detail in order to explain how he became the sort of person I shall be talking about. I am somehow convinced that all of us die the same sort of people as we are born [...].

Because of his [...] political campaigning, Pierre was expelled from the Lycée by the Director, who was opposed to Gambetta. But when the latter became Chairman of the [Council of] Ministers,

Pierre returned to the Lycée and on the staircase met the Director who was just leaving, having been relieved of his duties. Pierre was triumphant! Soon after that was the death of Charles Dickens, and Pierre wept as he sat in class. The teacher asked him, "What's the matter, d'Alheim?" and he answered: "Haven't you read that Dickens has died?"

When Pierre was no more than seventeen, his mother gave him the complete works of Diderot, despite her husband's advice to wait a while before presenting him with such a gift. She was a niece of the Bobrishchev-Pushkin brothers,[4] who had been Decembrists and were exiled for many long years to Siberia. When one of them returned from there and settled on the family estate of Plekhanovo, not far from Yasnaya Polyana, the precentor in the village church did not dare intone the prayer "For the Tsar's family and all the ruling house." Because from the place where he was sitting Bobrishchev-Pushkin showed him his massive fist and stared at him in such a way that the precentor took fright. That was why they never prayed for the Tsar in Plekhanovo [...]. Tatyana's grandmother was a Georgian princess, and it was from her that she inherited her beauty. She was a really beautiful, intelligent and kindly woman. All the children positively adored her. From Pyotr's letters from London and other places where he went on holiday, one can tell what a total trust he had in his mother [...]. From Pyotr's letters to his mother [...] it is also evident what a penetrating mind he had, and how well he understood all the people with whom he came in contact.

Later, when Pierre was studying at the Sorbonne, where he read philosophy and at the same time attended the school of oriental languages and diplomacy, I believe he was the Paris correspondent for the newspaper *Vestnik Lota*. The family wanted him to have a diplomatic career, but he soon gave that up: he wanted to be a writer. That ambition had been alive in him ever since he was a child of course, because he had never wanted to speak Russian with his mother at home, and always wanted to know [his own native] French to perfection. He studied Russian at the École des Langues Orientales, when he was already about nineteen. In those years he had taught French and Russian literature at some open evening courses in Popencourt, lecturing on Diderot and Tolstoy.

Evidently he spoke so convincingly about Tolstoy that one of his audience who worked in a barber's shop gave it up and went back home to the Pyrenees where [...] he managed to enthuse several young friends and together with them founded a Tolstoyan colony right on the frontier with Spain. They resolved to refuse to do military service, and the colony was a sort of commune. In 1909 when Pyotr travelled around France for his work on Louis XII,[5] he visited this commune. It was by now very well organised, like a socialist colony, and was called "Estagel." I recall that one of a group of young anarchists came from there, who were arrested and of course sent to the guillotine. On the ringleader (who was nicknamed "Aimons la Science"), in a little suitcase he always had with him, the police found Pierre's book *La passion de maître François [Villon](The Passion of Master François [Villon])*[6]. These anarchists could perhaps be described as "coquillards"[7] or "Volga outlaws." I remember they organised an armed raid on a bank.

Pyotr was aged about twenty when a girl-friend of his sister, Maria Espejo, from a family of Russified Spaniards, tried by hook or by crook to seduce him, and eventually she got her way by inviting him to visit her studio. He told me afterwards that as he left, he had a clear sense of having fallen into an abyss. However, he saw it as his duty to marry Espejo, even though she was almost fifteen years his senior. His parents were against it of course, and he had to wait till he came of age. He and his family fell out, and he left home almost without any luggage except for one suitcase filled with the collected works of Diderot. A year later he married Espejo, and they left for Brussels.

There, together with a group of new friends from Belgium and France, the sons of communards,[8] he organised some popular evening courses under the title "La jeune garde libérale de St. Josteunud," called after the suburb of that name. It was maybe from this little cell that the Maison du Peuple eventually arose in Brussels. In the cell along with Pierre their worked a man called François Fonceau, who was later known as the author of the play *The Wedding of Mademoiselle Belmans*, and also von der Welde,[9] who read political economy and was the youngest in their circle. Much later, when he was a prominent socialist, there was a lot

Pyotr d'Alheim, c. 1900.

about him that Pierre disliked. We met von der Welde in 1903, I think, in Paris, in the salon of Menard d'Orian,[10] at a time when he held very progressive views [...].

Menard was also a great friend of Gambetta. She was a deputy and had extremely close dealings with Victor Hugo. Uncle Ivan d'Alheim had for a long time been friends with this family [...]. Georges, the grandson of Victor Hugo, was married to the daughter of Menard d'Orian [Pauline]. [...] We met von der Welde at a large gathering where, as they say, "le tout Paris" was in attendance. When Mme Menard introduced them, Pyotr reminded von der Welde of the start of his career, but the man by now had great illusions about himself and did not deign to recollect. Then Pyotr reminded him how during a political demonstration von der Welde and another member of their central committee had one evening ran to a well-known Brussels lawyer during dinner and begged him to hide them from the police. The man did so, and opened up his wine cellar to them. Pyotr did not need to recount the rest of the story in their hostess' presence, because at the very outset von der Welde exclaimed, "Of course, of course, I remember. So you and I are old acquaintances." But their hostess nevertheless grasped the point of the story and burst out laughing. She generally appreciated Pyotr and enjoyed discussions with him, despite the fact that on more than one occasion he asked her: "How do you combine your socialist convictions with the fact that at the same time you manufacture weapons?"

I recall how once, on returning from Moscow, we called to see her. The salon was full. It was her *jour fixe*. She seated Pyotr down next to her and asked him about events in Russia (if I am not mistaken, it was the spring of 1906). Then suddenly she exclaimed, "Whenever I listen to d'Alheim, it seems as if the windows have suddenly been opened and a breath of fresh air blows in [...]." Not that we were at Menard d'Orian's very often, but hers was the only salon where I enjoyed singing. Both husband and wife were agreeable people who naively imagined themselves to be socialists.

[When] Pyotr returned from Belgium, there were various contretemps between him and his wife. At the same time Pyotr was enrolled for army service and, as they say, "il a opté pour la France" [i.e., he "opted in favour of France"], despite the fact that his father was not a French citizen, because on arrival in France, his father began concentrating on his painting and forgot about everything else. So Pyotr became a French citizen. He joined his regiment as a volunteer and served for a whole year. Probably he inherited a military streak from his forebears, the de Limousins, because his detachment (he was then a noncommissioned officer) was the only one in which not a single soldier reported sick during the whole period of the manoeuvres, and they had taken place in the south during the worst heatwave. He refused to allow wealthy soldiers to dine in town, and since they had the means they were required to improve the general menu of their comrades. The soldiers were altogether very fond of him and called him "père Dalin."

I do not know his attitude towards religion. I think it was similar to my own. His mother passed on to me a prayer by Pyotr that she wrote down when he was a child. He prayed God that everyone whom he loved should love him in return. I now wonder though: Whom did he not love? He loved everyone, he strove for close contact with people and suffered at the impossibility of conversing with them in a way such that "les esprits s'épousent." His letters to his mother reveal his negative attitude to militarism, to the leaders' injustices and their carping at the lower ranks of common soldiers.

During his stay in Brussels, he got to know the family of Madoux, manager of the newspaper *L'Étoile Belge*, whose Paris correspondent he later became. The son of Madoux was an artist and constantly at odds with his father. In 1895 he removed with his whole family to Paris, and they often visited us at Varya's studio [...]. In 1891, Pyotr published a small brochure with the [Belgian] publisher Savine about the coquillards, i.e., about their jargon and the ballades erroneously attributed to the poet Villon. He was already thinking about Villon, although he only managed to write and publish his work on him with Olendorf in 1899. The wife of Olendorf turned out to be the same Anna Cornelli with whom Pyotr had been friends as a child.

When we came to Paris with Uncle Ivan, Pyotr had been living apart from his wife for a long time. We got to know one another more or less by chance. He did not visit his father, since our uncle had long been divorced from his mother. [But] after his death Pyotr began to visit us very frequently, and he also brought along his brother Serge Murat. This brings us up to the period when our joint work together began. (SV, 108–16.)

Voice Studies in Paris

It was in 1895 that Maria Olenina and Pyotr d'Alheim began their collaboration. At that time the young singer was studying with the Paris voice teacher Julie Vieuxtemps[11] (known before marriage as Mademoiselle de la Blanchette). Olenina had begun lessons with her immediately on arrival in Paris, in 1893.

Olenina-d'Alheim:
On arrival in Paris with Uncle d'Alheim, I went [...] to a young woman professor. She was strongly recommended to me and was the pupil of two celebrities: Mme [Rosine] Laborde and [Gilbert-Louis] Dupré.[12] I later knew two [of Dupré's] pupils: Emma Calvé[13] and Marie Dupré. [Gilbert-Louis] Dupré was a famous tenor, who amazed everyone with the clarity of his diction, and his pupil managed to pass this on to me, which of course was not so easy. After all, I was Russian. But still, whenever I sang at Pyotr's *conférences*, I pronounced the French text so well that one of the chief artistes of the Comédie Française announced that her young pensionnaires [boarding pupils] would do no harm to take a few lessons in French pronunciation from Mme Olenina. It all proved that my professor, then still unmarried and called de la Blanchette, knew her job.

Every summer I followed her to the country village where she spent her vacations, surrounded by her pupils, and where her own Professor Laborde also lived in summer. I remember that in the second summer Mme Laborde had the idea of putting on a sort of concert in the ancient local church. I was to perform Schubert's "Ave Maria." Two days beforehand, I suddenly completely lost my voice. In the same village the family of a Doctor Landowski were also spending their vacation. He was a Pole who had fled after the Polish uprising. Doctor Landowski tried every way to restore my voice, but all in vain, alas. Then I decided simply not to speak at all for two days and take part in the mass all the same. When it was my turn to sing, everyone in the church grew tense. They all knew, of course, that I had lost my voice. Then, to everyone's amazement, my voice suddenly rang out clear and strong.

I should mention that it always had the ability to sound like the flute stop on an organ, so it was well suited for singing in church. Mlle Blanchette was overjoyed of course, and Mme Laborde wanted to take me over as her own pupil. Seeing my own teacher's agitation, Uncle Ivan advised me to sign a contract with her, which I did, and we began studying the operatic repertoire. Of course, she could not have been pleased with my resolve to became a concert performer. "C'est très humain," as the French say. (SV, 119–20.)

A contract was duly signed up, and the lessons continued. Despite the success of these studies, however, Olenina's overall dealings with Vieuxtemps were not altogether problem-free. Vieuxtemps regarded her main aim as making an opera singer of her young Russian pupil, and she could envisage no alternative course for her to follow. Indeed, at that time there was only one way forward for young singers—via the opera. However, Maria Olenina's destiny lay elsewhere, in the direction of chamber performance. This was predetermined by two factors—first of all, the actual nature of her talent, and secondly, her meeting with Pyotr d'Alheim.

Olenina-d'Alheim:

In the spring my teacher, Madame Vieuxtemps, took me to see Massenet, and then to one of the directors of the Brussels Opera. Both these men told her I was made not for the [opera] stage but for the concert platform, because I delved into all the minutiae of the text, both musical and poetic.

I do not think that Mme Vieuxtemps was altogether pleased with this verdict—I had a contract with her, according to which I was obliged to pay her 20 thousand [francs] as soon as I joined one of the major theatres: the Opéra Comique[14] in Paris, La Monnaie in

Brussels, or the Mariinsky Theatre in St. Petersburg. But she did not despair and took me to see the director of the Opéra Comique. He evidently found me of interest to the [theatre], and after auditioning me, scheduled another meeting when I was to bring along the role of Carmen. After I returned home, somebody—I forget who —told me that once I signed a contract I would have to sing everything that the directors offered me.

I remember even now, that when our mother was still alive, she [optimistically] wrote to our aunt that my father and she would not be distressed if I joined the Opéra Comique. For some reason she imagined that this meant operetta. In general my wish to go on stage was not to my parents' taste—at that time there were still so many aristocratic prejudices. (SV, 117–18.)

Now I must recount what it was I sang for my teacher in Paris. For her pupils' concerts she used to invite one of the lesser known, not the most celebrated, composers, and we pupils all had to sing this person's works at these concerts—for example, people like Pessard and Chaminade.[15] [...] I must say something about the evening devoted to Pessard. He immediately realised I was not just a society singer, but a real artiste, and at that concert he had the idea of leading me out on stage himself. But I showed my probably naive and ingenuous character, and in response to his kind gesture I answered: "Merci, but I can manage to walk out on stage myself, without assistance." (BNB, 38–39.)

The contract with Vieuxtemps was not fulfilled in the way that the latter envisaged. Many years later, in the year 1920, Maria Olenina still owed her money for lessons she had taken with her back in the nineteenth century. After lengthy litigation, in 1920, she offered Julie Vieuxtemps a financial scheme in order to liquidate her debt. The scheme was accepted.

Julie Vieuxtemps to Olenina-d'Alheim:
Madame, in reply to your letter received yesterday, I confirm that I accept the method of payment suggested by you.

The sum of 500 francs shall be paid immediately, after which you will pay in monthly instalments of 100 francs until the basic debt, the interest, and legal expenses are fully covered. Following this all disputed questions between us shall be considered as regulated and settled.

Please accept my best wishes.

Julie Vieuxtemps.

(J. Vieuxtemps, letter of 21 November 1920 to M. Olenina-d'Alheim, GMMC, fond 256, no. 952.)

The Mussorgsky *Conférences*

So ended the dealings between teacher and pupil—consisting of four years of lessons and over twenty years' litigation, but all of which prepared Olenina for a career that Vieuxtemps had never remotely dreamed of. At that time, in 1895, the young singer was on the threshold of that career, and the course she was embarking on was utterly unusual for France. This consisted of so-called "lectures" or lecture-recitals (*conférences* in French)[16] on Mussorgsky. These events began almost by chance. When Pyotr d'Alheim's friends introduced him to the works of Mussorgsky, he was delighted not just at the composer's artistry, but also at his views on art that coincided with his own.

Very shortly it was decided to introduce Mussorgsky to the people of Paris, and the d'Alheims began preparing their *conférences*. Apart from Pyotr as *conférencier*, these were to involve Maria Olenina and the pianist Charles Foerster, a pupil of Liszt and friend of Paderewski.[17] Much later, while writing her memoirs in the 1950s, Olenina wrote Pyotr Suvchinsky[18] a letter telling him about the history of those first *conférences* starting in 1896:

Olenina-d'Alheim:
Esteemed Pyotr Petrovich,
    You asked yesterday who was still alive of those who attended Pierre d'Alheim's first *conférences*. I have brought you a notebook in which he collected all his articles and announcements, and also the list we kept of our first audience. I gradually keep recalling that time (and I also remember Debussy, among other things).

In 1894 [?] d'Alheim was editor of (the Russian section of) *Le Temps*. Robert Godet was also there (for England). (Maybe you know his book *En marge de Boris Godounoff*.) They became friends, and once Godet—he was a friend of Debussy and of de Brayer[19] whose name you will find in the list—asked d'Alheim to translate a few scenes from *Boris*. He and de Brayer were thrilled by it at that time, and Debussy too most probably.

In early 1895 d'Alheim introduced me to Godet, who heard that I sang, and was very keen to arrange some *conférences* with performance of works by Mussorgsky, his songs. D'Alheim eagerly took up this idea, since he too was enthusiastic about Mussorgsky's genius. It was then that he began writing his book....

In October of 1894 he was sent as correspondent of *Le Temps* to attend the funeral of Alexander III. In Petrograd[20] he met up with Bessel, who told him that Mussorgsky's whole works were worthless and offered to sell them to d'Alheim for 600 roubles.... D'Alheim did not have such a sum, and a year later he published his book on Mussorgsky in Paris. You can read about this in this large notebook.

In 1896, Debussy did not attend a single session. At that time he was working on *Pelléas*, and all of us and his friends were surprised at his stubbornness, and others—not his friends—made ironic comments. From the article "Moussorgski et Debussy" which you ran through yesterday, you know what we thought of Debussy and about his accusation of Mussorgsky's [illegible].

When I met with him in 1911, we never exchanged so much as a couple of words. I never had the ability to come out with polite phrases, "donner du cher maître," etc., and Debussy was very shy. Because of that we simply stared at one another, and that was how our meeting ended.

I have brought you this large notebook in the belief that it will interest you. In a few days' time, after the holidays, I will visit you. I shall be specially glad to meet your wife. We may even become friends.

Best wishes.

Olenina.

(BN.)

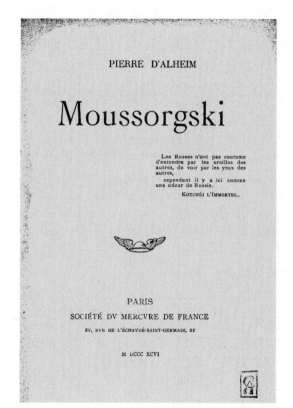

PIERRE D'ALHEIM

Moussorgski

Les Russes n'ont pas coutume
d'entendre par les oreilles des
autres, de voir par les yeux des
autres,
cependant il y a ici comme
une odeur de Russie.
KOTCHÉI L'IMMORTEL.

PARIS
SOCIÉTÉ DV MERCVRE DE FRANCE
XV, RVE DE L'ÉCHAVDÉ-SAINT-GERMAIN, XV

M DCCC XCVI

☞ The title page
of Pierre d'Alheim's
book, *Moussorgski*
(Paris: Société du
Mercure de France,
1896).

The *conférences* of 1896 were a major event not just for Parisians, who were discovering Mussorgsky for the first time, but for Olenina herself. This was the start of her career as a singer, and the first step towards creation of the "House of Song." It was at this time that her personal artistic philosophy was formed, based on the idea of the performer's renunciation of self in the service of the composer, the audience, and of artistic truth. Abandoning all thought of herself and her artistic ego, she saw her task as lying in total submission and immersion of herself in the composer and the poet's conception. In Olenina's view, any performance based on such a philosophy can never be premised on the idea of financial success, nor can it tolerate any cheap publicity.

Olenina-d'Alheim:
I was always opposed to any publicity, believing it to be incompatible with an artist's dignity. I valued the success I had with my

listeners, and at the end of my career I never even concerned myself with celebrity. That comes mainly as the result of painstaking advertisement, and I rejected that and we never spent any money on it. Pyotr was of the same opinion as myself. At all my concerts we took money only for the actual tickets; all the rest (the notices, the programmes) was provided and was not on sale. And it was like that even before the House of Song was founded.

We were convinced that great composers created their works for everyone irrespectively—just like God, the creator of the universe, who according to the Gospels showers sunlight and rain on all people, both the evil and the good. And the creative geniuses of this earth act in the same way. And if at some difficult moment any of them ever maintained that "it takes a genius to understand a genius" (it was Balzac who said that, I believe), [I think] he would have agreed that in fact we do not know where geniuses are born and bred. After all they are not cultivated in a nursery. That is why we made a rule not to fix high prices for our tickets. Such a system is not very profitable, of course, but [it follows] the saying that "friends are more important than money". (SV, 29–30.)

That same spring of 1895 we went to Belgium—Pyotr, Varya and I. He was very interested in Varya's artistic talent. He, Varya and I had good connections with the artistic world in Belgium, and he wanted to introduce her to one of the artists well known at the time. He began with Courtens. Pyotr was going to go to the sea [at Noordeijk]. We decided to follow him and set Varya up there for the summer. At Noordeijk I saw the sea for the first time. In the evenings it seemed to be made of fire, and all of us took our shoes off and dabbled our feet in the waves that glistened as they rolled inshore. On the return journey, from Brussels we called in at Ostend. It was late in the evening. The sea could not be seen, but I could hear its deep dull sighing and unconsciously recalled Beethoven's "Moonlight" sonata.

When we returned to Paris, my future mother-in-law often invited me and told me about Pyotr's childhood, and also about the terrible year when the troops from Versailles broke up the communards. They dug a deep trench around the Parc de Monceau, into which they thrust everyone who got in their path. One morning the

Murat family servant was walking along with some shopping, and the soldiers seized her and shoved her into the trench. Suddenly an officer in command of the squad noticed her and shouted out in fright, "What are you doing there?" Quickly he hauled her back out of the trench: it emerged that the girl was from the same village as he.

We spent the summer of 1895 not far from Paris, where Pyotr worked on translating all the Mussorgsky songs to be included in the lecture programmes. I helped him as much as I could. At the same time he had to go into Paris each day, where he worked for two newspapers. Once he returned quite ill—it turned out he had typhoid. It was a very hard ordeal for me. I wondered whether I could save him by my care which was probably inadequate. But fortunately Pyotr recovered, and I too came back to life.

Sergei Murat visited us at that time, though not for long, and then Varya returned from Holland after a very good summer's work. In October, when we were back in Paris and Pyotr was preparing the first French biography of Mussorgsky,[21] our father came. Pyotr could not take him around Paris at night to the Moulin Rouge and other fashionable bars of the time, he was unable to break off from his work. But a friend of Pyotr's, Jacques Dariel, chief secretary of the newspaper *Le Soir*, with whom he then shared an apartment, undertook to stand in for him, and together with Varya they took father to the Moulin Rouge and other night bars of Paris. I of course did not join their merry company, and I had never visited Paris by night before.

In early December father returned home, and we prepared our *conférence*. Pyotr's book came out with Mercure de France[22] publishers at the end of November, if I'm not mistaken. In January in the studio there were meetings of writers, musicians, and other artists on invitation from Pyotr, Robert Godet, and de Brayer. I recall that Mallarmé[23] was very interested in Mussorgsky, and many others too.

Debussy did not attend these meetings, and nor was he present at the *conférences* either, not one of them. He was then busy with his *Pelléas* and was maybe unable to tear himself away from his work. Neither Godet nor de Brayer could even get Debussy to look through the score of "Boris." When he finally heard Mussorgsky

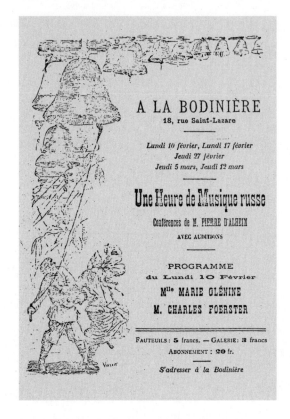

⤳ Poster announcing the first Mussorgsky *conférences* in Paris given by Mlle. Marie Olénine, M. Pierre d'Alheim and M. Charles Foerster, 10, 17, and 27 February and 5 and 12 March 1896.

A LA BODINIÈRE

18, rue Saint-Lazare

Lundi 10 février, Lundi 17 février
Jeudi 27 février
Jeudi 5 mars, Jeudi 12 mars

Une Heure de Musique russe

Conférences de M. PIERRE D'ALHEIM

AVEC AUDITIONS

PROGRAMME
du Lundi 10 Février

Mlle MARIE OLÉNINE
M. CHARLES FOERSTER

FAUTEUILS: 5 francs. — GALERIE: 3 francs
ABONNEMENT : 20 fr.

S'adresser à la Bodinière

performed by me, he wrote a remarkable review of me. That was in 1901, in the spring, when I gave a Mussorgsky evening together with Cortot, and Debussy was at that time critic for the *Revue blanche*. (SV, 118–19.)

The Mussorgsky lecture-recitals, or *conférences*, in 1896 raised a response not just in Paris, but also in faraway Russia. The musical press there appreciated a Russian singer's success in Paris, and the success of Russian music there made a considerable impression. For the Parisian, and later the Brussels, public these *conférences* were their first acquaintance with Mussorgsky's vocal works. Public understanding and appreciation were also encouraged by the appearance of d'Alheim's book, which in the words of *Russkaya muzyka'lnaya gazeta* presented a series of essays "touching on those external and inner forms of Russian life that are reflected in the compositions of Mussorgsky." The *conférences* were timed for the fifteenth anniversary of the composer's death. Each programme consisted of two parts—a lecture by Pyotr d'Alheim, followed by a concert section performed by Maria Olenina with Foerster as accompanist. Essentially, this marked the beginning of Olenina's career as a concert performer.

In order to understand the reaction of the French, and later the Belgian, public to these presentations, one has to appreciate the degree of their knowledge—or, rather, their ignorance—of Russian music. This was true of listeners in the West in general. The first serious critic who tried to introduce his compatriots to Russian music was Hector Berlioz. His own personal contacts with Glinka enabled him to *tell* Parisians about Glinka as a composer of genius, although at the time there was no chance of actually hearing his works. Later on, sheer good fortune enabled Dargomyzhsky to perform some of his own compositions for Belgian music-lovers. This in itself would have changed nothing, however, had Dargomyzhsky not aroused a certain interest in Russian music among Belgian performers. However, a Belgian music-lover called Louise Merci d'Argenteau[24] began performing works by Borodin, Rimsky-Korsakov, Balakirev, Mussorgsky and Cui in her concerts. Yet even these performances were isolated episodes.

In the late nineteenth century, when the Paris World Exhibitions began taking place on a regular basis, there were more opportunities for Parisians to acquaint themselves with Russian music. At the 1878 exhibition in the Trocadéro concert hall the Russian Concerts were given with Nikolai Rubinstein as conductor. However, even he emerged as a not altogether unbiassed advocate: his concert programmes hardly included a single work by the New Russian School. Among contemporary composers only his brother Anton Rubinstein[25] and Tchaikovsky were included, and Glinka and Dargomyzhsky were represented only in the form of a few extracts.

Ten years later, at the 1888 Exhibition, on the initiative of the publisher and promoter Belyaev,[26] the same hall in Trocadéro was the scene of Russian concerts conducted by Rimsky-Korsakov. This time the picture was somewhat broader. The programmes included works such as Rimsky's *Antar*, Borodin's *In the Steppes of Central Asia*, Mussorgsky's *Night on Bald Mountain*, symphonies by Glazunov, and other works. Yet although listeners at these concerts received a first introduction to this Russian music, it was a somewhat unbalanced presentation, since no vocal compositions were performed—or else their Russian texts were incomprehensible and thus inaccessible to the French audiences.

On the few occasions when a few isolated works of Russian vocal music actually figured in the programmes of French and Belgian performers, and where they were published with texts in French, these were only compositions by Tchaikovsky and maybe César Cui. True, these programmes often included Russian composers' settings of verse by French poets. But Mussorgsky's music was probably in the worst predicament of all, and its uniquely Russian spirit, unusual rhythms and harmony seemed to offend against all the principles of musical tradition to which the Paris public were accustomed.

It was at that time, and against this background, that the *conférences* on Mussorgsky began, painstakingly prepared in the form of what we would now call lecture-recitals. For these events Pyotr d'Alheim prepared special translations, and it was here that young Maria Olenina first appeared and displayed her sparkling talent. As one writer, P. Weimarn, commented, this introduction to Mussorgsky's works for the voice was not just a spontaneous random event but had a "practical" and programmatic character. Mussorgsky's music now sounded more comprehensible and it was heard often enough for people to get to know and accept its unconventional features. Furthermore the music was performed with such talent that it could not be ignored, and in the programmes against each item were the intriguing words "1-re audition" —first performance. (*Russkaya muzykal'naya gazeta*, March 1896, 400.) Yet all of this occurred at a time when Mussorgsky had not yet been appreciated even at home, in Russia.

Olenina-d'Alheim:
At that time, in 1896, both before and during the *conférences*, reports from Paris reached various towns and newspapers in Russia, and Vladimir Stasov wrote some detailed articles on the subject. And when all these articles about us and the promotion of Russian music, in which we played an active part, appeared and were passed on to Pyotr via "À presse la presse" [a newspaper cutting service], I did not even bother to look at them.

I [always] was a sort of holy innocent [*yurodivaya*] or under some spell, and even now I admit that I am more interested in issues concerning the whole of mankind and its fate on this earth, and much less concerned with individual, personal questions that are limited in scale. But even if I was uninterested in what they wrote about me personally, one might wonder how I could fail to be concerned by what people thought about Mussorgsky whose work I so much loved? Yet to me it was enough to know and love his work. To find out what other people said about him somehow did not concern me.

And although all these reports could affect our subsequent activities for good or ill, I never gave the matter a thought. I knew that our future work depended solely on our pockets: if there was money to continue our promotion of Mussorgsky, everything would go well; if there was no money, everything would collapse, no matter how they praised us. And I was certain we would be equal to our task, and that my performance would be beyond reproach. I was sure of this, because I gave my entire heart and soul to my performances, and so far as my voice was concerned, I knew how to use and control it, and I had no fears at all on that score. (SV, 120–21)

The *conférences* went off with great success [...]. [Pyotr] d'Alheim was a speaker of rare talent. He never read, but spoke freely, and his fairly light baritone voice had a certain captivating quality.

Almost all these sessions were attended by Pyotr's wife Maria Espejo. Probably she took a liking to me, because soon after that she agreed to a divorce with Pyotr. We did not ask her for this at the time, and actually got married much later, in 1898, in order to pacify old Murat who was very anxious that our marriage be legalised. Our dealings with Espejo were highly unusual. She continued to be fond of her divorced husband, and came to see us at Bois le Roy. She remained on the friendliest of terms with me right until her death. And in 1926, when I was in Moscow and she lay dying in France in an old people's home founded by Rothschild, she ordered that her last three hundred francs be handed to me. I did not enquire where she was buried, and somehow I never concerned myself with such questions. Nor would I now even think of going to my father's grave at Telebukino, where he was buried in 1910.

I cannot comprehend any cult of the dead. I love life and not death. Ever since [Pyotr's] death in 1922, I have not been to visit [his grave] more than five times. The first time was soon after the burial—no, not so soon, only six months later, when Lyova Tarasevich came in October and wanted to visit Pyotr's grave. I think about Pyotr constantly, and I am tormented by such pangs of conscience that it was only the need to continue his cause that gave me the strength not to despair. Because of this up till now it has been so difficult to keep my promise and describe our work together. Had he not met me, he would have completed all his writings, some of them only conceived, and some unfinished. I cannot forgive myself for my truly thoughtless egoism—yet Pyotr realised that without him I could not cope with my task, and he sacrificed everything for it, to ensure its ultimate success.

Often he used to say that perhaps he himself was not called on to be creative, but to direct the work of others. But I wonder whether these words were really sincere? In his heart of hearts was he not anguished at the impossibility of creating something of his own? How easy it is for me to recall my childhood, and how difficult and bitter are the memories of life with Pyotr! I know only that he allowed me to experience and understand what true friendship was, i.e., what is loftiest and most valuable in human life. He was a friend to me. And when I was left on my own, I involuntarily sought for such friendship again and I could not find it. Talking about [friendship] I cannot help recalling the song by Hugo Wolf to words by Mörike "Wo find' ich Trost?" But in this song it is not simply love that is described, it is Christ's loving friendship for people. And I often think how injured He must have been just before His death, when He told his disciples: I now call you not my disciples, but my friends; and then soon His favourite disciple John and his brother and mother asked Him to let them sit, the one on His right hand and the other on His left, when He entered the Kingdom of Heaven. What a blow, I believe, that must have been to Him. (SV, 121–23.)

I have not said yet how we went on after the *conférences*. In May Pyotr left as a correspondent for his paper to attend the coronation of Nicholas II. I remained in Paris in order to arrange a matinée performance of Mussorgsky at *Le Figaro*, as Pyotr had advised me. Probably he had already negotiated with the chief editors of *Figaro*, or maybe they approached him, I somehow don't recall. I think they did (approach him), the success of the talks was indeed quite remarkable. So there I was starting negotiations with the editorial secretary and telling him that Mussorgsky was the favourite composer of the young Tsar. I don't myself know now why I said that. Later on in Moscow I heard that in a whole list of operas submitted to him, *Boris Godunov* was the only one that the Tsar crossed out.

Those taking part in the *Figaro* morning concert were [Jean] Noté,[27] the baritone from the Paris Opera, myself, and a choir from the Russian church. In the programme we included the final scene from *Khovanshchina*, and I believe it was Mangen, the chef d'orchestre from the Opera, who conducted. I remember that at the rehearsal Noté could not cope with Dosifei's[28] descending scale, and Mangen asked him: "Monsieur Noté, avez-vous oublié comment on chante une gamme chromatique?" The programme was compiled by myself, and this was the first programme that I personally put together. The matinée was a great success. Soon after that I too got ready to leave for Moscow. (SV, 126.)

Journey to Russia

The d'Alheims' journey to Russia took place in 1896. Apart from Moscow, they visited St. Petersburg, Istomino, and Nizhny Novgorod. One encounter on that journey produced a deep impression on Olenina. This was her meeting with the folk-storyteller (*skazitel'nitsa*) Fedosova[29] during the All-Russian Exhibition at Nizhny Novgorod.

The lamentations (*prichitaniya*) performed by Fedosova reminded Olenina of her childhood impressions of Istomino bound up with a tragic episode when a ferry sank on the River Oka. As a child Maria had also seen a peasant-woman called Darya drown. The woman perished with her own twelve-year-old daughter Dunya and with her old mother looking on.

Olenina-d'Alheim:
When Darya was dragged to shore, Dunya threw herself on her grandma's neck and both of them started wailing. Each of them pronounced her own words, but they sang their lament with one voice. It was the first time I heard lamenting like that. Later on I attended a peasant gathering, a women's meeting, and heard the bride weeping and lamenting. [Alexander] Olenin's collection has one such lament noted down. (SV, 93.)

Now, in Nizhny Novgorod, it was no longer a little girl listening to Fedosova, but a mature singer who imagined what it might be like to adopt Fedosova's manner of performance for herself.

Olenina-d'Alheim:
My husband was sent as correspondent by the magazine *Le Temps*. In the summer we and Alyosha [Turgenev] met in Nizhny

Novgorod, where Pyotr was supposed to write an article for his journal. He had arranged with a Russian journalist who resided permanently in Paris and was returning there before we were, that he would hand the article in to *Le Temps* for him. But having heard no news for a long time, Pyotr decided to go to Paris himself. There he discovered that instead of handing the article in to the editors of *Le Temps*, his colleague had given or sold it to *Figaro*, and himself left on vacation for Les Sables d'Olonne.[30] Pierre was forced to go there himself in order to settle accounts with this pleasant monsieur.

In Nizhny at that time there was the folk-storyteller Orina Fedosova—from the Vologda province, unless I am mistaken, or maybe from the Olenetskaya. I well remember her performances in the town's grand theatre, which was almost empty because hardly anyone was interested in such artists. A few officials appeared, and she was demonstrated—actually demonstrated—by an official expert on Russian epic tales [*byliny*] and songs. He was very perplexed when she came out on stage for the first time and announced, "Can't all the audience come and sit closer to me, or otherwise they're all high up and far away. Let them come down. They'll hear better, and it'll be easier for me." Up on high, of course, there were students and the less well-to-do public. The learned gentleman [...] tried to explain to the old woman that there was no way of fulfilling her wish, but she would not give in, and she started singing only when the poorer public from the upper balcony were grouped together in the front rows.

She sang some widow's laments. The professor asked the audience to note that after each "couplet" she performed peculiar "*fioriture*" with her voice—"What 'fury-turies' are you going on about, old fellow?" Fedosova retorted. "Those are tears and sobs." After that she sang one of the old epic tales and also repeated it the following day, but with a few changes in the nature description. My husband and I went to ask her why she changed the text of the tale in this way. "Yesterday it was dull, you see, and rainy. But today there's a bit of sun. And so the story came out different," she explained. Yes, Fedosova was an unusual artist, in the best sense of the word. (SV, 91–92.)

Title pages
of Maria Olenina-
d'Alheim's book
on Mussorgsky, *Le
Legs de Moussorgski*
(Paris: Eugène
Rey, 1908).

Fedosova's performance was so important to Olenina that she talked about it in various ways at least three times—in her book *The Mussorgsky Legacy (Zavety Musorgskogo)*, in her memoirs "Snovidenie i vospominaniya" ("Dream and Recollections"), and in an interview that she gave to the present writer.

Olenina-d'Alheim:
I visited her [after her performance]. During our brief, friendly conversation, speaking in the marvelous language of a folk story-teller, she initiated me into the most secret, concealed parts of her performer's gift. She taught me what singing is in *nature*, in human nature.

At that time I did not fully understand her. Her phrases set my thoughts working, and it was only much later that I understood them in a light for which my eyes were at that time still unprepared. (ZM, 35.)

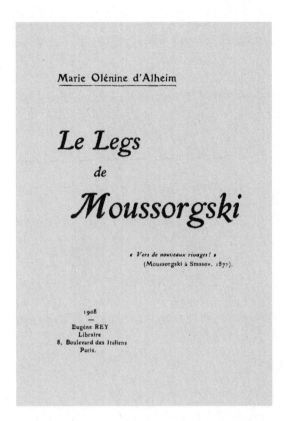

Marie Olénine d'Alheim

Le Legs
de
Moussorgski

« *Vers de nouveaux rivages!* »
(Moussorgski à Stassov. 187?).

1908
—
Eugène REY
Libraire
8, Boulevard des Italiens
Paris.

"One has to understand," the storyteller Ryabinin[31] said in 1870. "And then your voice starts running," said Fedosova the tale-teller in 1896. (ZM, 31.)

Meetings and conversations with Fedosova confirmed and strengthened Olenina's own ideas about the relationship between words and music in vocal interpretation. Her conclusions after hearing Fedosova's performance were extremely interesting: her thoughts on the creative act of artistic performance reveal to us how such an act of musical creation came about in her own case, and they also explain to some extent the effect it had on her listeners.

Olenina-d'Alheim:
In our time—a time of revival—surely the first task of the performer, which we have to approach willy-nilly, consists in "making room" for song in the natural expression of feeling. Of course, I can

And its Russian translation, *Zavety M.P. Musorgskogo* (Moscow: Muzyka i zhizn', 1910).

no longer recall the folk storyteller's actual words, because at that time I failed to ascribe to them the meaning they later acquired for me. The thoughts prompted by her developed, and this continued over a long period, although I was really deeply interested in this question. A powerful impression touches that centre in our soul where feelings are born, and along with them the need to express and demonstrate them. If the impression is relatively weak, it will be released in words. A more powerful and sudden impression will reveal itself as a cry, and in this respect the foundation of our nature remains constant. But in this cry the ability of a "civilised" person to express inner feelings stops short. However, in a person who has preserved his communion with nature, a feeling just as powerful—and not just a physical but also an emotional one—evokes "singing" […].

Isn't this exactly what folk tale-tellers do when they are invited to "lament" over a dead person? They, as it were, fill out that blunted sense of grief—a feeling that is no longer active yet still lives on in the hearts of those who call on their assistance.

From the age of twelve Fedosova had been to funerals and weddings. Later she also attended the farewell ceremonies for army recruits, who were lamented over as if they had died. Fedosova kept a whole volume of "lamentations," and highly expressive they were [...].

Doesn't the creative artist do exactly the same thing, the only difference being that nobody actually asks for this service? The expression of his grief hovers in concert halls and theatre auditoriums. [...] Who else but the performer [...] can return to Nature and promote a more correct view of things? And if this attracts him, if he realises that absolute primacy rests with the creative artist [i.e., the composer], if he wants to worthily share his own powers with him in fleshing this out—then let him turn to the performance of Mussorgsky [...].

Tell your grief within yourself. *Shout* about it to yourself as you surrender to it—and *sing* of it to others. And if you do so, you will be in a state to perform *The Little Orphan* [*Sirotka*] superbly and with appropriate feeling. (ZM, 36–39.)

In Russia, the year 1896 was filled with important events. One of them was the tragedy that took place on the 18 May at Khodynka Field, just outside Moscow. Olenina evidently arrived in the city shortly after it occurred.

Olenina-d'Alheim:
Our aunt and Varya still remained in Paris and followed after me somewhat later, along with Lyova Tarasevich. In Moscow Pyotr was expecting me with such impatience that he could not wait, and he set off to meet my train at the nearest station. But then his train was late by several minutes, and in that way we missed each other. I went on directly to the Turgenevs's apartment. Our aunt Bakunina, the mother of Sonya, lived with them. I was of course afraid to mention to her the death of my unfortunate young cousin Kolya. This grieved her greatly: she was of course expecting that I would stay with her and have a weep over him. But I did not want to remind her of his terrible death: he was exiled to the Vologda Province after he flogged an old cook to death while in a drunken state. And he himself was killed while in exile by some peasants that he rudely chased out of a tavern. About two hours later Pyotr finally returned from his unsuccessful journey to meet me. (SV, 126.)

At that time rumours were still going around Moscow of the accident that had just happened on Khodynka Field[32] during the national fete and celebrations to mark the coronation. Because of the disgraceful organisation, more than a thousand people had perished. Pyotr witnessed what happened. The cause of it all was thievery on a grand scale. A few years before, a French exhibition had taken place on Khodynka Field, and of course a fair number of wells had been dug there. The organisers of this recent popular fete had not filled in these wells, but simply covered them over with planks and turf, which was of course more economical for them. All the theatre-booths erected for the amusement of the public were surrounded by a huge area which people had to enter one by one between two buildings. These entrances were constructed like a funnel, with the walls of the two adjacent buildings on a slant.

The gifts presented to the public to commemorate the coronation were not available in sufficient quantity—also a piece of thievery of course—and to cover it up they began distributing the gifts before sunrise. There was no military band going around in groups and dividing up the crowd, as at the coronation of Alexander III. They claimed the Tsar had said he wanted to be totally united with his people, and for that reason they had [dispensed with] everything—including soldiers and police.

When the crowd found out that the gifts were being distributed, they rushed through the entrances into the central area because that was where they were being handed out. You can imagine what happened. People crushed one another in those stupidly constructed entry funnels, and others all around the Khodynka Field fell into the wells after the flimsy planking cracked under their weight. In each of these traps they found about thirty or forty people.

Pyotr saw all this, without realising at first why a lot of people came running off the field in terror, trying to escape. He described this "popular feast" in his book *Sur les pointes*. This was a very brief and cursory biography of all the Romanov tsars, starting with Mikhail and ending with Nicholas II. [The book] was strictly prohibited by the censorship in St. Petersburg.

At home in the country we saw one of the elders who had been invited from every locality to attend the coronation. He was the godfather of my sister Varya. He had three coronation medals, but he wore only two of them, claiming that the third had been "stained with the people's blood." The whole incident on Khodynka Field was kept secret from the Tsar. The banquets and ceremonies were supposed to continue, but the dowager Empress and the Procurator of the Synod spoke out against it. They demanded all festivities be halted and that requiem mass be celebrated in every church. [However] a group of Grand Princes got the upper hand, and the first solemn ceremony was held in the French Embassy. As always at such official gatherings, there were no seats in the salons and everyone including the Tsar and Tsarina circulated on foot.

And only one person, the Ambassador of China, was seated in an armchair and claimed to be unwell. The Tsar stopped in front of him and began talking with him. The Ambassador (whose name was Li Hong-Zhang[33]) had no qualms about mentioning the accident and opined that "of course, the guilty ones have already been hanged." Then General Boisdefferre,[34] a former friend of Alexander II, said gravely, "Your Highness, in all civilised countries such accidents occur when there are too large gatherings of people, at the coronation of Louis XII…." Then he stopped short, and everyone present averted their gaze.

The following day Li Hong-Zhang spoke with the correspondents of leading European papers and prophesied that there would be terrible wars in the near future in the whole of Europe, followed by the almost total ruin of many countries. "Only one country will hold out," he said, "and that is Russia. But it will turn in another direction." The Chinese diplomat was like Voltaire. He himself did not speak any European languages, but talked only via interpreters, although it was apparent that this was a piece of fine diplomacy on his part. (SV, 127–28.)

Moscow failed to provide the d'Alheims with any really interesting musical meetings, in particular there were none connected with Mussorgsky's music. After the Paris *conférences* and the *Figaro* morning concert, Olenina expected to receive approval and support in Russia for her activities abroad. But Moscow provided none of this. It was friends in St. Petersburg who helped convince her that the campaign for Mussorgsky should be continued both in France and in Russia.

Olenina-d'Alheim:
After a few more days' stay in Moscow, we went to Istomino for a holiday. Then, at the end of September we were in St. Petersburg, where we were greeted with open arms by all Mussorgsky's friends —those that by now existed there. Alexandra Molas rejoiced at my success and at my wish to continue promoting Russian music abroad.

By that time the score of *Boris Godunov*[35] with Rimsky-Korsakov's new orchestration had appeared. Alexandra Nikolayevna was indignant with her brother-in-law: "That score is never coming into my house!" she said. She told us a lot about Mussorgsky's difficult final years, about all his friends' criticism of his work, their complete failure to understand what he was then composing, and about his final break with them.[36] She recalled how Mussorgsky, who was very fond of them [the Molas family], was sitting with them at the tea-table one evening. Suddenly, hearing the voices of two members of the Handful in the hall and not knowing how to avoid meeting them, he lifted up the tablecloth and hid under the table! Alexandra Nikolayevna meanwhile hastily took the new guests into another room in order to allow Mussorgsky to leave the house.

She arranged a soirée at her home for us at which I sang the fountain scene with the tenor Kedrov. I sang *The Nursery* to her, and she told me I had conveyed to her what it was that Mussorgsky required: "When people listened to his *Nursery* he wanted people not simply to laugh, but also to be moved, and I could never really understand him properly." I was very touched by her candid preference for my performance, and I told her that a French composer, Alexandre Georges, had said that "When I hear about Mishenka in the corner,[37] I cannot help the tears coming to my eyes."

Stasov was not yet in Petersburg, but Mily Alexeyevich [Balakirev] said of the new orchestration of *Boris*: "It was quite unnecessary. The composer's orchestration was incomparably better suited to this drama of the people. Rimsky can be pardoned though—he has such a large family." Balakirev had a sense of humour which was not malicious, though still fairly caustic, and he did not always spare himself either. I remember, just when I was singing to him his "The moon is gliding so quiet and calm, and the young warrior goes forth to battle; the Caucasian horseman loads his gun, and the maiden then says to him…" [Balakirev began laughing]. At that point in the song there is a small phrase in the accompaniment that is fairly amusing and seems to introduce the twitter of this maiden, and it was this that set Balakirev laughing. He had composed the song as a young man.

Both he and Cui advised us against promoting any long-forgotten works by Mussorgsky in the autumn [in Russia]. They said it was too early and the season had not yet started. Cui also advised us not to content ourselves with the works of just Mussorgsky, but to compile a programme [of works] by the Mighty Handful. But we were unable to stay on in St. Petersburg and wait for the start of the season; by now virtually all our funds were in a sorry state. Also neither Pyotr nor I felt like giving up on our campaign for Mussorgsky, and for him alone. So we had to leave and return home.... (SV, 128–29.)

Even before her arrival in Russia, Balakirev took a very pessimistic view of Olenina's prospects so far as performing there was concerned. Knowing as he did the usual Petersburg bureaucratic obstacles in the way of any unknown young artist, he wrote to her brother on the subject.

Mily Balakirev:
  [...] You state that your sister wants to come to Russia to perform as a singer. But in order to carry this off successfully, one first has to do a lot of disgraceful creeping around the local directors and critics. Furthermore, she will probably have to sing publicly something from the peculiar immortal works by *Novoye vremya* composers Ivanov and Solovyov. But they won't be content with that. She will have to assure them in advance that their musical genius sends her into a veritable swoon, and to prove it she will have to present some of her programmes from Paris and Belgium, which might convince them of her sincere reverence for their work.
  Cruel times have now begun. There is not a word of truth to be found anywhere, and any honest person should get out of here while the going is good and find some burrow and sit there and keep quiet [...].

                                                                    Balakirev.

(Undated letter to Alexander Olenin, AAO, 23.)

Despite the disappointment of not being able to perform in St. Petersburg, the d'Alheims returned to Paris on the wings of new inspiration: their work had received the full support of precisely those people whose opinion they most valued. As before, they had no money, but they did have plans. These plans were for a new series of *conférences* on Mussorgsky that took place in late 1896 and early 1897.

Olenina-d'Alheim:
We had insufficient capital for promoting Mussorgsky, and Pyotr sat down to work on his book on the Romanov tsars and the celebration on Khodynka Field. He worked in his studio in the evenings, and we sat there as well, and sometimes by about two o'clock in the morning Varya would jump up and start hurrying Pyotr, saying that the Petit Poucet [Tom Thumb] restaurant would be closing in an hour. Then all three of us would dash down the street to the Petit Poucet and order ourselves a salade parisienne and beer. The Taraseviches were also[38] in Paris living on the rue Monsieur le Prince. They had a little daughter Yulia, a pretty curly-haired infant. In spring we took our Marianna along too. Hawkins[39] and his wife [also] used to bring their daughter to our studio. (SV, 137.)

The friendship between the Tarasevich and Hawkins families created a microclimate that was extremely vital for the d'Alheims' activities —an atmosphere of friendship, artistry and mutual support.

Olenina-d'Alheim:
Our daughter stayed with a wetnurse, and we collected her only in 1897. Aunt Katya lived with us. All our meetings took place in the studio. The Taraseviches were often at our home; we became friends with them back in 1894 when Varya and our uncle returned from Russia after the death of our mother.

We were also often visited by the artist Welden Hawkins, an Englishman, and his young Italian wife. Pyotr got to know Hawkins in a quite unusual way: Hawkins once came looking for some seconds [for a duel] and appeared at the editorial office of *Le Temps*. He knew someone there and this acquaintance introduced him to Pyotr, saying that of course d'Alheim would agree to be his second. But Pyotr first of all asked, "Is this a serious duel, or is it simply *sans résultats?*"—"Absolutely serious," Hawkins told him. I don't recall whether the duel ever did take place, but from that time onward Pyotr and Hawkins remained friends and their friendship lasted for a long long time.

The Taraseviches were accompanied by Anna's beautiful sister Katya Kudasheva. Much later her son was married to the young poetess Maya; after her husband's death, and after the 1917 revolution she married Romain Rolland. (SV, 116.)

I recall this young company with such a sense of joy. The Taraseviches were leaving for Russia for the summer, and the Hawkins and ourselves decided to spend summer in the Ardennes. Pyotr rented some accommodation sufficient for us all, near a large farm in a place called Vavrey. This village was situated close to Rochefort, almost on the frontier with Belgium and near the famous grotto of Han.

Pyotr wanted somehow to arrange a new series of *conférences* on Mussorgsky and an exhibition of pictures by Hawkins. He had some good friends in Brussels. Towards the end of the year our *conférences* actually began. The first was in the "Maison d'Art" [House of the Arts], an utterly bourgeois society institution. (SV, 136–37.)

For the programme cover Hawkins produced a portrait of Mussorgsky and of myself. (BNB, 59.)

I very clearly recall that first début of mine in Brussels [on 22 December 1897]. Our friends the Madoux were of course there among the audience, and also all Pyotr's other friends and old comrades. The public would not quiet down, although we performers and the lecturer were already on stage. This time instead of Foerster the accompanist was Charles Henusse,[40] a young professor from the Brussels Conservatoire. Pyotr said nothing, patiently waited for silence, and only then began his talk on Mussorgsky. After the concert it turned out Alfred Madoux had not realised why Pyotr did not begin speaking; he imagined he must be feeling ill, and got terribly worried. Then there was a group of spiritualists who attended the *conférence* and afterwards came up to ask whether I was aware that Mussorgsky had been standing there beside me on the stage. They did not ask me personally about this, but they asked Pyotr; I don't know what answer he gave.

The *conférence* went down with great success. We were asked to give a second one in the Maison d'Art. At this I sang *The Nursery* and all the merry songs. Pyotr definitely wanted to arrange a third one for the general public, and he hired the hall of "La Grande Harmonie" and invited several singers from the opera to take part. This *conférence* turned into a large-scale concert, and it ended so

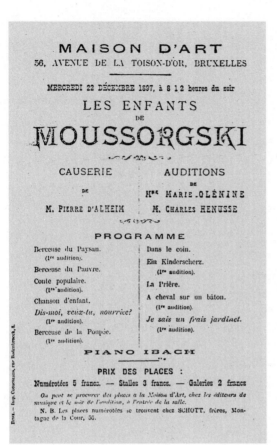

late that several people who came in from the suburbs had to return home on foot. I have kept one of the posters from that evening. Pyotr ordered them on Japanese paper, and the whole text was printed in bright red. This was my first performance before a general public. (SV, 137–38.)

In 1898 the *Russkaya muzykal'naya gazeta* carried an article on "The Parisians and Mussorgsky" by P. Weimarn, in which he wrote about the *conférences* and the d'Alheim husband and wife team's role in introducing the French public to Mussorgsky. While giving d'Alheim credit for his book on Mussorgsky, which appeared in Paris in 1896, the critic observed that such a major task was beyond the ability of a mere biographer.

P. Weimarn:

In order to achieve a presentation of Mussorgsky's vocal compositions, a performing talent was needed to confirm the speaker's theoretical expose.

Fortunately, a talent second to none was available in the person of our compatriot M-me Maria Olenina, who resides in Paris and is one of the most musical and serious concert singers of our time. Moreover she has no rival in the vocal interpretation of Mussorgsky....

I have before me several [...] published reviews by critics in Paris [and Brussels], and the unanimity, ardent sympathy, and often even the enthusiasm expressed by critics of *La Réforme*, *L'Étoile Belge*, *Le son*, *Petit bleu* and others leaves no doubt about the strong impression that the whole performance produced on them and on the audience. In particular, they were all thrilled by the scenes from a child's life, published under the collective title of *The Nursery*, and then by "The Little Orphan" ["Sirotka"] and "Svetik Savvishna" in which according to one critic one hears cries from the soul vented by a composer under the impact of scenes drawn from nature. They were also no less shaken by the artistic realism of other pictures, such as the *Dances of Death*, *Sunless*, and others. (*Russkaya muzykal'naya gazeta* 2 (1898), 186–87.)

Olenina-d'Alheim:

Altogether the three *conférences* went off more than successfully, and Pyotr wanted to put them on in other towns in Belgium, Flanders and Holland, but it turned out it was too late. Then we had a difficult time: our money had run out, and all that was raised from the first two *conférences* had been used up on the last one, for which the tickets were sold cheap, and the whole organisation cost a tidy sum.

Of course we could have gone back to Vavrey, but we had not settled with the hotel for our room and meals. We were left simply hoping something would turn up. And at that point Varya arrived from Istomino; she had been back to Russia at the same time as the Taraseviches. Now she arrived and promptly fell ill. And that was the position we found ourselves in. We had said good-bye to all our old and new friends and were living incognito. Our only hope was that aunty's pension would soon arrive, but that too was delayed. So then I sent a telegram asking my cousin Petya Olenin,[41] the son of Uncle Sergei, to send me a loan of a hundred roubles, or a hundred francs—I forget which. At any rate, he immediately carried out my request. He and I were always good friends.

Our new acquaintances in Brussels included, first of all, several music critics, then the chairman of the Academy of Arts, von der Starpen, who had thrown a large dinner in our honour. There we had got to know Verhaeren,[42] Clauze[43] (a splendid artist), and many others including Joseph Lambeaux,[44] a sculptor who was famous at the time. In Brussels there is a museum named after him. No, we did not get to know him then; Pyotr knew him earlier, when he lived in Brussels and was correspondent of the *Étoile Belge*. When Joseph Lambeaux had completed his enormous work in high relief entitled "Human Passions," King Léopold[45] wanted to see it and came to Lambeaux's studio. Observing that the crucified Christ was placed lower than Death, which reigned over everyone, he asked the sculptor to make the necessary adjustment and place Christ above Death. But Joseph said modestly, "Your Highness, that is how I see and feel it. I cannot alter it." Nor did he. He was something of an eccentric; that was how people regarded him. For instance, he did not like discussing art, and he found that in Paris "how well they can talk about art. Oh, how well they can talk!" He himself preferred to work. I did not return to Brussels [at that time]. I sang there again only in 1920.

And now I will tell you about someone who came to ply her trade there in my place and, what is more, performed there virtually under my name. We learned about this, if I recall aright, only in 1912. This was a Russian singer under the name of Onegina-d'Alheim who sang in Brussels. They said she had a good voice and maybe some people even mistook her for me—after all, I had only sung there once and about twelve years had passed since then. They may not have remembered me, and to foreigners Onegina and Olenina might well sound the same. After that she also travelled around the Russian provinces and Siberia under the name of Onegina-d'Alheim. I remember that someone once arrived from

Tomsk and told one of our Moscow acquaintances that he had heard me there, whereas in fact I had never been in Tomsk. None of this would have mattered, but what I very much disliked were her antics in Brussels: she apparently went down on her knees before Verhaeren and generally played the buffoon. And if they really did take her for me, then that was really unpleasant. At the time they advised me in Moscow to take her to court for appropriating my name. But courts of law are not at all to my taste, and I lacked the resolve to do that. Soon after that I was told that on arrival in Moscow she had fallen sick with typhoid and had died in hospital. (SV, 138–39.)

Back to Brussels in the year 1898. When we were finally able to leave, all three of us first of all went back to Vavrey and stayed there until February. Then we had to go to Paris, to Pyotr's relatives: his [word omitted] was very dangerously ill. He died in March, and it was in March, a few days before his death, that the mayor blessed us and we became husband and wife. Also in March, at the end of the month, Balakirev summoned us, believing there might now be some hope of arranging a concert in St. Petersburg. But that journey was eventually a failure; as I recall, it was either difficult, or else something else prevented Mily Alexeyevich from arranging the concert; I cannot recollect properly. (SV, 140.)

The reason Olenina's concert did not take place demonstrated how right Balakirev was about the predicament of the New Russian School in St. Petersburg, and about Olenina's prospects for a part in the all-Balakirev benefit evening that was organised to assist the Free Music School. Balakirev wrote to Alexander Olenin on the subject.

Mily Balakirev:
Unfortunately, I am forced to forgo your sister's part in the Free School concert for the following reason: The German Opera, which thanks to patronage from on high, has engaged the Mariinsky Theatre and Orchestra for the whole of Lent, long ago published its repertoire and organised subscriptions, although the 11th March had not actually been booked by them. In consequence, I chose that evening for our concert in the certainty that there would be no

obstacles to its taking place. Meanwhile, however, it turns out that
as soon as actual performances were discussed, the German Opera
took up every day of the second week with performances addi-
tional to the ones covered by subscription tickets. The musicians
say things will continue like that, and it is more than risky to count
on the 11th March being left free. Consequently, it could easily
happen that your sister and her husband come all the way from
Paris to St. Petersburg on a wild goose chase, which would be hard
on their pockets especially in view of their limited resources. This
dreadful situation has forced me to cable her my refusal; the reasons
I am explaining in a letter to her sent off along with this one. What
times we live in when a Russian artist has no chance to give a concert in St. Petersburg! If the matter is settled in any way, I shall not
fail to let you know. Your affectionate and respectful

Balakirev.

(M.A. Balakirev, letter of 23 February 1898 to A.A. Olenin,
GMMC, fond 39, no.127, 26.)

Olenina-d'Alheim:
We returned to Vavrey, where Hawkins and Varya were painting
away at their pictures, and Aunt Katya (who had only just returned
to us), Raphael, Hawkins's wife, Marianna and Jacqueline were
playing, reading and generally enjoying the springtime. Pyotr sat
down to write his third book ("François Villon"), but found he
lacked various essential information, and he could only obtain it
in Paris. So he went off there and stayed with his mother. Very
soon after that he summoned me, maintaining that he could not
work in peace on his book without me. His mother then moved to
the small apartment and left us her own. I moved to join Pyotr
there. I remember him waking me at night and reading me the
book chapters he had just written. He worked best of all at night.
(SV, 140–41.)

Alexander Olenin, who remained in constant touch with the
d'Alheims, received occasional news of Maria's concerts and told
Balakirev about them. To a letter describing the concerts and *conférences* in Belgium Balakirev responded on the 9 January 1898.

Mily Balakirev:
Dear Alexander Alexeyevich,
   I received your kind letter [...]. I am greatly cheered by the news of your sister's successes abroad, and I shall eagerly await the notices that you promise to send, and which I have not yet received [...].

                                                          Balakirev.

(GMMC, fond 39, no. 127, 27.)

Olenina-d'Alheim:
In the autumn a new newspaper appeared; its chief editors were Jacques Dorel [and] Bouillon (I simply cannot recall his very strange name). Pyotr was once again forced to take up the journalist's yoke with them—we had no other funds left. Dorel obtained the capital for this newspaper from some naive Greek. The man wanted to set up an "honest newspaper"! It collapsed in March, but the start was brilliant: it was situated on the fifth floor on the Place de l'Opéra, and in the evenings its title glowed brightly and attracted absolutely everyone's gaze. After this whole enterprise came to a halt we had a fairly lean time. In winter and spring Camille de Saint-Croix organised some popular evenings, with singing, dancing, etc. All this took place in various small halls in one of the plebeian areas of Clignancourt. I also took part in these evenings, and our Mussorgsky promotion had to be put on one side again.
   That same winter the whole of our company had to move back from Vavrey to Paris. Neither Hawkins nor we had a studio any more; [then] with great difficulty he found himself another. In Vavrey we sold almost all our furniture to cover our debts. Varya and our aunt then went back to Russia. And little Marianna and I stayed at Pyotr's mother's apartment. By the late summer we had to ask Varya to come and collect our little girl—I could not deal with her properly. She was what the French call "turbulente," and when one acquaintance of ours took her to the Parc Monceau she started to "mettre sur le flanc" [terrorise] all the other children, as he told me. I thought it would be more beneficial for her to run free at Istomino in the company of my brothers' children. So we decided to send her off to stay with them.

Pyotr finished his book and in spring it was offered via Saint-Croix to Olendorf, but was published only at the end of the year. One young musician and composer Georges Soudry[46] immediately wanted to write almost a trilogy on the life of François Villon using Pyotr's book. Pyotr persuaded him to start just with the prison where Villon was locked up, and immediately wrote a libretto for Soudry. (SV, 140-42.)

At the time when [Pyotr's] book *La passion de maître François* [*Villon*] appeared, there were not so many editions as they produce nowadays—one or two impressions and that was it. And Pyotr's book was published only once. Olendorf was a Jew and he did not know the second part of Pyotr's book, but he was so entranced by the first part that he decided to start the 1899 season with it. That season the whole of his publishing house was supposed to expand and move to the Chausée d'Antoine. The book was supposed to appear immediately after the publishers were installed in their new location, that is, in early November.

The first part had already been printed when Olendorf read part two in which Villon's presentation of the "Passions of the Lord" were described—the "Jeux de la passion" as they are called in French. After which he immediately decided to hide Pyotr's book under a bushel [...] and *La passion de maître François* [*Villon*] appeared only in the first half of December, and it spent no more than half a month in the bookshops during the children's Christmas book season and then disappeared altogether. The promise given by the publisher was not fulfilled.

When I asked Olendorf in 1921 whether the publishers wished to publish a second edition of my husband's book, they told me they had no such desire and were ceding all the rights back to me. Some time later, I met an artist at the house of an acquaintance who, as soon as he heard my name was d'Alheim, asked the host whether I was related to Pyotr, the author of a book about Villon that had so thrilled a writer friend of his called Pierre Mac-Orland. We were introduced, and he undertook to inform his friend that I now had the rights to Pyotr's book. Mac-Orland knew that the first edition was sold out, and regretted that another edition had not been announced. He himself was a reader [i.e., an in-house consultant] for Crès (which was at that time also a large publishing house).

They must have found out about this at Olendorf's, because soon after I received a letter from the secretary of the Writers' Society informing me that the editors of Olendorf publishers were "begging on their knees" that I return the rights on my husband's book to them. I replied that "I find one brigands' assault on d'Alheim's book is sufficient. I shall apply elsewhere regarding a second edition."

The second edition of the book soon appeared with Crès a year before the author's death. [Pyotr d'Alheim] died on 11 April 1922. Shortly prior to that I had let a music publisher in London have the translations of all Mussorgsky's songs that Pyotr made back in 1896. Just before his death I received from London the sum of over two thousand francs. I used that money to bury my husband.

There was also a piece of betrayal over his translations: his (Pyotr's) friend Robert Godet wanted to mix his translations in with his own, to which I refused to agree. [Then] he made an agreement with this London publisher. I do not know whether all the translations ever appeared that they bought from me, but that was what I wished. I believe I was visited by the son of Bessel[47] who asked me to allow them to add to their edition of Mussorgsky's songs all Pyotr's texts, printed on separate pages. Had he not then offered me three hundred francs, I would probably have agreed.

First of all, as I knew, through my own good grace Bessel had earned quite a tidy sum from the "mere paper" (as he called the whole of Mussorgsky's work in 1894), and he might have rated Pyotr and my own promotion [of Mussorgsky] as worthy of a more appropriate sum. [Secondly], I always hated money. I altogether failed to understand how Bessel could have made me such an offer, and why he did not place Pyotr's translated words beneath the actual Russian text in his new editions of Mussorgsky.

Then I realised that in putting out this edition, he had probably not thought of this, and maybe he had contracts with other translators. [...] Back in 1896 [Bessel] had travelled to Petersburg and signed up a contract for a translation of *The Nursery*, which the critics were then writing about with such rapture. He even told Pyotr at that time: "You are doing the work and we shall make use of your splendid propaganda, and we already have a contract with a publisher." Be that as it may, the French texts with which

Mussorgsky's posthumous existence began—not in heaven, but on this earth—have not appeared to this day in editions of his works; they exist only in my small brochure entitled "Four Concerts." (SV, 134–36.)

In the year 1894 Paris was on the boil because of the Dreyfus affair,[48] which divided not just the whole of Europe but the entire world. By 1898 it had grown to become a major political crisis, and the d'Alheims also involved themselves in the controversy:

Olenina-d'Alheim:
[...] The Dreyfus affair began, and everyone was divided into two camps. We, of course, were on his side. In the paper *Le Temps* the main lead-writer Présanse was a *dreyfusard* as well. The Menard family also formed into two camps: the parents were for him, and all the *dreyfusards* gathered at their house—Colonel Picard, Zola, Penlevé and others. But their daughter, Pauline Hugo (who lived on the [top floor] of her parents' *hôtel*) was influenced by Léon Daudet[49] and was against. On the lower floor at the request of Mme Menard, I sang Mussorgsky's "The Field Marshal" ("Polkovodets") for all the Dreyfus partisans.

Pyotr meanwhile took part in every demonstration in support of Dreyfus. He was also at a writers' meeting after they had condemned Zola. At this gathering people wondered how the writers ought to protest, and Pyotr said: "Our plain duty is for everyone to sign with 'J'accuse.'" Then a well-known and very talented author called Mirbeau[50] said, "Anyone would think that d'Alheim was an favour of sacrificing himself." Pyotr made no answer to this.... On several occasions during the trial there were incidents involving our friend the artist DeGroux.[51] (SV, 142.)

Meanwhile the Paris and Brussels musical critics talked increasingly of the unusual singer from Russia who kept performing unknown music by Mussorgsky. The d'Alheims' activities in promoting Mussorgsky's music in Paris and Belgium continued and began to attract attention in Russia. One commentator was the Moscow music critic Kruglikov.[52]

Semyon Kruglikov:

For a long time now, via the foreign journals, I have been following the remarkable activities of the *artiste* whose name stands at the head of the present note. For five years now, partly in Brussels, but mainly in Paris, she has been promoting Russian vocal music with untiring energy…. The d'Alheim couple are drawn especially towards Mussorgsky, and they have done a great deal for him. He [Pierre d'Alheim] has published an interesting study of Mussorgsky as a separate volume, and has made splendid translations into French of the texts of his operas and songs. She has studied to perfection all that Mussorgsky has composed for the singing voice. And in this she shows one concern—not just for the vocal repertoire for such a voice as hers, but for demonstrating the *whole* of Mussorgsky to a western public that had no conception of him.

In a long series of evenings in which both of them figured— the husband as an inspired speaker and commentator on the songs advertised by the poster, and she as a brilliant and refined executant—there have been sessions lasting many hours and demonstrating total self-sacrifice. Forgetting utterly about herself, this singer has tirelessly sung an entire opera from beginning to end with all the parts, both male and female. So it was, for example, in the Brussels Maison du Peuple in front of a two-thousand strong crowd of working people who were ecstatic at Mussorgsky's *Khovanshchina*, which Mme d'Alheim sang starting at eight o'clock and ending at one in the morning. (*Novosti*, 12 November 1901.)

However, Olenina had no wish to limit herself to performances in France and Belgium. The time had now come for Russia itself to hear this Russian singer.

III

THE TIME HAS COME TO SING FOR RUSSIA

Russia — 1901-1902

First Concerts in Moscow and St. Petersburg

n late 1901 and early 1902 Olenina-d'Alheim gave her first recital performances in Moscow and St. Petersburg. These concerts were preceded by correspondence with Balakirev and Cui in which the singer sought their advice and assistance before making her début in her homeland. Balakirev's surviving letters help to recreate the atmosphere of these preparations. Realising how much her career depended on their success, Balakirev showed considerable concern, writing letters of recommendation, cautioning Olenina against possible mistakes, and boosting her own self-assurance. The latter, in view of Balakirev's own character, was no easy matter, since he took a very glum view of the prospects for a serious musician in Russia, especially in St. Petersburg. At Olenina's request, on 4 September 1901 he wrote her a letter of commendation to Semyon Kruglikov.

Mily Balakirev:

Gatchina, 4 September 1901

Dear and esteemed Maria Alexeyevna,

I hasten to carry out your wish and am forwarding to you a

letter to be handed to Kruglikov, which I am sending unsealed in order that you may read it.

He has great understanding as a musician, and I am in no doubt that even without somebody's recommendation he would be capable of appreciating you. But as a person, for all his honesty, he is totally lacking in character and I therefore doubt whether he could do anything for you. Among the management of the Philharmonic School of which he has been director until now, no one has given a fig for his opinion, as I was forced to conclude. He is amiable but very feeble.

In a week's time I am moving into town, and if you now write to me at my town address (on Kolomenskaya Street), then I shall receive your letter without problem.

I would very much like to know whether anything came of my letter to [illegible], with which you presented yourself and when you were so careless as to injure your foot. I would also very much like to know whether you received my registered letter which your brother unfortunately sent to Tula.

Devotedly and with sincere respect,

Balakirev.

My sincere greeting to dear Alexander Alexeyevich.

(AAO, 33.)

Olenina consulted Balakirev about the programme for her forthcoming appearances. With touching self-abnegation, for the sake of her success, he was prepared to sacrifice his own compositions and omit them from the programme. Yet, although aware that Olenina's career opened a new page in the history of Russian music, he was at the same time unable to foresee the direction her career would take, and he still held out hopes for her future in opera.

Mily Balakirev:

St. Petersburg, 7 October 1901

Esteemed Maria Alexeyevna,

You ask my advice regarding the selection of items for performance in your concert. At this remove, it is hard for me to offer you counsel. It seems to me you should sing what you are specially

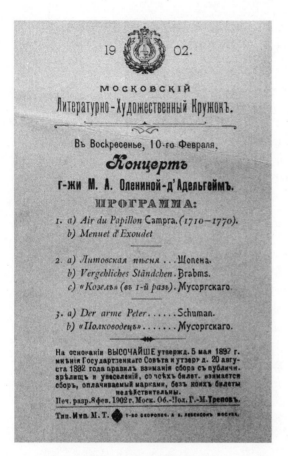

19 02.

МОСКОВСКІЙ
Литературно-Художественный Кружокъ.

Въ Воскресенье, 10-го Февраля,

Концертъ

г-жи М. А. Олениной-д'Адельгеймъ.

ПРОГРАММА:

1. *a) Air du Papillon* Campra. *(1710—1770).*
   b) Menuet d'Exoudet

2. *a) Литовская пѣсня* . . . Шопена.
   b) Vergebliches Ständchen . Brabms.
   c) «Козелъ» (въ 1-й разъ). Мусоргскаго.

3. *a) Der arme Peter* . . . . . . Schuman.
   b) «Полководецъ» . . . . Мусоргскаго.

На основаніи ВЫСОЧАЙШЕ утвержд. 5 мая 1892 г.
мнѣнія Государственнаго Совѣта и утвер? д. 20 авгу-
ста 1892 года правилъ взиманія сбора съ публичн.
зрѣлищъ и увеселеній, со всѣхъ билет. взимается
сборъ, оплачиваемый марками, безъ коихъ билеты
недѣйствительны.
Печ. разр.8 фев. 1902 г. Моск. Об.-!!ол. Г.-М.Треповъ.

Тип.Имп.М.Т. т-во скоропеч. а а. левенсонъ москва.

The pro-
gramme of one
of the first recitals
given by Maria
Olenina-d'Alheim
on 10 Februrary
1902, at the
Moscow Art
Literary Circle.

good at, and you yourself are the best judge of that. In any case,
I believe that you should not sing such songs as, for instance, the
"Doppelgänger," which are suitable only for male voice— as also
are Glinka's "Night Patrol" ["Nochnoi smotr"] or Dargomyzhsky's
"The Old Corporal" ["Staryi kapral"]. As for my own songs,
it would be sensible and politic for you to refrain from singing
them.

I sincerely wish you success, and for that it is essential that you
please the circle of people you have landed in. I very much fear that
in view of his utter feebleness and indolence Kruglikov is unlikely
to set things moving for you. Meanwhile, if things go in your
favour, you could land a good engagement with one of the private
Russian opera companies, from where it would be easier for you

to set yourself up on the official stage [i.e., in a state, Imperial theatre]. I shall be very interested to know how things go for you.
With sincere devotion,

Balakirev.

(AAO, 35.)

Not long before Olenina's first appearance in Moscow at the invitation of Kerzina,[1] Balakirev attempted to iron out one more problem and sent her a warning.

Mily Balakirev:

St. Petersburg, 20 October 1901

Dear and much esteemed Maria Alexeyevna,

I am very glad to read in your letter that your affairs are sorting themselves out in Moscow. But you exaggerate the importance of my letter, which was simply meant to give you the opportunity of appearing before Kruglikov not just as a distant relation, but as a serious artiste.

As regards the assessment of your talent, they will do that for themselves, without heeding my opinion of you, and I am sorry that you did not inform me whether you sang for them and what impression you produced. Since Mme Kerzina invited you to take part in the concert, one must assume that she has heard you.

As you await the arrival in Moscow of Nikolai Andreyevich [Rimsky-Korsakov], Vladimir Vasilyevich [Stasov] and others, the aim of the present letter is to warn you that I broke with these gentlemen completely a long time ago. In talking with them you would thus do better not to mention me. You should pronounce my name only if you have to, and only by the way, otherwise you risk causing yourself harm quite needlessly. Meanwhile I wish you great success.

Your sincerely devoted,

Balakirev.

Pass on greetings to Kruglikov. (AAO, 34.)

Finally, on 26 October 1901, Olenina-d'Alheim sang at an evening organised by the Moscow Circle of Russian Music-Lovers. A few days later, on the 14 November (some sources say—the 13th), she gave her first complete solo recital in Moscow. This was the start of frequent concert visits to Moscow, and she was given a warm reception.

Semyon Kruglikov:
First of all I must confirm that foreign opinions about Mme d'Alheim as a singer are not at all exaggerated. Based on them, I even expected less than I actually heard [at the concert on 26 October]. She is the very image of a performer of song, a genuine Kammersängerin as the Germans say.

The voice may not be one of special power, there is no striking beauty of timbre, but the tone is cultivated, well produced, carries freely, and it is flexible, clear, substantial and colourful. The diction is superb—every word was clearly audible without any exaggerated emphasis. The declamation was striking—every phrase—the fruit of thoughtful artistry and a vivid and immediate talent. She has an utterly exceptional ability to capture the mood of a piece and enter into the character of the person depicted. And throughout all this she shows impeccable musicality.... (*Novosti*, 12 November 1901.)

Russkaya muzykal'naya gazeta:
[...] Mme Olenina-d'Alheim is one of those artists of the heart, of deep penetration, and of rare variety—in the final analysis, an artist seemingly constructed and created to clarify life's troubles. Her voice may not be so great in range, but she uses it fluently, without deliberation, and without arousing fear for any particular note or problem of vocal fioritura.

Thanks to her exceptional talent, the singer's concert produced a sensation. She is altogether a major artistic phenomenon. [...]

Apart from compositions by Mussorgsky, his *Nursery [Detskaya]*, *Sunless [Bez solntsa]*, cradle songs and others, Mme Olenina performed songs by Cui, Tchaikovsky, Bizet, French songs of the sixteenth century, and she introduced [the public] to Schumann's *Frauenliebe* and songs by Schubert. Mme Olenina strikes one with her talent as a chamber singer; her singing has the imprint of an amazing understanding of styles and epochs. We can be proud of artists such as her. (*Russkaya muzykal'naya gazeta*, 47 (1901), p. 1199.)

Olenina's concert in St. Petersburg was a more complex affair. In his letter of 1897 to her brother, Balakirev was very pessimistic about how she would be received by the Petersburg public.

Mily Balakirev:
   I am very glad to hear of your sister's successes and am deeply sorry that the anti-musicality of St. Petersburg, which has developed mainly thanks to the increasing influence of Conservatoire teachers in the city, encourages no hope that our servile public will appreciate her as they should. Yet I know of no other singer so musical and talented as your sister. (M.A. Balakirev, letter of 26 September 1897 to A.A. Olenin; AAO, 21.)

In a letter of 17 August 1901—i.e., less that half a year before her first concert in St. Petersburg—Balakirev repeated his earlier doubts and even warned Olenina of the danger she could be facing there.

Mily Balakirev:

4, Novaya Street,
Gatchina.

Esteemed Maria Alexeyevna,
   You ask for my advice regarding your intention to give a concert in St. Petersburg. However, I am very unfamiliar with this sphere of musical activity, and my rare contacts with it always produce a vile impression on me. But your promise to act precisely according to my directions fills me with fear and obliges me to be specially circumspect in my advice.
   I will tell you the whole unattractive truth about our concert life, but I would ask you not to regard my opinion as incontrovertible and to check it. So far as I understand, in order to be successful in St. Petersburg, it is essential that an artist has an *excellent* foreign passport, and also the active support of musical reviewers. Usually artists reckoning on a major success send their agents in advance. They [the agents, i.e., impressarios] work on relations with the local reviewers, and a month before the artists step out on the concert platform, the papers begin sounding off in expectation of the eighth wonder of the world and also report flattering reviews of them in the foreign press. The most influential paper here is *Novoe*

Maria Olenina-d'Alheim, Moscow, 1901–1902.

vremya,[2] whose reviewer is famed for his incompetence, musical ignorance and unscrupulousness, and also claims to be a talented composer, and for that reason any singers and conductors who shun his music are subject to a severe thrashing.

There has been more than one revelation in the papers of such vile deeds by Maestro Ivanov, but in view of the present awful decay of moral standards the public still continues to believe *Novoe vremya*. So, as you can see, our public are not fastidious in ethical matters, and in matters musical they have become ignorant ever since the authority of the conservatoires and music schools firmly established itself in their opinion.

If you find these conditions for your success excessively tedious, then the best method [...] would be for you to address a letter to César Antonovich Cui (His Excellency, at 38 Fontanka), as director of the symphony concerts of the Imperial Russian Musical Society, and to ask him to give you an engagement that would provide you with the means to come here to take part in one or two of these concerts. If this is arranged, then the attitude of the public to your appearance on the Petersburg concert platform will determine whether or not you should give *your own* concert.

Unfortunately, *I do not live in Petersburg musician circles*, and am thus unable to provide any tangible assistance. My attitude towards them, and theirs to me, is such that my protection could actually be harmful, especially in the opinion of the most influential local paper *Novoe vremya*, which the late Saltykov-Shchedrin[3] felicitously called "the scholarly, literary and political newspaper *Pomoi* [Hog-wash]."

This is all I can say in answer to your question.

My best greetings to your brother Alexander Alexeyevich, and please ask him to write.

With deep respects and sincere devotion,

Balakirev.

(17 August 1901; AAO, 30–32.)

Balakirev's advice to approach César Cui turned out to be useful. With his assistance, Olenina gave a concert on 17 December 1901, with Evgeny Bogoslovsky[4] as accompanist. Her success with this début in St.

Petersburg was only a modest one, although in view of the unusual seriousness and complexity of her programme (consisting of Early French songs, Schumann, Schubert, and Mussorgsky) and the huge number of encores, it could be said that the audience actually gave her a warm reception. However, there was an equivocal review in the newspaper *Novosti*, which seemed to praise the second half but slate the first half of the programme. And the scattering of criticism and praise gave a veiled but negative picture of the recital. However, the main thing missing from the critic's remarks was any appreciation that both the young singer's recital programme as well as the performance were something entirely new on the Russian concert platform.

Nevertheless, this fact was well understood and clearly established by César Cui in his own review. He was the first one to state—although in slightly different terms—that Olenina's recital marked the first appearance in Russia of a new genre of musical performance—that of *chamber* or Lieder singing, with herself as the first Russian chamber music singer.

César Cui:
"Music and the Theatre"
  Yesterday's song recital in the Small Hall of the Conservatoire was a major event for musical St. Petersburg. In the person of Mme Olenina-d'Alheim we encountered an extremely talented and original artiste. This was a genuine revelation.
  Her originality lies in the following:
  First of all, she gives her recitals alone, without the aid of piano soloists, violinists, 'cellists, and the results are genuine *evenings of song* [emphasis supplied both here and below] without any superfluous admixtures.
  Secondly, at these concerts she performs whole *groups of songs* by the same composer. Thus, yesterday, she performed eight songs by Schumann and ten by Mussorgsky, as a result of which there was a completeness of impression and a possibility to appreciate the composer from many sides.
  Thirdly, Mme Olenina sings everything *from memory*. Yesterday, together with her encores, she sang forty songs, which in fact barely accounts for a quarter of her immense repertoire.

Fourthly, Mme Olenina is an artist of conviction. She does not follow the public, she does not chase after success and does not toady to public taste. She sings what she herself values, what is dear to her, and in the promotion of any music she displays remarkable independence and boldness. Sufficient to say that—*horribile dictu* —she sings Mussorgsky. [...]

Mussorgsky has been particularly unsuccessful in St. Petersburg: his operas are forgotten. [...] Performers of songs are also no fans of Mussorgsky. Indeed, in his songs there is so little love (of ten songs performed by Mme Olenina, only one was a love song); moreover, they are so difficult rhythmically, so difficult in intonation, phrasing, expression. [...] But the fact that they are both musical and performable was proved yesterday by Mme Olenina—only for that one needs to have her love, her understanding, and her talent. Mussorgsky and Schubert were the most successful in yesterday's concert.

Mme Olenina has a medium-strength mezzo-soprano voice, beautiful, high and even in all its registers. Her technique is superb and consists in splendid diction, phrasing, rich, varied and subtle nuances, and a rare ability to impart various timbre to her voice— now metallic, now gentle and caressing. Every nuance of human feeling is equally accessible to her—both a childlike, touchingly naive lisp that evoked smiles of sympathy (Mussorgsky's *Nursery*), and profound, fateful and soul-shaking tragedy (Schubert's "Der Doppelgänger"). [...] (*Rossiya*, 18 December 1901.)

After her concert on 17 December, Olenina decided to give an independent recital without counting on the "subscription" audience of the Russian Musical Society. Balakirev considered she should give such a recital only if her début in the Small Hall had been a roaring success. And since this was not the case, he tried in a letter of 18 December to persuade her against taking the risk.

Mily Balakirev:
Esteemed Maria Alexeyevna,
   I have caught an awful chill, I am sick and am spending almost all the time in bed. Yesterday I was barely able to get out to see your

A sense of purpose. Maria Olenina-d'Alheim, Moscow, 1901–1902.

Mr. Bogoslovsky who before leaving for Moscow wanted to talk with me—albeit through the door.

I invited him in and asked him about your concert. According to him, you were received coldly, although you had a certain success. Today I rushed with special interest to see how the local critics had treated you, and as I expected, *Ivanov slated you completely.* Unfortunately, I could not get hold of an issue of the paper *Rossiya,* which is not permitted for retail sale, but they did bring me the *Peterburgskie novosti,* which praised you only for your performance of Mussorgsky, but otherwise the critic does not see fit to compare you even with the "charming" Varby, who it seems did not disdain to give a public performance of songs by Messrs Ivanov and himself —i.e., Koptyaev (the reviewer for *Sankt-Peterburgskie Vedomosti*).

I don't know what they wrote about you in *Rossiya,* but in any case *Rossiya* is not enough for you to rely on for your concert activities in St. Petersburg. I must confess that your intention of giving your *own* concert in the Credit Hall, which Bogoslovsky told me about yesterday, *deeply depresses me,* since I expect nothing of this concert *other than a large deficit.* Would it not be better for you to go back to Moscow again?

Your sincerely devoted

Balakirev.

(Letter of 18 December 1901; AAO, 33–34.)

With her characteristic sense of purpose and aplomb, Olenina reacted to Balakirev's gloomy prognosis by straightway applying to the Petersburg police chief for permission to give a concert in the hall of the Credit Society "for her own benefit," i.e., at her own expense. This independent concert would decide whether Olenina should perform in Petersburg again in the future, or else limit her concert activity to Moscow. It was a question of winning over her own Petersburg audience, and it was a battle which she was intent upon winning. Alexander Olenin recalled the event.

Alexander Olenin:
On the 13 November 1901 my sister first performed in Moscow. Her performance was an extraordinary, unprecedented success. It was

the event of the season. Cui invited her to perform for the Russian Musical Society in St. Petersburg, of which he was then director. In S[t] P[etersbur]g she did not have such success, and the majority of critics were even negative in their response. But this did not perturb her in the least, and then at the beginning of 1902 she announced her own concert there. Mily Alexeyevich [Balakirev] had taken a fond and watchful interest in her first performances, and he was extremely nervous. When she announced her own recital in St. Petersburg, he was almost horrorstruck, and feared a total fiasco.

I made haste to attend this concert—without my sister's knowledge, incidentally, so as not to alarm her in any way. After all, this was going to be a battle royal. I bowled straight along to M.A. [Balakirev's] from the station. He was terribly glad to see me and immediately set me up for the night in Adrian's room. He was not at all surprised by my arrival, and believed that at such a moment in my sister's career I should be with her, and he fully approved my decision to keep out of her sight. We agreed to sit together at the recital, and to meet in the hall just before the start of the concert.

After that I left M.A. I remember that as I walked out onto the street, I bought a newspaper in which I found a huge swashbuckling article by Stasov à propos of my sister's concert: "Who will win —Moscow or Petersburg?" At the appointed hour M.A. and I met in the hall of the Credit Society. There were twenty minutes to go before the start of the concert, and the hall was virtually empty. M.A. was terribly on edge, and groaned: "It's going to be a failure, you know, and not just Maria Alexeyevna's failure, but the failure of genuine art. She shouldn't, she shouldn't have risked it." And he kept on saying the same thing in as many words.

The first bell rang, and suddenly the public began pouring in, and in half an hour the hall was packed. There was not a single spare seat. You should have seen Mily Alexeyevich's joy, although he immediately started scolding the public for their habit of coming late. "They should not have let them into the hall," he grumbled, but it was obvious he was just saying that for the sake of it, from an excess of feeling.

After the first few [items] there was concerted applause, and at the end of the recital it turned into a wholehearted ovation. M.A.'s face simply beamed with happiness. Incidentally, when my sister sang Schubert's "Ungeduld," M.A. recalled that Rubinstein used to accompany this song brilliantly. He asked the name of my sister's accompanist. [...] And in the interval, after my sister performed Schumann's *Dichterliebe*, he said, "You know, Bulich (the writer) said that he didn't know what was more brilliant—either 'Ich grolle nicht' itself, or the performance." After innumerable encores, I finally made my way to the artistes' room, and the public began to disperse.

It was a total and gigantic success. With all its encores, the concert ended at about one o'clock at night. As M.A. and I walked out onto the street, he hired a cab, and to my astonishment not to his own address at Kolomenskaya Street, but to Liteiny Prospect. It emerged that he was determined to call on my sister to congratulate her. That was typical Balakirev, the head of the fighting "Mighty Handful."

My sister was staying with her husband's relatives the Bobrishchev-Pushkins. When we arrived there, everyone was seated and enjoying a fine supper. M.A. warmly congratulated my sister, but refused any food and asked if he might simply have a glass of milk. He had to wait for it quite a long time.

Soon after that concert, I left for the country. [...] (A.A. Olenin, "Moi vospominaniya o Balakireve," ms., pp. 356–57. See also AAO, 99–101.)

Between concerts in Moscow and St. Petersburg, the d'Alheims had to return to Paris. There were two reasons for this. Firstly, Olenina had long ago been invited to appear in a concert for the Paris Philharmonic Society; and secondly, they needed money to continue their journey around Russia, and they hoped to raise a loan in Paris.

Olenina-d'Alheim:
When we returned [to Paris] after the first concert in Moscow on the 14 November 1901, and after the Philharmonic evening when we had to return to Russia, Pyotr asked [name omitted in ms.] for a

small loan in order to give a whole series of concerts, instead of contenting ourselves with just one or two. She and her husband happily agreed: we could apply in Moscow on their behalf to their firm's representative and collect up to maybe five thousand roubles.... Again I don't recall whether it was roubles or francs, since it was not quite the same thing. But it was all the same, because we hardly even made use of this loan.

At the house of Menard d'Orian we met a close friend of the wife of Paul Clemenceau,[5] she herself was an Austrian Jewess. This journalist friend of hers was a correspondent for the Vienna paper *Neue freie Presse* and during the Dreyfus affair he was expelled from France. His name was Frischauer. On hearing that we were returning to Moscow, he brought and handed to Pyotr a letter of recommendation to one of his good friends in Moscow. "He is a very influential person and I am sure he will be useful to you," he said. Pyotr of course thanked him and put the letter away in his wallet. On our way back to France in May already, we suddenly read it. First of all we were puzzled that Frischauer, who was an utter and irreversible left-winger, recommended us to Mr. Gringbut, the chief editor and owner of *Moskovskie vedomosti*, a glaringly monarchist paper. So much for Jewish solidarity!

In Paris we again met up with Frischauer, and he told us he had recently had a letter from his friend in answer to his own, because as soon as we had left he had written to Gringbut himself asking him to help in every way. "My friend writes that it was absolutely unnecessary for him to help you, and that Olenina-d'Alheim's performances in Russia could be likened to a triumphal procession." (SV, 139–40.)

Meeting with Lev Tolstoy

The d'Alheims' stay in Russia was significant not just because of the concerts, but also because of precious hours of association with Russian friends, meetings with Balakirev, Stasov, Molas, Cui and others. In 1901, the d'Alheims also visited Lev Tolstoy at Yasnaya Polyana.

Olenina-d'Alheim:

Pyotr talked a good deal with Balakirev, unlike myself. Later on in Moscow as well, I never took part in disputations simply because that tires the voice. But the fiancée of Sergei Lvovich (he was Tolstoy's eldest son, if I'm not mistaken)—I cannot recall her name —told Countess Tolstoy that it seemed to her that I was very stupid. The Countess herself told me this when we were at Yasnaya Polyana.

This is how we found our way there. It was after my first concert. This was in November. In Paris I had been invited to sing in the second concert of the recently founded Philharmonic Society (I should have sung in the first one too, but since I was in Moscow then, Litvin[6] sang instead). On returning from Paris, we first went to St. Petersburg [where] Cui had invited me to give a recital in the Hall of the Conservatoire, as he was a professor there.

[Then] we went to spend the holidays on the estate of Pyotr's mother, who had settled there some couple of years before that, after finally returning to her homeland. Sofia Andreyevna [Tolstoy's wife] was travelling in the same train from Moscow. On hearing that we were in the same railcar as herself, she invited us to her compartment and also invited us to come to Yasnaya Polyana, where all her family members were divided into two camps: one was in favour of Mussorgsky and myself; and the other, if not against me, was in any case opposed to Mussorgsky.

The most opposed was the eldest daughter, who at that time was married to Sukhotin, and this Sukhotin was related to the d'Alheims. Lev Nikolayevich [Tolstoy] knew this of course, and afterwards kept teasing Tatyana: "I've just met your cousin d'Alheim!" In fact he did meet him once in the winter. Pyotr was on his way from Tula to his mother's, or on his way back, I don't remember. It was late in the evening. Seeing a rider in the distance, Pyotr asked the driver who it could be. "None other than the count himself. He goes riding almost every day, in all weathers." It turned out to be true. Recognising Pyotr, Lev Nikolayevich stopped his horse and tied it up behind the sleigh, and he himself sat down next to Pyotr and that way travelled about ten versts [about 5.7 miles] with him.

I think Tolstoy had already read Pyotr's book [about Villon]. It had come out in 1899, and very likely either Olendorf or Pyotr him-

Lev Tolstoy.

self had sent it to him. So they were able to have a good long chat. Among other things Lev Nikolayevich asked Pyotr what he thought of the attacks on great artists like Dante and others in his book *What Is Art?* Pyotr answered that, knowing him to be a good huntsman, he realised that [Tolstoy] was sniping not at the Gods themselves, but at their idols. Tolstoy was silent for a moment, and then suddenly, without the slightest mistake, recited Baudelaire's poem "Les Phares."

Lev Nikolayevich was very sympathetically disposed towards Pyotr [during our visit to Yasnaya Polyana], and all that day talked only to him. After dinner and before tea in the evening I sang. But first of all I must tell about my meeting with Lev Nikolayevich.

We arrived at about eleven o'clock, before lunch, which was not attended by our host. I talked for quite a long time with the Countess. It was now that she told me about her future belle fille's opinion of me. And since she herself told me, it is quite possible that meant she was not in agreement.

After lunch Tolstoy himself arrived. The Countess introduced me to him first, and as you can imagine, I peered at him hard with my short-sighted eyes. Afterwards someone told me that he liked it when people looked him straight in the eyes. After meeting [manuscript error; read: After greeting] Pyotr, Lev Nikolayevich sat him down somewhere in the drawing room and they became engaged in a conversation that evidently interested him, because at about three o'clock he suddenly suggested that all his guests come on a sledge-ride to the abattis (I believe this was the woodland surrounding Yasnaya Polyana). Tolstoy wanted to show Pyotr a spring "which never freezes." I don't remember properly, but I think they provided Pyotr with felt boots so that he could get down the fairly deep gully where the spring was. I had my own felt boots on. As we approached the gully, Lev Nikolayevich asked: "Who wants to come down the gully with us?" Nobody wanted to and everyone refused apart from Sergei Lvovich [and ourselves]. I of course ventured down as well, although the snowdrifts were fairly deep, and there were about twelve degrees of frost. After climbing down the gully, the four of us walked a few more paces. Then, stopping by the spring, Tolstoy said, "Here we are," and fell silent. A few minutes later, Pyotr glanced at him and saw that Tolstoy was weeping. [I believe that] for him the never-freezing spring was somehow like a symbol of his own self.

On our return we sat down to tea, and Lev Nikolayevich seated himself opposite me. Maybe the Countess had already told him that I was by no means a fool, and he had decided to examine me himself. The table in their dining room was very long and narrow, so I could easily see my *vis-à-vis* despite my bad eyesight. Addressing me he suddenly said, "Do you think that a totally deaf composer can create works of genius?" I was taken aback by this question, and no doubt I looked so surprised that Tolstoy did not wait for a reply and said, "Oui, je comprends, je comprends."

Then he went off to his own room, but came back when every-one was already at dinner, and sat down next to Pyotr. Among the guests was one of the admirers of his talent, some doctor[7] if I'm not mistaken. With Pyotr seated next to him, Tolstoy whispered to him: "Regardez ce monsieur. Il ne se sert pas de sa main droite, mais la tient dans la poche de son pantalon... Ô, non. Il inscrit tout simple-ment toutes mes paroles... Comment y parvient-il? Il faut admirer son étonnante..." ["Look at that gentleman. He isn't using his right hand and keeps it in his trouser pocket.... Oh no, he's simply writ-ing down every word of mine.... How does he manage it? One must admire his astonishing...."]

After dinner, but not immediately, at about nine o'clock, the Countess led me over to the grand piano. Goldenweiser,[8] to whom she immediately introduced me, was already sitting at the piano. He was a very sensitive musician, a brilliant virtuoso, and as I later learned, a professor at Moscow Conservatoire. He was very friendly with the family of Tolstoy and often came to Yasnaya Polyana. I sang some Mussorgsky, thought not just him, but some Schumann and Schubert as well. Lev Nikolayevich liked the latter most of all, he loved his "Creation" and it moved him.

After that I sang some of the *Nursery*. [Tolstoy] said he could not understand how music could depict motion. I answered: "In the same way, I think, as the words of a writer." I also sang "The Little Orphan" and "Eremushka's Lullaby," but then went back to Schubert.

Suddenly I thought, why not sing "The Field Marshal" with its French text—I had not had time to learn it in Russian. In manuscript I had "The Field Marshal" transposed lower and Pyotr had called it "La guerre." Maybe Goldenweiser was unfamiliar with this work of Mussorgsky's. People did not know a lot of his work at that time, and only heard of it from me. As I finished singing "The Field Marshal" Tolstoy exclaimed: "Whose composition is that?" And everyone was thrilled by it and thought that it was written by some French com-poser. But when I pronounced the name of Mussorgsky, Tolstoy said, "How is it that people keep telling me Mussorgsky is a poor com-poser? After all, what we have heard just now was more than splendid." It then occurred to me that Mussorgsky's opponents ought to have hanged us.... We never went to Yasnaya Polyana [again]. (SV, 129–33.)

Confirmation of the debates about Mussorgsky's music that took place in the Tolstoy family can also be found in the diary of Tatyana Sukhotina-Tolstaya. The d'Alheims' visit to Yasnaya Polyana, which Sukhotina wrongly dates to 1903, is described by her in very prejudiced terms. Her remarks about the d'Alheims are so unobjective and even malicious, that they would scarcely be worth quoting, were they not indicative to some extent of Russian artistic life at the time. How little and how poorly even the cultural élite of Russia knew about Olenina and her husband's activities. And how ignorant they often were regarding some of the best representatives of Russian national music, especially Mussorgsky!

T.L. Sukhotina-Tolstaya:
Olenina-d'Alheim and her husband came and she sang a lot while we were there [in Yasnaya Polyana]. She has a small and ugly voice, but great artistry and ability to sing intelligently and with meaning. She sang Schumann and Schubert and then some repulsive Mussorgsky, whom she and especially her husband love and think highly of. Her husband is a sort of thoughtless learned parrot. I think he is extraordinarily stupid and dull. They have a daughter aged eleven, whom they have abandoned with some aunt, and after having her they decided to have no more children so as to be free to serve their art. He writes novels that I gather are indigestible. She earns a huge amount of money with her concerts, they live in hotels and believe that this is real living. (T.L. Sukhotina-Tolstaya, *Dnevnik* (Moscow, 1987), 442.)

We in fact know how pathetically small was the "huge amount of money" that Olenina earned with her concerts. We also know how fastidious the d'Alheims were in matters of money and publicity. The very mention of her visit to Tolstoy might have served as a useful advertising gimmick had Olenina regard that as a moral thing to do, and if she had wanted to exploit it as some well-known performers did.

Olenina-d'Alheim:
The following year the splendid harpsichordist Wanda Landowska[9] came with her husband, and we of course went to her first recital and got to know them. Wanda—[or rather] her husband Lev—

suggested arranging some joint concerts with Wanda in all the major cities of Russia. He had heard by then of my "triumphal procession through Russia," as the manager of *Moskovskie novosti* called my concerts—it was a glaringly monarchist paper, but more about this anon. I did not accept the proposal of Landowska's husband [since] I already had concerts scheduled in Moscow.

Being a truly splendid harpsichordist, she [Wanda Landowska] could not fail to please Sofia Andreyevna, who immediately invited her to Yasnaya Polyana. The Landowskis spent many days there, and almost all the holidays. On their return, Wanda in an interview told about their stay with Tolstoy and was amazed that of all the pieces she played to him—and she had played great masterpieces by Bach and other composers—such a great writer liked Couperin's "Old Men's Dance" most of all. It is a nice piece, but why did Tolstoy keep asking her to repeat it? She was very surprised at this. It was the wife of Sergei Lvovich (he was by then married to her) who revealed to us the reason why Tolstoy so much preferred the "Old Men's Dance": "On Landowska's last visit, when everyone had gone out onto the porch to see her off, I forgot to take my warm shawl and went back into the dining room to get it, and there I saw Lev Nikolayevich dancing round the table. He was skipping from one leg to the other and singing a phrase from the "Old Men's Dance" to which he had fitted the words: "Ils sont partis! Ils sont partis!" ["They've gone! They've gone!"]

It was understandable, since it was mainly the Countess who was taken up with Landowska, and Wanda's husband must have bored Tolstoy good and proper.

Wanda's husband talked with us about Tolstoy in a critical manner that was commonplace [at that time] and stupid. But this did not prevent [him] from publishing a poster for his wife's tour of Russia showing a scene of "Wanda Landowska playing for Tolstoy" and the poster also carried a photograph of Lev Tolstoy listening to her. I do not know who arranged that, and I did not ask. But when she returned and was preparing for her concert tour, she invited us to visit her, and if I remember rightly, Pyotr replied that we did not like the poster showing a celebrated author as "homme sandwich" and therefore did not wish to be further acquainted with them.

(SV, 133–34.)

Maria Olenina's meetings in Russia further confirmed her sense of mission—to promote Russian music and assist its performance both in Russia and abroad. She discussed with Balakirev the possibility of organising some Russian concerts in Paris, which of course would include work by Balakirev in the programme. Later, in 1903, Balakirev became keen on the idea of Kazanli[10] as conductor of these concerts. Much to the regret of both Balakirev and Olenina, however, they encountered difficulties in realising this plan.

Mily Balakirev:

Gatchina, 8 July 1903

Dear and greatly esteemed Maria Alexeyevna,

Today at last I received your answer to my request concerning Kazanli. It is a great pity that there is no hope of organising two Russian concerts in Paris under his baton. It appears that Germany is much more accessible for Russian music, than France.

A few days ago I received a book [...] [of concert programmes for 1873–1903] that was sent to me probably because I was among the foreign composers whose works were performed in these concerts. Running through the programmes of these concerts I saw that they were of a sort suited to the leisure garden, like the summer concerts in Pavlovsk under Galkin. And meanwhile Colonne is all the rage in Paris thanks to the fact that the Parisians have no need of serious music. It will be interesting to find out what sort of conversation we have with Chevillard,[11] but I am almost convinced that Dolina's recommendation will be for more important to him than my own.

In any case, bear in mind that since he is on duty, Kazanli can only travel abroad to conduct concerts during the Christmas or Easter holidays, i.e., between 4–20 January *New Style* or between 3–13 April, also *New Style*.[12] Of course, he could also take leave in summer, but there are no concerts in summer because the public leaves. [...]

Sincere greetings to your husband and to dear Alexander Alexeyevich. I heartily wish you good health and all the best.

Balakirev.

(M.A. Balakirev, letter of 8 July 1903 to M.A. Olenina, AAO, 42–43.)

The Problem of Money in the Arts

To the end of his days Balakirev took an affectionate interest in Olenina's success and did everything he could to help her extend her activities. Later he attempted to arrange a concert tour for her in Germany, where his own music was played fairly frequently. A concert was also due to take place in Berlin, but it was cancelled because of Olenina's somewhat brusque character. She was often quite uncompromising where her own views were concerned, and these sometimes bore the heavy imprint of her ideology. The episode that led to cancellation of the Berlin concert began quite peaceably.

Mily Balakirev:
Dear Alexander Alexeyevich,

Not so long ago I received news from Berlin that our publisher Zimmermann[13] who lives there wants to organise a series of small concerts in Berlin in the autumn or winter, whose number will depend upon their success. He intends to perform in them a series of piano pieces by myself and Sergei Mikhailovich [Lyapunov],[14] and also our songs which he has published. He has decided not to allow editions by other publishers for performance in these concerts, which are being organised exclusively to popularise his own editions.

Now he is looking for a performer of the songs. He has found a very good pianist, Sapelsky, who has a good name abroad and is well disposed to our compositions. He is looking for a German female singer with a good name, who is well known in Germany. [...]

It occurred to me to advise him to invite Maria Alexeyevna [Olenina-d'Alheim] for this, as a brilliant performer of Russian songs who, since she is totally unknown in Germany, will not present Zimmermann with any difficult conditions. Unlike any German singer with an established name who will rip Zimmermann off for a tidy sum and then proceed to ruin our songs because she is unfamiliar with Russian music, which takes more than an ability to give a brilliant performance of Mozart's "Veilchen," Beethoven's "Adelaide" and other pearls of German music.

I do not know whether he will listen to me. At the same time I wrote to Maria Alexeyevna, from whom I unexpectedly received a

gift of the book she has published on Mussorgsky. In my letter I
said that in case she was invited by Zimmermann, she should try
and reach an agreement with him that gives her opportunity to
acquaint the Berlin public with her supreme talent. She shouldn't
be put off by the narrowness of the programme. If she is successful
she can then give her own Lieder-Abend in Berlin, in which she
can perform Mussorgsky's *Nursery* and anything she wants.

I am asking for your assistance, so that you can convince her
not to let the grass grow under her feet while she still has a voice,
and not to miss a chance, if one presents itself, to introduce herself
to Berlin, from where (if she is successful) the whole of Germany
and Austria will open up for her concert activities.

I happen to read in the papers from time to time that she still
wants to present herself in the Moscow Concerts, but it is galling to
even think of that. Moscow has more than enough with Sionitskaya
or some other ordinary singer of that sort. But if she still really wants
to enjoy [...] success in Moscow, it will be incomparably easier to
achieve this after a success in Berlin. [...]

Yours wholeheartedly,

Balakirev.

(Letter of 8 June 1908; AAO, 61–64.)

In reply to his letter Balakirev received an outright refusal from
Olenina who was infuriated at his suggestion: she had no wish to be
involved in an enterprise merely designed to line the pockets of its
organisers. Olenina was remorseless in her campaign against the rule
of money and exploitation in the arts.

Mily Balakirev:
Dear Alexander Alexeyevich,

I have just received your letter, and I gasped when I read of
Maria Alexeyevna's views on the subject of concert organisers. *Of
course, and beyond any doubt,* they organise concerts *to earn money,*
just as performing artists (including, of course, Maria Alexeyevna
herself) and composers appear in public *with that same aim*—
hoping to derive material benefit from the gift God gave them,
which, if it is skillfully and practically presented can bring hand-

some rewards, whereas without an impressario no artist can achieve any success.

I cannot fathom what horrors of exploitation your sister imagines are contained in Zimmermann's proposal. To fill out his portrait I can tell you the following: he has spent a lot of money on publishing our compositions, supposing them to have great artistic worth, and because he quite naturally wants to help to popularise them among the public.

Can your sister really demand that a publisher *unselfishly* serves art *for the sake of art*, as though he doesn't need to eat or drink or keep his family? After all, even your sister does not invite the public to her concerts for the sake of art, she charges them money. So how can she condemn a publisher who wishes to introduce the public to nothing other than the *musical works that he has published*?

What exploitation can Maria Alexeyevna be talking about, when nobody in Germany knows her name, and when by inviting her on my advice, Zimmermann may end up out of pocket? And if she is successful, the road in Germany will be opened up for her concertising, and she can perform whatever she sees fit.

You are puzzled at Zimmermann's demand that *exclusively his editions* should be performed in the concert. But just think what would be the point of him using his concerts to promote the editions of Bessel and Jurgenson, who will not so much as say thank you, while for the sake of this venture he himself could very well end up making a loss. Let Messrs Bessel, Jurgenson and others *exert themselves to popularise their own editions*; it would be ridiculous to demand this of some outsider.

I shall be sad if your sister rejects this opportunity—perhaps her only one—to do a bit of concertising in Germany without any loss to herself, and maybe even with some profit. And when I advised Zimmermann, I chiefly had in mind to give Maria Alexeyevna a chance to show herself in Germany.

In a letter I recently had from Zimmermann, he tells me he is in correspondence with your sister, which means she has not yet replied and turned him down. And you would be benefitting her, and Zimmermann and the art of music, if you can persuade her to take a sensible view of all this.

If her opposition to exploitation were logically applied, then she herself would be bound to bake bread from her own flour, so as to avoid being exploited when she buys bread at the shop. [...]

These are arguments which I have hastily tried to sketch out for you, so as to provide you with material for further polemics with Maria Alexeyevna.

Yours wholeheartedly,

Balakirev.

(22 June 1908; AAO, 64–67.)

The concert in Germany fell through, and Olenina clung to her "radical" views to the end of her life, although she was forced occasionally to depart from them. After a concert tour in London in 1912, which of course was a commercial venture and could not otherwise have taken place, Olenina categorically condemned the whole institution of concert tours—the reason being that they were expensive, and this forced the entrepreneurs to raise the price of tickets. It would therefore be better if concert tours did not take place at all. It seemed to escape Olenina's attention that all this would be a great loss for music itself, and that music would be inaccessible to the general public altogether if her views were taken to their logical conclusion.

IV

INTERNATIONAL CAREER

*Russia, France, Belgium, Switzerland
& England — 1903-1908, 1912*

lenina's concerts in Moscow and St. Petersburg marked a break-through in her artistic life. From now on she ceased to be merely a Russian singer resident in Paris; there now began the *international* career of a *Russian* singer. From 1901 onward, Olenina divided her time between Russia, France, Belgium and Switzerland, and in 1912 she made an extended tour of England.

Meanwhile, in Paris and Brussels, the name of Olenina-d'Alheim and that of Mussorgsky became synonymous. Such was the tenor of an article by Bellaigue[1] in the Paris *Revue des deux mondes* of 1901, and also of a fundamental review by Calvocoressi[2] in his article in *Le Guide Musical* for 1906, which summed up the decade's achievements since the first *conférences* on Mussorgsky.

Calvocoressi:

Mme Olenina-d'Alheim and M. Pierre d'Alheim were pioneers in the promotion of Mussorgsky's fame [in France], and I suppose that Mme Olenina-d'Alheim felt a flush of justified pride when she put at the head of her programme: The 54th Concert of Music by Mussorgsky. This long and patient labour of theirs has not been in vain, for the celebrity of Mussorgsky in France today must be

111

BECHSTEIN HALL.

FRIDAY EVENING, MAY 31st, at 8.15.
TUESDAY EVENING, JUNE 4th, at 8.15.
MONDAY EVENING, JUNE 10th, at 8.15.
WEDNESDAY AFTERNOON, JUNE 12th, at 3.15.

MARIE OLÉNINE D'ALHEIM

WILL GIVE A SERIES OF

. **Vocal** .

Recitals

At the Piano

M. MARCEL LAISNE.

BECHSTEIN GRAND PIANOFORTE.

TICKETS - 10s. 6d., 5s., 2s. 6d.

May be obtained at the Box Office, Bechstein Hall, usual Agents, and if

CONCERT DIRECTION DANIEL MAYER, Chatham House, George St., Hanover Square, W.

Poster announcing a series of vocal recitals given by
Maria Olenina-d'Alheim in London, May–June, 1912.

⁀ Alfred Cortot.

ascribed to the activity of these two disciples of his. The wife's main medium has been the concert; her husband's—that of the book, the brochure and the spoken word. In this way the couple have gradually spread and reinforced the fame of this composer's works [...]

Mme Olenina-d'Alheim is able to execute this very special music with an intelligence, assurance and enthusiasm that deserve the highest praise. In a single moment she can pass from the smiling insight required in performing the *Nursery*, to the tragic tension that suits a performance of the *Songs and Dances of Death*. And of course she is the very singer that Mussorgsky would himself have chosen.

(M.D. Calvocoressi, *Le Guide Musical*, 1906, vol. 23–24, p. 438.)

The d'Alheims associated and collaborated with the finest musicians in France. During this period began Olenina's many years of collaboration with Alfred Cortot,[3] Darius Milhaud,[4] and later her friendship with Nadia Boulanger.[5] In 1901 Claude Debussy published a review of her concert with Cortot in which she performed only songs by Mussorgsky. Olenina's own rendering of part of Debussy's text read as follows:

Claude Debussy.

Claude Debussy:
The composer [Mussorgsky] could never have wished for a more faithful interpreter. Everything in her performance was expressed with a precision that bordered on the miraculous. In the *Nursery* one cannot fail to notice the little girl's prayer before going to sleep, the tender excitement of a child's soul and even the enchanting mannerism of little girls when they imitate grown-ups. In the "Doll's Lullaby," one imagines that every single word, prompted with such amazing sensitivity, is able to evoke pictures filled with a mysterious magic peculiar to children's fantasy. (*Revue blanche*, 15 April 1901; quoted in Olenina's manuscript that diverges slightly from the original.)

Her partnership with Cortot and Milhaud introduced Olenina to the very heart of Paris musical life. For almost a decade she took part in regular subscription concerts mounted by Cortot's concert organisation [Association des concerts A. Cortot], and Cortot and she became close friends. He invited her to perform Mussorgsky songs with orchestra, and he himself performed with her as pianist. We also know of these two artists' collaboration from their correspondence.

Alfred Cortot:

22 December 1904

Dear Friend! Could you sing at my 7th concert, on the 19 January, Mussorgsky's "War" [i.e., "The Field Marshal"] in Rimsky's orchestration, since we have nothing else, and the *Nursery* with piano? Please let me know quickly. My sincere respects to you and your husband. Clo sends greetings to you.

Alfred Cortot.

(GMMC, fond 256, no. 3919.)

Alfred Cortot:

Dear friend,

The other day after your concert I left for Orleans and could not call on you to applaud and shout "Bravo." I know only that it created an immense impression, as indeed it should have done. Many thanks to you again. My sincere friendly greetings to you both.

Alfred Cortot.

(GMMC, fond 256, no. 1173.)

Olenina's artistic development as singer and musician reached its apogee in the 1910s. Confirmation of this comes in contemporary reviews by music critics, and in assessments of her art by the finest musicians of the time. In 1910, for example, Cortot gave his verdict.

Alfred Cortot:

In the course of these few hours spent with you in rehearsal and at the concert, you have brought me genuine joy—a joy I can compare only with what I experience when I play with Casals.[6] When you sing and I am unable to hear you [i.e., when I am away], I suffer an "artistic trauma." (A. Cortot, letter of 20 December 1910 to M.A. Olenina-d'Alheim; GMMC, fond 256, no. 1175.)

Similar assessments are contained in the letters of Darius Milhaud, who not only accompanied Olenina but saw in her the ideal interpreter of his own works.

 Darius Milhaud.

Darius Milhaud:
I would like to tell you once again how sorry I was not to be in
Paris when you performed my *Chansons hébraïques*. I wish to thank
you once again for including them in your programme since it is
a great honour for me and my music to have you as its interpreter.
(D. Milhaud, letter (n.d.) to M.A. Olenina-d'Alheim; probably 1925, when the work was written,
GMMC, fond 256, no. 1411.)

Darius Milhaud:
I shall come with great pleasure tomorrow at four o'clock to rue
Faustin Hélie. It is a great honour and joy for me to think that
you perform my music. I remember how when I came to Paris ten
years ago, I attended the concerts you gave with Cortot in the Salle
des Agricultures. I remember going away thrilled, with a mixed
feeling, and with a feeling of deep sorrow as I told myself that
never, never would such a wonderful singer as yourself take notice
of my music. And now the dream of my youth has come true....
I would like to write some songs for you for which [...] the two of
us together will choose the text. (D. Milhaud, undated letter to Olenina-d'Alheim,
GMMC, fond 256, no. 1412.)

Living abroad did not mean that Russian affairs failed to concern Olenina. She not only promoted the music of Mussorgsky, but did everything to assist the collaboration of French and Russian musicians. Balakirev's dealings with Alfred Cortot, for instance, occurred after Olenina put them in touch. In October 1904 Balakirev thanked Cortot for his "kind letter forwarded to me by Mme la Baronne d'Alheim" in which Cortot wrote of his wish to play some works of Balakirev in his concerts. (See draft of letter in archive of M.A. Balakirev, Russian National Saltykov-Shchedrin Library, fond 41, inventory 1, no. 651.)

In her concerts in Paris and elsewhere Olenina invariably performed music not just by Mussorgsky, but by other Russian composers who were close to her heart and with whom she maintained constant close links. Of living Russian composers, the closest to her remained Balakirev.

Mily Balakirev:
Much esteemed Maria Alexeyevna,

My songs have at last appeared in print, but are only on sale separately at present, and I hasten to send you two songs dedicated to you. I hope that you like them.

The German text will enable you to perform them in Germany, which will be a complete novelty for the German public, and you will have no competitors. When they come out in a single album, I shall not delay in sending you copies.

My best regards to your husband and I wish you a merry time over the forthcoming holidays.

Yours with sincere devotion,

Balakirev.

(Letter of 15 December 1904 to M.A. Olenina-d'Alheim; GMMC, fond 256, no. 792.)

Olenina was always noted for her liberal opinions and, like many Russian intelligentsia, she sympathised with those at the bottom of the social ladder. The revolution of 1905 and period following only served to increase her concern with problems of social justice. If educated Russians perceived the events of the revolution in their direct political context, for Olenina all these stirring Russian problems were refracted through music—her chief mode of self-expression and communication with reality. And the music of the Mighty Handful appeared an ideal medium for such communication. Where the poetic text of vocal compositions was concerned—especially those of Mussorgsky—Olenina weighed up and gave meaning to every word. And although her judgements may today strike one as naive (which they doubtless were), their realisation in Olenina's interpretation carried a quite sophisticated expressive conviction which contemporaries confirmed as very typical of the singer.

Olenina-d'Alheim:
Do you remember Khovansky's baritone aria in *Khovanshchina*—"The camp of Streltsy is asleep" ["Spit streletskoye gnezdo"]? I cannot at all agree to it being given to the boyar informant Shaklovity. Probably, Rimsky-Korsakov found that a single aria does not make up a character role, and he simply tacked it onto the part of the informant. I do not think that this is what the author wished. Did he not give the last word to just such a witness—the Holy Fool in *Boris Godunov*? If he had wanted to entrust his main statement, his final word, to another person, in the final scene of the drama, after the departure of Dmitry and all the crowd, he could have brought back or left on the road not the Holy Fool, but the old monk Pimen. I have often sung that aria "The camp of Streltsy is asleep" in recitals...

Mussorgsky predicted the future fate of all princes and wealthy people, and in *Khovanshchina* he entrusted a woman, the schismatic Marfa, to tell this prophecy to the world: "My prince, you shall know want and hardships, great toil and sorrow. In that toil, amid scalding tears you shall learn all the truth of this earth." But not everyone has understood this prophecy, and it has to be said that it is like that with all pronouncements by poets and other thinkers: although people understand their meaning, they somehow treat it lightheartedly, without fear, like a series of poetic inventions. In general people do not like to hear and understand the truth.

The tsarist censorship somehow sniffed out that this same truth is contained in *Boris*, and gradually they began removing *Boris* from the stage. They didn't beat about the bush with a minor clerk like Mussorgsky. But they overlooked the truth contained in

Khovanshchina and in his other [works], because they appeared after Mussorgsky's death and were presented by someone in office, a Conservatoire professor.

And [the censorship] overlooked yet another eagle that came flying from the cage of another person in office, the chemistry professor Borodin. [This was] in three of his songs: "The Sleeping Princess" ["Spyashchaya knyazhna"], "The Song of the Dark Forest" ["Pesnya tyomnogo lesa"] and "The Sea" ["More"]. The "Song of the Dark Forest" is a set of reminiscences of the Pugachev rebellion.[7] The song called "The Sea" was written when a political exilee made an unsuccessful and tragic attempt to flee from the island of Sakhalin. In progressive circles they heard about this, and Borodin wrote his "The Sea." But the censors still forbade its publication with Borodin's words. The [composer] had to insert a new text in which a "young merchant" replaced the young revolutionary. I did not realise this and yet still could not make up my mind to sing "The Sea," although I loved Borodin's music. But you know, I have never found trades-people sympathetic. However, one day an old pupil of Rimsky-Korsakov, Semyon Kruglikov, told me about the story of "The Sea" after I told him I did not like the text of this song by Borodin. And it didn't take me much thought to alter the words in my own way and restore the real text as well as I was able. Kruglikov could not remember it properly, and knowing the sense of the words, I simply made them up, and that was how I sang it. And I was glad because it's a splendid composition, one of the composer's best. This was in 1914, unless I'm mistaken.

And the police chief did not interfere. Generally they—the police chiefs, that is—did not interfere much, only on two occasions. The first time was in Nizhny Novgorod when he forbade me to sing Chopin's "Lament for Poland," and I then replaced it with the aria "The camp of Streltsy is asleep." And the second time it happened in Odessa after the elections to the First Duma [i.e., 1906]. They had elected a Kadet,[8] a rich Jew, and the Jews for some reason were trying to get round the authorities. I don't know what they arranged or how, but at my concert not only the city police chief turned up, but the railroad police chief as well, which had never happened before, and there were policemen standing inside the

doors of the hall. So what forbidden things were there in my programme? There was that same "Lament for Poland" and a Jewish
song "Shabashnaya" ["The Sabbath Song"], and I was to sing it
both in dialect [i.e., in Yiddish] and in ancient Hebrew.

Then, just before the start of the final part of the programme, an
official from the police chief appeared in the artistes' room and
demanded that I refrain from singing these songs. I refused of course
and told him: "You can write a report if you want." He was embarrassed and walked away with his report, and I immediately walked
out on stage. My brother Alexander was accompanying me. We had
just taken up position when the electricity in the hall was suddenly
turned off. I told my brother: "Begin playing. You know by heart
what I have to sing now." The public protested a little at first, but
when they heard the first chords on the piano they quietened down,
and I sang both songs, and after that I whispered to my brother:
"Play Beethoven's 'Mignon'." After the first couplet, the lighting
began to go on again, and after the final one, it was fully restored.
There were big ovations, of course. But next day we left, and the
chief of the railroad police was there at the station. (SV, 98–101.)

The story told by Olenina about Borodin's song "The Sea" has not
been confirmed in subsequent editions of the composer's vocal works.
For instance, in the edition of 1947 edited by Pavel Lamm,[9] the com-
mentary makes no mention of any other text allegedly "restored" by
Borodin. The song was written and first published in 1870 and subsequently republished many times without alteration. The 1947 edition
was based on the composer's final manuscript and contains no essential changes affecting the hero of the song; evidently he really was a
merchant. Nevertheless, Olenina's mention of this story and the very
fact of the singer's detailed attention to the text of the song are eloquent evidence of her approach to the works she performed.

In the texts of the songs Olenina sang no detail was so insignificant
as to be ignored—seemingly the most minute details were carefully
thought out and worked over. In 1963, after hearing the Moscow singer
Viktor Rybinsky perform Mussorgsky's "Svetik Savvishna," Olenina
made a series of comments that confirmed the detailed thought that
underlay her understanding of the song text.

Olenina-d'Alheim:

It's good that he [sings] in the same tempo all the time. All the time, all the time, like speech, with speech accent. After all, he cannot speak like other people. Incidentally, when I sang this, I always thought of Mussorgsky himself. He too was just the same sort of *yurodivy* [holy innocent] confronting life and its beauty. So that here you have to completely... When Mussorgsky himself performed [this song] he told one performer (there was this general who was very fond of all the Mighty Handful, and this general [complained to Mussorgsky]: "I'm choking, gasping for breath. I can't take a breath anywhere"). From start to finish, it has to be like speech, and without emphasising the feeling anywhere. [You have to sing it] the same all the way through, absolutely the same.

I'd like to find out somehow, I'd still like to find out whether the sister of Pavel Lamm is here because she probably saw various notes by Mussorgsky himself. What did he say? Svetik Savvishna? Svet Ivanovna, or Svet Ivanova? That would be enormously important. (Tumanov: Why, Maria Alexeyevna?) (Olenina-d'Alheim hums) "Svetik Sávvishna, Svet Ivánovna"—he really is a sort of complete holy fool. (Olenina explains that both Savvishna and Ivanovna are patronymics, so it would be logical for Ivanova to be the surname.) Anyway, he has woken up. His feelings have awakened, so one really has to know: if it's Ivanova, then that means he has a flash of realisation, rather than if he says Ivanovna. He was like that semi-conscious, that poor old *yurodivy* [from *Boris Godunov*?], because he kept on saying the same thing. They kept telling him, but he kept on with his own ideas... (See verbatim account of Olenina's master classes in Moscow 1963, pp. 309–27.)

Despite having spent almost fifty years abroad, Olenina nevertheless remained very Russian. Her splendid speech manner and love of the Russian language never faded despite years of separation from the land where she grew up. But a Russian singer needed a Russian public. This idea gradually ripened and finally led to one of the most important stages in her life—to the creation of the House of Song, the "Dom pesni," which was set up while vocally she was still in full blossom. How exactly did Olenina herself sing?

Olenina's Performance Style

Olenina's singing was unfortunately never recorded on disc. "First of all," she told me in 1963, "I was concerned with other things: concerts, new programmes, and there was neither the money nor the need. Later, after Pyotr died, there was no money at all, and it was too late to think about it. Apart from which, I never did trust any machines, including the microphone." The result is that we can discover what sort of artist Olenina was only by indirect means—via memoirs, articles and reviews. Nevertheless, these provide a fairly detailed picture of how contemporaries perceived the vocal artistry of this highly original performer.

In his article "À propos of Mme Olenina-d'Alheim's concerts" written after her Moscow début in 1902, Stasov ranked her alongside "the marvelous, original and talented Os[ip] Af[anasyevich] Petrov,[10] Iv[an] Al[exandrovich] Melnikov[11] and Fed[or] Ign[atyevich] Stravinsky.[12] " "It is to this same family of original, unique national talents," Stasov wrote, "that Maria Alexeyevna Olenina-d'Alheim belongs. She appeared after all of them, as the most junior." (V.V. Stasov, *Izbrannye sochineniya*, vol. 3, 284.) Almost from the very outset, Olenina began gathering a public of her own, who remained faithful to her. In the same article Stasov cites the critic of a Moscow German-language newspaper which observed that "Mme Olenina-d'Alheim has managed to create about her, here in Moscow, a whole throng of inspired constituents; with each concert this throng increases, and the day is not far off when only people with antediluvian ideas will be capable of dismissing the wizardry of her singing." (Stasov, *Izbrannye sochineniya*, 285.) However, perceptions of the singer's art were always contradictory. So how *did* she sing? What was it that attracted some listeners, yet aroused the criticism of others?

Many of Olenina's contemporaries report that her voice was not a large one, that it had no specially beautiful timbre, and that her vocal manner was not beyond reproach. Leafing through the pages of her press reviews, one is struck by the variety of opinions, although the verdict on her actual vocal endowment was fairly unanimous and probably well justified. Among the comments on Olenina's voice one finds statements such as the following from *Moskovskie vedomosti*: "Her voice, which was not remarkable for its beauty and power before, has now faded even further"; or in the *Daily Telegraph*: "if only her intonation was always faultless and the tone of her voice equally distributed over its range." At the same time, one has the impression that the vast majority of listeners failed to notice these faults; César Cui spoke of her "rare ability to impart various timbres to her voice— sometimes metallic, sometimes gentle and caressing"; "her technique [is] superb and resides in her splendid diction and phrasing." Furthermore, the singer's voice and manner were often positively appreciated, and more often than not her faults were perceived as insignificant at the side of her virtues. Here are some typical pronouncements about Olenina's voice:

Khronika:

Does Mme Olenina have an unpleasant voice? Yes. Are her high notes raucous, strident and like a tin-whistle? Yes. Are the low notes dull and flabby? Yes. No evidence of schooling? None. Does she climb [up] her "chest voice" to the middle [register] so that the timbre emerges like that of a ventriloquist, or does one have the impression of a melodramatic gypsy performance [...] ? Yes, but...
(*Khronika*, 15 (1916), 11.)

Musical News:

The first of four recitals which are being given by Marie Olénine d'Alheim proved very attractive. The artist is one of Russia's leading singers, possessing gifts of a very high order and a voice of exceptional purity. (*Musical News*, 8 June 1912.)

Fyodor Stepun:[13]

Everyone can remember her recitals, first of all in the Small Hall of the Noble Assembly, and later in the private premises of the Maison du Lied set up by her and her husband. She sang not only in every European language, including Yiddish dialect, but also from the depths of every nation's heart. If only the spirit of her recitals could some day become that of the League of Nations, then Europe would be saved.

Maria Alexeyevna never was a first-class singer (she had a small and not markedly pleasant voice), nor was she a first-class stage actress in the spirit of Chaliapin.[14] But she was a real "priestess" of art in the full sense of this ample word. Despite the fact that Maria Alexeyevna was a very independent personality, on stage she produced the impression of a medium. For those closely acquainted with the d'Alheims, this came as no surprise. For them it is no secret what an enormous role Pyotr Ivanovich played in his wife's artistry. (F. Stepun, *Byvshee i nesbyvsheesya* (New York, 1956), Vol. 1, 313.)

Yury Sakhnovsky:[15]
The impression is all the more powerful because it accumulates gradually, and as usual in Mme d'Alheim's recitals it reaches its climax only towards the end of the concert. At the start of the recital I had occasion to observe those who were hearing Mme d'Alheim for the first time. She sang the Lermontov-Dargomyzhsky called "Song of the Gold Fish" ["Pesnya zolotoy rybki"]. These listeners pulled faces, they began exchanging looks that were at first disbelieving, and later indignant. What on earth was all this? What sort of voice did she have? None at all! And what a chill breath there was in her performance. The disbelief continued during three Schiller settings by Liszt. How was it she was so popular? Quite incomprehensible. But then came the turn of Schumann's "Waldesgespräch," better known under the title of "Die Lorelei." At the end of the ballade Mme d'Alheim seemed reborn, and listeners heard the fatal enchantress, the Lorelei herself. The performer's voice rang out with authority and power, and in a second every listener's eyes glowed with the fire of happiness—a spark from the creative fire of Schumann-d'Alheim had entered their souls. I place these names side by side as creative equals not just on the basis of that one performance of "Die Lorelei." After that followed "Die beiden Grenadiere," which I personally have heard at least forty times on the concert stage, but it was only this time that I understood Schumann himself. [...]

The text of the ballade contains not a word about his [the Grenadier's] death, but Mme d'Alheim's revelation consists precisely in the fact that his death takes place in her performance even as we watch: she falls silent on that last premortal exclamation, and then comes death in Schumann's final concluding chords. Listen to

this ballade in Mme d'Alheim's performance and you will understand the profundity of Schumann's talent. (GMMC, fond 256, no. 12, pp. 1–2.)

Russkoe slovo:
To speak of the performance is superfluous. As usual, it was
uneven, sometimes sinking to the level of a correct and noble interpretation by a cultivated artist (Wagner), but more often rising and
elevating the audience along with it to supernal heights of artistic
revelation. (*Russkoe slovo*, 8 March 1912.)

Morning Post:
In these songs [Mussorgsky's "Serenade" and "La Berceuse de la
Mort"] Mlle d'Alheim's interpretive efforts achieved their most
telling significance, which evidently arose from her professional
enthusiasm for the music of Moussorgsky. The technical difficulty
of sustaining a placid *mezza voce* or a high degree of vehemence
occasionally overcame her powers of musical definition. Her voice,
which is of mezzo soprano range and quality, showed a rich tone,
sometimes of a peculiar softness and always conveying a natural
and temperamental expression. (*Morning Post*, 5 June 1912.)

As we see, opinions of Olenina's voice sometimes differed like night
from day: from descriptions of an "unpleasant, raucous voice, with
flabby low notes," top notes like a "tin whistle," and "uneven performance," to mentions of a "richness of timbre, a voice of exceptional
purity, especial mellowness, natural and emotional expression." It is
evident that foreign critics placed less emphasis on Olenina's vocal
inadequacies and, as a rule, remarked on the power of her interpretation, whereas at home in Russia they often criticised her voice. It is evident that Olenina was not a first-class vocalist. Nevertheless, her fame
and popularity were exceptional, and they were based on a peculiar
"musical-declamatory expressivity," a sincerity and ability to "dissolve"
completely in the text and music of a song. These qualities of Olenina
were well described to me by Madeleine Milhaud, the composer's
widow, when I visited her in Paris in December 1991: "Olenina-d'Alheim
was absolutely pure—like gold. She seemed not to belong to this world
of ours, but she was well aware of it." We sat in the Milhauds' apart-

ment on the Place Pigalle. Doubtless Olenina herself had been here on more than one occasion—the Milhauds had lived here since time immemorial and even held on to the apartment during the Second World War, when they lived in America. I imagined Olenina standing there by the old upright piano at which Milhaud composed his *Chansons hébraïques* that were dedicated to her. "She was very Russian," Madame Milhaud told me. "Not very tall, thin, and full of energy. She was without age. She lived in her own world. And it was not important whether she had a good voice or not: it was impossible to criticise her—she was above criticism."

The Singer's and Composer's Concept

From her first public appearances until her last concerts, which she gave in Russia in 1926, Olenina's interpretations were notable for their deep understanding of the composer's conception, and all her vocal and technical resources were placed at the service of this. Here is what the music critics had to say.

> Yuly Engel:[16]
> Every word, every sound composed by the creator of *Boris Godunov* is evidently immensely close and dear to this artist; they are deeply imprinted in her artistic awareness and subconscious; and once imprinted there, they are then recreated as something of her own, something personal, newly created and thus capable each time of gripping one with a new force and directness. [...] Mme Olenina sang truly gorgeously, uniting the ecstasy of first enthusiasm with the unshakeable firmness of habit, and the more she continued, the better it became. (*Russkie vedomosti*, 9 March 1912.)

> *Daily Telegraph:*
> Her interpretations derive great value from their consistent sincerity, and by the means of that asset she won the warm approval of all who attended her second recital in the Bechstein Hall. For depth of insight and intimacy of expression, her version of

Schumann's tender *Frauenliebe und Leben* was one that few singers could surpass, and it was noticeable that, while the feeling was everywhere appropriate, no significant points were overemphasised. [...] At the end of the programme came two groups of the Moussorgsky songs which the singer made peculiarly her own. (*Daily Telegraph*, 7 June 1912.)

Teatr i muzyka:
The most gifted executants who possess an excellent technique, an excellent voice, with excellent shades of nuance, usually perform every composer identically. They give good prominence to good music. Mme Olenina-d'Alheim sings each composer in an individual way. She is caught up by the power of the piece she performs, by the power of the epoch, the power of the composer's gift, the power of his nationality and individuality. Her artistic communication sets her to one side as executant and conveys instead the *piece performed*, conveys to you *the work itself*.

[...] If you carry in your soul the slightest ability to rise for a few moments above deadly routine, after hearing Olenina you will go away with a feeling quite unlike any stereotype "impression of a concert." [...] Mme Olenina has contrived to avoid the common fate of most talents, and has retained that precious unspoiled gift which our great musicians delighted over in her very first performances. How this happened, we cannot know. But we do know that as a young singer, almost in her youth, she interpreted Mussorgsky to the French, and she continues to reveal to us the treasures of music from all over the world. (*Teatr i muzyka*, 9 December 1915.)

Olenina succeeded in creating her own special style of performance, which influenced the taste of her contemporaries and also transcended the limits of her own time. The main stylistic feature of her artistry was a blending of poetry with music, text and musical development, an ability to "tell the song." The singer's voice was able to undergo total transformation and achieve maximum expressivity in the re-creation of a particular artistic image. Those who heard Olenina often confirmed this quality as possibly the main reason for her success.

Baku:

Without possessing any remarkable vocal resources that deserve recognition—quite the reverse: by very modest means—Mme d'Alheim has used the strength of her enormous talent and inspired performance not just to enter the very front rank of concert singers but to create special techniques of vocal communication. Their special quality lies chiefly in a characteristic manner of *declamatory expression* [author's emphasis] and in a colourful eloquence of musical phrasing which in this singer achieve extraordinary force and significance. (*Baku*, 16 February 1916.)

PriazovJky Krai:

When the artist introduces the names of Mussorgsky, Medtner, Borodin or Schumann into her programme and plunges into musical depths of passion and haunting spiritual spectres, her voice undergoes miraculous transformations. Depending on the mood experienced, it can be sharply modified to its physical limits. Unbeautiful and falsetto-like in its natural form, it becomes extraordinarily typical and appropriate in everyday and humorous scenes, for instance, in the *Nursery* cycle, in "The Sauce-box" ["Ozornik"], or Mussorgsky's "Gopak" and others.

At significant, solemn or broadly lyrical moments, for example, in the Ravel-Engel "Hebrew Song" and elsewhere, her voice becomes warm and lovely, especially in its middle register. It can become [...] chesty with sounds that are hoarse and terrifying at moments of tragedy, in Medtner's "Invocation" ["Zaklinaniye"] or Mussorgsky's "Trepak," for instance. Olenina has yet another timbre, used predominantly in Mussorgsky's cycles "Songs and Dances of Death" and "Sunless," which we could describe as mystically horrified. And here we reach the ultimate limit of artistry: stage play comes to an end and aesthetic masks fall away. (*Priazovsky krai*, 14 March 1916.)

KavkazJkoe Jlovo:

Her singing is amazing in its flexibility, mobility and technique (the trill in the song by Martini), and in its artistic ability to use vocal material and colour it with a variety of timbres. In the singer's voice we can hear now a whisper, now death's chill voice from beyond the tomb, now the song of birds in a woodland thicket, now the exact sound of the flute—what the French describe as "voix flûtée"— and now the "mighty might and free freedom" of the song of the dark forest.

Mme d'Alheim is a great singer because she is a remarkable artist; her singing in the narrow sense is part of her unique artistic personality. Here is an artistic spirit capable of "knowing all, feeling all, and seeing all," and able to transform everything into imagery —touching as the prayer of the little orphan, or the lullaby to a "peasant's son," anguished as the death of a man forgotten on the field of battle, or death's trepak dance with the drunken muzhik; mystically macabre as death in the guise of the field marshal reviewing the fallen warriors. Her world of personification has no limits. (*Kavkazskoe slovo*, 22 October 1915.)

Rech':

Normal criteria, and a customary view of the art of the voice based on certain recognisable features of technique and tradition are inapplicable to this singer. [...] It is not here that the power and beauty of her vocal communication lie, but in its unique freshness, in the cogent logic of her artistic conception, flexible and varied as the pieces she performs, in the subtlety and inspiration of her expression, in the absence of any cerebral purposiveness in execution, in her captivating directness and simplicity, in her elegance of taste.

And all these purely spiritual facets of her performance somehow upstage any material and merely acoustic aspect. (*Rech'*, 17 January 1916.)

In the reviews by Pierre Lalo and Claude Debussy mentioned earlier, there was emphasis on Olenina's ability to get inside the composer's idea and conception. Both critics talked about her faithfulness to Mussorgsky in her performance of *The Nursery*, and about her ideal penetration into the composer's inner world. The same idea is echoed, too, in reports about other pieces which she performed.

Olenina's striving for artistic substance led her to a composition and structure of recital programmes that were unusual for her time, and she eliminated anything of a random sort or aimed at mere effect. Olenina's programmes were always built around a central idea. Like all serious musicians, the singer thought first and foremost about *what* she was performing. Hence the thematic unity, psychological and historical focus of her recitals. Thus, for her concert in the Small Hall of the Petersburg Conservatoire on 11 January 1917 she had the happy idea of including a "Pushkin" section, in which she performed songs by Glinka, Dargomyzhsky, Borodin, Rimsky-Korsakov, Rachmaninov, Cui and Mussorgsky to words by Pushkin. Today such a theme for a concert would arouse no surprise and would be regarded as a perfectly conventional "monographic" feature. However, in Olenina's time, vocal evenings were usually filled with "occasional" works that lacked any unifying sense. Olenina's thematically integrated approach had an almost revolutionary impact—certainly, that was how contemporaries viewed her Pushkin concert.

Vechernee vremya:
The first part of yesterday's recital consisted exclusively of works set to verse by Pushkin. The introduction was Glinka's "There is a desert land" ["Est' pustynnyi krai"], inscribed to the memory of Pushkin. [...] Thanks to this, the idea of Pushkin was sustained throughout, and he blended in with his composers all the more closely. There is no need, of course, to speak of Glinka ("One wondrous moment I recall" ("Ya pomnyu chudnoye mgnovenye")) and Dargomyzhsky "The youth and the maiden" ("Devushka i smert'"), "Oriental Song" ("Vostochnyi romans")). More rarely performed is Borodin's "Towards your homeland's distant shores" ["Dlya beregov otchizny dal'ney"]. Yet this showed a most perfect unity of spirit, thought, mood and sound between the poet and the creator of the music. Especially remarkable was the fact that this song was written by Borodin under the impact of Mussorgsky's death and was dedicated to his memory. Olenina remembers this and she made us recall it too. [...] The song was performed with the simplicity of genius and a youthful freshness of feeling. (*Vechernee vremya*, 12 January 1917.)

Priazovsky krai:
Olenina usually starts her concerts in antique spirit—with the yellowing pages of Glinka and Dargomyzhsky; then come some

Old French or Scottish chansons, Old Russian restorations... Yet, charming though it is in its pristine sincerity, this antique genre is, essentially speaking, the most unpropitious for this singer. For despite a light patina of emotionality, there is here a predominance of externally depictive elements and pure beauty, so to speak. [...]

Olenina's repertoire, which has the genius of Mussorgsky at its centre, is exceedingly broad, with a marked encyclopaedic tendency to take in the whole art of song. (*Priazovsky krai*, 14 March 1916.)

During Olenina's tour of England, critics unanimously commented on the unusual substance of her performances. For instance, the *Pell Mell Gazette* on 8 June 1912 claimed that one rarely encountered a singer whose programmes were so rich and varied in content as the previous day's fourth and final concert by Olenina-d'Alheim. The national press wrote in similar vein.

Daily Telegraph:
The programme designed by Miss Marie Olénine d'Alheim for her recital in Bechstein Hall last night was of unusual interest for those who care for good songs. [...] There, surely, is history presented in an illuminating way; and when to this Goethe group the singer added four different settings—by Schubert, Schumann, Liszt and Wolf [...] it will be seen that the interest was even more psychological than historical. [...] Miss d'Alheim certainly did wonders in carrying through such a programme so well as she did, for she is not by nature too well endowed with purely vocal graces. [...] It is her interpretations which matter. (*Daily Telegraph*, 7 June 1912.)

Saratovsky vestnik:
To place on a programme works by Glinka, Dargomyzhsky, Olenin, Chopin and Mussorgsky, and not to offer a single song from the so-called public favourites, was an idea that could only occur to a true artist, an artist who senses her obligation towards her art; and Mme Olenina-d'Alheim is just such an artist, a true servant of art. Thanks to her, Western Europe (England, France, Belgium [...]) has been introduced to the works of the most original Russian

genius, Mussorgsky. But the artiste has introduced not just Mussorgsky to Europe—she has also introduced the composer to his compatriots and made them like him. [...] Using her ability to speak to people and to their hearts, and with a profound perception of Mussorgsky's bidding [...] Mme Olenina placed on her programme only works that are capable of "shaking" people. And since her task is not to show herself off, but to reproduce as fully as possible the composer's idea, her programmes are utterly unlike conventional concert programmes. (*Saratovsky vestnik,* 29 September 1916.)

Olenina's singing was a blend of the intellectual and emotional, in which the primary factor, to use the Mighty Handful's own expression, was a *sense of artistic truth.* Contemporaries also noted her characteristic artistic conviction. She sang each work in the way she did because she was filled with "that indomitable certainty of her own artistic rightness, which is so typical of this remarkable artiste"—as Yuly Engel wrote in the paper *Russkie vedomosti.* And as they listened to Olenina, people knew that this was the only way in which one could, and should, sing whatever work it happened to be.

Yuly Engel:
How full [...] of that infectious conviction was her rendering of Mussorgsky, which occupied almost the whole of the evening! It included the entire series of songs entitled "Sunless," the whole of the *Nursery,* and extracts from *Khovanshchina* and *Boris Godunov,* and a whole series of individual songs. Mussorgsky was the first creator of Mme Olenina's fame, but she too has done much for Mussorgsky by her insistantly blazing propaganda. (*Russkie vedomosti,* 9 March 1912.)

A special atmosphere reigned at Olenina's recitals, which reflected the singer's approach to performance as a process of total "immersion" in the music she was singing. On the platform, Olenina produced on many the impression of someone in a state of trance. This was precisely how the poet Alexander Blok perceived and described it in a letter to Sergei Solovyov[17]:

Alexander Blok:

Dear Seryozha,

Yesterday evening Lyuba and I expended a lot of nervous energy. There was a concert by Olenina. At first I was seized by a sort of dreadful inner quaking, and after the German songs I was so tired that I only listened to the Russian ones with difficulty. Among other things, she sang the "Erlkönig," the "Doppelgänger" and "Die beiden Grenadiere."

Fortunately there were no "Songs and Dances of Death" but there was Mussorgsky's *Nursery.* Lyuba was completely shaken, and it had the same effect on mama. [...] Something happens to Olenina when she sings. It seems to me, she will not live long. [...] Returning home I intended to write about her for *Vesy.* [...]

(A.A. Blok, letter of December 1903 to S.M. Solovyov, in A.A. Blok, *Sobranie sochinenii v vos'mi tomakh* (Moscow-Leningrad, 1963), Vol. 8, 72–73.)

Blok's plan to write on Olenina, mentioned in the letter, was not realised and his prediction that Olenina would not live long did not come true: she lived for a mere hundred and one years. However Blok's reaction to the magic of Olenina-d'Alheim's singing was often experienced by many other observers. Often at the end of a programme, the atmosphere was so electrified that the public rushed up to the platform, and a few exalted listeners would try to touch the hem of the singer's dress or her hands. Olenina herself, however, wanted nothing of the sort and even attempted to fend off the applause after each item.

Olenina-d'Alheim:

If I tried to train my audience not to applaud me, this was simply with the aim of achieving two seconds of silence after each item on the programme. And that silence, if you like, actually intoxicated me—if one can refer to a moment of supreme happiness and joy as intoxication. Applause robs the performer of this happiness. I am also convinced that during that fleeting moment of silence, the work which has just been heard retains its influence over the listener, and it is utterly unreasonable to cut it short with hand-clapping. The influence [...] is destroyed by such clapping; it spoils it, and it also spoils it for the performer and for the audience as well. (SV, 34.)

Even in the twilight of her concert career, Olenina produced the same unforgettable impression of something utterly out of the ordinary. In conversation with Doda Conrad,[18] one of the last living witnesses of her singing, whom I visited at his home in Blois, near Paris, on the 11 December 1991, I asked what condition Olenina's voice was in 1931, and whether she could still sing. He told me the following:

Doda Conrad:
When I first heard her in my life ([it] was in 1923 or 1924), she had one of those voices which was completely without timbre, no vibrato at all. All the singers who would hear her would despise her, but still there were some things that I will always remember. [Tumanov: Expressiveness?] Not only that. Even vocally. *The Nursery*, and also things like "Berceuse de la mort" [i.e., the Lullaby from *Songs and Dances of Death*]. She would not sing it really, she would...you couldn't explain...she would shout sometimes, she would yell. She had strange dresses and she would raise her arms on the platform. And she looked like a bat; she had big sleeves, she looked like a bird. It was very tragic and very impressive.

She [already] couldn't sing Schubert or something of that kind, that was impossible (she did it in her youth), but when she did Mussorgsky or Olenin or even Grechaninov[19] [whom] she didn't like [...], Medtner (Balakirev I didn't hear, nor Rimsky, nothing of that sort because those were too much bel canto), it was really unforgettable. There are many singers who sang much better, who disappeared completely from memory, but she stays. With all her defects she was a character.

First of all, you couldn't classify her; you couldn't say: she sings better than somebody else, one couldn't say that; or she had a more beautiful or more ugly voice, you couldn't say that—it was quite different. She was [...] beyond criticism. Beyond comparison. She had fanatic admirers. But always among poets and writers, people like that. Painters and only some musicians. What she sang extraordinarily was "Meyerke, mein Sohn," the third Jewish song by Ravel, "Yisgadal" also, all the three. She sang that very well. She was not Jewish, but she sang Jewish music in an extraordinary way. [Her] Hebrew songs by Darius Milhaud [...] were unforgettable. (DC, 3–4.)

Andrei Bely and his wife Asya Turgeneva in 1912.

A most interesting account of the impression produced by Olenina's singing was given by the writer Andrei Bely[20] in an article included in his collection *Arabesques* (*Arabeski*) published in 1911. Bely's statements have both philosophical and aesthetic import. The article in question, entitled "A window on the future" was actually written in 1904, at a time when Bely's philosophy and Symbolist aesthetic were in the process of formation. Its five subheadings are characteristic: "The Vortex" (madness and the world's chaos, "we are beings that have arisen on the cold crust of a fiery delirium"); "The Symbol" ("In art we perceive ideas, tracing the image back to the symbol. Symbolism is a method of depicting ideas in images"; Nietzsche on the drama as symbol); "The Mystery" ("The mystery gave us the forms of musical drama." Nietzsche "sought salvation in music, calling the music drama [of Wagner] the last link that completes culture," but "Wagner is only one of the pioneers proclaiming to us the union of poetry with music"; the true blending of the two occurs not in the music drama but in song). The last two sections of Bely's study are called "Olenina-d'Alheim" and "The Concert." In the latter Bely describes a performance by Olenina before an audience consisting of bourgeois "people in suits." The contrast between the earthbound auditorium and the singer's loftiness and simplicity is the leitmotif of the chapter. Here we actually "see" how Olenina, the priestess of art, used to sing.

Andrei Bely:
When she is before us—this depictor of the soul's profundities—when she sings her songs to us, we dare not say that her voice is not beyond reproach, and that to start with it is not very large.

We forget about the qualities of her voice because she is more than a singer.

The relation of music to poetic symbols deepens these symbols. Olenina-d'Alheim conveys these deeply buried symbols with remarkable expressivity. She highlights her attitude to the symbols she conveys by an unique facial expressiveness. The poetic symbol, rendered more complex by the relationship of a music that is transformed by the voice and nuanced by mimic art, is boundlessly expanded. [...]

Outside drama and the opera, we cannot conceive of an art that more fully unifies poetry with music. But by the complexity of the resources they need for their execution, drama and opera weaken the directly pulsing stream of Eternity. Modern drama and opera threaten to collapse under the burden of complicated technique. [...] Should not a nascent mystery take on the fiery form of lyric prophecies?

The absolute blending of music with poetry is possible only in the human soul. That is why [...] the appearance of Vladimir Solovyov,[21] of Nikisch,[22] and of Olenina-d'Alheim are significant for our culture. [...]

Olenina-d'Alheim unfolds before us the depths of the spirit. [...] Across all this lies the shadow of a prophecy of the future. [...]

The mysticism that gushes forth from ancient songs in performance by Olenina-d'Alheim may turn out to be a lever with which people will subsequently overturn the whole of reality. [...]

That is why the complexity of the symbolic ideas touched on by Olenina-d'Alheim's singing imposes on her the imprint of religious celebration. (A. Bely, *Arabeski* (Moscow, 1911), 142–44.)

Being close to Russian Symbolist circles, Maria and Pyotr d'Alheim were familiar with the religious philosophical system of Rudolf Steiner[23] and his anthroposophy and eurhythmics, which at that time became an object of extremely widespread enthusiasm among poets, artists and people involved in the arts. In the world of art itself there were attempts to connect the idea of a Steinerian distribution of energy and the art of performance. One of Steiner's most fervent proselytes, for instance, was the great Russian actor Mikhail Chekhov,[24] who saw the task of anthroposophy in raising humanity to a higher spiritual plane, elevating people above their everyday physical existence. There is evidence that Pyotr d'Alheim also interested himself in these ideas, and one presumes the same was therefore true of Maria Olenina herself. However, the question of Steiner's actual influence on her performance is an obscure one; there is nothing to confirm that Olenina actually altered her manner of performance or started singing in any way differently after her encounter with anthroposophy. Doda Conrad told me that although he was in close contact with her during the 1930s and later 1940s, he never recalled her so much as mentioning Rudolf Steiner's philosophy. Nevertheless, Andrei Bely certainly emphasised a mystic force at play in Olenina's rapport with her audience.

Andrei Bely:
With a mask tightly bound over his face, someone's slack and care-free black contour slips among the folk illuminated by the electricity of the concert hall. Ladies glide above the abyss, pointing their lorgnettes and fanning themselves. The tails of tightly buttoned suits wave above the abyss. Everyone without exception stops up the gaping depths of his soul with a mask, so that no draught blows from the soul's chasm. Whenever there is a breath of Eternity, these folk are afraid of catching the fever of the world.

Somebody whispers to someone: "She's a talented singer."... Is that all?

No, no, *of course, not only that*. But don't ask any questions, don't tear the shroud from the soul, when nobody knows what to do with that furtively approaching depth. [...]

But quiet, quiet.

Somewhat awkwardly the tall lady in black walks onto the platform. There is something oppressive about her silhouette, something too ample for a person. She should be listened to amidst abysses, she should be seen in the break between stormclouds. In the harsh lines of her face simplicity is combined with an ultimate exclusivity. The whole of her is simplified, and excessively strange. Strange eyes burn us with their excessive glint, as though she were approaching the stars through the gaps of a befogged life.

She sings.

About something we have forgotten, but which never forgot us—about the dawn of a golden happiness. [...] Her groaning, just like the lament of a winter blizzard about how brother was slain by brother... From distant universal spaces sounds the plaint of lonely old Atlas holding up the world.

"Ich unglücksel'ger Atlas! Eine Welt,
Die ganze Welt der Schmerzen muß ich tragen..."

Someone should help the old titan. Raucous old Atlas, swaddled about with stormclouds on the horizon, where are you fleeing to and taking the horizon away from us, in order to weep again about your loneliness? [...]

What seemed transparent and showed a glimpse of world abyss has now faded again and shows nothing. There she stands with muted urgency. A shapely firtree, crazed with grief in its frozen entreaty.

But she is leaving. A thunder of applause sounds in her wake. The impulses of a titan have no purpose among midgets. Great feelings and small deeds.

The masquerade resumes. Dresses rustle. Mask enquires of mask: "Well, what did you think?" Mask answers mask: "Amazing."

Animated speech and too frolicsome gestures. The student has clapped his hands off. The men in suits jump up. The flaps of their clothing wave.—

—Once again, the ominous dancing of masked personages above the same abyss.

When she sings, there is a breath of profundity. But if you wish to plunge into those abysses, in the process you are bound to smash against a surface.

When will all this end? (A. Bely, *Arabeski* (Moscow, 1911), 144–46.)

Andrei Bely's emotional contrast of the spirituality and profundity in Olenina's singing with the world of bourgeois philistines was basically a philosophical one. Bely was saying that Olenina's singing was, as it were, directed not only towards its immediate listeners, but also towards the future. And essentially, that was indeed the case. Olenina's activities were one of the reasons for a significant change in public attitudes towards vocal chamber performance, which in Russia at the dawn of the century became a new and serious form of music-making. Usually people are not conscious of such changes and their causes at the time when they actually occur. However, musicians and critics among Olenina's contemporaries did realise that a new tradition was being created thanks to her artistry.

Novoe vremya:
Mme Olenina is our only concert singer with her own ideology. In this area we usually rest content with singers among whom only

very few think about any idea at all. Good concert performance is a difficult art, it requires a fine finish, an ability to switch quickly from one mood to another. Mme Olenina is undoubtedly talented, and if not everything she does is equally successful, her performance is always original. She is an example to our young Orpheuses that the cult of chamber music is not a figment of the imagination but a great service to art. (*Novoe vremya,* 12 December 1916.)

The First Russian Chamber Singer

We can in fact speak of Olenina-d'Alheim as a singer who deeply influenced the creation of a *tradition* of Russian vocal chamber performance—both in her manner of singing, in her interpretation, and in the atmosphere created by the performer during the concert. This certainly comes to mind when one thinks of such singers as Zoya Lody, Alexander Dolivo, Georgy Vinogradov, Nina Dorliak, Viktoria Ivanova, Zara Dolukhanova and Boris Gmyrya[25] (the latter successfully combined the opera stage with concert performances) and others who, willy-nilly, consciously or unconsciously, followed in the steps of Olenina-d'Alheim. I recall that in 1965 Gmyrya sang Schubert's *Winterreise* cycle in the Grand Hall of the Moscow Conservatoire,[26] prefacing his performance, as Olenina used to do, with a request not to applaud. Of course, the link with Olenina's tradition lies not just in what was possibly no more than an incidental external detail. The main point in common lay in something far more important which Gmyrya himself did not suspect when he once told me of how he took part in an All-Union singing contest. In the second round, after he had performed "Der Leiermann," Zoya Lody visited him in the artistes' room. She congratulated the young singer and told him he had achieved what she had always striven for when singing Schubert's masterpiece. This significant meeting of two generations acquired an even greater piquancy when one recalls that several decades prior to this the critic of the newspaper *Birzhevye vedomosti* commented on a similar meeting of generations when Lody was compared with Olenina; that early commentator was perhaps unaware that the meeting he witnessed was a bridge between the late nineteenth century and our own time, between the modern Russian school of chamber singing and one of its chief founders, Maria Olenina:

Birzhevye vedomosti:
Such concerts as the one that took place on the 9th January in the Small Hall of the Conservatoire are correctly described by the talented young singer Mlle Z. Lody as "evenings," without using any of the banal old-fashioned names. One feels like adding: an "evening of song"—like the ones that were once given by Mlle Olenina-d'Alheim, and with whom yesterday's singer shares something in common. It is true that the Moscow artiste was more nervous and passionate than Mlle Lody, but the charm of the latter is her "tender sincerity" which is just as typical of her. Still, there is some common ground between d'Alheim and our chamber singer in their ability to "tell the song" and to use phrasing of such subtlety that the public listens with rapt attention. (*Birzhevye vedomosti*, 12 January 1919.)

Thus, apart from subtle phrasing, a common feature with Russian chamber singers was their treatment of the text as a prime element in the composition. In just the same way, according to the Mighty Handful, the word was for them a guiding principle in their musical compositions. But how did the ideology and practice of the art of Russian chamber singing develop? What of the chronology by which these artistic ideas were handed down from one generation to another? If we trace the various generations and the link created in the early nineteenth century that leads down to our own time, and if we locate Olenina's place in this sequence, we can understand her special role, and her particular influence on the aesthetics of our time.

Maria Olenina's grandmother Anna, whose beauty was celebrated by Pushkin, took singing lessons from Glinka, who was the first Russian national composer and founder of a tradition of Russian vocal chamber performance. Of course, this fact in itself could not have influenced Olenina-d'Alheim's actual singing. However, it played a certain role in her awareness of herself as a singer, since in the Olenin family the notion of the link between Anna Olenina, Pushkin, and Glinka had a deep symbolic significance and was a frequent topic of conversation. One of the first Russian chamber singers, Alexandra Nikolayevna Molas, had studied singing with Dargomyzhsky, another Russian composer who continued the Glinka tradition and established the idea of the primary role of the text in song— "I want the word directly to express the music," he maintained.[27] Later, as an artist, Molas was closely associated with Mussorgsky and sang a lot of his music, and Mussorgsky shared with her many of his ideas on the art of performance. Although she hardly ever appeared on the concert platform, Molas was both a voice teacher and a musical public figure. In 1880 Maria Olenina became her pupil, and one recalls that Molas discovered in her performance of *The Nursery* something which its creator had sought for, and which Molas in her time had been incapable of producing. As one sees from many reviews, music lovers and critics perceived in Olenina certain particular features that had earlier been absent from Russian vocal performance: a special attention to the text, a holistic view of programme building, intelligent and expressive interpretation, the artist's total immersion in the world of the work performed, and the subjection of vocal resources to the task of artistic expression. The influence of Olenina on vocal performance was clearly felt by her contemporaries in the early years of the twentieth century. In effect, Olenina-d'Alheim established in Russia and abroad a Russian genre of chamber song performance with a style, form and aesthetic norms that extended well beyond her own personal activity. Later on in the 1960s Olenina personally met and corresponded with such singers as Gmyrya, and the younger Galina Pisarenko and Viktor Rybinsky[28]— the latter two artists were introduced to her ideas on performance at actual master classes.

The singing career of Olenina-d'Alheim nominally lasted for about forty years, from 1898 to 1935. Its most intensive period came to an end in 1922, however, with the death of Pyotr d'Alheim. After that her concerts only occurred sporadically. To be even more precise, one is bound to recognise that the crucial turning-point in her career was in 1918, when the activities of the House of Song came to an end. We are thus talking about a relatively short period of only twenty years. Yet how much was achieved in that time!

How best to describe the spirit and impact of this remarkable artist's activity? While recognising her brilliant talent, her educational and other musical public activities, one is bound to say that perhaps her most important feature as a singer was her awareness of the future and her forward-looking view—"towards new shores," in the words of Mussorgsky's own rallying call. When I myself met her, she was aged ninety-four and still talking about the presentday and future prospects of vocal chamber performance, and she spoke as a person still actively engaged in modern musical life—this was the essence of Olenina. In Russian musical culture she was a connecting link: having come to music just after the death of Mussorgsky and in the final years of the Mighty Handful as an active group, Olenina was a link between our musical culture of the past and its present and future, a tie between the nineteenth century and the twentieth.

V

THE HOUSE OF SONG

Russia & France — 1908-1918

*Towards new shores! Unfearing, despite
the shoals and underwater rocks
—onward towards new shores!*
(Modest Mussorgsky, letter of 1872
to Vladimir Stasov)

lenina-d'Alheim always regarded her art as a mission in life. And she saw herself as an instrument or tool with whose assistance music could rise from the mute pages of the score and begin to live a life of its own, transformed into sound for the benefit of its audience. For Olenina this was true of everything she sang, but it was especially true of all Russian music, and even more particularly of Mussorgsky. Despite her active and fruitful performing career abroad, Olenina realised that her life's main work still lay ahead of her, in Russia. She had long sensed the unusual nature of this mission, and the fact that she herself would be called upon to play a leading role. All this led to the creation of the House of Song (Société de la Maison du Lied). At the time of the very first *conférences* on Mussorgsky, the fate of Russian music, the Russian musical public, and the music of Mussorgsky in Russia were concerns that constantly occupied Olenina's mind and gave her no rest.

The House of Song was thus conceived as an artistic enterprise designed to stimulate musical enlightenment, promote and propagate classical and modern vocal chamber music, and also to study the problems of musical perception and assist the education of young musicians. "The constitution of the House of Song Society described its

144

basic task as being to unite the audience and performers of music (principally of song, or the Lied) in a joint collaborative activity based on a common understanding of art; the Society also aimed to study composers and poets of all lands and to undertake the instruction of musical performers." (E. Alekseyeva, "M. Olenina-d'Al'geim," *Sovetskaya muzyka* 1 (1960), 11.)

The whole of Olenina's earlier life and her whole development as a singer and personality were invested in the concept and creation of the House of Song. Some of this prehistory was described by Pyotr d'Alheim in the first issue of the monthly magazine *Dom pesni* (The House of Song).

> Pyotr d'Alheim:
> The idea of the House of Song is not a recent one; the concept was quietly nurtured and was close to being accomplished. But owing to a fatal combination of circumstances, it had to be consigned again to the realm of secrecy, which according to our law is tantamount to nonexistence.
>
> Twelve years went by [from 1896, when the first *conférences* on Mussorgsky took place, till 1908 when the House of Song was set up]... The idea for the House of Song once more arose and emerged from its hiding place untainted—for no one knew of it—and began to arm itself for the battle that lay ahead. (DP, 1 (1 February 1910), 11.)

At the very outset Olenina had been aware of the limited audience they had reached with their *conférences* in Paris and Brussels, and she felt the need to appear before a wider audience than that assembled in the Brussels Maison d'Art. She wanted to put her art to the test, if not before the general public, then at least before ordinary music-lovers.

> Olenina-d'Alheim:
> My first popular concert, organised by the artistic section of the Maison d'Art in Brussels, was given on 2 February 1898.
>
> This was at the time when Mussorgsky, forgotten in his home country, was coming to life abroad.—In Paris the audience at the first few concerts consisted mainly of musicians, writers, and artists (not "amateurs," as someone recently stated).
>
> The more variegated Brussels public was divided: at the Artistic and Literary Circle there were folk from high society, some financial

Excerpt from Pyotr d'Alheim's opening article in the first issue of the monthly *Dom pesni*, 1 February 1910.

ДОМЪ ПѢСНИ.

Идея „Дома Пѣсни" зародилась не теперь: она давно была лелѣена въ тиши, и была близка уже къ осуществленію; но, благодаря роковому стеченію обстоятельствъ, ее опять пришлось водворить въ область тайны, что, по нашимъ временамъ, равносильно небытію.

Прошло двѣнадцать лѣтъ. (Знаменательный циклъ въ зарожденіи и развитіи мыслей отмѣченный многими, между прочимъ, Бальзакомъ).

Идея „Дома пѣсни" вновь возникла, вышла не тронутой изъ своего тайника—ибо никому не была извѣстна — и стала вооружаться на бой.

Вооружается она въ пустынѣ, влекомая необходимостью жить, проявить себя, восторжествовать—и когда же! въ наше удивительное время, когда стала предосудительной идея всякой борьбы, не оправдывающейся стремленіемъ къ мистической непреложной силѣ единственнаго божества, не знающаго атеистовъ: Золота.

Она же задалась цѣлью доказать обратное, т.-е. что идея сама себя оправдываетъ въ достаточной степени, когда бы и гдѣ бы она ни зародилась,—въ области ли художественной передачи или художественнаго творчества. Моцарты, Бетховены, Шуберты, Шуманы, Вагнеры, Мусоргскіе эти паріи проходящіе отверженными по улицамъ нашихъ спекулятивныхъ центровъ; на самомъ же дѣлѣ они единственные крупные капиталисты въ области искусства—настоящей родины своей, гдѣ пространство и жизнь безпредѣльны.

* *

and hereditary aristocrats, military, big-time merchants and industrialists; in the Maison d'Art they were aesthetes.

I did not concern myself to flatter anybody's taste. Then, as now, I believed that the prime requisite for anyone striving after genuine artistic success was to present only really superb works and to use them to test the hearts of one's listeners [...] to appeal [...] to those profound feelings that are usually dormant in the secret recesses of our hearts. (M. Olenina-d'Alheim, "Narodnye kontserty po vpechatleniyam s estrady," DP, 6 (1910), 4.)

As we know, the concerts in Brussels and Paris were a success. "The work of Mussorgsky," wrote one critic in the paper *Art Moderne*, "was accepted, understood, and keenly felt by this unusual audience, which showed surprising tact and sensitivity in understanding this utterly new art and emphasised its most amazing beauties." (Cit. in DP, 6 (1910), 3.) A quite special event was the concert mentioned by Olenina, in the Paris Maison du Peuple, which started at 9 o'clock in the evening and finished at 2 in the morning. The main work in the programme was *Khovanshchina*, "individual scenes of which produced the most unexpected impression. In the course of that evening, none of us—neither the artistic creator [i.e., the composer], nor the performers, nor the public—were let down by a single moment of failure, weakness or distraction." (Cit. in DP, 6 (1910), 3.) If this was true of a concert given in Paris, what would the response be to such a concert back in Russia?

The way ahead was not easy however. In 1902, in Russia, Olenina was let down by precisely those Russians she had most counted on. Most of "educated" Russian society reacted to the work of Mussorgsky with total incomprehension. She recalled how the organiser of a popular performance of *Khovanshchina* in a village maintained to her that Mussorgsky's opera and the character of Dosifei were intended as a satire on religious fanaticism.

Olenina-d'Alheim:
"Just imagine," said the woman organiser, "the day after the performance a deputation of religious schismatics who are quite numerous in this area, came to see me expressing their gratitude."

"But that seems to me quite natural" [I said].

"But the fact is, they understood nothing of this drama. They took everything seriously! They totally failed to see the funny side of Dosifei's role and the satire against fanaticism!"

I have to admit that I was utterly disarmed by the genuine naïveté with which this was said. I couldn't think of a single word to defend Mussorgsky and his audience, since I felt it would be fruitless. I decided to ride the situation by simply smiling vaguely. (DP, 6, (1910), 4.)

This and other similar incidents strengthened Olenina's urge to "contact once again that social milieu which sometime or other had to be won over, since it was there and only there that an artist could find [...] treasures still untapped." (DP, 6, (1910), 4.) Olenina was quite uncompromising in the tasks she set herself, and she also showed quite unprecedented honesty with herself. Her first serious encounter with the Russian public on 26 October 1901 was one that she later recalled.

Olenina-d'Alheim:
What did we expect to achieve in our first concert given before the Russian people? Hitherto I had met these people only in their own true field of activity, on the land, and it was there that I had learned to know and love them.

As I stepped onto the platform, I made a commitment to myself to give an honest account of all that I experienced in the course of that evening.

I had put together a programme as usual without any "outward" success in mind, and aiming only at the sort of success that interested me. By gradually preparing them, inspiring their trust and diverting them away from the sensations of their ordinary surroundings, my task was to awake in my audience an inner activity that is essential if they are to become genuinely involved in the phenomena of art. As soon as this trust is acquired, as soon as you have achieved the essential condition for people to leave their normal surroundings behind, you have to lead your listeners to the pinnacles of art, by following a certain rhythmic sense of feeling.

The first part was made up of lively songs by Mussorgsky and ended with the "Gopak." During it, as in Brussels, I sensed the support coming from the public, who were sincere and impulsive. But for me the essential part was the second part which was devoted to the most gripping works.

And I have to confess—despite the outward success, the applause and ovations—I was not successful in the sense that I understood. I could not rise to full height. I was forced to stop half-way and limit myself to the outward, dramatic features of what I was performing. I made several attempts to rise up and draw others after me and failed, and while I attracted public attention, I stood there before Mussorgsky in the position of the soldier who calls to his sergeant: "Sergeant! I've caught a prisoner!"—"Bring him over here!"—"I can't, he's holding on to me!"

The third part of the concert was especially important to me. I brought to the people of the city what I had learned from those in the country. I performed part of the epic song (*bylina*) about the Volga and Mikula, in which a Russian Homer praises the power of productivity and sets it before another power capable only of destroying. But I did not feel that I had been understood. The next few lyrics "gave pleasure." But all the same I felt I was standing before an audience that was too brightly lit by electric lamps and was blinded by them, and together with their leaders they had lost the valuable ability to look inside themselves, an ability which makes the people, who remain poets and musicians, in touch with nature, into a Teacher of Teachers.

I am stating all this perfectly frankly. (DP, 6, (1910), 4.)

It was clear to Olenina that she must meet with her *own* audience, meet with them regularly, and increase her psychological contact with them. At the same time, what she observed in Paris was a growing commercialisation and embourgeoisement of art at the Popular Concerts. An urge to find her own audience in Russia as well as in the West led Olenina to the idea of the House of Song. And after convincing herself that there was no public for vocal chamber music in Russia, and that this public therefore had to be sought out and discovered, the House of Song was created. Initially it pursued aims identical with those of the first *conférences* on Mussorgsky.

Olenina-d'Alheim:
As you know, the House of Song was founded in 1908 in Moscow. Pierre wanted to arrange a series of lectures together with other Russian intellectuals. And the first such lecture did take place! Its contributors were Rachinsky,[1] Lurye[2] (the editor of *Russkaya mysl'*), Bely and myself. Its theme was: symbolism in art.

I perfectly remember that first lecture, because one of the participants—Lurye, I think—turned the [podium] upside down. As I walked out onto the stage, I noticed with surprise that it had been built for only one person [and] that the person who had mounted the dais was not the one who was supposed to be speaking about the [thesis], but the man who was meant to speak at the end of the session about the synthesis. How glad I was that I included in my programme Schubert's song "Mutter Erde," [which contained the words] "With what pleasure I shall bury everyone and inhume them in the earth!"

Not long before the actual lecture Valery Bryusov came and joined us—he was invited by Pierre. Looking through a chink, he observed that really we already had quite a large audience, and I answered him rather sharply and said: "We need some oarsmen to start off with, later we can do our own rowing." All the same he was at the rehearsal for the lecture and took part in the discussions.
(BNB, 81–82.)

The lecture Olenina was talking about, took place on 6 November 1908, and the participation of Andrei Bely was no coincidence. He was a poet with a special interest in the role of song in the art of poetry, and his speech actually dealt with two themes: "Song and the Modern Age," followed by "The Life of Song." On the 21 November Bely gave a second lecture for the House of Song audience. This time his theme was "Symbolism."

From its very inception, the Symbolist movement had paid considerable attention to the phenomenon of song. The d'Alheims' home was thus a frequent meeting place for Symbolist poets as well as for other litterateurs in search of a meaning and a place for art in human life. Apart from Bely, others who attended included Vyacheslav Ivanov, Alexander Blok, and Sergei Solovyov.

☙ Maria Olenina and Pyotr d'Alheim, c. 1908.

Andrei Bely:
I met with her at Grigory Rachinsky's; Pyotr Ivanovich [d'Alheim]
bowled me over totally; and the singer captivated me by the
grandeur of her simplicity; after that the Rachinskys and I [...]
used to rush and dive into her dressing room during the intervals,
in order to collect a flower from her, or be treated to conversation
with her over supper following the concert; thus our acquaintance
slowly grew into a rapprochement. (NV, 391.)

For Bely, song was a vital synthesis of art forms, and he wrote on
this subject on various occasions. Seeking to establish a link between
all artistic phenomena, he perceived song to be one of the loftiest manifestations of the creative spirit, capable of transforming human life. To
Bely, one of the manifestations of this was the artistry of Olenina.

Indeed, her concerts were a major musical phenomenon of the first decade of the twentieth century, and as one critic recently commented, "Olenina-d'Alheim was Andrei Bely's favourite singer. He saw in her an effective embodiment of the true mission of art—to penetrate the depths of phenomena."[3]

The d'Alheims' activities largely followed the same course as the Symbolist quest to create a synthesis of the arts. One such attempt was Vyacheslav Ivanov's[4] theory of "syncretic theatre" (*sobornyi teatr*), which notionally combined together music, poetry, painting, word and action. Ivanov talked of the spectator's involvement in the act of art and of a collective "orchestra," in which the viewer would participate in a theatrical action designed to draw in and involve all people. In this sense the House of Song was extremely close to the ideas underlying Ivanov's theory. There was talk, in fact, of creating a whole network of "houses of song," in which a mass audience would be joined together in a general act of musical art and recited poetry.

The first Moscow lecture was the start of the evolution of the House of Song, and it marked a step down the road from individual "*lecture-conférences*" to a serious organization of musical enlightenment with its own constitution, and pursuing a variety of activities, first of all in Moscow, then in Petrograd (starting 1916), and with plans for branches to be opened in a series of European capitals. Now, many years later, one can see what a significant influence the House of Song had on the development of integrated monothematic vocal chamber concerts in Russia, and possibly also abroad. The lecture-recital became a common occurrence in the activities of Russian and Soviet philharmonic societies; and finally the musically illustrated lecture-concerts of our own time began with similar events organised by the House of Song.

To start with, there were Olenina's own recitals arranged under the aegis of the House of Song; in 1910 a monthly magazine called *Dom pesni* began to appear; and from 1912 onward, when the "House of Song" became the "House of Song Society," its activities became even more varied. The House of Song effectively provided a solution to Olenina's dual mission of musical performance and education. First of all, by means of subscription concerts she acquired a regular and stable audience and a flexible organisational tool that enabled her to put

Maria Freund.

together substantial programmes without having to worry about their commercial success. Secondly, the organisation of the House of Song made it possible to realise one of Olenina's major ideas—that of actively involving the public in the performing process.

A typical season of the House of Song usually consisted of two or three cycles of six or seven concerts each, and taking place during the autumn and winter period. The mainstay of the programmes in each cycle were Olenina's own solo recitals. One evening would be set aside for some other singer, male or female (in 1908, for instance, this was Anna Stenbok;[5] in 1913 it was Maria Freund[6]), and one concert in the

An excerpt from her recital programme during the 1913–1914 concert season of The House of Song.

SAISON 1913 — 1914

DEUXIEME CONCERT DE

MARIA FREUND

PREMIÈRE PARTIE.

Komm susser Tod.

Bach.

Komm süsser Tod, komm, sel'ge Ruh'!
Komm, führe mich in Friede,
Weil ich der Welt bin müde.
Ach, komm, ich wart'auf dich'
Komm bald und führe mich
Drück mir die Augen zu!
Komm sel'ge Ruh'!
Komm süsser Tod, komm, sel'ge Ruh'!
Ichwil nun Iesum sehen
Und bei den Engeln stehen.
Es ist ja nun vollbracht,
Welt, darum gute Nacht,
Mein' Augen schliess' ich zu!
Komm sel'ge Ruh'!

Der Wegweiser.

Muller.   Schubert.

Was vermeid ich denn die Wege,
Wo die andern Wand'rer gehn,
Suche mir versteckte Stege
Durch verschneite Felsenhöhn?
Habe ja doch nichts begangen,
Das ich Menschen sollte scheun;
Welch ein thörichtes Verlangen

season was performed by Olenina with a programme of items requested by members of the House of Song Society.

In Moscow the House of Song evenings usually took place in the Small Hall of the Conservatoire; a few were held in the Great Hall (for instance, the pupils' concerts which in 1913 included performances of the second act of *Rama*, Lermontov's *The Demon* and scenes from *François Villon in Prison*). In Petersburg, the Moscow programmes were usually repeated in smaller halls, which better suited Olenina's acoustic ideals.

According to the addresses printed on the programmes, the head office of the House of Song was in Moscow, initially at 22 Smolensky Boulevard, and later, after 1913, at 8 Tverskoi Boulevard. Bely indicates another address: "The House of Song later settled in Gnezdnikovsky Lane: spacious blue and blue-grey walls with exactly similar blue and blue-grey furniture; with bluish-grey and greyish-blue curtains." (NV, 394.) It was here that orders were taken for subscription tickets, and where

СЕЗОНЪ 1913—1914

ВТОРОЙ КОНЦЕРТЪ О-ВА

19 ноября 1913.

МАРІЯ ФРЁЙНДЪ

ПЕРВАЯ ЧАСТЬ.

Приди, желанная смерть.

Бахъ.

Приди, желанная смерть, приди, благословенный покой! Явись и уведи меня въ мирную обитель, ибо этотъ міръ утомилъ меня. Ахъ, приди, я жду тебя! Скорѣй ко мнѣ, уведи меня. Закрой мнѣ глаза! Приди, покой благословенный! Приди, желанная смерть, приди, благословенный покой,

У меня одно желаніе—видѣть Іисуса, предстоять съ ангелами. Все въ жизни свершилось, прощай, земная жизнь. Я закрываю глаза. Приди, благословенный покой.

Дорожный столбъ.

Мюллеръ.   Шубертъ.

Что мнѣ до тѣхъ путей, по которымъ идутъ другіе странники, я ищу сокрытыя тропинки на засыпанныхъ снѣгомъ высотахъ,

Я ничего не совершилъ такого, чтобы бояться людей, какое пустое стремленіе влечетъ меня!

Дорожные столбы на путяхъ указываютъ города, а я странствую безконечно, нигдѣ не отдыхая, ищу себѣ

editions of *Dom pesni* were prepared for the press. The transformation of the plain House of Song into the House of Song Society in 1912 was a significant event in the development of this unique organisation. The chief aim of the Society was to give the public a more active role, and from now on the membership indeed played a greater part in several activities—organisational, artistic (Society members' request programmes), financial, and even executant (with the commencement of pupils' concerts). All these activities were concrete steps towards realising the philosophy of a "syncretic" art, which the d'Alheims had nurtured ever since their first *conférences* on Mussorgsky. Moreover, although not the sole focus of Society activities, Mussorgsky certainly remained among their central interests and his music figured in almost all their programmes. This was true too of the House of Song concerts that were later performed in Paris—after Moscow and St. Petersburg —and in 1912 in London.

⌒ The announcement of concerts given by Maria Olenina-d'Alheim and Maria Freund in November 1913.

ДОМЪ ПѢСНИ,
основанъ въ 1908 году
М. Олениной д'Альгеймъ.

ВЪ МАЛОМЪ ЗАЛѢ КОНСЕРВАТОРІИ
Во вторникъ 12 ноября, въ 9 час. вечера:
КОНЦЕРТЪ
М. ОЛЕНИНОЙ д'АЛЬГЕЙМЪ.

Программа составлена публикой О-ва «Домъ Пѣсни»
(1912—1913).—Глинка, Даргомыжскій, Чайковскій, Му-
сргскій, Оленинъ,—д'Энди, Пьернэ, Дебюсси, Гретри,
Берліозъ, Равель (Lienel Melech Malchel),—Моцартъ.
Бетховенъ, Шубертъ, Шуманъ, Вагнеръ, Шпенъ.

Партію ф.-п. исполнитъ Е. В. Богословскій.
(Рояль Бехштейнъ изъ депо А. Дидерихсъ).

ВЪ МАЛОМЪ ЗАЛѢ КОНСЕРВАТОРІИ
Во вторникъ, 26 ноября, въ 9 час. вечера:
КОНЦЕРТЪ
МАРІИ ФРЕЙНДЪ.

Программа: Debussy, Schumann, Schubert, Chopin, Bizet.
Партію ф.-п. исполнитъ Е. В. Богословскій.

Мы напоминаемъ членамъ О-ва 1913 года, что они
пользуются скидкой въ 25%, при условіи покупки билетовъ
въ Бюро О-ва, на билетахъ отъ 8 р. 10 к. до 1 р. 60 к.

7

The Philosophy and Aims of the House of Song

The educational ideas that occupied Olenina's mind in her youth were supported and confirmed in her collaboration with Pyotr d'Alheim starting with their very first *conférences* on Mussorgsky. The d'Alheims also linked their educational aims with those of making art materially accessible to a general public.

Even as a child Olenina developed a critical attitude towards the idea of money and profitable earnings. With the years this turned into a general conviction that art was actually corrupted by money. Olenina often talked and wrote on the subject.

Olenina-d'Alheim:
It is utterly impossible for the working people to enjoy works of artistic genius, and in this lies a great and terrible injustice. It is

Исполнителю пѣсни приходится сначала выступать
въ симфоническихъ концертахъ. Наше дѣло улучшить,
перемѣнить такое ненормальное положеніе вещей. Вы
скоро услышите въ этой самой залѣ прекрасную испол-
нительницу Марію Фрёйндъ, она знаменита въ Парижѣ,
но здѣсь никто еще о ней не знаетъ.

Вы, конечно, оцѣните ее и представите ее московской
и всей русской публикѣ.

Что же касается отдаленнаго будущаго,—вотъ мое
желаніе: пусть мысли, любимыя мною такъ, неизмѣнно
переживутъ меня. Я хочу и жду себѣ въ послѣдователи
только тѣхъ, кто, отрѣшившись отъ себя, безъ всякаго
расчета, всецѣло посвятитъ себя своему искусству и
будетъ въ уединеніи работать и готовиться, чтобы сумѣть
въ будущемъ упрочить жизнь «Дома Пѣсни». Если кто-
нибудь изъ нихъ пріобрѣтетъ необходимыя качества,
чтобы стать во главѣ его послѣ меня, то я буду вознагра-
ждена за всѣ мои труды мыслью, что, имѣя въ рукахъ
такое вѣрное орудіе, познавъ всѣ завѣты великихъ нашихъ учителей, понимая призваніе исполнителя пѣсни
и опираясь на кругъ избранныхъ слушателей, онъ смо-
жетъ въ своей жизни, продолжая мною начатое дѣло,
сдѣлать гораздо больше меня, такъ какъ на самомъ
поприщѣ самое трудное—это открыть путь.

Вспомнимъ на сегодняшнемъ вечерѣ пѣсни, въ ко-
торыхъ слышенъ одинъ и тотъ же грустный стонъ вѣчнаго
изгнанника художника-творца.

И послѣ приблизимся еще разъ къ тому, кто есть
истинный основатель «Дома Пѣсни».

Пусть прозвучитъ его пѣсня изгнанія, пѣсня изгнанія
русскаго художника-творца.

very, very wrong that only the people who already profit considerably from those who work can enjoy not only art, but all manner
of other good things in this world. If Christ reappeared among men
in our age, he would be deprived of everything—because he would
be a simple working man. In order to [...] make my idea clearer,
I would add that art should enter into everyone's life and be
absolutely linked with it [...] even though at present it is not yet
able to fulfil this purpose. (SV, 33.)

The artist too should be freed from money, Olenina believed. Only
then would he cease striving to turn his art into a means of enriching
himself. This was another aim pursued by the House of Song.

Olenina-d'Alheim:
Our task was to show that the aim of art does not lie in such jour-
neys [i.e., concert tours], which first of all demand large expenses

and because of that cease to be purely artistic but become a form of commercial enterprise depending on impressarios, because the latter are forced to recover the money they have spent, are they not? Hence the need to give these concerts in the very largest halls, with very expensive advance publicity. (SV, 31.)

I have always been [...] against advertisement, and believe it is incompatible with the dignity of the artist. My success with my audience was dear to me, and I never bothered about celebrity once my career was over. Fame is obtained chiefly through advertising, and I renounced that, and we did not spend money on it. Pyotr was of the same opinion as myself. At all my concerts, money was only taken for the tickets, all the rest (notices, programmes) was provided, not sold for profit. And it was like that even before the foundation of the House of Song Society. We were convinced that great composers created for everyone alike, just as God the Creator of the universe according to the Gospel sends sun and rain to all people, to the evil and the good. Earthly creators of genius act in the same way [...]

That is why we made it a rule not to set high prices for our tickets. Such a system is not very profitable, of course, but [it follows] the proverb: "Instead of a hundred roubles, better a hundred friends." [i.e., "Friends are more valuable than money."] (SV, 30–31.)

Indeed we did have good friends—not a hundred, of course, but they did help us so far as they could. For they realised the meaning and aim of our work, and I became very fond of them. Closest among them were Lev Alexandrovich Tarasevich and his wife, whose maiden name was Stenbok-Fermor. We got to know the Taraseviches in Paris. Lev was at the medical faculty and later worked with Mechnikov. Anna had studied singing I forget with which professor. She [later] took an active part in the work of the House of Song and was the responsible editor of its Russian-language monthly journal. She also took part in concerts and led the House of Song voice school. She had a very pleasant, not too low contralto. (SV, 30.)

Obviously, my brother Alexander understood and appreciated the principles on which the House of Song operated. At first he had other ideas about the duty of performing artists, but he very quickly realised the aim we were pursuing. Varya, of course, knew

Here, at 8 Tverskoi Boulevard in Moscow, the head office of
The House of Song was situated in 1914–15.

everything from the very start, she was with us in Paris and
attended our first *conférences* on Mussorgsky. She also helped us so
much in our personal life: when our daughter fell sick with tuberculosis and we had to send her to Davos,[7] Varya dropped everything and went to join her, which I was unable to do, as the House
of Song concerts in Moscow had already been announced. It was
very difficult for me, and I remember that throughout the entire
season I had to sleep in a sitting position in order to avoid the most
dreadful headaches.

That was in the 1908–1909 season, and about eighteen concerts
were advertised [...] Anna Stenbok performed the programme of

only one concert, and I sang all the other seventeen. And neither unhappiness, nor headaches prevented me [...] [But this was] no special feat. I simply believed that no events, happy or sad, should interrupt the obligation I had taken upon myself. (SV, 30–31.)

For Olenina there was nothing more important than her art. Neither personal interests, nor family, nor her daughter, nor her husband could distract her from this. And in this *total* commitment there was even something terrible. The pace of life and work load that Olenina took upon herself were only possible for someone who abandoned the norms of behaviour of an ordinary human being who loved those close to her. The period when the House of Song began functioning coincided with a worsening in the condition of the d'Alheims' daughter Marianna, who was sick with tuberculosis and who died in 1910. This was preceded by a period spent in sanatoriums and clinics, when the girl was left without her parents for the simple reason that the House of Song concert series had been advertised in Moscow. There is a record of all this in the "Black Notebook," which most probably relates to the period between 1908 and 1910 and thus covers the 1909–10 concert season.

Olenina-d'Alheim:
When the Murats left, I travelled with them as far as the frontier. And when I got back, I found Marianna in bed and I immediately got in touch with the Pasteur Institute and summoned our friend who was also a friend of Lyova Tarasevich, a Sicilian called Malteritano, or Malteri as we dubbed him. [...] He advised me to send Marianna to Dulec Place, to Dr. Spengler, who had discovered a new medication for tuberculosis which he called *tuberculin*.

I summoned Pierre, and at the end of August he took our patient to Switzerland. The first winter in [illegible] Marianna had terrible headaches, but she quickly began recovering there, and Dr. Spengler was evidently proud that his tuberculin medication worked so splendidly. He was going to demonstrate Marianna in Paris. We went to see her in June when we got back from Moscow, and we found her strong and cheerful.

Домъ Пѣсни
La Maison du Lied

Къ новымъ берегамъ! Мусоргскій.

Vers de nouveaux rivages! Moussorgski.

ДОМЪ ПѢСНИ.

LA MAISON DU LIED.

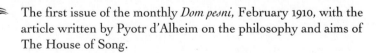

The first issue of the monthly *Dom pesni*, February 1910, with the article written by Pyotr d'Alheim on the philosophy and aims of The House of Song.

However, soon after that she started haemorrhaging and took to her bed. And when Pierre brought Asya [Turgeneva] from Brussels he had to reproach her: she wanted to get Andrei Bely to come from Moscow. Poor Asya immediately understood his reproaches and burst into tears. And when she entered Marianna's room with tearstained eyes, Marianna said, "You'd do better to take Asya away with you, she'll find it difficult here." And Pierre left with Asya, and I stayed to await his return. *We had to return to Moscow, where the HS concerts had been advertised.* [author's emphasis] (BNB, 76–79.)

Thus, when Maria Olenina was faced with a choice between something personal and something relating to her art, she chose the latter. For her to *sing* "Death's Lullaby" was more important than any other personal distraction—even the actual death of her daughter.

The philosophy and aims of the House of Song were set out in the first issue of the monthly *Dom pesni*, which began appearing two years after the organisation itself was set up. As an epigraph for each issue, as well as for its whole activity, the journal adopted Mussorgsky's rallying call "Towards new shores!" The creators of *Dom pesni* thus saw their aims not merely in preserving the achievements of the Mighty Handful in the later nineteenth century. They saw themselves as a vanguard moving forward into the twentieth century—towards new shores. Indeed the whole of Olenina's life was an expression of this aspiration and was demonstrated in her performances. This was also stated in the editorial "manifesto" article in *Dom pesni*.

Dom pesni, February 1910:
The idea of the House of Song first saw the light of day through the agency of a musical interpreter [i.e., Olenina.] who abjured the chase after profitable concert tours.

Her task consisted not just in filling a concert hall with public once, twice or half a dozen times, in collecting a certain tribute from them, and then moving on somewhere else where she could count on further quarry.

It was not a matter of converting the precious virgin metal of the masters into ready cash, but one of turning that same cash,

Maria Olenina-d'Alheim with Evgeny Bogoslovsky and
Pyotr d'Alheim.

their own inalienable property, to their own service [...] a matter of striving for the posthumous fulfilment of their ideals. [...]

It had to be explained to everyone that for an artistic work to be realised and to live, an intimate cooperation between the *creative artist*, the *interpreter* and the *listener* was essential. [author's italics] (DP, 1 (1910), 1.)

The founders of the House of Song saw the basis of their activity in this trinity of composer, interpreter and public. And from there triune relationship came the idea of an ideal public and an ideal interpreter. The latter was described by Olenina in her book on Mussorgsky.

Olenina-d'Alheim:
The executant is a living book. And it depends on him himself where and how that book is read. It depends on him to direct the reader's [i.e., the listener's] thoughts towards the thought of the author [...]; it depends on him to convey the thought of the author, absorbing it in such a way that the light refracted off the blank page illuminates those present. (ZM, 52.[8])

Thus, with the help of the interpreter, the creative artist not only creates, but "*discovers* his audience among people created in his own likeness... And it is these people who make up the real audience in the field of the arts. Those who talk about the need to educate and direct them, manage them, initiate them into the mysteries of art, are nurturing unrealisable dreams: they want to become gods. But there have been no gods for a long time. This audience must educate themselves, manage themselves." [author's emphasis] (DP, 1 (1910), 1.)

In conclusion the editorial article expressed the hope that the public "will now be able to comprehend our idea better and help us create and sustain this House of Song, which will doubtless mark a new stage in the evolution of modern art." (DP, 1 (1910), 1.)

As its very title implied, the central idea of the new organisation lay in song. "In the House of Song," wrote the newspaper *Kubansky krai* in 1912, quoting Olenina, song was regarded not "as a secondary form of art." On the contrary, it had a primary place reserved for it, because "an incorrect understanding of the true meaning of song is prejudicial to the loftiest interests of art." Song is the surest way of establishing a spiritual union between creative artist, interpreter and listener, which alone gives life to works of art. Comparing instrumental music with vocal, Olenina wrote: "Musical instruments convey that inner music of the soul which does not submit to the word, no matter how brilliant that word is; song introduces into musical harmonies the voice of a human being, not some fictional hero, but the voice of the artist himself who initiates us into his cherished secrets. The performer of song embodies the actual thought of the creator. *His mission is to absorb all the convolutions of the artistic concept, and without explaining or distorting anything, to convey faithfully what appears as a newly born impulse of the poet.* Without impatience, with perfect self-control, the executant must allow time and the works themselves to prepare the mood of the audience, banish anything frivolous, and seizing their whole attention, permit the one person to speak who has that right. And then he, the creative artist, will bare his soul before us." ("K novym beregam," *Vechernee vremya*, 27 November 1916.)

The activities of the House of Song Society were truly all-embracing. However, a primary place was obviously reserved for Olenina's recitals and others performing programmes of vocal chamber music. But in addition to concerts, the House of Song also organised lecture cycles on various subjects connected with music, poetry, and the psychology of art. Another novel feature were the lessons and educational programmes, which gradually supplemented the already established lectures and concerts. Of inestimable importance too was the publishing activity of the House of Song: from the very outset it printed bulletins several times a year before the start of the season, announcing the programmes, giving translated texts of the works to be performed, and also news and announcements about the work of the House. Eventually these activities expanded even further, about which more will be said below. One of the most important aspects of the House of Song's work, and the one which had the greatest resonance abroad, was its Russian and international competitions which resulted in the creation and publication of some highly interesting poetic and musical compositions.

 Charter of
The House of Song
Society published
in 1912 in Moscow.

Concerts at the House of Song

The concert activity of the House of Song was striking in its range. Between 1908 and 1910 their publishing section printed and issued twenty-one concert programmes. By 1913 the membership of the Society had grown to almost nine hundred (564 full members and 320 candidate members). At that time it was planned to start a second series of concerts. After performances in Moscow and St. Petersburg, almost all concerts were repeated in Paris, and Olenina's own recitals in England in 1912 were made up entirely from programmes performed during various Russian seasons of the House of Song.

The concerts included a wide range of composers. There were purely Russian programmes consisting of works by Glinka, Dargomyzhsky, Borodin, Balakirev, Rimsky-Korsakov, Cui, Lyapunov, Tchaikovsky, and of course, in first place, Mussorgsky. Western European music was

— 8 —

10.

Общество для достиженія поставленной имъ цѣли: 1) устраиваетъ а) закрытые концерты, закрытыя исполнительныя собранія, лекціи и чтенія, испрашивая, однако, предварительно устройства таковыхъ разрѣшеніе подлежащей власти, б) конкурсы на гармонизацію народныхъ пѣсенъ и музыкальные переводы, 2) издаетъ музыкальныя произведенія и переводы пѣсенъ и сочиненія по вопросамъ, находящимся въ связи съ цѣлями, преслѣдуемыми Обществомъ, 3) организуетъ преподаваніе (уроки, лекціи и проч.) для подготовки исполнителей.

Примѣчаніе: Концерты устраиваются въ небольшихъ, пригодныхъ для камерной музыки, залахъ съ тѣмъ разсчетомъ, чтобы число слушателей не превышало 700 человѣкъ; въ виду этого, въ случаѣ необходимости, концерты и проч. повторяются для отдѣльныхъ серій членовъ.

11.

Дѣлами Общества завѣдуютъ: а) Правленіе, б) Общее Собраніе.

12.

Правленіе состоитъ изъ учредителей и 2 членовъ Общества, избираемыхъ Общимъ Собраніемъ, простымъ большинствомъ голосовъ.

represented by Schütz, Bach, Gluck, Beethoven, Berlioz, Grieg and others. There were also evenings devoted entirely to Schumann, Schubert, Wolf and Liszt. Further programmes included work by contemporary Russians such as Stravinsky, Medtner and Olenin. In various seasons, the House of Song also gave special concert presentations that included Russian epic song (*bylina*), round dances, and old ballades. One such production in the 1913–14 season was a "Seventeenth Century Divertissement" put on by Pyotr d'Alheim. The programme included performance of Alexander Olenin's "Khorovody" (Round Dances). But the main genre presented in House of Song concerts was actual song.

Olenina-d'Alheim:
Nevertheless, too often people wrongly regard song as a second-rate form of art. There are many possible explanations for such a

Concert programmes for the season of 1913–14 announced in The House of Song's Bulletin.

ДОМЪ ПѢСНИ.

МОСКВА. Смоленскій бульваръ, 22.

MAISON DU LIED.

à MOSCOU. Boulevard de Smolensk, 22

Телефонъ 252-20.

Программа концертовъ сезона 1913 – 1914 г.

Четыре Liederabend'а М. А. Ольениной д'Альгеймъ.
I, II, III (въ программу ихъ войдутъ: Bach: Arien von Mat-
thoeus—Passion und Johannes Passion. — Schütz (Motets).
Lieder von Beethoven, Schubert, Schumann: *Frauenliebe
und Leben, Aus Wilhelm Meister*, Franz Liszt, Hugo Wolf.
Gabriel Fauré, César Franck.—Глинка, Даргомыжскій,
Рубинштейнъ (Персидскія Пѣсни), Балакиревъ, Римскій-
Корсаковъ, Бородинъ,—Мусоргскій (*Дѣтская, Деревен-
скія пѣсни*).—Глазуновъ, Ляпуновъ, Стравинскій.—Пѣсни,
которыя получатъ премію на 8-мъ конкурсѣ «Дома Пѣсни»).
IV. Сочиненія Николая Метнера (партію ф.-п. исполнитъ
авторъ).—V.Liederabend Анны Стенбокъ (Григъ, Синдингъ,
Järnefeld).—VI. Представленіе (постановка Пьера д'Альгеймъ): а. Дивертисментъ XVII вѣка (пѣніе и танцы).—
б. *Улица* А. Оленина (хороводы).—VII. Программа по
выбору публики.—Партію ф.-п. исполнитъ Е. В. Богословскій.

view. The main ones, it seems to us, are the following: the careless-
ness with which some composers "set to music" poems that randomly come their way, both ones of artistic value and other that are
utterly worthless; the disdain of many opera singers for the melody
and text of anything performed without stage makeup; a frequent
lack of conscientiousness in compiling programmes, and the
strange inexplicable fact that many people perform songs not from
a sense of vocation, but merely because for one reason or another
they failed to make their way on the [opera] stage.

Be that as it may, such an erroneous understanding of the
importance of song is inimical to the higher interests of art. It is via
the song that most surely of all there can arise that close spiritual
union between *creative artist*, performer and listener, which alone
can bring works of art to life. (*Byulleten' "Doma pesni,"* 1912, 5.)

One cannot fail to be struck by Olenina's intensive concert activities documented in the House of Song programmes, and by the fact that at the height of the season her recitals—and solo recitals at that— were given at very close intervals. They occurred every two weeks, and sometimes each week. Moreover, practically all these concerts had a wide-ranging repertoire. A good example can be found in the 1910 season. Between the 31st of January and the 30th of March Olenina sang in Moscow and St. Petersburg seven *different* programmes with Charles Henusse as accompanist. On the 31st of January in Moscow there was Bach, Beethoven, Schubert and Liszt. On the 11th of February in Petersburg—Glinka, Dargomyzhsky and Schubert's *Die Winterreise*. On the 15th of February in Petersburg—Bach, Gluck, Beethoven, Liszt, Berlioz and Mussorgsky. On the 18th of February in Moscow—the 66th Mussorgsky concert, consisting of 14 songs. On the 11th of March in Moscow—Tchaikovsky, Borodin, Balakirev, Lyapunov, Rimsky-Korsakov, Rubinstein, Grieg, Chopin (in Polish), Liszt. On the 17th of March (Petersburg)—Mussorgsky, Cui, Balakirev, Liszt, Chopin. On the 30 March in Moscow, Olenina gave a so-called popular concert with a quite unusual programme: the epic songs "The Volga and Mikula" and "John Chrysostum," the premiere of some folk songs by Alexander Olenin, and also works by Mussorgsky, Schumann and Schubert. The title of this concert reflected its intention: this was a concert for the people. To mark the occasion an article entitled "The Public Concert" appeared in the journal *Dom pesni* and announced that "only seats in the first seven rows will be on sale at the usual prices: Row 1—8 roubles, 20 kopecks; row 2—5 r. 20 k.; rows 3 and 4— 4 r. 20 k.; rows 5–6—3.70; row 7— 3 r. 20 k."

In order to enable everyone to participate in this enterprise, by way of exception, we are offering to the public 75 entry tickets at 75 kopecks. The remaining 400 places will be allocated free of charge to societies of workers.

The works included in the programme are creations of that popular spirit which is preserved unspoiled by their brilliant creators. (*Dom pesni*, 1910.)

At the end of the 1910 season Olenina repeated some of the pro-grammes in Paris. Here too there was the same concentration as in Moscow and St. Petersburg: between the 28th of November and 19th of December, on Mondays the Salle des Agriculteurs was host to four different recitals at intervals of one week. The piano part was played by Alfred Cortot on three evenings, with Alexander Olenin accompa-nying on the fourth. Each evening had its own specially thought-out programme combining Russian with Western music. On the 28th of November, apart from Bach, Beethoven, Berlioz and Liszt, there were Mussorgsky's two cycles *Sunless* and the *Songs and Dances of Death*, and also some folk songs. On the 5th of December there were 8 songs by Balakirev, 9 by Liszt, and 7 by Chopin. On the 12th of December there were performances of Schubert's *Die Winterreise* and Mussorgsky's *Nursery*. On the 19th of December there was an evening of folk songs: "The Death of Roland," songs by Burns (from the third competition organized by the House of Song) and folk songs set by Alexander Olenin (from the fifth competition).

All this might suggest that Olenina was uninterested in contemporary music. To some extent this was indeed true, except for some programmes which included works by Medtner, Alexander Olenin, Glazunov, and Stravinsky. Medtner himself accompanied Olenina, who was one of the first performers of his "Invocation" and other songs. In the music of Stravinsky, Olenina was attracted by the popular, folk element. His modernistic idiom was not something she could closely relate to how-ever. Nevertheless, the very fact of her engagement with Stravinsky's vocal works, as well as her later performances of Debussy, Milhaud and Poulenc, meant that she was not a singer who narrowly confined herself to the nineteenth century, and it was yet another mark of her function as a vital link between the nineteenth and twentieth centuries.

Lectures in the House of Song

The educational activity of the House of Song was not limited to music alone. For the creators of the Society, music was unthinkable without poetry and the other arts, and any understanding of music

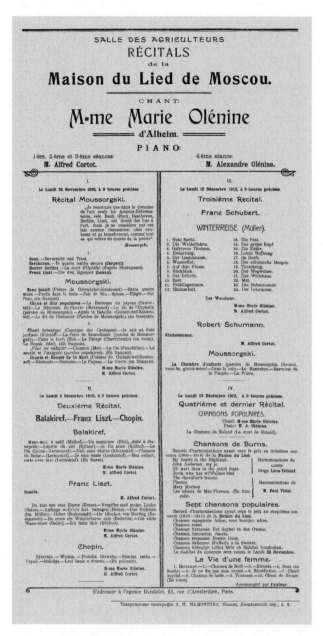

Poster announcing series of the Maison
du Lied de Moscou recitals given by
Maria Olenina-d'Alheim in November-
December, 1910.

was incomplete without a knowledge of psychology and the philosophy of art. Therefore the lectures that were a constant feature of each
season and which took place in the form of specific thematic cycles,
were devoted to problems of Russian and Western music and poetry, as
well as more general aspects of artistic theory. The lecture-recitals of
the House of Song had their own particular atmosphere quite unlike
what the public were used to. At his first lecture there Andrei Bely was
struck by the way in which the stage was set up.

Andrei Bely:
Notices were hung up; all the tickets were sold out; the daises in
"demicirculaire" were set out according to special plans. It was evident that the fantasy of "Merlin," as we called him, [i.e., Pyotr
d'Alheim] had been at work on the podiums: the legs of the lecturer
had to be covered in a way that allowed him to gesture to right and
to left, leaning on his elbow also to right and left; and as lecturer I
was given a course in meloplastics [i.e., musical gesture]; and he took
me off by cab to the Conservatoire (the Small Hall) to show me how
the daises were set out—for Maria and for me, to right and left—and
between them, set back, was Bogoslovsky's instrument; the "triangle"
style, had probably been designed by him that night. (NV, 397.)

The season 1909–10 provides typical examples of the House of Song
lecture series. Over that period alone members were offered no less
than six different cycles of lectures. On Mondays, for instance, there
were the lectures by Artur F. Luther in a series on "World Poetry," dealing with German lyrics. In them he talked about Klopstock, Bürger,
Günter and other predecessors of Goethe as well as Goethe himself.
Then followed Schiller and the poetry of Romanticism (Novalis,
Brentano, Eichendorff, and Uhland), after which the lecturer discussed
the poetry of "universal sorrow" (Platen, and of course Heine).
    On Thursdays there was a lecture cycle given in French on the
"Psychology of Art." The lecturer was Pierre d'Alheim and he devoted
his seven talks to an "analysis of feeling in the field of performance."
The series on "Analysis of Feeling" touched on the d'Alheims' most
important ideas about the correlation between the composer as artist-

creator, the executant and the audience. The lectures were accompanied by readings from Victor Hugo, Lamartine, Alfred de Vigny, and Paul Verlaine. In an analysis of Racine's *Phèdre* there was discussion of the "decay of emotion." The problem of "emotions studied from the viewpoint of their communication by the performer" was discussed in lectures about Gluck's *Orfeo* and illustrated by the singers Anna Stenbok and Louisa Schwartz with Charles Henusse at the piano. In these lectures d'Alheim managed to express not only his own view on the art of performance, but also something more concrete: essentially he gave an account of how Olenina actually sang.

Pyotr d'Alheim:
The performer's basic, primary feeling (or Faith) takes on the character of self-abnegation. In fact, his mission is one of incarnation [embodiment]. He must yield himself to the work performed and in his awareness he must live only in and through it.

This sense of self-abnegation, as it increases, changes form and turns into inspiration [spiritualisation]—a supreme elevation which, as it increases, becomes an active force of influence...

It becomes clear to him [the performer] what comprises and sums up his *mediumistic mission* [*missiya posrednichestva*—author's emphasis], and with what reverence he must accept the treasure entrusted to him by the artist-creator; how he must preserve it, trying to extract nothing from it for his own benefit; and how he must make the public accept this treasure in all its pristine entirety.

[...] Here all feelings flow together in a full and final self-renunciation: the artist is dead to the world, and he lives in a constant, uninterrupted communion with the ideals of his great teachers.
(DP, 4 (1910), 5.)

D'Alheim's lectures touched on some current problems of the art of performance that are no less relevant in our own day: the link between music and text, and the relation between music and gesture. The lectures were illustrated by the performance of some unusual works which in themselves became cultural events. An account of this can be found in one of the Petrograd newspapers.

"Lectures by P.I. d'Alheim":
A few days ago the third lecture on art by Pyotr d'Alheim took place
in the hall of the Petrograd Music School (13 Troitskaya Street). [...]
The lecturer [inter alia] paused to discuss the activity of this institution [the House of Song] in 1914 in the field of research and the
application of the laws of musical speech, which have now been fully
worked out and defined. By way of illustration to the lecture there
were presentations of *Mimiambi*[9] from the third century B.C. and an
18th century farce, *The Corsair-Harlequin*. [...] These works were
offered in order to acquaint the public with the House of Song doc-
trine concerning the close link obtaining between word and gesture.
Mr. d'Alheim maintains that Mussorgsky's *The Nursery* records
intonations not only in the melody, but also in the instrumental
accompaniment, and also gestures that emphasise these intonations.

("Lektsii P.I. d'Al'geima," *Novoe vremya*, 28 January 1917.)

In the third cycle of Monday lectures, starting on the 30 November
1909, there was an attempt to analyse the German Lied as a genre.
Sixteen lectures given by Oskar von Riesemann[10] were entitled "The
Development of German Song as an Artistic Form." From the art of the
Minnesinger and Meistersinger, Heinrich Albert and his predecessors,
from Eccard[11] and Schein[12] to the songs of Hugo Wolf and Richard
Strauss, listeners could follow the evolution of a musical genre that had
a major influence on the song and vocal art of Western Europe and
Russia. Individual talks were devoted to J.S. Bach, Handel and Gluck
(3rd lecture); Weber, Haydn and Mozart (5th lecture); Beethoven,
Schubert and Schumann (6th, 7th and 9th lectures). The next three
talks were on Mendelssohn and Brahms, with the final five lectures
devoted to Wagner and his influence on German song.

A series of lectures in French by Serge Murat took place on
Saturdays, and was devoted to the French lyric in all its diversity,
including modern French poetry and the lyric verse of the trouvères
and troubadours. "Song and Romance in Eighteenth-Century Russia"
was the title of a lecture cycle by Evgeny Bogoslovsky. Finally, there
were some talks by N.V. Dosekin on "The Autonomy of Arts" which
rounded off the House of Song lecture programme for the 1909–10
season. Taken all together, such a lecture programme would have
enhanced the season of any modern-day philharmonic society.

Lessons and Courses at the House of Song

Olenina-d'Alheim began giving tuition in singing while still in Paris, long before the House of Song was opened. These teaching activities were fairly limited, and she had no desire to devote her life to this. Nevertheless, in the course of time her interest in teaching grew, especially as she increasingly realised how her own approach to the art of singing differed from that of the conventional vocalist, who was occupied primarily with his or her own voice and only then with the music. Olenina gradually became aware that performing singers should be educated in a way quite different from the accepted method. It is not surprising therefore that soon after the House of Song opened, it began to advertise voice lessons with an aim and character determined by Olenina's own views on singing.

> Announcement:
> Singing lessons at the House of Song are offered, based on the principles practised by Maria Olenina-d'Alheim since the very beginning of her musical career, and which she has always steadfastly followed.
>
> The application of her methods to various voices and temperaments, both with persons commencing their musical education, and with those disadvantaged by a false start in their studies, has produced such results in a short time that the House of Song has decided to extend its activities in this direction.
>
> Obviously, in doing so, it is concerned only with those striving to devote themselves wholly and unreservedly to the performance of the greatest works of art, or those wishing merely to acquire the necessary basics enabling them to delve more deeply into these works, reproduce them and convey the pure enjoyment of art to others and themselves.
>
> This tuition has as its object only works of chamber music in their infinite variety: songs (Lieder, chansons) and works of a religious character—solos from oratorios and cantatas.
>
> This method, whose direction is sufficiently familiar from the House of Song concerts, is not suitable for persons preparing for the opera, in view of the theatrical singing tradition and repertoire.
>
> In Moscow, the regular course of tuition is conducted by Mme Anna Stenbok. All pupils undergo a qualifying examination with

Mme Olenina-d'Alheim, who directs their studies during her annual sojourn in Moscow. (DP, 14, 6.)

From notices that have been preserved, we know of another course also offered by the House of Song. This was concerned with a programme to extend the Society's concert repertoire: "As of next year [1914], the House of Song is organising courses in mime and dance, which will gradually provide an opportunity to introduce into the programme forgotten treasures of the 17th and 18th centuries." (DP, 7 (1913), 16.)

Publishing Activities of the House of Song

From its very first evening in 1908, the House of Song in Moscow began issuing programmes of its concerts which provided detailed notes on the musical, poetic, historical and aesthetic content of the works performed. Unlike commercial concerts, these programmes, as Olenina always emphasised, were not on sale but were distributed to the audience free of charge. The House of Song opened up an editorial office in Smirnov's house in Maly Gnezdnikovsky Lane that soon began handling all the Society's publishing affairs.

Publishing activities quickly expanded their scope. Starting with the actual programmes, they then extended to publication of the House of Song *Bulletins*. These came out several times a year in the form of a brochure of 20–30 pages in small format and contained translated texts of songs, information about the composers and musical style of works to be performed, and about all aspects of the Society's work (including its new publications). An example was a detailed report "On the Public's Programme Votes," which provided exact figures on the voting for each work considered for the request programme. Most probably the publication of such data began after one curious episode. One of the programmes compiled on the basis of popular votes was criticised in the St. Petersburg newspaper *Novoye vremya*, which carried a note hinting that the results of the vote had been tampered with and "massaged." Olenina considered it her duty to answer such accusations. Her letter was signed exactly three weeks before the February Revolution of 1917.

Olenina-d'Alheim:
Dear Sir and Editor! Kindly print in you worthy newspaper my letter
of disavowal concerning two points in a note printed in issue No.
14695 of 1st February of this year in the section "Theatre and Music."

The note in question insinuates that: 1) the vote count printed
in the programme of the last concert of the House of Song Society
seems confused and fails to correspond to the figures given, and
2) the programme in general is composed exclusively of pieces that
were performed in the course of the season. To this I must respond
as follows: The programme was compiled from the works of authors
that received the largest number of votes, for which the voting slips
will be [once again] checked by a special commission appointed by
a general meeting of the Soc[iet]y, and the result of this check will
be communicated to members of the Society, since the accusation
of tampering with voting slips is for me, if not for the author of
your note, a question of honesty.

As regards the second point in your note, there is no need for any
special refutations, since the programme contained the following items:

1) Tchaikovsky—"Sred' shumnogo bala"
   ["Mid the noise of the ball"];
2) Rimsky-Korsakov—
   "Spliu, no serdtse moyo chutkoye ne spit"
   ["I sleep, but my sensitive heart is awake"];
3) Schumann—"Je n'ai nul fiel"
   [French translation of "Ich grolle nicht"];
4) Schubert—"Der Erlkönig";
5) Mussorgsky—"Gadanie Marfy"
   ["Marfa's Prophecy" from *Khovanshchina*];
   "Spit streletskoye gnezdo" ["The camp of Streltsy is asleep"];
   "Pesn' yurodivogo" ["Song of the Holy Fool"];
6) Beethoven—"In questa tomba oscura"

—none of which were performed in any of the four previous recitals.
With sincere respects,

M. Olenina-d'Alheim.

(M.A. Olenina-d'Alheim, letter to editor of *Novoe vremya*,
2 February 1917; ms in UAA, fond 89–136, no. 4.)

The handwritten copy of Olenina's letter to the Editor of the newspaper *Novoye Vremya*.

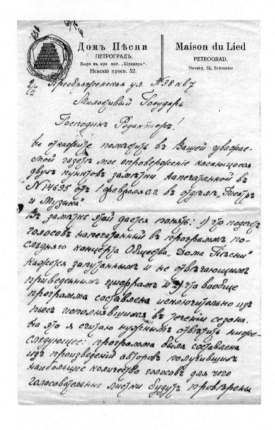

These public request concerts became a tradition in the House of Song. The names of *all* voters were published in the *Bulletin* and gave Society members a sense of genuine participation in creating these concerts. But there was something more important in this as well: public request concerts were just another aspect of that union between the composer, interpreter and audience, which in Olenina's view was a sine qua non of living art. The *Bulletin* also contained a list of House of Song members, notes of the elections to membership of the Board and Auditing Committee, full season programmes and also information of an "ideological" character.

Dom Pesni

Following her wish to use the last meeting of the House of Song Society in order to bid farewell to its members for this season, Maria Olenina-d'Alheim will perform songs on this evening which especially influenced her decision to cease conventional public recitals and to found a society aimed at uniting in a conscious and consistent form the three factors essential for the total revelation of the essence of a work of art—its creator, performer and listener.

(*Byulleten' "Doma pesni"* 7 (1913–14), 12.)

The scale of the House of Song publishing activities expanded significantly when the monthly journal of the Society began appearing on 1st February 1910. The aim of the new periodical *Dom pesni* was to address a broader circle of readers. The monthly included articles relating to Society activities, and also articles, extracts from books, and pronouncements about art by "artist-creators of all countries and of any age." According to Olenina, Pyotr d'Alheim himself was the author of much of the material printed, and the journal became an important manifestation of Russian cultural life of the time. On 6 to 8 pages of large, newspaper format, successive numbers of *Dom pesni* published articles by Hector Berlioz, the French critic André Chevrillon, Pyotr d'Alheim, and pronouncements by J.S. Bach, Beethoven, Schiller, Liszt, Mussorgsky, Wagner and other artistic figures, and also the text of works by Mussorgsky translated into German and French, announcements of current musical events, advertisement of Society competitions, etc.

It is of interest that many materials in *Dom pesni* were printed not just in Russian, but also in French and German. The d'Alheims had plans to open branches of the House of Song in other important European centres.

A special, "programmatic" place in the monthly journal was occupied by Hector Berlioz's article "On the Modern State of Singing" (written for the *Journal des Débats*, to which he regularly contributed as music critic) and a large work by French musicologist Camille Bellaigue under the title "Studies of Mussorgsky." Both works were printed in serial form and spread over several issues during 1910–11. Berlioz's article criticised the "modern state of singing" with reference to two basic aspects of the art—namely, treatment of the voice and interpretation.

Hector Berlioz:
At the present time in view of the prevailing system of singing tuition in Europe, out of every ten self-styled singers it is barely possible to find two or three capable of singing even a simple song well, that is, absolutely correctly, accurately, expressively and powerfully, with a pleasant and pure voice. Suppose that one such singer is told: "Here is an ancient song, very simple, very touching, its tender melody does not modulate and moves around modestly in a single octave. Sing it to us." It is very likely that our singer— perhaps even a celebrity—will ruin this poor musical flowerlet with his performance. And as you listen to him, you cannot help recalling the country girl who sang that same ancient song so artlessly, but oh, how well. (DP, 1 (1910), 3.)

The author goes on to describe the various defective ways of interpretation, talking about so-called "naively stupid," "banal," and "stupidly mannered" inane singing, full of every "piece of nonsense that enters the singer's head." But an even greater disaster is the "criminal" singing that "demoralises the public and lures them down a dangerous path by an alluring, capricious performance, a brilliant but false expressivity that outrages both taste and common sense." (DP, 1 (1910), 3.)

The critical ideas expressed in Berlioz's article were very close to those of Olenina, not only because they confirmed her own notions about meaningful and simple performance, criticising any mannerism and striving for outward effect. In his article Berlioz also attacked the use of immoderately large halls (he was talking mainly about lyric [i.e., opera] theatres), the system of "paid or unpaid applause," and also the preferential treatment given to "the interpretation rather than the work, the throat rather than the thought, and material substance rather than spirit." (DP, 2 (1910), 3.) The article led on to the idea of the self-abnegation of the interpreter who walks out onto the platform not in order to show off his voice and artistic sophistication, but to become an *honest* mediator between the composer and the audience. This was also the very point emphasised in a *Dom pesni* review of a Beethoven concert given by a Czech quartet which, in the reviewer's opinion, was a model of behaviour for the artist.

> Pyotr d'Alheim:
> How rare in our time are concerts in which artists abandon all vanity and all desire to dazzle the audience with their talent, where they disdain success as something too easy and achievable by the false brilliance of superficial virtuosity, and where—instead of this —in their artistic sincerity and honesty they achieve a total self-suppression in favour of the inspired creator whom they are called on to embody. (DP, 4 (1910), 4.)

Of course, d'Alheim's ideas were fully shared by his wife. Olenina also stood strongly behind another idea advanced by Berlioz: his critique of large halls that provoked singers into forcing the voice and, as he maintained, "failed to create conditions for making an impact on human organisation [sic!]." When I met Olenina in Moscow in the mid 1960s, she talked indignantly of the immensity of such halls as the Palace of Congresses in Moscow's Kremlin, or even the Grand Hall of the Conservatoire. "In a hall that is too large," she maintained, "the musical sound fades, its musical impact on one's hearing is weakened, and the composer's ideas are distorted." These same ideas, which Olenina repeated with characteristically obsessive frequency, can be found also in her manuscript called "Dream and Recollections."

Olenina-d'Alheim:

[...] We always shared the same opinion as Hector Berlioz, that very large halls are not suitable for the performance of artistic works, since in these halls the sound loses its quality, cannot retain its full strength, as it exceeds the distance that physical laws intend for it. It does not produce that sense of excitement that grips listeners at a closer distance, and as always, it ends up with the poor audience being deprived of that feeling because poverty prevents them from buying a seat in the first few rows. Berlioz was right when he told the director of the Paris Opera: "We can never understand one another: we are artists, whereas you are men of commerce."

Berlioz campaigned vehemently against large theatre and concert halls and proved very well by example their unsuitability for listening to works created by an artistic genius. He told how he himself had once come out of the opera after listening to *Orfeo* and was struck by the fact that he had felt none of the excitement that he expected. Yet when he heard *Orfeo* again, one week later, in the hall of the Conservatoire with the same performers and even without scenery, he was shaken by it, like all the rest of the audience. The latter hall accommodated not more than six hundred listeners.

So as to make his arguments even more convincing, Berlioz wrote: "Imagine that you are listening ecstatically in a small drawing room to a superb Beethoven quartet. And then gradually, the room increases in size, and the distance between you and the performers also increases till it reaches the stage where you have to strain your ears so as not to miss the most delicate pianissimo. Such a strain is tiring, and imperceptibly the effect on you of Beethoven's masterpiece is reduced, and your rapture becomes a mere piece of cerebral reflection on the genius of the composer. At that stage, you can bid farewell to any profound inner excitement!"

When I gave my last series of recitals in 1935, I addressed the audience and underlined to them the betrayal of great geniuses by talented performers because concerts continue to be held in huge halls. The following day I received a letter from a group of young people who had attended my concert. They told me they agreed with me because they themselves recently confirmed that not every-thing was equally audible in a large hall: they had been in the back rows at a concert by a famous violinist and when they left, they did not have the sense of pleasure they had counted on. (SV, 32–33.)

A significant space in *Dom pesni* and other publications by the Society was reserved for material about Mussorgsky. There were arti-cles about him, exposes of the content of his operas, information on the performance of his music in Russia and abroad, quotation of the composer's own statements, and new translations of the text of his works into German and French. But perhaps most significant was the already mentioned reprint of Bellaigue's study of Mussorgsky, originally written in 1901. This was among the first French works on the com-poser. In 1893, just a dozen years after the composer's death, one Albert Soubies[13] had written a lengthy essay on Mussorgsky emphasising the importance of his music which at the time was largely unknown in France. Three years later, in 1896, Pierre d'Alheim's ample monograph appeared, and then, finally there was the essay by Bellaigue.

Camille Bellaigue:
Not content with dedicating to him part of his time and labour, M. Pierre d'Alheim has found by his own hearth and created a superb female interpreter for his favourite composer. For this artistic cou-ple their concern for the unknown genius became almost a sacred obligation, a sort of family legacy. They have both made him cele-brated—the one by his lectures and articles, the other, even more eloquently, by her singing.

I shall never forget the day when they both first revealed Mussorgsky to me. It was one winter's day in a modest apartment. The woman's beautiful voice sang—first of all an extract from the opera *Khovanshchina*: Marfa's prophecy. Slowly, in words that I did not comprehend, but which were immediately translated for me—and in sounds that were strange to me, yet comprehensible in them-selves—the melancholy cantilena prophesied his gloomy destiny to a hero still unknown to me. When she finished singing, the artiste was silent for a few instants, and then began again.

This time a joy lit up her face and enlivened her voice—it was a brazen almost malevolent joy. In wild rhythm she sang the love song of a peasant woman. Then we heard heroic ballades, hymns with a dusky brilliance and austerity that inspired terror, hymns of warfare, blood and death. After them followed other songs, even more heartfelt, and maybe even more electrifying…

And finally we heard the composer himself moan as he lay dying on a hospital bed, the abandoned and unacknowledged singer of so many deaths. "A roomlet so silent and cramped…"[14] the voice sighed in its mortal agony, and it genuinely seemed to us then that in the walls of that room there was concentrated all the beauty of that strange music with all its horror. (DP, 4 (1901), 4.)

In his account of the life and work of Mussorgsky, Camille Bellaigue underlined the composer's "realism," which he heard as something quite different from "pure music." Hence in fact the predominance of vocal works in Mussorgsky's output. Yet even Mussorgsky's instrumental music is "concrete," with an air of real impressions about it, and devoted to real events. (Thus, for instance, the "Impromptu passionné" of 1859, written under the impact of Herzen's novel *Who Is to Blame? [Kto vinovat?]*.)

Camille Bellaigue:
And here is Mussorgsky himself telling us about the origins of his "Intermezzo,"[15] written first for pianoforte, and later orchestrated and dedicated to Borodin. Once in the country, on a splendid winter's day, the composer saw a crowd of peasants sliding and falling in the snow. "This was all so beautiful," Mussorgsky recounted, "so picturesque, and serious, and amusing. And suddenly," he said, "in the distance there appeared a crowd of young women, walking along an even path singing and laughing. This picture flashed into my mind in musical form, and unexpectedly the first Bach-like melody composed itself, pacing up and down: the jolly, laughing peasant women occurred to me in the form of a melody from which I later composed the central part, or *Brio.*" (DP, 4 (1901), 4.)

One cannot help recalling Maria Olenina's story of an incident in her own childhood, when she too watched a peasant procession on one of the feastdays (see pp. 5–6): these were the same impressions of peasant life that Mussorgsky was talking about. Of course, it was not this which determined her amazing ability to "get inside" the imagery of the composer's songs and create an entire gallery of such images. But their common surroundings and the impressions which formed them both as artists are certainly another link in their spiritual kinship.

Bellaigue's observations about Mussorgsky's three most important cycles (*The Nursery, Songs and Dances of Death*, and *Sunless*) were based not just on the musical text itself, but first and foremost on his impressions of Maria Olenina's performance of them, and discussions with her and Pyotr d'Alheim about their content. Here are the critic's thoughts on death in Mussorgsky's work and on the death of Mussorgsky, which were inspired by Olenina, and which formed the conclusion of his study.

Camille Bellaigue:
In Mussorgsky's works people do not die as in some German ballade—a distant and fantastic death. In Mussorgsky death is something commonplace and terrible, it pursues humanity from the cradle up. Once, when the great artiste who introduced us to this scene [the "Lullaby" in *Songs and Dances of Death*] sang the work at a concert, a young woman wearing mourning came up to her and said in a dispirited voice, "Madame, it was staggering, but you should not sing such things in front of an audience." Maybe she was right… The music of Mussorgsky is astounding and almost intolerable not just for people afflicted by sorrow, but even for those before whom it is unfurled like a tableau.

Here we are, almost at the end of our sad, terrible and often gloomy excursion. Mussorgsky himself soon has to die. His final cycle of songs *Sunless* is his last sob, his last gasp. Verlaine's bitterest wails of despair, with which he inspired contemporary music— Reynaldo Hahn's "From Prison" or Debussy's subtle flowing song "Il pleure dans mon coeur comme il pleut sur la ville"—are not at all comparable with the unremitting despair which floods and totally smothers these few bars of Mussorgsky […]

None of those people celebrated by the Russian musician is left alive. Tsar Boris is dead, dead too are the schismatics [...] beneath the snow the little *muzhik* sleeps the sleep of the tomb, the bones of soldiers glisten white on the field of battle, and in a house without children a little bed stands empty. Dead at last is the sorrowful creator of so many unhappy heroes, and it seems as though in the walls of his room, all these dead folk have gathered round his hospital bed to be present and pay tribute at his death. (DP, 8 (1910), 6.)

The activity of the d'Alheims before the foundation of the House of Song first introduced the name of Mussorgsky to the French public. This occurred around the turn of the century. Now in the 1910s, the editions of the House of Song registered the spread of Mussorgsky's music in the western world.

"Mussorgsky Abroad":
Many people were attracted by the fact that we placed Mussorgsky's own device ["Towards new shores!"] at the head of our journal. And from various quarters people have been sending us information about the performance of his works during this last winter.

Boris Godunov was produced in Turin, Naples, Genoa, at the Opera Khediva in Cairo, and in Buenos Aires...

The songs of Mussorgsky have been performed almost everywhere in France, and always with success. We are told about concerts in Angers, Nancy, Le Havre, Rouen, Limoges, Nantes and Paris, where they have been performed. Among the performers we can name Mme Annette Dupré, Mme J. Henning, Mme Felia Litvin, Mme Robert, Mme Babian, and Mme Schütz.

Works for pianoforte. The *Pictures from an Exhibition* have been played in Paris by G.M. Dumesnil.

Choral and Symphonic Works. The Society of St. Cecilia in Bordeaux included in its programme the *Defeat of Sennacherib*. The overture to *Khovanshchina* was performed in Lausanne and in Rome, the polonaise from *Boris Godunov* in Liège, the *Night on the Bald Mountain* in Reims.

These reports are far from exhaustive, but they fairly eloquently show the growing success of Mussorgsky abroad. (DP, 4 (1910), 4.)

⁀ Medal
minted in France
as a homage to
Mussorgsky.

It is impossible to detail all the important materials and publications issued by the House of Song. But probably most significant of all were those connected with the competitions, both Russian and international, which were organised by the Society.

The House of Song Competitions

Between 1908 and 1913, eight competitions (five Russian and three international) were organised. Typically, the main themes of the competitions were musical translations into Russian and other languages of the principal works of vocal chamber music and harmonisation of folk songs of various nations. This direction for the competitions was defined by the dearest interests of the House of Song's founders—i.e., especial attention paid to the poetic text of a vocal work, and the popular sources of vocal music.

Members of the competition juries included such celebrated musicians as Sergei Taneyev,[16] Alexander Grechaninov, Mikhail Ippolitov-Ivanov,[17] Nikolai Medtner, Alexander Goldenweiser, and the critics Kruglikov and Kashkin.

Olenina regarded the poetic text as an equal partner to the music in any composition. She was always absorbed by the problem of the audience's understanding of a text. Hence her reflections on the original text and its translation, which were reflected in the House of Song competitions. In her approach to the dilemma of whether to prefer the original or a translation Olenina remained ambivalent. The statement in a recent essay that she always tried to ensure that listeners "apprehend a work in its original language" did not quite reflect her true aims.

(E. Alekseyeva, "Olenina-d'Al'geim," *Sovetskaya muzyka* 1 (1960), 105.)

Olenina-d'Alheim believed that "one has to be more or less a German to convey Schubert and Schumann; a Hungarian to convey Liszt; a Russian to convey Mussorgsky." (ZM, 44.) But she strove to ensure that the Russian audience understood the Germans and the French, and conversely, that the French should understand the Russians. For this purpose, first-class translations were essential.

Olenina-d'Alheim:

The performance of Mussorgsky in Russian requires great sensitivity. However, it must be admitted that the art of musical translation is still in its infancy—if one allows at all that it has actually been born. [...]

Obviously, it is difficult to require of a translator that he should be inspired. His work is limited by obstacles such as the poet never knows; nevertheless, it is essential for him to preserve the rhythm of the feeling expressed. If the translator sticks to literal translation, he subjects the singer to genuine non-sequiturs in the expression of feeling. [...] Yet if he cleaves to the spirit of the composition, he can mislead a singer who, while trusting the verbal rendering of feeling presented to him, may harm the actual musical measure indicated by the composer. The most splendid performer may be led astray by that other interpreter—the musical translator. [...]

While awaiting the appearance of a poet so dedicated to art as to conscientiously undertake the ungrateful duties of musical translator, [...] the singer himself must revise the text placed before him. [...] The singer must study foreign languages at least sufficiently for the needs of the music, and he must also get to know and study his own language more deeply; only then will he be in a state to carry out the frequently needed corrections. (ZM, 52–53.)

The first of the House of Song's competitions for the best translation took place in 1908–9. As one could have foretold, its object was to produce a musical translation—in this instance a text of Schubert's cycle *Die schöne Müllerin*. Eight competitors each received 500 roubles for a Russian text of individual songs in the cycle. In the second competition, six translators shared the prize—for a translation into Russian of twelve song settings of Goethe. These translations were not immediately published—the House of Song competitions were still only gathering strength.

With the third competition publication of the results began. The harmonisation of ten folk songs to words by Robert Burns produced for the third competition in 1909–10 by Count S.L. Tolstoy (the son of Lev Tolstoy) was published by the Russian Music Publishers (Moscow-Berlin) with an author's preface in Russian, German and English. For a harmonisation of four Burns songs, a prize was presented to the Parisian Paul Vidal.[18] These songs appeared in a Collection of Folk Songs published by Jurgenson[19] in Moscow (the French translations were by the House of Song; Russian versions were by the translator Sviridenko).

After A.F. Luther received a prize for his translation of twelve Mussorgsky songs into German, an international competition was announced for a harmonisation of seven folk songs.

"Concours de la Maison du Lied" 1910–1911:
P[iano]f[orte] accompaniment for seven melodies (French, Russian, Flemish, Scottish, Italian, Spanish and Jewish).
1. The melodies to be harmonised will be printed in this newspaper.
2. The prize is 500 roubles. It has to be awarded. In the event of the jury not agreeing to award the prize for one single manuscript, the prize may be divided up for individual songs.
3. Manuscripts shall not previously have been printed or publicly performed.
4. Manuscripts must carry no indication of the author's name, address, place of residence, and must bear one single *motto*. In addition, a sealed envelope must be sent bearing the same motto and containing the name and address of the author.

5. Manuscripts must be sent by *registered* post. Similarly the envelope if it is sent separately.

6. Manuscripts for the competition must be sent to: House of Song, Moscow, P.O. Box No. 6, before 1–14 October 1910. Manuscripts dispatched later than this date will be returned to their authors.

7. The result of the competition will be announced in November, and interested parties will be written to.

8. The composition that receives the prize becomes the property of the House of Song. It will be performed in a concert of the House of Song and published within the period of a year...

(DP, 7 (1910), 6.)

One of the contestants in this competition was Maurice Ravel. As the Society's *Bulletin* announced, in the fifth competition "the prize was shared between Maurice Ravel (French, Spanish, Italian and Jewish songs), Alexandre Georges[20] (Scottish and Flemish) and Alexander Olenin (Russian)." Their arrangements appeared in 1911 "in a collection of folk songs published by the House of Song as *Seven Folk Songs*. French and Russian translation. Jurgenson Publ., Moscow." (*Byulleten' "Doma pesni,"* 7 (1912–13), 4.) Many years later Ravel decided to orchestrate his arrangement of the Hebrew song and wrote about this to Olenina,

> Maurice Ravel:
> Dear friend and Madame,
>   At the beginning of this year I was going to orchestrate the Hebrew melody that won a prize from the House of Song. On the cover of this edition there was the address of the publisher Jurgenson. In this connection I applied for permission for this orchestration to the journal *Musique russe* (*Russkaya muzyka*), 3 Moskovskaya Street. [...] There they advised me to write to the representative of Jurgenson publishers, M. Forberg, 19 Galstrasse, Leipzig. A few days later I received a reply from M. Forberg: The House of Song collection "Folk Songs" does not figure in the Jurgenson publishers' catalogue. A month later, a Madame Roche-Sey (of Bordeaux) sent me a postcard also from Leipzig, where they not only gave her the same answer, but also said that the collection in question is [also] not registered in the Durand[21]

Maurice Ravel won the prize for four song
arrangements, including the Jewish song,
"Méjer'ke main Suhn."

publishers' catalogue. In addition to which, all requests concerning
this collection sent to Jurgenson publishers and Moscow have
remained unanswered.

I will be most grateful to you for an explanation of this mystery,
since it will be a pity if these compositions remain buried for so
long, and nobody can even find out where the tomb is![22]

May I use this opportunity to thank you for the splendid
souvenir discovered on the desk in my room at Madame Madoux's.
Please accept my apologies for not thanking you earlier.

Respectfully yours,

Maurice Ravel.

(M. Ravel, letter of 21 June 1924 to M.A. Olenina-d'Alheim,
GMMC, fond 256, no. 4925.)

The text and melody of the Jewish folk song included into the Fifth Competition of The House of Song for the arrangement of seven songs.

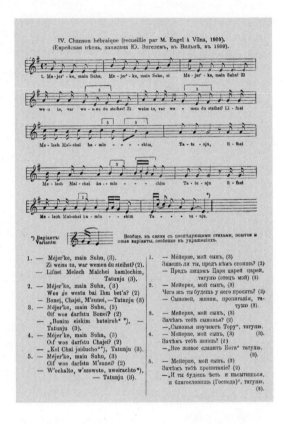

In late 1913 the House of Song issued a three-language edition of the works submitted for the sixth international competition, in which the prize of 500 roubles was shared between Albert Groz (for a setting of Colin Muset's "The reed-pipe"), Gabriel Pierné[23] (setting of a twelfth-century Provençal ballade), Alexander Olenin (Polish and Russian songs), and Roland Saint-Aulère (an English song setting).

Unfortunately, after 1913 the House of Song competitions went into abeyance owing to the Society's financial difficulties, although this was in itself nothing new, since from its very inception the House of Song had struggled hard to stay financially afloat. However, with the onset of the First World War and during the war the Society's affairs became even more problematic. Nevertheless, over six years their competitions had played a not insignificant role in musical life both in Russia and beyond its borders.

Olenina-d'Alheim:

When in 1935 I gave my last recitals, I had nothing left either. Pyotr and I, with his help, had also pointed out a new path to our artistes and colleagues, and but for the 1914–18 war the House of Song would have opened in Paris and in London. Pyotr already had everything prepared. But soon after the war he died, and it would have been beyond my powers to carry on the cause. [I did have] an assistant, but she quickly became scared, just like that disciple of Jesus I have just mentioned [...][who] was about to follow him, but then became scared and renounced him. Of the ones I did call on, many seemed to understand, but were unable to drag themselves out of the slough of prejudice and all sorts of traditions and routine; they had snuggled into that nice warm slime and were afraid to leave it, and it was so difficult to stir their brains! (SV, 35.)

———————

When World War 1 broke out, the House of Song was faced with all manner of difficulties, primarily financial ones, and after the 1917 Revolution and particularly by 1918 its activities were radically curtailed. The minutes of the final meeting of the Society's board make sad reading. It took place at a time when the d'Alheims" departure for France seemed to have been postponed indefinitely "because of the times we are undergoing," and when they still seemed able to achieve something inside Russia.

MINUTES OF THE HOUSE OF SONG SOCIETY BOARD MEETING: The meeting opened at 7.00 p.m. [on 17/4 February 1918] in the apartment of Board member A.V. Tarasevich at, 11 Savyolovsky Lane. Present were: President of the Society M.A. Olenina-d'Alheim, Board members, A.V. Tarasevich, P.I. d'Alheim, K.I. Tikhomirov, Society member V.V. Ruzskaya and candidate member N.N. Alexeyeva [...]

The meeting heard the report by President M.A. Olenina-d'Alheim about the Society's planned activities in the forthcoming summer season. The President reported that in view of her non-departure for abroad because of the times we are undergoing, she proposed not to curtail the Society's normal activities in the summer. A problem is perceived only in searching for suitable premises; such accommodation is however being offered to the Society by Society member V.V. Ruzskaya. This accommodation consists of a villa located on Pogonno-Losinyi Island in the Bogorodsky region of the city of Moscow, plot 87–39. [...]

It was resolved: to accept the President's report and take over for the Society's use the villa offered by Society member V.V. Ruzskaya, for which deep gratitude is expressed to Mme Ruzskaya [...]

(Draft ms. of minutes of House of Song Society, GMMC, no. 2751.)

The resolutions of that last meeting of the Society's board were never realised: In November of 1918 the d'Alheims left Russia, and so ended the last Russian page in the history of the House of Song. The House of Song was a unique organisation in its time, and not only in its own time. It was notable because, without being in any sense an élite organisation, it never reduced the problems of artistic performance to a commonplace level. Despite its proclaimed intention to "discover" rather than to educate its own public, the House of Song gradually turned into a constantly expanding society of sympathisers interested in musical enlightenment. It would be hard to exaggerate the House of Song's aesthetic, educational and cultural influence on Russian (and also partly on foreign) musical life, and its programmes are a model of their kind in Russian musical education.

It is also of importance that the Society created by Olenina in fact became the most congenial platform for her own supreme artistic self-expression and development. It was in the concerts, competitions and educational activities of the House of Song that she honed and polished her own talent, and it was here, in the halls ot the House of Song, that Olenina's voice found its fullest and most brilliant expression and sounded with the greatest dramatic significance which impressed itself on the memory of contemporaries as a unique artistic phenomenon of its time.

VI

FORTY YEARS
IN EXILE

Paris — 1918-1959

Departure from Soviet Russia

he Revolution of 1917 found the d'Alheims still in Russia. Being French citizens and perceiving no special danger to themselves, they were in no rush to leave and never really thought of doing so. So what if there was a revolution? The intelligentsia were of liberal persuasion and looked forward hopefully to the future. However, after the events of October 1917 a gradual process of flight and emigration began that increased as time went on. The old familiar Russia was living out its last few days. This became especially clear once the Civil War began, and in 1918 the d'Alheims realised they too must leave. According to Olenina this was less for political motives than because of Pyotr's illness. Nevertheless, there is reason to suppose that they sensed their continued stay in Russia could be fraught with danger, although Olenina-d'Alheim subsequently denied this. That same year the estate of Istomino was requisitioned and confiscated. In her memoirs Olenina retrospectively attempted to justify the hardships that they and others had to undergo.

Olenina-d'Alheim:

I cannot say that [I regretted the loss of Istomino]. One somehow imagined that this was inevitable after the revolution, and after all, I sympathised with it heart and soul. And after father's death my brothers had sold off quite a lot of land and also left for abroad. Alexander spent a couple of years in the Pyrenees, and Pyotr was everywhere—in Italy, in France, and I think he even went to Egypt. The one among us who was fondest of his nest and of the whole land here was Alexander. He maybe felt bitter at having to move to Kasimov, which he had never liked. But Alexander loved the people and was always for them, and he suffered because of their arduous life, so that he too was not inconsolably miserable. At that time we were in Moscow, where the House of Song recitals were continuing.

Alexander told us about the requisitioning of Istomino and about the great difficulty he had in finding sufficient cartage for the move into town (the authorities did not confiscate all the furniture and the rest of the goods). I applied to the Commissariat dealing with the preservation of historically valuable items on various Russian landed estates. Unless I am mistaken, the person in charge was the wife of Trotsky. I approached her and told her about the problems my brother, one of the people's composers, was having. She promised to take care of him. No more than a week later, my brother informed us that to his great surprise fifteen carts had come to Istomino from Kasimov, and he had been able to transport everything on them into town. There he lived with his family until 1922 and then moved to Moscow, acting as imagination prompted him, according to a letter he wrote. In Istomino and especially in Kasimov his artistic fantasy had probably started going to sleep, but despite very difficult living conditions in Moscow after the upheaval he was able to compose many superb works, especially in the last years before the Patriotic War [i.e. World War 2]. He loved his native land with all his being. In one of his cycles "Autumn" this love is expressed with especial vehemence: after a dream of some southern land there is an immediate transition to "No! No! As the son of a cold land, I was nurtured by it, and its storms and misfortunes are also mine. And I will not, and I cannot, part with it." This was written in 1901 in Istomino. Alexander always used to say, "I am of best use in the place where I was born." He not only used to repeat this proverb, but also acted according to it. (SV, 96–97.)

Despite some privileges granted by the new authorities, the picture painted by Olenina in her later memoirs is a somewhat bleak one.

Olenina-d'Alheim:
I am going to recall my departure from the USSR in November 1918. At that time all foreigners were requested to leave the "Land of Soviets."

Which one of the commissars was it that I met then? Was it Kerzhentsev,[1] the commissar in charge of theatres? Anyway, he gave me a note, a sheet, or rather a state-certified "Order to all civil and military authorities" to assist us in our movements, and so forth.

That was in the summer. In Moscow the arrest of foreigners had just been halted, but it was rough going for them in the provinces. Yet I wanted personally to warn my brother who had already moved from Istomino to Kasimov that his son Yury had perished (he was an officer, and like all other officers who had held secret meetings, he was arrested and executed). That summer we were living in the Losinoostrovsky Forest, and when my husband heard that all Frenchmen were being arrested in Moscow, he wanted to return and join his own people. (BNB, 64-65.)

Pyotr's Sickness and Death

What Olenina described as a polite "request" to all foreigners to "leave the 'Land of Soviets'" turned out to be a general round-up of all Frenchmen. Moreover her brother Alexander had to be personally warned of his son's death—evidently in order that he could take some measures to secure his own safety. It is also evident that the d'Alheims were actively striving to get out of Russia on the insistence of Pyotr. (In her later reminiscences, however, Olenina often talked of the guilt of those who left their homeland. This was one of her favourite topics, and of course her attitude hardly endeared her to Russian émigrés in Paris at a time when she herself was in dire need of support.) Pyotr d'Alheim meanwhile suffered from a protracted grave illness. The diagnosis was a terrible one—progressive paralysis and cerebral affection as a result of syphilis, which he contracted in his youth, and that had not been properly cured. One wonders whether the d'Alheims realised in Russia what the appalling consequences of this terrible illness would be and what lay ahead of them.

After a most difficult journey in the winter of late 1918, the d'Alheims finally reached Paris, where Pyotr's condition got worse. On top of all this, there were disagreements with the owners of the apartment that they rented, which quickly turned into a full-scale legal dispute. Their arduous passage from Russia back to France had been an ordeal scarcely easier than it was for actual fugitives from the Soviets, and they had barely recovered from this before they were pitched straight into a financial and family crisis. All this occurred at a moment when because of having to care for her sick husband, Olenina's performances virtually came to a standstill. They now entered on a period of genuine poverty. Darius Milhaud and Alfred Cortot both helped them in their distressed circumstances, and they did their best to ensure that Olenina could resume her performing career. Cortot's letters to her were full of concern and sympathy. As an old friend, he realised that the most important thing for her was to continue working.

Alfred Cortot:
I was very distressed by your letter that brought the sad news of your own and Pierre's health. But there is one thing I do not understand: Is the separation that you write about caused by material circumstances, or does it arise in the interests of the patient, whom you obviously would like to keep with you?

However difficult it might be to take a decision either way, it is essential that you keep a hold on yourself and control your actions in order to start work once again.

I promised you to have a talk with Dandelot, but at the moment he is away from Paris. He knows about you and is enthusiastic, so a mere letter from you will be sufficient. You can write to him

Facsimile of the letter written by Alfred Cortot to Maria Olenina-d'Alheim, 26 August 1919. [Translation is found on p. 200.]

at Val-André—Côtes du Nord. In addition, you can also write to Michel at 7a Piccadilly, London, to Henn at 2 Place Neuve, Genève, and to Wolf at rue de la Mésange, Strasbourg.

These are the concert agencies that could be useful to you. Obviously, you can write to them and refer to me, and if you consider it useful, I for my part can also talk to them about you.

Be assured, my dear friend, that I deeply share your sorrow, and please make use of me in every respect.

Yours,

A. Cortot.

(A. Cortot, letter of 14 August 1919 to M.A. Olenina-d'Alheim, GMMC, fond 256, no. 1177.)

However, Olenina was in no position even to consider active work. By the time Cortot wrote the 14 August letter to her, Pyotr had to be confined in hospital (hence the separation mentioned by Cortot), and gradually but relentlessly his condition got worse. Cortot for his part continued attempting to get Olenina back onto the platform. Less than a month later he wrote again.

Alfred Cortot:
By the same post I am sending off recommendations to each of the concert agents whose addresses I let you have. In Paris, you should also see Mangeot, the director of "Monde Musical," 72, rue de Méromesnil—he will probably be able to help you, as also will Robert Brussel of "Beaux-Arts," 3 rue Valais.
    I have warned Blair Fairchild of the disagreements with your landlord. I hope he will be able to intervene.
    Be assured of my true and respectful friendship.
                                                                            A. Cortot.

(A. Cortot, letter of 26 August 1919 to M.A. Olenina-d'Alheim, GMMC, fond 156, no. 3921.)

A few days following his letter of the 26 August, Cortot offered Olenina direct financial assistance, claiming with his usual delicacy that the offer actually came from an unidentified friend; it is not hard to guess that this was Cortot himself.

Alfred Cortot:
    A friend of mine who is deeply sympathetic to your misfortunes has detailed me to ask you whether you would be willing immediately—i.e., before the 1st October—to move your apartment to Fontainebleau and sell up your furniture here and now, which it is at present possible to do to your advantage. If you are in agreement, he is prepared to advance you the 3000 francs you need to settle the matter with your landlords, including the change of apartment, and to offer you an additional 1500 francs, which together with the income from sale of your furniture would enable you to get by for a few months until concerts again bring in what you need.

It is very difficult to break in this way [...] with a past that is full of cherished memories, but it seems to me almost essential, as it will in some degree restore your material comfort.

Please let me know of your decision. Be assured of the deep affection of
Your

A. Cortot.

(A. Cortot, letter of 11 September 1919 to M.A. Olenina-d'Alheim, GMMC, fond 256, no. 3922.)

Alfred Cortot:
In all honesty, I do not know what to advise you, since my own wish to solve your material problems as soon as possible does not allow me to forget that your landlords are tormenting you illegally.

I think that you should, on my behalf, ask M. Clément Delayet (2, rue du Conservatoire) to put you in touch with a lawyer from L'Oeuvre fraternelle des Artistes, Mme Megnen, who will be able to advise you better than myself whether you should agree or not to the offer that I made you in the belief that this would immediately get you out of your difficulties.

I am, dear friend, wholeheartedly with you and your dear sick husband.

Your Alfred Cortot.

(Letter (undated) to M.A. Olenina-d'Alheim, GMMC, fond 356, no. 3923.)

However, material problems continued, compounded by Pyotr's constantly worsening condition. Olenina did not manage to return to the concert platform, and almost two years later, her situation remained unchanged.

Alfred Cortot:
Alas, dear friend, either I am in error, or else you did not realise that I meant to fix up a meeting with you yesterday when I was at Pleyel's after lunch. I have to go to Britanny to see my mother who is unwell, and alas, I do not know how long I shall be detained

there. But before leaving for Britanny, I will let you know the
decision of "Beaux-Arts" which is still unclear, but which I shall
not leave in this situation.

Your respectful and still devoted

Alfred Cortot.

(Letter of 7 July 1921 to M.A. Olenina-d'Alheim,
GMMC, fond 256, no. 3924.)

Finally came the tragic dénouement. On the 11 April 1922, Pyotr
d'Alheim died after prolonged suffering. Doda Conrad, the son of
Maria Freund who had collaborated with Olenina in the House of
Song, told me of the horror of Olenina's friends when news came that
"Pierre d'Alheim became crazy. [...] Completely. [...] He was in an
asylum." In Conrad's account, the death of Pyotr was a grievous
tragedy and it more or less determined all of Olenina's subsequent fate,
which was one of desperate poverty, loneliness and abandonment.

Doda Conrad:
When he died, that was the first time my mother had contact with
Marie d'Alheim. [...] Marie d'Alheim called my mother and asked
her, because she was very poor already then, very poor, if my
mother could come to photograph d'Alheim on his deathbed at the
insane asylum in Ste. Anne. He died at Ste. Anne. My mother was
very impressed. [...] Marie d'Alheim also asked my mother if she
could bring a bed sheet because she had none. And my mother
came with a bed sheet and d'Alheim was completely naked. My
mother photographed him, and he was buried in my mother's bed
sheet because there was no other bed sheet. He had been crazy for
three years in an insane asylum. (DC, 1.)

In the final years before her husband's death, Maria Olenina
expended much energy attempting to publish an edition of his works.
Many of these efforts proved fruitless. However, Mussorgsky's songs
in his translation were published in London, and a second edition of
his book on François Villon appeared with Cresse publishers. The
money from this was used to bury him. To Olenina the death of Pyotr
d'Alheim meant more than the loss just of her husband; she had also

lost her inspirer, her Pygmalion, and her comrade-in-arms in a cause that both of them had regarded as the aim of their existence. In the many letters of condolence from musicians and friends, Olenina found generous words of appreciation for both his activities and his outstanding personality.

Maurice Ravel:
Dear Mme d'Alheim,

I was much pained by the unexpected news of your great sorrow.

The name of Pierre d'Alheim marks a highly important epoch in my life as a musician. I shall never forget the day—and it was so long ago—when you and he appeared and revealed the work of Mussorgsky to us. With all my heart I ask you to accept my deepest condolences.

Maurice Ravel.

(Letter of 12 April 1922, GMMC, fond 256, no. 1762.)

Alfred Cortot:
Dear friend,

Believe me, it is with such a heavy heart that we think in these grief-filled hours of you and of the cross whose weight you have to bear. In Pierre's person a rare and sensitive soul has departed this life. He possessed that exciting gift which is the mark of a great artist [...]

Yours, Alfred Cortot.

(Letter of 16 April 1922, GMMC, fond 256, no. 1178.)

Darius Milhaud:
My dear friend,

I regret that I cannot be in Paris tomorrow in order to attend the requiem for your dear departed husband, and to tell you that with all my heart I think of you constantly and with sympathy. [...]

Your ever devoted Milhaud.

(Letter (n.d.) of April 1922,
GMMC, fond 256, no. 1410.)

The death of her husband was for Olenina a dividing of the ways, and it left her without money, without close friends and, effectively, without any occupation. As is often the case in a crisis when one is abroad, her loneliness might well have drawn Olenina to her own people, to the Russian community. But émigré society turned its back on anyone like her who had the arrogance to compare and contrast themselves with the main community of refugees. As she later wrote in her "Short Biography" in 1946, "If my husband had not fallen dangerously ill, we would have remained in Moscow in 1918. He was very keen to open a people's theatre, and I—a school for small children" (KRAVT, 5). Olenina did her best to emphasise that she was a French citizen and that she had nothing to do with those who had fled Russia. Indeed, she did not disguise the fact that she supported the Bolsheviks, and believed those who had fled Russia deserved to be condemned. Not unnaturally, Russian émigré society reacted very negatively to this.

Olenina-d'Alheim:
My brothers did not leave Russia, and I am bound to take pride in this decision of theirs. I regret very much that so many of the intelligentsia left Russia.
Of course, the requisitioning of large estates and rich properties cannot have greatly cheered their owners. Many people fled in fear of the terror that accompanies all revolutions. Here, of course, the Bolshevik group could not prevent this. Only I think that Russian people of culture had a poor understanding of the historical move their people had made. [...] I know that among the "diaspora" as they term themselves, there are many good, intelligent and honest people, and I would be happy to see them admit their guilt towards their native people. (SV, 97.)
[...] I was in agreement with the Bolsheviks when still in Moscow, and Pyotr too. He wanted to stay in Moscow and told me that "now that the country has been liberated, we can do more and better work." He planned to set up a People's Theatre, where all the best works would be staged in the best translations into Russian. "Now I love Russia, as I do my native France." And when I brought him in a sick state to Paris, Doctor Ducoste who was treating him,

kept halting me and saying, "Madame, you talk in a way such that people will simply take you for a Bolshevik, and you know how they are hated here." (SV, 2.)

Generally I have to say that all the émigrés abroad totally ignored me, and even when I lived in a large atelier in Passy. [...] I sit here writing all this, and I am sorry that in 1917 Lenin did not imprison all the members of the Provisional Government in the Peter and Paul Fortress. Its president Rodzyanko together with the White Guardists could not have gone against *his own people*, and that is how it turned out. (BNB, 163–64.)

Doubtless Olenina, who was nothing if not candid, made no bones about speaking her mind on this subject whenever she talked with other Russians in Paris. Very soon therefore she found herself completely isolated.

The Maison du Lied in Paris

Now that Russia was caught up in the Civil War, there could be no question of the House of Song continuing its activities there. It was thus necessary to think of something similar as a substitute, at least in France. Soon after her husband's death Olenina at first took steps to resurrect the House of Song on French soil, and she tried to continue performing with the pianist Dorothy Swainson who lived in Paris. Doda Conrad later talked about this with me when I interviewed him in 1991.

Doda Conrad:
Then Marie d'Alheim (she was very courageous) created in Paris the Maison du Lied.
Alexander Tumanov:
What year was that?
Doda Conrad:
Nineteen twenty-three to twenty-four—those years. And she gave concerts in Paris. But she was already almost without a voice really, and she had a following of intellectuals, of literary people, no fol-

lowing at all of musicians, or she didn't give any singing lessons. But there were people like Darius Milhaud who were very close to her, and several other people, but very few. [...] Canteloube,[2] Ravel a little [...] Florent Schmitt[3] and André Caplet,[4] I think. [...] Who spoke a lot of Marie d'Alheim in those days was Emma [the widow of] Claude Debussy[5] because Debussy was very much interested in Mussorgsky. [...] Among her friends were also the Baruzzi brothers. [...] One of them was a music critic in the newspaper *Le Ménestrel*.[6] [...] That was a little circle around her, but very, very little, because she gave some concerts in a concert hall, the Salle des Agriculteurs, it's a small hall. But then later she had an accompanist called Dorothy Swainson [...] who had a studio in number ten, rue Faustin-Hélie[...] And on the last floor there was the studio where there could come probably forty or fifty people. So we all went there and paid, I think, five or ten francs because we knew that she was very poor. And this went on for five or six years. (DC, 1.)

Olenina attempted to revive the House of Song in Paris the same year that Pyotr died. In summer of 1922 a programme was announced for the fourteenth season of the "Maison du Lied," as it became known. The concerts continued from November 1922 till April of 1923 and took place in the studio at 10, rue Faustin-Hélie. The last concert was an exact repeat of one of the House of Song concerts in Moscow in spring of 1917. On the 18 September 1922, in a letter to an unidentified person, Olenina talked about renewing her activities within the framework of a concert series put on by the General Assembly of the League of Nations. And although many of her efforts bore no fruit, she did not give in.

Concerts were announced now under the title of the House of Song, now under the aegis of the "M.A. Olenina-d'Alheim Concert Association." Olenina most often performed together with Dorothy Swainson, sometimes also inviting other singers to her concerts—such as M. Alexandrovich for the scene between Marfa and Galitsky in *Khovanshchina*, or the singer Youra Guller for Bach duets. One of her concerts also involved the well-known singer Claire Croiza[7] who sang songs by Debussy and together with Olenina performed a scene from Monteverdi's *Orfeo*.

Dorothy Swainson in 1913. She took part in
the activities of The House of Song in Paris
in the 1920s.

From surviving letters we know that apart from Dorothy Swainson,
Olenina also performed together with Eugène Wagner, one of Paris'
most popular regular accompanists.

Doda Conrad:
He was a bearded gentleman who was *the* accompanist, like a sort of
a servant domestique. When somebody came—a violinist, a singer,
anyone—the manager would call immediately Eugène Wagner, and
Eugène Wagner would accompany. […] He was a little ridiculous.
With a long beard, he looked like Brahms. And he had a daughter

Announcement of seven concerts given by Maria Olenina-d'Alheim from November 1922 through April 1923 at Dorothy Swainson's studio, 10, rue Faustin-Hélie.

Société des Concerts
OLÉNINE D'ALHEIM

Quatrième Saison 1922-1923

SEPT CONCERTS

donnés au Foyer de la Société

10, Rue Faustin-Hélie (16e), à 9 heures du Soir

16 Novembre

1 La belle meunière (Müller) . . . . . SCHUBERT
   (conte pour lire en hiver)
   Version Française de Pierre d'ALHEIM.

2 Le Soldat (Andersen) . . . . . . SCHUMANN
   Rêve d'une mère (Andersen) . . . . —
   Le vielleux — . . . . — .
   Versions françaises de Pierre d'ALHEIM.

3 Rencontre dans la forêt (Eichendorf) . SCHUMANN
   Le Roi des aulnes (Gœthe) . . . . SCHUBERT
   Marie Olénine d'ALHEIM.
   Dorothy SWAINSON.

30 Novembre

BEETHOVEN : 2 cycles de mélodies et une œuvre
         de musique de chambre

who was a spinster, an old maid, who would turn pages. It was very funny. Here was a lady singing, beautifully dressed, or a violinist, even Enesco would make concerts with him, and here was this strange couple—Brahms with a badly dressed girl. (DC, 5)

Despite her age (in 1929 Maria Olenina turned sixty years of age) and contrary to Doda Conrad's view, she had not completely lost her voice. Indeed her vocal abilities still remained quite strong. There are documents recording that she was the chosen performer and partner with such musicians as Milhaud and Poulenc. When Milhaud composed his "Four Songs" to poems by Claudel,[8] two of them were sung by Olenina, and two others by Madeleine Grey and Jane Bathori.[9] In 1922, Milhaud accompanied Olenina when she performed his works, and later on he was to dedicate to her the *Six Chants Populaires Hébraïques*, opus 86. In the late 1920s the name of Mme Marie Olénine

19 Décembre
1 Chants populaires et Noëls anciens . . . .
2 Fragments de l'Oratorio de Noël, de Bach.

23 Janvier
MOZART et HAYDN. — DEBUSSY et RAVEL.
Psaumes et chansons hébraïques

14 Février
Avec le concours de M. ALEXANDROVITCH
1 MOUSSORGSKI : La Scène de Marthe et du
Prince Galitzine, du « Complot des Khovanski »
2 Œuvres d'Alexandre Olénine.
3 Duos des Maîtres italiens

2 Mars
Avec le concours de Mme Youra GÜLLER
BACH ET SA FAMILLE

17 Avril
Programme donné par Marie Olénine d'ALHEIM,
à « la Maison du Lied » à Moscou en 1917

Plusieurs de ces programmes comprendront des œuvres
de musique de chambre pour divers instruments.

La Cotisation annuelle est de 50 francs

d'Alheim still figured in some fairly important concert halls. For instance, she took part in a concert of modern and folk music in the hall of the Comédie des Champs-Elysées, organised by the managing committee of the Louvre, at which she performed songs by Poulenc, two Hebrew songs by Milhaud dedicated to her in 1925, and a Chinese cycle by Blair Fairchild[10]—all of this accompanied by Poulenc.

In February of 1931 Olenina marked the fiftieth anniversary of Mussorgsky's death with a concert that also formed a milestone in her own career. She wrote about it to Maria Freund.

Olenina-d'Alheim:
My dear friend,
On the 27 February I shall be singing at the Music Club which has organised a Mussorgsky Festival on the occasion of the fiftieth anniversary of his death. The 27 February also marks thirty-five

years of my own artistic career, which began on 10 February 1896, and the aim of that very first concert was to promote the music of Mussorgsky.

Can you come on the 27th? I shall be really happy to sing at this concert—and for my friends as well. Please let Paul and Sophie Clemenceau know about this. Also, tell them that I no longer go on Sundays to the avenue [illegible], simply because my life is too sad for that.

Who knows, maybe the 27th will be the last day of my long career, and I would like them to give me a cheerful burial.

Friendly regards to all your family,

Marie d'Alheim.

(BN.)

The dates mentioned by Olenina are highly symbolic: on the 15 February 1881, six weeks before his death, Mussorgsky made his last bow before the public at a concert at the Free Music School; exactly fifteen years later, in February 1896, the first *conférence* by the d'Alheims took place; and finally, fifty years after the composer's death and thirty-five after Olenina's début, on the 27 February 1931, was the concert and swan-song to mark fifty years of Mussorgsky's passing. The baton had been passed on, and the mission had been accomplished: the music of Mussorgsky was alive and had spread beyond the frontiers of Russia. Sadly, in Russia the name of Olenina-d'Alheim was unmentioned at the celebrations to mark the half-century of Mussorgsky's death.

There is no evidence how that concert went, and although it was not her last actual appearance, thereafter Olenina's singing career went into a definite decline. A natural alternative to this might have been an increase in her teaching activity, had it not been for her own particular character as a singer.

Although she made attempts to develop her teaching, Olenina never wanted to give mere voice lessons and concern herself simply with so-called voice production. She was always more attracted by teaching vocal *performance*. This indeed was what she attempted to do, and together with Jane Bathori she announced a "Mussorgsky interpretation course"—with "gesture and verbal expression as established by Pierre d'Alheim." The "House of Song Mondays" were to take place

Maria Olenina-d'Alheim, c. 1930. Drawing by
Doda Conrad in 1997 from memory.

in the studio of Jane Bathori on the rue Poncelet, and were announced
in connection with some concerts of Mussorgsky's music scheduled,
evidently, for February and March of 1931. This time Olenina planned
to appear as the lecturer or *conférencier*, as Pierre d'Alheim had done.
The performing role she left to the young artistes who, according to the
announcement, were to be trained for these Monday recitals. Indeed it
was Olenina's plan that the newly formed Paris Maison du Lied should
be a "house of the young." She herself however sang in another concert
on 27 February 1931, which she mentioned in her letter to Maria Freund.
The success or otherwise of the Monday concerts is something of
which we know nothing. If indeed they took place as planned, they

must have continued only for a short time: Olenina's notes and letters of the period make no further mention of them. Nevertheless, she returned again to the idea of appearing as lecturer twenty-five years later, in 1956, on the 75th anniversary of Mussorgsky's death.

Occasionally, Olenina's friends would send pupils to her who were studying the Russian repertoire and needed to have their Russian pronunciation corrected. The work was neither very interesting nor very creative, although she evidently found some release and outlet in it, as she told Suvchinsky.

Olenina-d'Alheim:
Esteemed Pyotr Petrovich,
I was very glad to see you on the 27th [May] at the Salle Chopin. Come and hear how I have taught Miss Tapeur to pronounce Russian. She is a pupil of Jane Bathori, and well deserves one's sympathy and attention.

As you can see, I am living not far from you, but seem not to be able to come and visit you. I keep thinking a lot about my biography [i.e., "Dream and Recollections"] and have already compiled it in brief.

Do come on the 27th, and we'll see one another and have a word.

Olenina-d'Alheim.

(BN.)

This letter, evidently written in the 1940s, reflects the sharp reduction in Olenina's activities and abandonment of active performing that had begun the previous decade. She no longer had the constant support of her husband, and there was no longer that faithful Russian public that had patronised the House of Song. Although it became increasingly hard to organise performances in the early 1930s, Olenina still sang in occasional concerts together with French artists.

In the year 1929, the Maison du Lied and the Olenina-d'Alheim Concert Association announced a series of five concerts in the Salle d'Orgue of the Paris Conservatoire. The artistic committee of the Association included some prominent French musicians, among them Nadia Boulanger. However, the composition of the committee kept

LA MAISON DU LIED

SOCIÉTÉ DES CONCERTS OLÉNINE D'ALHEIM

••••••••••••••••••••

Le Comité de direction artistique est composé, d'ores et déjà, de Mmes. Jane Bathori, Nadia Boulanger, C. Croiza, Marya Freund, Marcelle Gérar, Vera Janacopulos, Anne-Yann Roubane et Marie Olénine d'Alheim.

••••••••••••••••••••

La Société donnera, au cours de la saison 1929,

CINQ CONCERTS

dont les trois premiers sont fixés aux

Jeudi 14 Mars
Mercredi 17 Avril — Mardi 14 Mai
à 21 heures

Salle d'Orgue du Conservatoire
2 bis, Rue du Conservatoire

••••••••••••••••••••

*Les dates des quatrième et cinquième concerts
seront annoncées ultérieurement*

••••••••••••••••••••

La cotisation de membre est fixée à 50 francs par an et donne droit à une place à tous les concerts de la société.

Est membre d'honneur toute personne ayant fait don à la société d'une somme de cinq cents francs minimum

Les cotisations sont reçues au siège de *La Maison du Lied*, 10, Rue Faustin-Hélie (16me) et au

Bureau International de Concerts C. KIESGEN et E.-C. DELAET
Immeuble Pleyel, 252, Faubourg Saint-Honoré.

⌒ Poster under the aegis of La Maison du Lied announcing five concerts for the season of 1929 at the Salle d'Orgue du Conservatoire.

changing constantly, and Boulanger soon left it. Nevertheless Olenina did not abandon her efforts.

The pianist-composer Nikolai Medtner[11] was living near Paris, and despite the fact that his music was obviously remote from the artistic principles of the House of Song, Olenina tried in 1935 to engage his collaboration in the Maison du Lied. Needless to say, nothing came of this enterprise and Medtner wrote to Olenina about it.

Nikolai Medtner:
Dear Maria Alexeyevna,

Until the very last minute I was hoping to get to tomorrow's recital and for this reason have not yet answered your letter. I am unable to tear myself away from my work which has recently been absorbing all my energy. What a shame that concerts in Paris begin after nine o'clock, and we out-of-town residents who depend on the trains are forced to return so late at night that this affects our work next day. In addition to which, Anna Mikhailovna has developed hay fever and she hardly goes out anywhere.

We would both very much like to see you, dear Maria Alexeyevna, and if you were to find it possible to come to us in Bellevue, we would be happy. We were very happy to hear that the activity of the House of Song which is so dear to us is gradually getting under way, and with all my heart I wish it total success!

Only I do not quite understand in what way you imagine my active part in your enterprise? It seems to me that I am unsuitable here either as a composer or man of affairs... *

We both send you our sincerest greetings.

Your N. Medtner.

* But it would be better and easier to talk about all this in person...

(Letter of 12 July 1935, GMMC, fond 256, no. 1116.)

That same year, but after moving to London, the Medtners continued corresponding with Olenina, who kept them informed of the concerts and other prospects of the Maison du Lied. From a letter from Medtner's wife, Anna Mikhailovna, it is obvious that Olenina still dreamed of reviving it.

Anna Mikhailovna Medtner:
Dear Maria Alexeyevna,

Thank you very much for remembering us, and of course we read your letter and the prospectus of your Society with great interest, and we much regret that we cannot take any active part in this as we are not in Paris.

But we do hope to be in Paris, and we shall then definitely visit you. We do not yet know when this will be. We were very happy to see that you do not doubt how precious to us your performances and reminiscences of the House of Song are. May God grant that your new activities are crowned with complete success. We both send you our very best wishes.

A. Medtner

(A.M. Medtner, letter of 12 November 1935, GMMC, fond 256, no. 1406.)

All this time Maria Olenina was thinking again of translating the text of Mussorgsky's songs into French and English. Negotiations began with Soviet publishers, evidently, back in 1926 during Olenina's last concert tour to Moscow. Unfortunately very few details have been preserved about this tour, other than the fact that works by Alexander Olenin were included in the programme, and that he accompanied her. (Other sources, however, suggest that her accompanist was Abram Shatskes; see E. Alekseyeva, "Olenina-d'Al'geim," *Sovetskaya muzyka* 1 (1960), 11.) It is also known that Olenina's very extensive programme included folk songs, that it was a huge success, that the takings yielded 350 roubles per concert, and that Olenina spent a lot of time with her close friends the Taraseviches with whom she stayed during her visit. During her stay in the Soviet Union in 1926, there was also discussion of the possibility of reviving the House of Song. However, these plans came to nothing. One surviving document is a report submitted by Olenina, a sad relic of the period when even the most brilliant manifestations of Russian culture were destroyed to satisfy the idea of preserving the class "purity" of proletarian culture.

Olenina-d'Alheim:
REPORT ON REVIVAL OF THE HOUSE OF SONG:
In the year 1918 I submitted to the Commissariat of Education (Theatre Section) a project for a kindergarten to prepare and train artists from the very earliest age. In the event that my project was realised, Pyotr d'Alheim my husband, a French writer, intended presenting his own proposal for creation of a People's Theatre. From his youth d'Alheim dedicated much time to working on courses for the people in Brussels and Paris.

To our great disappointment, my project could not be carried out in view of the absence of sufficient funds for this enterprise. In 1926 I went to Moscow on invitation from Rosfil [Russian Philharmonic Society] for several concert appearances. I spent two months in Moscow and before departure attended a meeting of members of the House of Song society, founded by me and my husband, and also by An[na] Vas[ilyevna] Tarasevich. It was resolved to apply to comrade Lunacharsky,[12] who was then Commissar of Education, for permission to revive the activities of the House of Song.

No such permission was received from Lunacharsky. For what reason I cannot know. I heard that my own nobility background was maybe an obstacle, although I think that one should not [...] deny the nobility a chance to think freely of all prejudice. An example of this to all of us is Vladimir Ilyich Lenin. [...] (M.A. Olenina, Undated and unfinished draft ms., GMMC, fond 256, no. 4625.)

Even after refusal of Olenina's submission to the Soviet authorities, not all seemed lost. Over subsequent years, the question of the translations appeared solved: it was simply a matter of discussing final details, and the translation work could start. From correspondence with Pavel Lamm, it was evident that contractual, financial and artistic problems (such as that of iso-rhythmic renderings) were all discussed. Lamm wrote to Olenina on this matter on several occasions.

Pavel Lamm:
The Musical Sector accepted with great readiness my proposal to entrust you with editing the translations of [Mussorgsky's] songs into French and English. (Letter of 5 May 1928, GMMC, fond 256, no. 3935.)
   Regarding translation of the Mussorgsky songs I can only say that the principle of complete iso-rhythmicity must stand firm, but this does not mean that if the matter of translation is in the hands of such a Mussorgsky expert, connoisseur and admirer as yourself, there may not be exceptions in such cases. [...] In brief, I am reassured since I am certain that you will spare no labour, love and patience so as to alter the voice line only in the most extreme cases.
(Letter of 30 October 1929, GMMC, fond 256, no. 3936.)

Campaign to Return to Russia

Despite this, at the last moment, the whole plan fell through, and Olenina sought for other ways of realising her idea. At about this time, in the late 1920s, she began to think of returning to Russia permanently. Only there could she pass on her knowledge and artistic principles to a younger generation of performers. Only there would her work have an aim and meaning. It might appear that so far as the Soviet government was concerned, no one among the Russians living abroad was more suitable than her to make a home-coming with suitable official fanfare. Olenina's artistry was still fresh in people's memories, and her political reliability should have been beyond reproach or doubt. However, the moment turned out to be a highly unpropitious one: the Soviet Union was entering the 1930s, and Olenina was to embark on a long and arduous route marked by hopes and despair. In fact, her protracted campaign for the right to return to her homeland lasted for most of the rest of her life.

After her return visit to Russia in 1926, she had the idea that she might be able to work there while continuing to live in Paris and merely visiting Moscow and Leningrad for her concerts, as she had done up until 1918. Vladimir Stepun,[13] the actor brother of the émigré philosopher Fyodor Stepun, wrote to her on this subject in 1927.

Vladimir Stepun:
Dear Aunt Marusenka!
    Constantly thinking as we do about you and your life, we are often on the point of writing you a few lines. But our life, whose crazy rhythm you remember from your last visit, gives us no chance to concentrate and get ourselves organised for a few minutes. [...] ...
    About your coming here I can say the following: Much though we would like you to come, you must take this step only if you decide, under favourable circumstances, to stay here for good. [...] ...
    If you give six concerts to a full house, after subtracting from this sum the cost of the trip *aller et retour* and of organising the concerts [...] at 25 percent, the remaining 75 percent will leave you with the sum of 300–350 roubles per concert. But owing to the general shortage of money now in Moscow and an absence of interest in serious music (the masses prefer the cinema), if your concerts produce not 100 percent, but 50 percent, or even less, then it could be that you would net only 100 roubles per concert.

There is thus the question whether this will be enough to survive on, since on your last visit [...] there was no money left for your return ticket! It seems to me that you must weight up the pros and cons dispassionately. My opinion is as follows:

contra—an absence of guarantees, and the possibility of less than total success,

pro—apart from the subjective happiness of seeing you and hearing you, it is my conviction that if you wish, you can set yourself up here better financially than in France. But the most important thing is that you should have the wish to do so, and that, using your arrival in Russia, you should speak personally with Lunacharsky. But then of course, you would have to reckon on staying here for good. [...] ...

[In that case], apart from concerts [...] you will maybe have your own seminar at the Conservatoire. Lunacharsky will arrange some school for you to train young people: then you would have to be given decent living quarters where you could also give both private lessons and consultations on artistic performance. Only of course this would have to be set up very officially and precisely.

I think that if you had the Conservatoire, private lessons and a few concerts per season, you could easily earn 150–200 roubles per month, on which one could live quite decently. [...]

You are one of the few still surviving links with the past, with people who were near and dear and unforgettable, and who have departed to another world. And for that reason I would like to save and shield you from all difficulty by frankly stating my opinion about the present state of affairs. Decide for yourself, for man's life and the shaping of it are in his hands alone, and in those of God, his Lord and Master.

Your Volodya.

(Letter of 20 April 1927, GMMC, fond 256, no. 1905.)

Reading that letter later on, Olenina must have been surprised and touched at her dear friend's naïveté. Life had dictated something quite different, and work in the Conservatoire with private lessons and concerts was as yet a mere mirage, far beyond the horizon. However, at this stage, at the outset, both she herself and her friends and relatives in Russia were full of hope and enthusiasm. Here was some of the advice she received.

Vladimir Stepun:
Dear Aunt Marusya,

We have received your good letter and send you our love and kisses. In the next few days we are due to attend a meeting with Belyaev, Nina, Anyuta, Sarra Shakulova and Varya regarding a plan of action for your coming here.

But on my own part I would like to suggest to you the following: without putting things off, write a letter to Anatoly Vasilyevich Lunacharsky stating that you want to devote the rest of your life to handing on your experience, your knowledge and your artistry to your Russian heirs. Mention your previous activities and promotion of Mussorgsky, your art propaganda during the Russo-German war. Tell him that for twenty years you worked in Russia and that you want to complete it here and ask him to accommodate you in this wish, and ask whether he can offer you anything—whether a school, or courses, or demonstration concerts?

Also say that you had to leave Russia in 1918 because your husband was a French citizen, and also that he was so poorly that you had to take him back to his homeland for treatment.

I think that if you set all this out in an "impassioned" manner, forward your letter to me, and if I go to him myself and expand and develop your ideas, then maybe he will make you the best possible offer. Mention also about living accommodation and an instrument, which are essential to you, and also about the Conservatoire having invited you. This seems the very best plan to start with. [...]

Love and kisses, and awaiting your reply,

Your Volodya Stepun.

(Letter of 29 March 1929,
GMMC, fond 156, no. 1907, 1–2.)

It is sad to read all this advice on how best to meet the wishes of Olenina's highly placed "patron," and how to demonstrate her political loyalty and usefulness. The very thought of her having to *prove* to someone like Lunacharsky that Russian art needed someone like her is outrageous. We do not know whether she sent that "impassioned" message to the Commissar of Education. We do know, however, that Olenina was forced to continue campaigning for her right to return to Russia. In 1928 she should have come to Moscow to give a seminar on Mussorgsky, and in 1932 there was discussion of her working at Moscow Conservatoire as professor. The result each time met with an official refusal.

Pavel Lamm:
Dear Maria Alexeyevna,

I have just received your short note, from which I discern that, first of all, you will not manage to get to Moscow this season, and secondly, that you have not received my own letter. Both these facts are sad ones. I wrote to tell you that I have spoken about your case with Igumnov,[14] that there is no need to rush to Moscow specially because of the [Mussorgsky] seminars, and that you will in no way let anyone down [...]

The fact about Sovdip [i.e., the Soviet diplomatic service, dealing with entry visas] is a sad one, but it is very typical of this institution and is often repeated. I have heard rumours that they have been allowed to fulfil already signed-up agreements with foreign artists, but under no circumstances to conclude new contracts, and to terminate immediately any unsigned contracts no matter what stage they are at. At the moment, on the musical front we have a very difficult situation (all because of foreign currency of course). At the Conservatoire itself in the immediate future we have to expect some big changes in the management as well as in the professorial staff. Therefore, sad though this may be, it is perhaps better if you defer coming here for a time.

With New Year's greetings and wishing you all the best.

I kiss your hand.

P. Lamm.

(Letter of 31 December 1928, GMMC, fond 256, no. 1210.)

Alexander Goldenweiser:

Much esteemed Maria Alexeyevna,

Despite the fact that in the present academic year we have already allocated all our students among the teachers, and have invited some new ones, and thus the Conservatoire has no need to invite further voice teachers, nevertheless your offer strikes us as too artistically valuable for us to turn it down even temporarily. Therefore we shall clarify with the Commissariat of Education the question of your being invited, and will send you an official answer very shortly.

I was very heartened at the friendly tone of your letter and very much hope that I can really say to you "Au revoir—until we meet!"

Yours truly,

A. Goldenweiser.

(Letter of 1 October 1932, GMMC, fond 156, no. 3863.)

Alas, the Conservatoire could not find a professorial post for Olenina, despite the fact that her offer was so "artistically valuable." There are no grounds for doubting the sincerity of Goldenweiser's words. Olenina's candidature was obviously quashed elsewhere, maybe not even in the Commissariat of Education, but at even higher level. Subsequently, during the many years of her life in France, Olenina made renewed attempts to obtain permission from "on high" to return to her native land.

Surviving correspondence shows that on 18 June 1931 she wrote to the Soviet Embassy in Paris, requesting a meeting with the ambassador, with whom she wanted to discuss the possibility of being granted a visa to return to the Soviet Union. On the 7 July, the head of Chancery at the Embassy, N. Krasheninnikov, informed her the meeting would be the next day. But there was again no result—she was refused. A year later, in September of 1932, she made another attempt and wrote again to the Embassy, again without success. Requests were sent to highest level, with appeals to such persons as Gorky and Romain Rolland, but again the outcome was a series of further refusals. One wonders why a sixty-year-old singer could not be allowed back into the country. Olenina herself tried to explain this. But when one examines the details of the affair, it becomes clear that this was some sort of Kafka-esque bureacratic labyrinth governed by its own peculiar and inscrutable set of laws.

Olenina-d'Alheim:

In 1935 I wrote to Rolland and asked him to tell Gorky of my desire to return and work again in Moscow, and Rolland did this. And recently, as I was sorting various correspondence, I found two letters from his wife telling me that Gorky was delighted at my desire to return to Moscow. He immediately informed Molotov[15] and a short time later my brother wrote saying that there had been a meeting à propos of my returning home, at which Leonid Borisovich Krasin[16] and Bubnov[17] had been present, and it was decided to invite me for some performances. Of course, I would have stayed there. My brother and others too had already written and said that I could develop my activities in workers' clubs. [But] the trip did not take place. [...]

At that time comrade Kerzhentsev for some reason had his doubts, believing that I was already too old, and he wrote to say that there was nothing he could offer me. Maybe I could have gone there independently, simply in order to see family and friends, and as my brother told me: "Just come, and something will be found for you here." Leonid Krasin also did some agitating on my behalf. [...] But I did not go. There were three reasons for this. The first was that I was refused a visa. That is, I was not directly refused, but informed that this was not the right time for me to come. The second reason was that I had no money for the trip, and the third was my own natural shyness about insisting and imposing myself.

(SV, 116–17.)

From letters sent by Maya Kudasheva, the wife of Romain Rolland,[18] it is apparent that Olenina's prospects of returning to her homeland became more and more remote. It was increasingly clear to her celebrated patron and his wife, who had high-up connections with the Soviet rulers, that somewhere on "Olympus" the singer's return was disapproved of.

Maya Kudasheva-Rolland:

Dear Maria Alexeyevna,

I am writing to you only now, and not from Moscow, since there were an awful lot of urgent things to do which could not be postponed. So it was better to wait for a moment's leisure in order to do this. Ekat[erina] Vas[ilyevna] handed your letter to Rolland. I translated it immediately into Russian and handed the translation to Alexei Maximovich Gorky with whom we were staying. He is personally very interested in your desire and told me that he will hand your letter to Molotov. And he himself strongly supports your request.

A few days later Krasin rang and asked whether Rolland was doing anything for you. I told him that both Rolland and Gorky consider your activities as very much needed in the USSR, and that your letter was already in Molotov's hands. He seemed pleased with this, and I hope that he immediately informed you of this? If you still have no news of further developments and if it is necessary to remind them about it, write and let us know. But I imagine you are already getting ready to leave, and maybe have already left! (I am not sure whether it was correct to act via Molotov? I wanted to go via Neuhaus,[19] but Gorky himself decided it was better to give the letter to Molotov.)

All the very best. We wish you success! Rolland sends you his sincere greetings and asks you to pardon his not writing in person: our six-week absence has caused a lot of work to mount up for him, and his contacts with the USSR have increased tenfold. He has barely time to breathe!

Your M.P. (Katya)

(Letter of 7 August 1935, GMMC, fond 256, no. 4066.)

Maya Kudasheva-Rolland:

Dear Maria Alexeyevna,

Forgive me for not replying for so long. I am so loaded with work and get so tired that it is often hard for me to write letters. I have not sent your brochure and your own handwritten letters to Moscow—I simply fear they will get lost: apart from Alexei

Maximovich [Gorky] there is nobody to send your papers to—
and he has *thousands* of things to deal with and several secretaries.
One never knows what actually reaches him, and what will hold
his attention when it does reach him!

While in Moscow, it was easy to tell him *personally* about your
case, and we did that. He said then that he had handed everything
over to Molotov. But I do not know what happened after that.
Molotov too has thousands of things to do, even more than Gorky.
At any rate, I cannot bring myself to send your papers off from
here: if they get lost somewhere, it will be my fault. And Gorky is
not in Moscow at the moment, but in the Crimea.

I think that you must now clarify *who is directly responsible* for
your case, and apply the pressure there; I think that Krasin could
now do more than Gorky. Rolland will of course write a couple of
words to comrade Potyomkin,[20] so that he receives you, but I do
not know when this will be possible. [...] [illegible sentence re
Potyomkin's absence from Paris.] The fate of Europe, and perhaps
of the world, is decided there! And of course, this is not the moment
to distract his attention with the fate of one person: he will not
remember it, and it will pass him by.

My advice is: act via Krasin. I do not know where he is, but I do
know that he is sympathetic towards you. And he of course knows
all the ways and byways, who to act upon, and what depends on
whom, et cetera. We know absolutely nothing of this! My own
personal opinion is: in your explanations of your work plans and
aims, you ought to convey a more precise and real idea of the
methods and aims of your work. It would be even better if somebody else did this, if only Krasin himself. [...]

We cannot offer any other advice. (Rolland will still write a
letter to Potyomkin, but, I repeat, he is not in Paris at the moment,
and is probably preoccupied with quite other thoughts!)

I am sending back your brochure and papers. I wish you all
the best and hope that your case will be settled.

Your M.P.

If Krasin is in Moscow, and if you cannot reach him by letter yourself, Yulia and Volodya [Stepun] can *do this more easily than we can*,
since they are there on the spot. Write to them. (Letter of 11 October 1935,
GMMC, fond 256, no. 4067.)

It was indeed an inopportune moment for Olenina's return to the Soviet Union, since the political show trials were already starting up with all that that entailed. Repressions, terror and xenophobia were destroying all the tenuous contacts that linked the elderly singer with her country. Years went by, and the stream of letters from Russia diminished, and the people that promised to help with her return fell silent. And although this did not shake her belief that Russia was the only place on earth where social justice triumphed, and where art was uncorrupted (unlike the West, where she believed everything was becoming more and more commercialised), her yearning to return remained unsatisfied.

When Olenina started her campaign to return to Russia, she was already turned sixty. But as decades passed, and the Second World War came and ended, she was approaching eighty; all her ties with her homeland were broken; but the urge to return never left her. In 1946 she wrote to Moscow once again, this time addressing her letter to the Moscow musicologist Boris Yagolim,[21] who she apparently imagined had some influence at that time. As a member of the Moscow Conservatoire staff, Yagolim asked her to send her biographical data for a musical directory of "Russian musical personalities," which was being compiled under the editorship of Boris Asafyev.[22] To her letter she attached a "Brief Autobiography of M.A. Olenina-d'Alheim." Evidently she was convinced she had been finally forgotten in her home country and that a new generation needed to be told who exactly Olenina-d'Alheim was.

Olenina-d'Alheim:
Dear Mr. Yagolim,
[…] I hasten to answer and send you some data about my family. I was very glad of the chance to be in contact via you with the Moscow that I love. As it turned out I failed to get there and work as a professor, although a decision to invite me was taken at a special meeting with comrades Molotov, Bubnov, and Krasin during Romain Rolland's stay in Moscow. Gorky at his own request heard a report from Krasin about my activities and those of my brother (Alexander Alexeyevich [Olenin]). To this day I cannot fathom why after this decision I was refused a visa. And

how well my brother and I could have worked together. So much time has elapsed that it is better simply not to recall this failure which I have felt so painfully.

Here, after returning with my husband, since late 1919 I continued the campaign against wheeler-dealing in the arts, which was a constant aim of mine from the very start of my career. And now I continue to agitate for the government (*état*) to organise workers' clubs. I append a copy of this project to this letter. When they assure me that the realisation of this plan is impossible amid total ruin, I reply that it is time to stop treating art off-handedly like some poor hanger-on, and to realise that its power over people is certainly more valuable than any other, that without it humanity could not exist, and that in these dreadful times of ours it alone prevents people from sinking to the level of animals.

On Saturday, the 9 February I shall be giving a talk about this in the Russian Conservatoire here. I have decided to go as a professor there in order to find some young heirs to whom I can hand on all my accumulated artistic capital. Up until now I was unable to find them—my method of service to art did not suit young artists who are intoxicated by the spirit of commerce and desire to get rich.

If you could inform me about certain of my friends, I would be most grateful to you. Is Pavel Alexandrovich Lamm alive and well, who was working on a new edition of Mussorgsky's works from the manuscripts, and also his sister? I would also like to know whether Kirill Lvovich Tarasevich is alive. Vera Mikhailovna can tell you about him and all his family, and also about my pupils Alexeyeva and Maslenkova. Perhaps she knows something too about the family of my cousin Sergei Sergeyevich Olenin. It is so difficult not knowing anything for so long about relatives and friends close to me.

My sincere thanks to you, and my most cordial greetings.

M. Olenina-d'Alheim.

(Letter (n.d.) of February 1946 to B.S. Yagolim, GMMC, fond 256, no. 3282.)

In fact another thirteen years were to pass before Olenina-d'Alheim finally returned to Russia. However, although she scarcely ever appeared on the concert platform, the years of campaigning and waiting for this last journey home were not a time of total inactivity for her. On the 19 April 1942, she gave her very last public concert, in Paris, together with the French piano duettists Gouvy and Berteau. The programme included works by Bach, Beethoven, Schubert, Schumann, Wolf and Olenin. And so the Russian singer's concert career, which began so brilliantly in Paris in the late nineteenth century, quietly faded to a close there, half a century later.

But the end of her singing career did not mean the end of all musical activity for Olenina. She continued her correspondence à propos of a new Mussorgsky edition, and she tried to have Pyotr d'Alheim's unpublished works printed, and also thought about handing on her artistic legacy to a new generation of performers. She remained full of plans—from organising clubs for the workers to projects in support of young artists, and she continued writing letters to the papers and to the French Ministry of Culture. Back in 1937, her old correspondent Maya Kudasheva-Rolland mentioned one such article that Olenina vainly endeavoured to have printed.

Maya Kudasheva-Rolland:
Dear Maria Alexeyevna,

Please forgive my not having replied to your letter for so long—I have had absolutely no time to myself. Rolland has been finishing a gigantic book (about the works of Beethoven), and I had to rush and copy out the whole text. At the same time I have been copying his diaries, which he is distributing under seal to several libraries, for unsealing twenty years after his death. And all letters have been held up. Rolland went off yesterday to recuperate at a sanatorium, and now I have sat down to write replies.

I think that the very best thing would be for you to join the musical section of the Maison de la Culture. First of all, they will help you to apply your knowledge and strength in training young people; secondly, it will be easier for you via them to print your article. But it would be ineffective to write to the director of the paper: they are all too busy with other matters now! The letter would pass them by. Yet I am sure that in the Maison de la Culture you will immediately feel some terra firma beneath your feet. [...]

I wish you good health, dear Maria Alexeyevna, and I hope that you will be able to offer and achieve a great deal in your musical profession.

Your Maya.

(Letter of 8 May 1937, GMMC, fond 256, no. 4068.)

Ideas on Musical Performance

Despite the hardships of the war period, Olenina continued to live an active life of the mind, and she was full of ideas on musical performance, etc. We know very few details of her way of life. She received a tiny pension that was just sufficient to keep body and soul together. She had virtually no possessions. All the rooms that she rented (and she changed addresses often) were furnished "bachelor flats," or more often garrets. She was unable to buy herself any clothes and got by on gifts from charitable societies. Later she confessed that for many years she was unable to buy even a pair of stockings. Nevertheless, when she was turned eighty, she still felt a need to share her thoughts and experience with a new generation of musicians. In 1942 she had the idea of publishing a brochure in the form of an "appeal to young performers." Full of romantic phraseology about the selflessness of true art and the struggle against "wheeler-dealing in the arts," this unpublished brochure was subsequently slightly altered and addressed to the artists of the Soviet Union. Although several people involved in the arts and culture of France were familiar with her "Appeal" to young performers (including the Paris Conservatoire director Claude Delvincourt[23]), it was never actually published, since its main ideas were unconnected with art and were bound up with the author's own social and economic projects that were far removed from real life. Of far more interest were Olenina's ideas on the art of musical performance.

Among other papers, Olenina's correspondence with her pupil Tanya Slonim has survived, in which we can find expressed some of the ideas that were closest of all to Olenina's heart. Slonim's letter was written in answer to a fairy tale that Olenina had written and sent to her. (It was quite in character for her artistic interests to find an outlet in this unusual genre as well.) Evidently Olenina had sent her one of three of her Biblical tales, written in French and devoted to a series of social and moral problems, such as original sin, war and peace, the power of money, and justice. The surviving draft of Olenina's letter to Tanya Slonim touches on one of the central problems of her vocal interpretation: the performer's self-abnegation in favour of the music and the text.

Tanya Slonim:
[…] We have both read your story. It is a splendid—and not merely splendid, but also a profound and justified story, and it would be very useful for people to read it. But how to do that? It is in French, and here there is no suitable French press. I will try and translate it into Russian or English, but this is very difficult since my translating abilities are very mediocre. If anything comes of this, I will send it for you to inspect.

I have started singing a lot—I have to prepare for performances and recordings in May. I shall sing the whole of Mussorgsky apart from "The Flea" and other things purely for men. But I have not chosen any Glinka yet. Tell me what I could manage best. Your advice to me is a law not to be flouted.

You can not imagine how glad I was to see you, and how happy that you are just as cheerful as you always were.

I embrace you tenderly and firmly,

Your T. Slonim.

(Letter (n.d.), GMMC, fond 256, no. 1881.)

Olenina's reply was a sort of artistic testament from the singer to a younger generation of performers. She wrote with vehemence, passion and conviction about what she believed was most important for a singer—and not only for a singer, but for any musician. Reading this letter, one realises how much Olenina could have done for her art, if only she had been granted the chance to have pupils and others to continue her work.

Olenina d'Alheim:
Dear Tanya,
Here I am in Switzerland staying with Asya Turgeneva.[24] I am

still resting after Paris, where I had a lot of bothersome things to deal with. [...] Just before I left I heard from [...] that a parcel had been sent to me, but I was unable to wait for it—I already had my ticket. It will have to wait for my return. I am returning in June if I manage to carry out my intended programme—namely, to visit Geneva, give a lecture there to the women's club about the art of performance, about the many tasks of performers et cetera, and also to talk with Gorchakov (a publishing house in Geneva). If despite my arguments and the letter of praise from the director of the Conservatoire, he still does not want to publish my brochure (a book that performing artists need), then [I shall have to] send it to you. [The brochure in question is presumably Olenina's "Appeal to young performing artists."] What do you think of this?

I am very glad that you are trying yourself out on the stage, and are thinking about programmes and their composition. In this letter I am telling you all that I know from experience, and I can vouch for the correctness of it. I hope that you have begun waking from your sweet dreams and intoxication with your exciting external success, accompanied by applause and praise and so on. And I therefore think that my advice will help you to achieve true glory, even if it is not accompanied by great material benefits. I of course wish you an easier career than mine was in this respect.

Now let us talk about you: you undoubtedly have both musicality and a lovely voice. With this you can create much that is beautiful. But you must acquire other essential qualities, for which you must carefully fathom the secret of genuine and honest performance of works and their proper presentation. Think deeply about this, and when you find you have not only the desire, but the willpower and freedom, to *sacrifice your own self* in favour of the composers and their creations, then you can begin without any fear or doubt to build your programmes and perform them. I can predict in advance for you an all-transcending and all-consuming joy, with which nothing else in life can compare.

Now I am going to copy out for a you a few of my programmes. Soon, when I get my book *The Mussorgsky Legacy*, I will send it to you. You will be able to derive a lot from it, and in it, at the end, is a programme of "Songs of Goethe."

1. There are programmes that are easy to put together. These are
   the cycles, especially when they contain 20 or 24 items, such as
   in Schubert's *Winterreise* or *Die schöne Müllerin*.
2. There are programmes in which heroines appear whose
   personality has, as it were, become part of general tradition:
   Margarita, Ophelia, Ariadna, Alceste, Iphigénie. Here is one
   of my programmes of this sort:

PART I:

> "Ariadna's Aria"—Monteverdi
> "Iphigénie's Farewell to Clytemnestre"—Gluck
> "Iphigénie's Farewell to Achille"—
> "Iphigénie's Dream" (in Tauris)—
> "Alceste in the Temple" (from the opera *Alceste*)—
> "The Death of Ophelia"—Berlioz
> "Es war ein König in Thule"—Schubert
> "Gretchen am Spinnrade"—
> "Kennst du das Land?"—

* * *

PART II:—BALLADES.

> A. You can find, of course, old English ballades, and
> you must choose from them those where both the words
> and music are beautiful. You can take the ballades of
> César Cui, "On that wild cape"; as I remember, it is
> called "Menisk." There are ballades by Grieg. Then,
> something like a ballade is Glinka's "The Night Patrol,"
> Dargomyzhsky's "Palladin," Mussorgsky's "The Forgotten
> One" (ballade), Borodin's "The Sea," "The Sleeping
> Princess," "The Song of the Dark Forest." And by
> Schumann there are "Waldesgespräch" and "Balsatzar,"
> and Schubert's "Der Erlkönig," and Mussorgsky's "The
> Field Marshal" and "Death's Trepak."

* * *

B. Two arias by Bach with flute and other instruments. Only choose those with suitable words, i.e., those
that first sound as a rebuke to the straying human soul
in its blindness, and then as a consolation.

The programme I gave with this aim in mind worked
out well, with flute accompaniment. [...]

* * *

I think that *the word is the main thing*, and it can be pronounced
in all registers of the human voice. If the few things that I am telling
you in this letter open your eyes, and I think that after the horrors
of the last war it cannot be otherwise, because you have the heart of
a human being, and not of a vacuous *female*, and it will move you
to serve *in the same way in the sphere of art* to which you belong—
do not forget that it is essential that we work in such a way as to set
right, renew and purify everything in the realm of art.

I think that all these programmes and the way they are put
together are clear to you. Regarding others, I can say that I almost
always resorted to the line along which human feelings and
spiritual forces developed, and I followed their appearance, sound
and action in human life. I will write in more detail about this
later on.

Do not make up "sample programmes," for after all you are not
a sales clerk or a professor, and any idea and wish to "demonstrate"
or "teach" is bound to go against the purely artistic *phenomenon*
which you as a true servant of art are obliged to create in the hall
and in the souls of your listeners.

Here is another programme. I have remembered it just now. It
consists of works in which the poet-musician is an eternal, lonely
wanderer, pouring out his bitter plaint:

[...]
"Jesus in the Garden of Gethsemane"—Bach
(*Notebook of Anna Magdalena Bach*)
"Komm, süsser Tod"—
"Wonne der Wehmuth"—Beethoven
"Busslied"—

"Im Treibhaus"—Wagner
"Der Freund"—Hugo Wolf
"Auf ein altes Bild"—
"Wo find' ich Trost?"—
"J'ai perdu ma force et ma vie"—Liszt
"Svetik Savvishna"—Mussorgsky
"Within Four Walls"—(when I performed this song
    by Mussorgsky, I involuntarily thought of him
    himself and his malign fate.)
"Die alten bösen Lieder"—Schumann
"Le recueillement"—Debussy
"Aufenthalt"—Schubert
"Dead is she"—(*L'Orfeo*) Monteverdi

* * *

Here is yet another brief explanation of what should happen inside us during a performance. Let us take the simplest example: can anyone recount anything interesting and important in a room where a general conversation is going on or some instruments are sounding? Of course not, since their voice will be interrupted by others and their speech will emerge weak or disconnected, not as they wanted. When any interesting genuine work of art takes root within you and through its embodiment in you speaks out to listeners sitting in the hall, it needs total silence in your own internal room, and for that reason you must chase out of it all thoughts of anything else and be completely silent within yourself. Then the spirit of the work which you allow to take over within you will raise its voice in all its beauty and truth and using the strings of your inner lyre it will awake a stronger echo in some listeners, and a less strong one in others—that will depend on the quality of their soul. But the work itself will sound as it sounded in the composer's own soul.

There is no doubt that this is true of great creations by men of genius. Weaker compositions, created by merely talented composers, may excite and enlighten the human soul less. But since the main aim of all creative genius consists in addressing other people—and not only Mussorgsky desired and strove for this—then you will understand that one must avoid mediocre works, and never perform bad ones. That was the advice of Robert Schumann.

The silence can settle inside you when you truly forget about yourself and live only the life of that person, or that composition which you are performing. Perhaps what happens is something like the old Jewish belief, which you know, that the soul of a deceased person may settle in a living person and manifest itself in this world via them. I always believed that the system of "experience" (in the [Moscow] Arts Theatre) was a mistaken method, and that it should not be you who experiences, but the spirit that implants itself within you—the spirit of the composer with his own thoughts, or else of that person through whom the composer addresses himself to people.

When you are performing Gretchen, or Mignon, or Iphigénie, it is they who should be singing inside you, weeping, rejoicing or experiencing terror, and not you with your superstitions and nerves. And they must be so excited that as you walk off the stage, you are entirely filled with that excitement and cannot recover yourself and return calmly to ordinary life. In secret, I will tell you that this never actually happened to me, but I was filled only with a great joy such as a good hostess experiences when she lovingly receives a guest. As I walked off the stage or the platform, I could always speak calmly about other things, although the excitement aroused by the music just heard still reigned in the auditorium. It was free to act with full force on the audience, and *I did not interfere with it.*

If you can understand all this, and most of all, understand with your whole being, then you can hope for a fame that will blind us with its real light, and which will gladden me beyond words! I have so little hope left of passing on to anyone the whole of this psychology, which is essential for any honest performing musician…

I embrace you. My greetings to your dear husband.

Olenina-d'Alheim.

(Draft of letter of 1946(?) to T. Slonim,
UAA, Accession No. 89–200–2.)

Doda Conrad in 1937.

Olenina's thoughts today sound the same—or perhaps they have even greater relevance than they did in her time. How often nowadays one hears musical performers with big names for whom the composer and his music are a mere tool, or a pretext for the exhibition of their own talent. Olenina was always opposed to this. How many "artistically honest" singers—to use her own phrase—she could have trained if her life had turned out differently.

Olenina considered it her duty to assist young singers. Whenever she had got to know someone she regarded as a talented singer specialising in the performance of chamber music and oratorio, her immediate impulse was to send a letter recommending the young artiste to a reputable and trusted musician. One such letter went to Nadia Boulanger.

Olenina-d'Alheim:

Dear Nadia Boulanger,

I was told that you have returned to Paris. I would be glad to see you, but life is becoming increasingly complicated, and you, like myself, must be burdened with all manner of business quite unconnected with music.

I am writing to you about what I would have liked to tell you personally. The season of concerts of religious music is approaching (oratorios, masses, cantatas, etc.) and I know one singer, the possessor of a lovely contralto voice and a superb musician too, who specialises in the performance of works of this sort.

I utterly fail to understand why they continue as before to invite opera singers to take part in concerts [of this sort]. No matter how talented they are, they are not well acquainted with compositions written for concert performance.

The singer I am writing about is called Renée Fleuret. She is from Versailles (her address is: 33 rue Jean La Fontaine, Versailles, tel. 42–03). I am quite convinced that her participation in concerts would be extremely beneficial. Her repertoire is immense. She knows the works of Bach, Handel and other composers, both classical and contemporary. […]

Give Renée Fleuret a call. She will be happy to sing under your direction. She genuinely deserves to be supported, since she has a genuine talent and love for art. She loves art with the same love as we do, you and I.

As soon as the spring sets in, I will call and see you.

Amicably yours,

M. Olenina-d'Alheim.

(BN, Département de la musique, Nouveaux fonds,
Lettres, autographes, N.L.A. 50, no. 171.)

A Life of Poverty

For many years Olenina experienced material hardship. She never complained about these deprivations, which reduced her to an almost beggarly state. Not a single diary entry, not a single note in her reminiscences touches the subject. Yet it is hard to imagine how she actually managed to live from the early 1930s onwards. Her pride did not allow Olenina to ask for help, and her difficult and intolerant character kept those at a distance who were willing to assist. Doda Conrad recalled this period and talked of the years when Olenina "disappeared...in complete poverty." I asked him whether he remembered meeting her during this period

Doda Conrad:
Nobody saw her. And I found her at the funeral of Claude Delvincourt in 1954 at St. Augustin. I saw someone whom I recognised immediately—she was cross-eyed, completely cross-eyed—she looked...even old, she looked like a baby—round-faced. There are some Russian women [who are] old and look all round, like that. And I said "Marie! Que vous faites ici?" And she said, "Moi je vends *L'Humanité.*" She was [...] selling the communist [newspaper] *L'Humanité.* She became a communist. Outside in the cold, in the rain she was sitting there...

And my mother said, "We should invite her." So she [would come] every Wednesday for lunch. She came, but one had to give her the money for the subway. And eventually, as d'Alheim had been a French writer, I had a lot of [...] connections. I asked the [...] Académie des Beaux Arts if one could not give her a room and board at, as it was called, the Fondation Galignani. I put her in there. And even from there she had no money, she got a room and [transported] her papers and whatever belongings she had. That was in Neuilly, very decent, and I was there to settle her in there. She found it horrible. [...] Eventually she couldn't stand being in Galignani, she said she felt as if she were in jail.

At the end my mother couldn't stand her because she was, you know, first of all, very aggressive against my mother (my mother was very brilliant and loved her) [...] because my mother succeeded and I succeeded and she didn't. And we were, if you want, well to do, and she was humiliated because I, a young man, was taking care of her. She told my mother and me that she for twenty years never was able to buy a pair of stockings or a suit, she would be dressed by the poor people's stock at the mairie (city hall). They have charity things where people would give old clothes. And she wore only [clothes] of people she didn't know.

There were still at the beginning people like Mme Menard d'Orian and Mme Sauterot, rich ladies, who would help her a little. [...] Dagne Björnson Sauterot, the daughter of the Norwegian statesman and writer, was her admirer.

And she would come always on Wednesdays for lunch. [...] Those luncheons were amazing because in the conversation Marie d'Alheim was extremely proud and she never would think a minute that one might have pity of her or something of that kind. [...] Finally my mother could not stand her. She would come every Wednesday, so my mother would go out and I would have lunch with her alone, tête-à-tête. I had a great deal of admiration for her and respect for her, but she was a kind of a lost cause. One couldn't do something for her because she [would say] "I'm not going to... I don't do this... I will not... I don't sing this sort of music..." And so forth, criticising everything. [...] She belonged precisely to a certain circle which was my own or what I wanted for my ideals. We were always agreeing [with] each other. And so for instance when I am telling you about the whole idea of small halls it goes definitely in full agreement with her. (DC, 1–5.)

Olenina's diaries never mentioned the material hardships that in one way or another beset her throughout her life. The war years were especially difficult of course, and the postwar period was even worse. Sometimes help appeared unexpectedly. Among her surviving papers is a letter from Andrei Sedykh, the editor of the New York Russian language newspaper *Novoe russkoe slovo*.

Andrei Sedykh:
Dear Madam,
    My friend Michel Pobers informed me of you address, and on behalf of our paper I immediately sent you a parcel of provisions; I hope next month to send you another. At the same time I took the liberty of passing your address to the Society of Russian Artists in Hollywood, which helps artists in Paris by sending parcels.

Please accept, Madam, my sincere respects.

A. Sedykh.

(Letter of 22 December 1945, on letterhead paper of
Novoe russkoe slovo, GMMC, fond 256, no. 2139.)

Olenina ended up in such dire straits that she was reduced to selling off her dearest possession—the music of Mussorgsky. Her letter to Claire Croiza sounded like a tragic call for help:

Olenina-d'Alheim:
Dear friend,

Forgive me about the score of *Boris*: I was going to come and see you on Saturday, but I met a person who offered me more than a hundred francs. Because of the inescapable poverty in which I have lived for such a long time, alas, I have had to telephone you to tell you of this change and to apologise. So there we are.

You gave me some hope that perhaps I might receive an active membership card in our group. It would be splendid if with the help of this card I could be assisted with the cause that you are furthering, and which is undoubtedly of benefit to the young generation.

Having sacrificed so much in my life in the service of the Masters, I am a perfectly suitable person to show young performers the right path to follow. Can I count on your support which will help me emerge from the stagnation that is killing me? You know that I have absolutely nothing, and I cannot even feed [?] myself.

But do I really have to end my days in a corner, forgotten and needed by no one? It is for you to decide: you can do this.

I embrace you,

M. Olenina.

(BN.)

Olenina had extremely bad sight, close to blindness, but she was so poor that could not even order herself some glasses. A few days before leaving Paris for Moscow in 1959, she visited Maria Freund for probably the last time. On arriving home, she wrote to her faithful friend what she had discovered in a purse.

Olenina-d'Alheim:
My dear Maria!

Just imagine, I opened your purse only this morning when I was packing various small items into the case I am taking to Moscow.

How very kind of you! The more so when your own affairs are not so brilliant. Thank you, my friend. Now I can order some glasses for myself without waiting for money from the charity bureau which has still sent nothing so far!

But meanwhile I have to get ready to leave and also go to [illegible]. This means definitely that I shall not be able to drop in to kiss you goodbye. [...] If I manage to solve the problem of glasses inside eight days (the time needed to make the lenses), I will call in to see you.

I embrace you and thank you a thousand times.

M. Olenina.

(Letter of 1959 (n.d.), BN.)

"Dream and Recollections"

Yet, despite material problems, Olenina never ceased her creative activities in some form or other. In the late 1940s her friend Suvchinsky persuaded her to start writing her memoirs, and in 1948 she began work on the fairly voluminous manuscript she later entitled "Dream and Recollections." Suvchinsky took a lively interest in her progress on this work, and Olenina read him several extracts from her manuscript. In January of 1948 she also wrote to him on the subject.

Olenina-d'Alheim:
Esteemed Pyotr Petrovich,

I have heard that my manuscript "Trebnik"* will be returned to me in February, since the people who are bringing it have been held up in Brussels for several days. Up to now I was unable to think freely about my "Recollections" because of an immense amount of ghastly fuss and nonsense of every sort. Now everything seems to be settling down, but it would be better if we did not see one another till next week. Also, do not forget that I am never at home on Mondays and Fridays. So, come what may, I look forward to seeing you soon.

Your Olenina-d'Alheim.

(BN, Letter of 27 January 1948, BN.)

[* Evidently this refers to the manuscript of "Three Tales: Law, Word and Deed," on a Biblical theme, which Olenina tried to publish in Belgium. See mention of "fairy tales" in correspondence with Tanya Slonim, above p. 228–29.]

Only in 1956 was work on the first part of Olenina's reminiscences completed. At 87, she seemed immune to the normal penalties of old age and was full of energy which, apart from memoir writing, extended to planning a series of Mussorgsky evenings to celebrate the 75th anniversary of his death.

Olenina-d'Alheim:
Dear Pyotr Petrovich,

I called you on the telephone to enquire about your health, since there was a scaring report that "apparently you have died." I refused to believe this, but having heard from Vladimir Mikhailovich that you had been knocked over by some fool (there are so many of them these days), I called you up and heard that you were happily on holiday and that you will be returning at the end of the month. I am therefore writing to you with the idea that next week my letter will be awaiting you at home.

As you can see, I have again changed my place of residence. I have managed to fix myself up in the Galignani *maison de retraite* [old people's retirement home]. Otherwise it became very difficult for me climbing up to the sixth floor about five times a day. Here I can think and read and write quite calmly.

I have finished my reminiscences, and have sent the Russian text to Ehrenburg[25] in Moscow. If he finds that they deserve publication, I shall be happy. He is the chairman of the Society of Lovers of French Literature. But just as it was with Pyotr d'Alheim, so the same is happening to me: although I am a French author, at the same time I am Russian and for that reason I find myself sitting between two stools—which is very uncomfortable.

The Fr[ench] text is finished, but I have interrupted the typing because I need my money for the projected *festival of the return from the dead of Modest Mussorgsky*, who is now alive for many years to come. You probably know that recently (in spring) there was a *commémoration de 75 ans depuis la mort* [a celebration of the 75th anniversary of his death], and it was, so to speak, official. And now I feel bitter that, having taken part in his resurrection, I have no way of celebrating this event which is such a joyful one for me.

I have therefore decided to organise an evening (in late November) as a sort of repetition of Pyotr d'Alheim's first *conférences* on the life and work of Mussorgsky in 1896. I shall also recall and mention those who took part and first worked at his resurrection, three Frenchmen, a Hungarian and a Russian woman who has not yet shuffled off this mortal coil. I shall appear as "*conférent*" and some young (contemporary) admirers of the great Russian genius will perform a large programme.

That is why I have held up the typing of my "Recollections" and am keeping the 40,000 fr[ancs] that I have under lock and key. This sum, unfortunately, will not be enough, since to organise the conc[ert] they are asking 70,000 for one concert! Whatever their genius, this can be hardly afforded by the poor artists. And so I am having to apply for public assistance, i.e., friends and acquaintances, for them to subscribe or whatever else they wish, to rustle up the necessary sum for this festival, and let me have it in the form of a loan, i.e., it would be returned to them after the concert which will be by invitation, with "participation aux frais" at 200 fr. par example. These invitations together with a programme and small message of appeal from Ol[enina]-d'Alh[eim] to her old audience, will be distributed as widely as possible. I think this plan of mine might be a success. What do you think?

My "Recollections" have turned out rather unlike usual writings of this sort, and they are a form of self-psychoanalysis (what a long and awkward word!). Only the first part has been written, the second will be more detailed and will touch mainly on the activities of the House of Song in Moscow.

I am rounding off this already long letter, and probably you are already tired of reading it. I am glad that you are restored to health, and I hope you have had a good holiday away from the stinking Paris air. [...]

M. d'Alheim.

(Letter of 1956 (?) to P.P. Suvchinsky,
at 89 Boulevard Bineau, Neuilly, BN.)

We know that Olenina was unsuccessful in her attempt to print the manuscript of her recollections, which are full of interesting information and conclude with the first *conférences* in Paris and Brussels. Her failure was perhaps due to the belletristic form of the work. As its title suggests, "Dream and Recollections" was written in the form of a description of a dream vision. Olenina falls asleep and in her dream imagines herself arriving in Russia. There, on board a steamer, quite by chance she meets a fellow passenger who remembers her performances in Moscow before the Revolution, and the singer then recounts to him various episodes from her life. The chaotic exposition of material, which typifies the whole manuscript, caused problems in understanding the chronology. This was a major fault if one bears in mind that these were memoirs, purporting to give a coherent consecutive account of events. After completing the Russian version of her recollections in 1954, Olenina offered them without success to various publishers. In her search for an interested publishing house, she started corresponding with the well-known Russian born American musicologist Nicolas Slonimsky,[26] who at that time was working on the second volume of his dictionary of musical personalities and wanted to include a whole series of figures unmentioned in Soviet publications. Among them was Olenina-d'Alheim.

Nicolas Slonimsky:
Esteemed Maria Alexeyevna,
    Many thanks for your letter. Your name is of course legendary —I have only just received the first collection of articles by Cui, which includes his review of your concert in December 1901! In his volume on Mussorgsky (1930) Calvocoressi talks about the importance of your recitals in Paris in the 1890s. So you can easily imagine how pleasant it was for me to receive concrete news of you!

I greatly appreciate your information about your brother.

Is there any chance of obtaining his compositions? This would be very valuable for my work.

I will be most grateful to you, too, if you could send me a separate biography of Pierre d'Alheim. His name should be included in the musical dictionary. Your personal biography I should receive shortly from Fyodor Antonovich Erlanger. My dictionary (a new edition of "Baker's Biographical Dictionary of Musicians") is still in the process of preparation, so that there is still time for me to include new materials. Do you have any information on the "small" composers of Belyaev's circle? When and where did Antonov, Nikolai Shcherbachev (Stasov's friend), Andrei Shcherbachev and Kazachenko end their days? Did you know Ilyinsky? I believe he died in 1919.

Once again, sincere thanks for your letter and your assistance with my work. With sincere greetings,

N. Slonimsky.

(Letter of 14 February 1954, GMMC, fond 256, no. 1886.)

Nicolas Slonimsky:

Dear Maria Alexeyevna,

Thank you for your letter and your help with my work. I hope that you will soon receive further information from Moscow about your brother's compositions.

I have made enquiries about the state of affairs in the Chekhov Publishing House. From my information, the rule about manuscripts being presented in typewritten form is not absolute. I believe that they would be glad to accept your manuscript written by hand—it is clear to any educated person that your memoirs have historical value. But is it not a risk to send your only copy by post?

Of course I am ready to assist the printing of your memoirs in any way, but it seems to me that the proposal to Chekhov publishers should come from you personally. Why don't you talk to Fyodor Antonovich d'Erlanger about copying the manuscript? He has a Russian typewriter, and maybe he knows someone who would undertake to copy-type your manuscript for an agreed sum.

I wish you every success with your manuscript. I am sure that

Alexandrova will answer your letter and give you exact directions regarding the manuscript. But it seems to me that for the time being I should not write to Alexandrova—indeed, it would be somehow awkward to explain to her who Olenina-d'Alheim is—after all, I repeat, your name is a legendary one.

   With sincere greetings,

N. Slonimsky.

(Letter of 6 April 1954, GMMC, fond 256, no. 1887.)

   In the 1960s, at the time of my association with Maria Olenina, she was still hoping to find a publisher for her "Dream and Recollections" and she asked for my help. At that time she gave me part of her archive, including a copy of her "Dream," which served as one of the stimuli for writing the present book. Many pages from her memoir manuscript are in fact reproduced on these pages.

   When Suvchinsky heard of Olenina's plans for a 75th anniversary celebration of Mussorgsky's death, he suggested the idea for a broadcast concert to mark the event. The two letters below demonstrate Olenina's attempts to follow this up—her last attempts in Paris, probably, to do something for the cause for which she had lived—the promotion of Mussorgsky's music.

Olenina-d'Alheim:

Dear Pyotr Petrovich,

   Thank you for your kind letter and for your good advice. It is very sensible, and any practically minded artist would definitely follow it up. But you offer me it, forgetting that I have never been practical by nature, and as you may recall my saying, I am a *yurodivaya* ["holy fool"], and that is indeed the case: I always do everything in my own way, and not like other people.

   I wouldn't even dream of a large hall, and I cannot stand them, just as I cannot bear the radio, and I cannot even imagine myself saying anything coherent in front of a micro[phone]! Would there suddenly be peace on earth because of a word from me on the radio? If that were the case, I would not only not refuse, but would even shout over the radio so that as many people as possible could hear me.

The plan I have for my *last* service to Mussorgsky totally excludes any idea of profit and money: they were always my enemies and they still are! No. If I wished for anything, then it would be to live again amongst those works that I have performed so many times in the course of my difficult career. I would like to rejoice and celebrate the revival of Mussorgsky in the year 1896, in which I played such a devoted part.

As for the microphone and radio, I remember that once in Moscow they tried to make a recording of a peasant collective from Ryazan. But nothing came of it. The participants (it was a women's chorus) really failed to understand how it was possible to sing in front of a machine. So the organisers gave up the idea of any preliminary recording, and the women sang straight from the stage.

But even if I refuse to appear on radio, the young singers who will take part in our small concert could repeat it splendidly on the radio. [...]

M. d'Alheim.

(Letter of 1956 (?), BN.)

Soon afterwards Olenina wrote to Suvchinsky again about his plans for a radio broadcast.

Olenina-d'Alheim:
Dear Pyotr Petrovich,

I have not been able to walk for three days: I hurt my knee— Vladimir Mikhailovich told me via one of the pensioners in the house that he will come himself, and I am waiting for him.

I wanted to tell you, however, that regarding my plans to celebrate the renaissance of Mussorgsky, you are right and I was wrong. You advise me to do this on radio, but I have an instinctive fear of all these machines, and I therefore replied that I could not appear in front of a microphone. Apart from which, I had too strong a wish to relive those splendid experiences I once had on the platform, and to find myself again among the works of Mussorgsky that were my [illegible] friends.

But in fact it is not a case of my pleasure, but of what would be most beneficial to Mussorgsky himself, since the campaign for his original works still goes on, as you know. I must take this up again.

You advise me to turn to Schaeffner[27] and Schloezer.[28] I am
quite prepared to do that, but I cannot help wondering why these
two have long ago forgotten the way to poor old Olenina, who
should have given up all this several decades ago. Should they
really have abandoned me because I could no longer sing and was
inactive? I have just heard that Schwab, who was also disloyal to me,
has died. And ultimately, is there any agreement on what now ought
to be done to defend Mussorgsky against all these unforgivable
encroachments by his blind friend Rimsky-Korsakov? After all they
continue producing *Boris Godunov* all around the world in an
orchestration that was rejected by Balakirev and Madame Molas
(the sister-in-law of Rimsky-Korsakov with whom I studied before
coming to Paris in 1890). Perhaps Schloezer and Schaeffner are on
the side of Rimsky-Korsakov, who never realised the vileness of his
behaviour, and that lowdown editor who prompted him to distort
Mussorgsky's creation?

Write and tell me what all this means. Anyway, I am waiting for
Vladimir Mikhailovich, and when he comes we'll have a talk. I am
afraid to ask you to join him, as you did in 1948, in persuading me
to write my memoirs, since I live quite far away, although it is not
all that distant...

May I express to you my profound sympathy and gratitude for
awakening me as you did in 1948, in connection with the whole of
my past. I had really gone to sleep.

Your M. Olenina-d'Alheim.

(Letter of 10 September 1956, BN.)

Enrolment in the Communist Party

On the 6 August 1945, following Hiroshima, Olenina joined the French
Communist Party. Only the communists, she believed, could save the
world from the atom bomb. For her joining the Party was not at all a
random act. She herself points out two reasons for taking this step:
the first was currently relevant—because of the American atom bomb
—while the second was a matter of principle: "I agreed with the
Bolsheviks while I was still in Moscow." Olenina in fact held radical

political views all her life, and joining the Party was the natural culmination of this at a time when her "political struggle" had eclipsed
almost all her other interests in life.

Olenina's main motive—her *idée fixe*—was a hatred of money,
which she viewed as the root of all evil in this world. Money corrupted
art, commerce was always unclean, the trader was always a con-
temptible human being, and profit defiled everything it came in contact
with (one recalls her correspondence with Balakirev on this topic).
Olenina herself was above money, her art could not be bought, better
proud poverty than the defilement of art by the vicious power of gold.
Olenina's conversations, letters and reminiscences were full of these and
similar slogans and catch-phrases. They logically brought her to the
point where she joined the Communist Party, and they also played a
destructive role in her own artistic career. Concert tours allegedly filled
the pockets of the impressarios who organised and made profit by
them—so away with concert tours! Thus, instead of giving recitals all
over Europe, Olenina only once appeared in England, and gradually her
concerts became rarer and rarer. She always had a mass of plans that
required material support, but she was utterly impractical—and was
proud of this—and not one of her major projects came to fruition. In
the long run, her renunciation of concerts based on commercial success
(the "fat profit" as she called it) and her general "campaign" against the
commercialisation of art slowly killed that very art whose interests she
thought she was defending. Her life on the concert platform turned out
much shorter than it might have been, had she not so resolutely followed the message of her own sermons. There were times in her old age
when she seemed to realise this, and she admitted her creative life could
have lasted longer, and that she was to blame for this failure.

The Break With Cortot

Of interest in this respect is the sad episode of Olenina's break with
Alfred Cortot, the friend who did so much for her during difficult
times. When I met both Doda Conrad and Madeleine Milhaud and
asked them about the reason for this, I got the same answer: Olenina

broke with Cortot in protest against his collaboration with the Nazi occupying force during the Second World War.[29] As Conrad recalled, "She hated him [...] because he was a collaborator with the Germans [...] and he was a Secretary of Fine Arts in the government of Pétain." (DC, 4.) However, if one reads Olenina's own letters, it becomes clear that she broke with Cortot far earlier, evidently in the late 1920s, and apparently for some quite different reason.

Judging by letters that have survived from Olenina to Cortot, their quarrel centred on certain accusations that she leveled against him. One concludes that she condemned him for having, as it were, sold out as an artist to the "demon of gold," exploiting his activities for commercial success. Seemingly she sent him a sharply worded letter and there was some animated debate between the two of them on the subject.

It is impossible to establish the exact chronology of Olenina's letters; they are undated and marked simply with the addresses of various apartments where she lived at different times. It is clear that their conflict lasted quite a long time. However, it is important to try and establish the time-frame for their quarrel as accurately as possible, since it contradicts the verbal evidence of Doda Conrad and Madame Milhaud.

It would seem that the conflict occurred in 1927, when Cortot sent his last-known letter to Olenina. Even without knowing the exact subject alluded to, any reader can tell that Cortot is bidding his addressee a final farewell.

Alfred Cortot:
Dear Marie,

Do not complain that I am unable to give you the advice that you did the honour of asking me for.

I can act in no other way, for I very much wish to preserve in my memory a recollection of my lasting admiration for you.

Yours respectfully,

A. Cortot.

(Letter of 24 June 1927, GMMC, fond 256, no. 1179)

There is mention of some conflict with her "one-time friend" Cortot in Olenina's letter to Nadia Boulanger of some twelve years later.

Olenina-d'Alheim:
Dear Mademoiselle,

[…] I thank you with all my heart for your efforts to help me.

As for approaching Mr. Cortot however… No, on no account. I would sooner prefer to die of hunger or sweep the streets in order to avoid dying of hunger than turn to this one-time friend who has done everything to make me realise his true character. After all, I have not yet sunk to an extreme of despair, and I am still holding up.

With great affection,

Yours, Marie Olenine-d'Alheim.

(Letter of 1939–40 to Nadia Boulanger,
BN, Département de la Musique, Nouveaux fonds. Lettres, autographes, N.L.A. 50, 170.)

The four following letters from Olenina to Cortot after 1927 reveal the tragic nature of the conflict with her former friend. The letters are published by kind permission of the Bibliothèque Musicale Gustav Mahler in Paris, where the archive of Cortot is kept.

Olenina-d'Alheim:

36, rue St. Sulpice, 6e

My dear Cortot,

I need to discuss with you a plan of action outlined by Pierre, who entrusted you and myself with its realisation.

We are not talking about our mutual conflicts—it would be better to forget that as past history. I want to revive an even more distant past by working in the way Pierre would have wished on what he did not manage to complete in his lifetime. I wanted to write you more than a month ago, but you were not there. I have sent my plan to Mr. L. See, but he forwarded it on to Mr. Huysman whom I have just seen. He found the plan an excellent one, but thinks he has not the necessary money for its immediate realisation. As for myself, I have studied the means of immediately starting work. Mr. Huysman told me that you talked with him about me, and of course the good that you always do. Thank you, and please let me know when I can see you to discuss the project and examine it with you.

Please be assured that my feelings towards you are just as friendly as before.

Marie d'Alheim.

(BMGM.)

This undated letter, evidently the first of four, was sent soon after 1927. Its tone is businesslike and any conflict is only mentioned indirectly. Olenina seems to emphasise that their disagreement should not affect their present common cause. Seemingly Cortot did not reply. A few years later Olenina wrote to him again, evidently attempting to re-establish their relations. The letter aimed at a reconciliation and recalled their earlier friendship.

Olenina-d'Alheim:

12 rue du Caporal Peugeat, XVII

My dear Cortot, friend of better days,

Does it not seem to you that it is time to end our enmity? So far as I am concerned, I have a very strong desire to see you again before I return permanently to my first homeland. It would be sad for me to leave not having seen all the people I love here. Now, thanks to the hazards of fate, I am going to get a chance to sing my "swansong," i.e., give four recitals with the valuable participation of Jean Duhème.

Most likely, I shall now have to reconcile myself to silence: doubtless, old age will soon begin knocking at my door. For sixteen years already I have been holding on to this bitter virtue, since apart from a handful of passing joys, I have had only suffering and sorrow in my life. Come, my dear friends: you will give me enormous pleasure.

At the first recital I shall perform Schubert's *Winterreise*. I constantly recall that evening when you and I performed this work.

As soon as my programme is ready, I will send you it.

With respect and affection,

Marie d'Alheim.

P.S. Once these concerts have been given, it only remains for me to finish reviewing Pierre's manuscripts, put them in order and classify his works. (Letter (n.d.) to Alfred Cortot, BMGM.)

Facsimile of the last letter written by Maria Olenina-d'Alheim to Alfred Cortot.

What departure was it that Olenina had in mind? It is clear that this letter could not have been written in 1959, before her departure for Moscow—at that time the ninety-year-old singer was of course in no condition to give concerts. The departure for her homeland was evidently one of her *plans* to return made in the 1930s. Her mention of "sixteen years" of suffering and sorrow also suggests the later 1930s, counting from the date of her husband's death in 1922; indeed the year 1938 was a time when Olenina was striving with all her might to return to Russia.

All Olenina's attempts at reconciliation with Cortot were in vain. However, the next letters convey a clearer picture of what actually happened between them, and we read of some accusatory letter sent to Cortot and of Olenina's later assessment of this "cruel" letter that led to the break in their relations.

Olenina-d'Alheim:
Dear friend,

Thank you for your generous wish to assist my search for paper, which I urgently need for the copies of Pierre's works. I read your letter with a lump in the throat, since I knew of your strong and friendly feelings towards Pierre, but I hoped and even thought that you might have reserved a small share of these feelings for myself as well.

Your long sense of offence at that letter, which I admit was a cruel one, has shown me my mistake and, believe me, this has caused me much pain. Doubtless, my own condition at the time which was more than terrible did not occur to you. Only [the memory of] Pierre has forced me to agree to survive him and attempt to complete the projects he conceived for those musicians to whom he sacrificed so much of his time.

Facsimile
of the last letter
written by Maria
Olenina-d'Alheim
to Alfred Cortot
(continued).

I learned my excessively direct manner of expression from
him, since he too was never a mild man, but rather severe both
with me and with you, and with everyone. He never condescended
to anyone, and said everything that he thought with absolute
sincerity whenever anything important was being discussed. For
that reason I am now trying to do everything possible and I thank
you for your help. I would be happy if you would help me in the
realisation of Pierre's projects. First of all I shall try to publish
a brochure for young people. It will contain Pierre's works, and
I hope that it will be of immediate benefit.

Goodbye, my friend, and I beg you to bear me due respect—
for the sake of our friendship which I shall value all the more.

Marie d'Alheim.

[P.S.] I heard of the death of your sister, and I very much wanted to express my condolences to you, but as you did not answer the letter that I wrote to you in summer, I decided that you do not wish to renew our relations even at a distance. That is why I decided not to impose myself on you. (Letter (n.d.) to Alfred Cortot, BMGM.)

The following letter was Olenina's last letter to Cortot and was probably written several years later than the three earlier ones. It seems to have been written in 1947, in the year of the death of Cortot's first wife Clo [Clothilde Cortot-Bréal].[30] The letter seems to draw up a balance-sheet of the whole of Olenina's life. Shortly before it was sent she and Cortot met personally, and possibly there was at least a formal reconciliation. But this evidently brought Olenina little repose and she continued to set down on paper her thoughts on the relationship between art and the world of business. In this she seemingly followed

Cortot and used the Biblical phrase about giving unto God that which is God's and unto Caesar that which is Caesar's; in this case "God" is art, and Caesar is the world of finance. Is this letter an admission of the bankruptcy of the ideology that Olenina followed all her life? One might at first imagine so, yet a few lines later the singer contradicts herself and maintains that if she could start over again, she would change nothing in her life.

Olenina-d'Alheim:

My dear Cortot,

I was very glad to see you and to convince myself that the memory of our former friendship has not totally disappeared from your heart. It would be a bitter thing for me to leave this world without being reconciled with all who were and who remain dear to me. It was all the more pleasant for me to honour you along with all you admirers (myself among their number) since I have come to the conclusion that you were right when you told me not to forget Caesar while still serving God. Because of my excessive pride I obstinately ignored Caesar, for which I have been cruelly punished, having been forced to halt in the very midst of my work and when my strength was at its height. And that was a heavy blow for me! Meanwhile, you continued boldly to serve art and its masters.

Now I have come to terms with everything and have no regrets; I am not going to act on my own again and am engaged only in classifying Pierre's posthumous works, to whose counsels I want to remain true to the end. If it were possible to start all over again, I think I would have changed nothing, but I would hope for better luck and success.

You and I have not seen one another for twenty years already. How time flies! It seems as if all this were yesterday—what a feeble sense I have of time, which seems not to exist for me!

I shake you by the hand most warmly and pay tribute to Clothilde's kindly memory.

With feelings only of friendship,

Marie Olenina-d'Alheim.

(BMGM.)

Our own dating of this letter to 1947 is confirmed by its text which refers to a lapse of twenty years since Cortot and Olenina last met. Yet even twenty years later, and despite her bitter admission of personal defeat, Olenina still clung to her ideological radicalism. This had started out with the ideas of the New Russian Music school and with a compassion with simple humanity; later it developed into a personal global campaign and continued to rule her mind to the end of her days. Joining the Communist Party was simply a logical culmination of this, yet it was also a niche and refuge that justified everything she herself had failed to do.

Return to Russia

Olenina clung firmly to the same views even after her return to the Soviet Union, although she quickly realised there was a deep gulf between the realities of Soviet life and her own ideals. Paradoxical though it seems, the factor which most of all assisted her return to the land of her birth was not a recognition of her contribution to Russian culture, but the fact of her joining the Communist Party. Her letter to Goldenweiser in the 1960s rehearsed the whole question again.

> Olenina-d'Alheim:
> [...] You know, I had long been striving to return to my country and continue my activity in Moscow, but all our requests to the Commissar of the Arts in 1926 were answered negatively. I say "our request[s]" because, if you remember, before my departure a conference was arranged in the Conservatoire of members of the House of Song, at which some of the professors and the director [of the Conservatoire] Igumnov were present. [...] Every time I asked for permission to return, I was turned down. I think that, as they told me in 1918, in my "file" there was a lot of slander, and supposedly in Lenin's circle they considered me to be a monarchist, and a ramping and raging one at that. Damn it all! And it turns out that comrades were guided by this until I last year had the idea

of sending them my Party card, and they only then saw absolutely everything in my "file" was a malicious fabrication. [...] (Letter (n.d.) of the 1960s to A.B. Goldenweiser, GMMC, fond 256, no. 474, 1.)

Olenina's concern and involvement in current events were a regular feature of her life. This even delayed her actual return to Russia, which might have taken place earlier but for the political situation in France.

Olenina-d'Alheim:

I returned [to the USSR] quite by chance—I saw in *Ogonyok*[31] a photograph of Elena Stasova[32] and immediately wrote about this to the editors of the magazine, but I got no answer. I forget through which institution it was in Moscow [...] No, I am wrong, I saw the photo in 1957, and I simply sent my letter to the Communist Party Congress, but it turned out she was in a sanatorium.

And then, in 1958 on the 13 May, de Gaulle was elected President of the French Republic, and there I was ready to leave for Moscow. I had 100 thousand francs, given to me by Angèle Sonet for the journey to Moscow; she knew I was anxious to get there, we were both communists. And then when de Gaulle was made President, and with rights which no presidents had before, I decided as a communist to stay so as to buy our paper *Humanité* and distribute it everywhere—in September the elections were due to take place... That is why I stayed on in Paris, in order to campaign for the candidates of our Party... (BNB, 173–74.)

After 1956 and the revelations about Stalin's "personality cult," which ushered in a "thaw" in the Soviet Union, there was new hope that Olenina might now manage to return to Moscow. Nevertheless, in order even to travel there on a visit, an entry visa was needed. But Olenina wanted to return to Moscow for good, and so began a new round of visits to the Soviet Embassy. But time was not on her side. She was approaching her ninetieth birthday. In Moscow lived her cousin Tatyana Alexeyevna Turgeneva, with whom she had been in regular correspondence in the postwar years; she regarded Tanya Turgeneva as her closest and dearest friend.

Olenina-d'Alheim was also very anxious that her arrival in Moscow be preceded by publication of her reminiscences. In her regular letters to Vladimir and Yulia Stepun, she more than once asked about their publication and conducted negotiations to this end. However, her memoirs were printed neither before her return to Russia, nor after it.

By spring of 1958, Olenina's visa was ready, and that autumn she was due once again to set foot on her native soil. However, as we know, her departure was delayed. She actually arrived in Moscow in early 1959, shortly before her ninetieth birthday—thirty years after she first expressed a desire to return, and thirty years after the time when she might reasonably have worked there. In effect, Olenina had returned to her country in order to die.

VII

THE LAST DECADE

Ruddia — 1959-1970

Moscow: The Last Decade

y the time of her return to Moscow, it seemed that Maria Olenina's years—or indeed days—were numbered. After all, what was the life expectancy of someone already turned ninety? But she continued to surprise everyone with her health and vigour. It was much too early to think of burying her. Thirty years before, she was considered elderly and approaching the end of her life. Indeed, one of her own explanations for being refused a permit to return to Russia was her advanced age—after all, by the end of the 1920s she had turned sixty. But Olenina was well practised in ignoring or overcoming conventional measures of time. On returning to Russia, the ninety-year-old astonished those around her by her smartness and alertness; she wore high-heeled shoes and had no use for a dressing-gowned existence. All this was later recalled by Natalya Solovyova:[1]

Natalya Solovyova:
Maria Alexeyevna's life in France had taught her always to be in form, although she was simply Russian and also liked telling people she was the illegitimate daughter of a coachman. When she arrived,

she drank a shot of vodka; she ate meat all her life; she showed no concern for her health, and she smoked. [Once] I was travelling out by train with her [to our dacha]. She lit up in the railcar, and they cursed and swore at her, but she reacted quite good-naturedly. There was a lot of the child about her right to the very end. She was very democratic—a democratic aristocrat. (Natalya Sergeyevna Solovyova, interview recorded in 1991; UAA, Accession No. 89–200.)

Olenina-d'Alheim always lived in a manner suggesting she had a great deal of time ahead of her. She was active and full of plans, and although she had not sung for a long time, in a certain sense she never ceased being what she had been all her life—a performer. During her remaining years (she lived to be over a hundred) she met with musicians, journalists, and figures from the world of art, she maintained a large correspondence, gave master classes, and lectured to students. In fact she lived in a manner that kept alive the main cause and business of her life, which was to seek out like-minded folk who shared her opinions and to whom she could pass on her ideas. And although age took its toll, Olenina never gave in. At the age of ninety, she seemed to be starting life all over again.

As Olga Solovyova[2] recounts, "on returning to Moscow, Maria Alexeyevna thought she would land among the circle of people that had been there in Istomino, or before her departure." In reality, everything turned out quite different. None of her old friends were alive, and nothing remained of her former life. Some connections still survived with people of the younger generation, but even they were getting on in years. These included the Stepuns, who had always been warmly disposed to her. Olenina had played a special role in Vladimir Stepun's life.

Vladimir Stepun:
Dear Aunt Marusya,
   Half a century ago, when I used to turn the music pages for your accompanists as a youth, you gave me your photograph with an inscription: "To V. Stepun—in the firm conviction that he will never forget me." And you were right—I never did forget, despite our long years of separation. And when I lay down in the evening

on my hard bed in solitary confinement in the Butyrka prison in 1938, I recall how I used to remember your recitals, and in my imagination I summoned up your image and would fall asleep with a sense of gratitude to you for all that you gave to us young people through your art. Both Yulia and I are full of sincere love for you, respect and admiration. (V.A. Stepun, letter of 30 June 1964, to M.A. Olenina, GMMC, fond 256, no. 4370, 2.)

In fact behind Stepun's confession there was an ironic symbolic subtext of which Olenina herself could scarcely have been aware. As he languished in the Butyrka jail and recalled her artistry, Stepun was really a Soviet variant of Mussorgsky's suffering hero—one of the insulted and injured whose wretched fate was celebrated with such pathos in the song of this artist who now returned to the Soviet Union, as Solovyova recalled, all "ready to build communism."

Olenina's closest contact in Russia was her niece Tatyana Turgeneva.[3] By the time of her return, Tatyana was living with her husband Gury Ametirov in a tiny room of fifteen square meters in a communal apartment in the building above the Sandunovsky Public Baths. When the authorities began enquiries as to who could accommodate Olenina, Tatyana Turgeneva agreed and on this basis Olenina was offered a flat in Moscow. For the time being however she stayed in the Turgenevs' cramped quarters, although she continued hoping she would have a room of her own in the promised apartment. In some ways, though, she was now worse off than in the Galignani old people's home. But the days turned into weeks and months, and the promise of an apartment remained a promise.

Finally Olenina became infuriated and announced that she was returning to Paris, since she still retained her French citizenship. At this point the demanding "foreigner" was resettled in the Hotel Peking. However, seeing that nothing essentially was being done, and that she was living utterly alone without any means of subsistence, Olenina did in fact leave and flew back to France. In those years, however, despite their anti-capitalist and anti-Western propaganda, the Soviet government remained fairly sensitive to Western public opinion, especially where cultural and artistic figures were concerned. There were fears that the story of Olenina's arrival and rapid re-departure might attract negative publicity among the French intelligentsia and among other Russian émigré artists whom the Soviet authorities were trying hard to coax back to their homeland. The Ministry of Culture, headed by the infamous Furtseva,[4] therefore began doing everything to ensure their shrewish elderly singer returned to Russia.

Olenina-d'Alheim was therefore allocated a state pension of 120 roubles per month, and a three-roomed apartment was set aside for her with the family of Tatyana Turgeneva in a building on Leninsky Prospect above the "House of Porcelain" crockery shop. Nevertheless, the initial period after her second return was an arduous one. As expected, particularly in one so old, Olenina found it hard to adjust to new conditions. It was particularly hard to get accustomed to her loss of independence, although in Tatyana Turgenev and her husband Olenina effectively acquired a new family. At certain moments she kept claiming she wanted to return to Paris again, but those around her realised that these were nothing but words.

Olenina's arrival in Moscow was an event unnoticed by the general public, and ignored even in musical circles. Some short notices appeared in *Literaturnaya gazeta*, *Vechernyaya Moskva* and *Komsomol'skaya Pravda* announcing her return to Moscow and giving some very general information about the forgotten singer. It was only in 1960, however, that the first serious articles appeared in specialised musical journals such as *Sovetskaya muzyka* and *Muzyka'lnaya zhizn'*. The central press hardly reacted however, which was an indication of the official status planned for the returnee artist. And musical officialdom responded to these signals. In one of her letters, for instance, Olenina-d'Alheim wrote that after the death of Goldenweiser she was totally unable to establish contact with the new director of the Conservatoire, who simply had no time for her.

Nevertheless, the articles published in musical journals had some effect, and soon Olenina was receiving visits from musicians, composers and journalists. She also began corresponding with several people. Her mind during this final period of her life was occupied by two central ideas. The first of these concerned her artistic heirs and the fate of chamber singing in Russia. "It will be awful to die without fulfilling [...] this task," she wrote in her "Short Autobiography" (KRAVT 5). The other idea was concerned with Pyotr d'Alheim and his works, which remained unpublished in Russia. After his death she had constantly thought about his unfinished work as though it were the continuation of her own. "I think constantly about Pyotr," she recorded in her "Dream and Recollections" (SV 34), and she was haunted by the idea that the work of the "Russian Frenchman" should become known in Russia, the country to which he dedicated most of his life.

It was with this in mind that she had approached Ilya Ehrenburg while she was still in Paris in 1955. She asked him to assist in securing publication in the Soviet Union of a Russian translation of d'Alheim's book on François Villon. Ehrenburg examined the French edition and became interested in the idea.

> Ilya Ehrenburg:
> Dear Mme Olenina,
>
> I understand that you would like the book *The Passion of François Villon* to be published in the USSR. I have read the book, and I like it very much, and I would very much like it to be published in Russian.
>
> Since you already have a translation, I will be grateful if you can send it to me.
>
> I remember you very well and recall those French ditties that you sang in Moscow.
>
> Yours most respectfully,
>
> I. Ehrenburg.
>
> (Letter of 7 May 1955, GMMC, fond 256, no. 2098.)

Reading this supposedly friendly and promising letter, one winces however at the reference to "French ditties." What did he mean? Was this a lack of respect or understanding for Olenina's work, or was it simply ignorance? Olenina-d'Alheim gave Ehrenburg a copy of the Russian version of d'Alheim's book produced by an unknown translator. But this turned out to be a mistake—it was her only copy and its fate soon caused her grave apprehensions. Ehrenburg left Paris and for several years never wrote her a single line about the book. It was only after returning to Russia that Olenina again approached the literary overlord again, and even then she sought for a tactful pretext and then sent him greetings for the New Year of 1962. Ehrenburg's answer was one of courteous gratitude; the manuscript was mentioned only in a postscript however.

Ilya Ehrenburg:
Dear Maria Alexeyevna,
My sincere thanks for your New Year greetings. May I too wish you all the very best for 1962. May it also be a peaceful one!
I. Ehrenburg.
P. S. I feel very guilty about the manuscripts you once handed me. I have still not managed to locate them in my large archive. I will return them to you immediately I find them. (Letter of 15 January 1962, GMMC, fond 256, no. 4137.)

Typically, there was now no mention of publication once the manuscript was found, but only of returning it to Olenina. Another period of total silence followed; the manuscript had evidently failed to turn up. Olenina's next letter was also timed for a national festival, and she sent Ehrenburg greetings on the anniversary of the October Revolution and timidly asked the highly placed writer for his advice on publication. Less than a couple of years after his previous letter, Ehrenburg now made no mention at all of the manuscript, which was doubtless lost. Nor did he even remember the name of his correspondent.

Ilya Ehrenburg:
Dear Olenina-d'Alheim,*
I thank you for your letter and congratulations. I hope that you are in good health. It is very possible that Pyotr d'Alheim's book could interest our publishers, but I would advise you first of all to show them the book, and then think about a translation. Usually the publishers themselves appoint a translator. Perhaps you should approach the comrades who published the Villon collection.
Sincerest good wishes to you,
I. Ehrenburg.
* Please pardon my having forgotten your name and patronymic.
(Letter of 13 November 1963, GMMC, fond 256, no. 4138.)

Now there was not only no mention of the lost manuscript, but not even a statement of willingness to assist in order, as it were, to atone for Ehrenburg's guilt. By now however Olenina had neither the energy nor the contacts to continue campaigning to get the book published. She was left simply with a sense of bitterness and outrage.

> Olenina-d'Alheim:
> [...] Yet this splendid book [*La Passion de maître François Villon*]— a masterpiece, as they said in Paris—has to this day not been translated into Russian. And I am cross again with Ehrenburg for losing the Russian translation of the manuscript, which I gave to him in Paris... What an unpleasant thing for a writer to do. (BNB, 117.)

Unable to carry out her ideas regarding Pyotr d'Alheim's works, Olenina tried conducting discussions with various people about musical performance from the standpoint adopted by d'Alheim. Her letter to Goldenweiser was written in this vein, for instance. In it she discussed workers' clubs, the unsuitability of large concert halls, and the harm of international competitions and concert tours—the whole panoply of politicised artistic problems that had occupied her throughout her life. In the same spirit she also wrote some unpublished "Notes on Van Cliburn"[5] in November of 1959. Here Olenina returned to the problem of the artist's freedom from the thrall of money that had exercised her at the dawn of the century. Now she took the theme up again with reference to modern times:

> Olenina-d'Alheim:
> I recently read a brochure about this young American pianist. He was awarded First Prize at the Tchaikovsky Competition, and the public and all the critics acknowledged the jury's decision as correct.
>
> I was not there in Moscow in 1958, and as I now read the brochure glorifying this young artist, I judge him not by these words of praise but by his own words. They tell me about his spiritual personality: it is certainly of a sort peculiar to only a few true artists and is encountered very rarely.
>
> It is now a year since this marvellous boy completed a tiring concert tour to which he doubtless assented against his own will,

yielding to the requests and influence of those around him—his dear parents, his professor, and also the "unselfish" intervention of the "kindly" organiser of that splendid concert tour. What words of Van [Cliburn] allow me to assert this so confidently? "It is not a matter of money," he said, "I don't need it." And when he was asked what he thought of performing immediately after returning from Moscow to New York, he replied: "I would rather it not take place."

Returning to his homeland, he naively imagined that he would be able to settle down to work, he was anxious to perfect his performing talent, and of course he had to agree with bitterness in his heart to a materially "profitable" concert tour. I am sure that he secretly foresaw the danger of such an exhausting ordeal, and only agreed to take the risk in desperation and with the normal daring of young people. In Moscow, everyone who appreciates his unusual performing talent is apprehensive for him about this difficult ordeal.

If Van [Cliburn] ever reads this note of mine, he should seriously think about its contents, and he should see it as a friendly warning and a wish to help him on such a dangerous and uncertain road.

I have the right to talk about my own experience, I am old and have already completed my career. If I could resist all the blandishments and keep my artistic conscience as clean as it should be, it should not be forgotten that I consciously opposed them. But he is pure and naive, he has never thought of such a struggle, nor does it occur to him now. ("Zametki o V. Kliberne," ms, November 1959, GMMC, fond 256, no. 3613.)

When I met Olenina-d'Alheim in 1963, her fixation on political problems—always highly radical—had by now reached an almost maniacal extreme. However, by this time, Soviet bureaucrats were becoming the target of her criticism, although "Leninist principles" were still something she spoke of with a slight gasp of reverential awe.

In reviewing the Soviet scene and artistic culture around her, she found by no means everything to her taste. When she discovered that in the Soviet Union they built and used those same large concert halls which she had always abhorred, she discovered for herself the bourgeois nature and class divisions of Soviet society. She was upset by the "gilded luxury" of the Bolshoi Theatre ("just like the merchants used to have"), and she feared the "corrupting role" of cultural exchanges with the West. But one of her most unpleasant discoveries was the pathetic plight of folk song in the land of triumphant socialism. On the radio one could hear pseudo-folkloric products by Soviet composers representing a popular culture that Olenina had always regarded as the main enemy of genuine culture.

Olenina-d'Alheim:
When I was young I particularly disliked average lowbrow songs and regarded them as vulgar. To my great distress, that type of song is very widespread in the Soviet Union and has even found its way into the countryside. There are some splendid songs that were created during time of war, on the actual field of battle—they are so closely bound up with the life of that time, like songs of the people in olden times, created under the influence of nature and the life of the people (the peasantry) of that time.

You say that these songs are maybe the very finest in a musical sense. Of course you are right, and all foreign musicians regard this as true of Russian folk song. I can say that when one knows the songs of the people in every country, then one understands and appreciates their beauty, which reflects the customs and character of this or that people. Just now a Brazilian singer with a phenomenal voice is performing here, and the entire musical public will be in raptures about her songs, yet they do not know their own folk songs.

(Letter of 1960s (n.d.) to A.B. Goldenweiser, GMMC, fond 256, no. 474, 1.)

Ironically, the "Brazilian singer with a phenomenal voice" whom Olenina offered as a model to the Soviet public was in fact Yma Sumac,[6] an artist famous in her time who was also a complete fake. In her repertoire she had not a single folk song, and her voice was "phenomenal" only with the assistance of a microphone! However, Olenina's attitude was unambiguous. Like very few people at that time, she called things by their proper names. As, for instance, when she wrote to pianist Heinrich Neuhaus telling him about the need for his article on Richter[7] amid "the crisis of the art of music that we are experiencing, and not just here but everywhere abroad…" From her letter to Neuhaus, we also learn of Olenina's own plans.

Olenina-d'Alheim:
I have already shared my impressions of your article with comrades in the main musical institutions section of the USSR Ministry of Culture. I took up contact with them recently à propos of the founding of a soc[iety] of friends of Mussorgsky in Paris on the initiative of his great niece Nina Kuteleva [illegible]. And a correspondence with them has started, whereas prior to this I always applied direct to Comrade Furtseva, and she handed all my letters to this section. I am in correspondence with [a Ministry employee called] V. Boni. Do you know of him? (Letter of 21 December 1963, GMMC, fond 256, no. 4289, 2–3.)

Olenina's plan to set up a society of friends of Mussorgsky extended beyond Paris to the Soviet Union itself. Through its agency she intended to "purge" Soviet performances of bourgeois influences —to "get rid of the bourgeois ideology adhering to all performers here," as she told Tatyana Turgeneva in summer 1963.

Olenina took a vital interest in the Mussorgsky Voice Competition[8] that was first held in December of 1964. One might naturally have expected such a celebrated performer of Mussorgsky to be included as a jury member. But her age was becoming more and more noticeable, and the competition organisers realised she could not stand the strain of jury work. In fact, Olenina heard none of the performances, and stayed at home all winter: after a fall in which she injured her leg in the spring of 1963, she spent a long time in hospital and in the winter was confined to her apartment.

Olenina actually asked that there be a radio relay of the competition, so as to have chance to hear the competition. But to set that up would have been a complex matter, apart from which the competition organisers were not anxious to have the intractable elderly singer as participant. Not without reason, they were put out by her reputation for candour and lack of diplomacy. After all, Olenina perfectly understood how these competitions functioned in which professors of singing sat on the jury while their own pupils were the competitors.

The established form of national and international competitions displeased not only Olenina but many others. One of her sympathisers in this was Boris Gmyrya, who had in his time received the blessing of

Olenina's successor Zoya Lody. It was with him that Olenina discussed the idea for another competition devoted to Schubert.

Boris Gmyrya:
First of all, I must apologise for the delay in replying to your kind letter with its very serious suggestion for organising a Franz Schubert competition. I returned yesterday from a concert tour, which I embarked on following a three-week illness (evidently "flu with complications"). Now everything is behind me and I have sung off my debts. I performed *Die Winterreise* everywhere.

It was pleasant to find that audiences everywhere received this far from entertaining cycle very well and with great sense of contact. And it is quite understandable that any musician, especially one who has artistic links with Schubert's music, would be happy for there to be many and frequent performances of the songs and symphonies of this genius, and for them to assist the aesthetic education of our glorious people.

The only thing that I fear, if I suggest organising this competition, is that they are *bound* to involve me as a jury member, and I am organically unable to bear these sessions at which one sits and witnesses the usual fuss in order to drag through perfectly decent performers who have influential teachers and others.

For this reason any suggestion for a Schubert competition might come from other people, [...] but not from myself. In the Mussorgsky competition I was unable to take part as a jury member, since my concert trip was planned up to a year and a half in advance.

Once again my deep gratitude for your kind words addressed to me. My best wishes for good health and untiring energy in harvesting the crops of musical culture. [...]

B. Gmyrya.

(Letter of 12 February 1965, GMMC, fond 256, no. 3832.)

During my own meetings with Olenina-d'Alheim in 1963 I introduced her to the young bass singer Viktor Rybinsky, who was preparing for the Mussorgsky Competition. He was one of the few who realised how much Olenina could impart to a singer performing Mussorgsky, and he consulted with her. In November of 1964, roughly a month before the competition was to take place, she wrote to Rybinsky and told him of the role in which they had invited her to participate:

Olenina-d'Alheim:
They have just brought me a copy of the newspaper *Pravda*, in which the names of the Mussorgsky Competition jury are published. I read with surprise that I was proposed as *honorary member* and, of course, without a right to vote. [...] I do not understand by what means I was appointed as honorary member, but despite how these things are always done everywhere, nobody asked me about it. People who behave like that are a set of oafs.

As I see, all the jury members are professors, and probably they have sent their own pupils to compete while they themselves vote for them. That is not the way to behave in a competition, and it is very clear why. Musicians and musicologists are invited onto the jury who are *not familiar* with the competitors. It's a matter of common sense. (Letter to V.P. Rybinsky of 10 November 1964, GMMC, fond 256, No. 4290, 3.)

The conduct of the Mussorgsky Competition was a form of litmus test for Olenina. It would demonstrate whether or not it was possible in the Soviet Union to pursue the sort of Mussorgsky promotional activity she had dreamed about. Her conclusion was negative, alas. The trauma of this discovery was so grievous to her that it played a partial role in her final attempt to return to France after the competition was over.

Lessons to the Young

For the time being life followed its course, and Olenina's attention was engaged by various young musicians. Her meetings with Viktor Rybinsky and other singers who visited her convinced her that young performers should know more of her own artistic philosophy. Some of her ideas were formulated in a letter to Rybinsky, and she also made notes for a small brochure "On Working with the Voice (Advice to Young Performers)" which was never actually published. Here are her remarks addressed to Rybinsky.

Olenina-d'Alheim:

Dear Viktor Panteleimonovich,

I want to remind you that for a real performer truly dedicated to his art it is necessary first of all to forget completely *about oneself*. If you recall, I pointed out to you one word in Pimen's recitative; that is the word "anonymous" [*bezymyanny*], and it was written by Pushkin. [...]

I also told you that in the *genuine* opera theatre of the future all performing artists will be *anonymous*. Let me explain what I mean. The theatre is like a monastery which people enter who have renounced their own selves. They take another name and become unknown to everyone apart from their close relatives. As they enter the theatre, singers undertake to "incarnate" various personalities, and because of that they cease to be celebrities and must forget their own names. That is why in the opera theatre of the future all artists will be nameless.

In addition to which, this will help them to rid themselves of braggardliness, of competing with their comrades and of bad feelings in general which have hitherto existed in our theatres. [...]

I can assure you that the performer's renunciation of self and of his various enthusiasms gives him such a sense of fulfilment and incomparable, profound joy, [that] all the outward noises of ecstasy and approval strike him as poor and insignificant. *Inner feelings* awake and work within him, and these feelings not only look, but also see; they not only listen, but also hear. It is they which direct one's thought and develop its sensitivity to everything truly beautiful. People with such vital inner feelings are still rarely encountered [...] (Letter of 10 November 1964, GMMC, fond 256, no. 4290, 1.)

Olenina's advice to young performers, "On Working with the Voice," exists in the form of a draft for an unfinished work, hence its fragmentary nature. We have omitted that part where the author talks about topics already mentioned, such as Berlioz's ideas on the size of halls and perception of music. Olenina's interesting, though fragmentary observations, on vocal technique, diction and manner of performance invariably turn around what to her was the all-vital link between music and the word, between declamation and singing.

Olenina-d'Alheim:

I would like to talk with you about working on one's voice. This will help all of you to understand how to develop, strengthen and prepare your voice for the performance of both classical and modern Soviet works. All of them are absolutely realistic, and thus singers should not need to obtain the type of tone required in performing Chaliapin's operatic arias.

Young students in conservatoires and other schools who have not yet started preparing their future repertoire can easily develop their voice, its sonority, flexibility and stamina. I can quote my own case as an example. [...]

After completing my training I continued developing my voice with a professor. I sang a lot of vocalise items, exercises and, on the advice of a well-known singer, I sang them on the vowel "i", because this vowel sets the vocal chords in the right position, and this helped me to free myself of the throaty sound which I used to have, like all Russians do. I discovered for myself various new devices and exercises to help my diction.

The French language uses various vowels, both open and closed, et cetera. In it the vowels "a", "o", "i" and "e" sound differently. In performing in this language I carefully observed all these phonetic differences, and when I performed publicly for the first time singing songs by Mussorgsky (in French), one of the old actresses of the Comédie Française claimed that "Our young actresses would do well to learn good pronunciation of our language from Olenina."

("O rabote nad golosom," GMMC, fond 256, no. 3509, 1–3.)

In another of her notes Olenina again emphasised the speech-related nature of all singing. For her, the ability to "tell" a phrase did not exist separately in its own right, but arose from a whole complex of psychological, scenic and aesthetic impulses:

Olenina-d'Alheim:

Imagine that you have gone to the theatre to hear Glinka's opera *Ivan Susanin*, for example. You have entered the auditorium, which is lit not by chandeliers but by reflected light. But you have arrived late and you walk past in front of the stage during an interval. Then the lighting is radically reduced, and at the same time the curtain quickly and silently rises. In front of you you see a dark forest in moonlight (in the theatre of the future there will of course be no footlights). Among the sleeping forms of Polish warriors you see a Russian, a peasant still in the prime of life.[9] He gets up and comes to the front of the stage and says quietly to himself: "They sense the truth." Then he sings and does not shout in a strident voice as our singers have to do in the Bolshoi Theatre. And the only surprising thing is that the Polish warriors do not seize Susanin and prevent him from finishing his aria. It is sufficient that in opera they sing as a *convention*, rather than speaking as people do in real life. (But I myself once heard a gypsy woman sitting at the entrance to a prison weeping and lamenting, and her lamentation gradually turned into singing.) Let us return to the auditorium of our theatre. As you listen to Susanin, you have a deep sense of his fate and you sympathise with him with all your heart. Because before you stands a man who denies himself and gives his life to save his motherland, and who realises that his final hour is at hand. ("O rabote nad golosom," GMMC, fond 256, no. 3599, 4–5.)

With an emotionality typical of her, Olenina's attention was directed entirely towards the future: the theatre of the future, even the acoustics of the future. (In her notes she reflects on the need to construct halls where even "in the back rows one must be able to hear the quietest 'piano' and see the most elusive expression on the faces of the performers.") For improving the acoustics of the halls of the future, Olenina suggests using old construction principles, recalling the acoustic clay echoing vessels used in the St. Sophia Cathedral in Kiev.[10]

However, more than anything else, Olenina thought about the singers of the future, those young people with whom she wished to share her thoughts and her experience. In March of 1961 she met with voice students of the Gnessin Institute.[11] She talked and told stories mainly about herself, although this actually left her dissatisfied: she wanted to hear the young people sing and to offer her reactions to this in the context of a discussion on interpretative problems. Olenina had long dreamed of doing this, especially in Paris as she planned her

Olenina's master class on Mussorgsky's *Nursery*, with pianist Vera Shubina and singer Galina Pisarenko, 1963.

return to Russia. However, of course, since these were public presentations, and especially in view of her own impaired hearing, the realisation of this ambition was impossible.

Thus, when in 1963 I suggested to Olenina that she might work on some songs of Mussorgsky together with Galina Pisarenko and Viktor Rybinsky, she accepted the idea with great alacrity. I was nervous as I took my microphone to the first of these master classes. My previous encounter with Olenina had been to tape a detailed interview with her for the magazine *Sovetskaya muzyka*, which commissioned me to write an extended article on her life with "live" details narrated by herself.[12] To my great disappointment, nothing came of this interview, because Olenina's memory was too fragmentary to produce any consecutive account. I was therefore concerned as to how this meeting with the singers would work out. I was worried that Olenina's age might cause the same disappointment as with my interview. However, her professional memory, which had earlier won her a unique reputation, turned out to be just as sharp as ever. She remembered every word and every note and every single rest in *all* the songs of Mussorgsky.

The master classes Olenina gave opened up a whole new world to us, demonstrating her private "artistic laboratory." It was like the restoration of an old picture when modern viewers suddenly realise: "Lo and behold! So this is why contemporaries were so thrilled!" Now the magic of Olenina's performances became clear to us; one could see *how* she achieved what she did. The article that appeared in *Sovetskaya muzyka* following these master classes was a first attempt to understand in specific concrete terms the method she followed in her own creative work. Although it was printed in abbreviated form and without musical examples, the article (or more precisely, my own work on it) convinced me that a complete print-out of these tape-recorded classes should one day be made available to music-lovers and professional musicians.

The master classes included work on all six songs from *The Nursery* ("With Nursey," "In the Corner," "The Beetle," "With the Doll," "Evening Prayer," "The Hobby-Horse"), which were performed by Galina Pisarenko; five other items by Mussorgsky, "The Goat," Boris's Monologue and Pimen's Monologue from *Boris Godunov*, and "The Classic" and "Svetik Savvishna," were sung by Viktor Rybinsky. The accompanist was Vera Shubina.[13] The setting and atmosphere of the master classes was dominated by a sense of Olenina's enormous benevolence, and of rapt attention on the part of every listener. All of us realised we were in effect taking part in a journey by "time machine," which transported us all back from the mid 1960s to the end of the last century.

The master classes were so closely bound up with nuances of Russian speech intonation, lexicon, phraseology and syntax, and with often untranslatable elements in the Russian text of Mussorgsky's songs, that they cannot be rendered properly in English. The complete text of these classes is therefore published in Russian in the Appendix (pp. 309–27) for the benefit of readers who know Russian. Here we shall limit ourselves to a few examples and generalisations that convey an impression of how Olenina interpreted the songs of Mussorgsky.

Without attempting to summarise the master classes, one might note that Olenina's approach to the material was based on a consideration of the total musical, psychological and textual intricacies of each work. More than half a century before her meeting with Pisarenko and Rybinsky, she gave a remarkably accurate formulation of how she envisaged the source of imagery in Mussorgsky's songs.

Olenina-d'Alheim:
He [Mussorgsky] hears and listens, sees and observes, and his music is the speech of the characters that he depicts; and this speech is so faithfully conveyed that it evokes vivid images. As one listens, one sees them. In the *Songs and Dances of Death* and *The Nursery*, all the characters who sing, speak, babble, laugh or weep, are characterised and sketched with such bold lines, they are portrayed in such varied and bright colours, and these colours are rendered into sound with such definition, that a few bars are sufficient to bring these characters to life and allow them to fully express themselves. One instant and they emerge from their silence, a few words and they return again to their silence. But this is enough for them to imprint themselves on one's memory. The melody is their words, the harmony is their movement, and both of these are indissolubly bound by a fervent, secure yet flexible rhythm, like the rhythm of nature itself. (ZM, 6.)

Quite striking was Olenina's attention to the text, in which she had worked out and comprehended every single word. The text provided, as it were, the guiding force both in her understanding of the music's structure, and in her explanation of how to plan a performance. By fortunate coincidence, in all the works included in the master classes, Mussorgsky was the author of both the words and the music, which enabled one to see a special correspondence between music and text. This was one of the guiding principles for many Russian composers, starting with Dargomyzhsky. Certainly it was a vital component in Mussorgsky's artistic creed.

The music's direct link with the "personalities depicted" is the key to a truthful interpretation. With the help of this Olenina decides on the tempo, intonation and dynamics of the music. An example are her statements about tempo in various items of the *Nursery*. In the first song of the cycle ("With Nursey") the singer explains that the initial "fast" tempo marking is due to the fact that the little girl wants to hear

✑ "The Nursery"
title page, drawing by
Ilya Repin.

about the dreadful wolf (or bogeyman—*buka*—in Russian), and she is attracted by scary tales. So she speaks ever so quickly, because she wants to hear as soon as possible: "Tell me, Nanny dear, tell me the story about the fearful, dreadful *buka*...." But when they get to the *buka*, Mussorgsky for an instant seems to halt the movement. Even though she wants to hear about the *buka*, the girl is also slightly afraid. Then again she patters away: "how he wandered in the forests, how he carried small children off into the woods and ate them up, including the bones, and you could hear their cries!" But at this point she is scared stiff again and begins pondering what she knows about the *buka*, and she starts singing more slowly and quietly. She reflects on what the children might have done wrong—and for that reason Mussorgsky places a pause. And when it becomes clear that the children themselves were to blame (they "offended their old Nanny [and] disobeyed their parents"), the little girl talks about this with more speed and conviction. She consoles herself: she will not be like those naughty children. And she hastens to dismiss the unpleasant impression: "Or else: better tell me about the Tsar and his Tsarina." This she now sings happily and calmly. She likes imagining their large, rich palace and is amused that wherever the Tsar stumbles a mushroom springs up. And the bit about the Tsarina's cold is also amusing and sounds long and drawn-out: "The Tsarina always had a ba-a-a-ad cold." Then she goes off into a merely amusing story, and puts the other frightening tale to one side, because even though she likes scary experiences, she is still a bit afraid and not certain whether it is worth listening. And so, Olenina concludes, the tempo keeps changing all the time depending on what catches the little girl's fancy at any one moment. Although at the start of the song there is a general tempo indication of *allegretto* that continues unchanged to the end, these precise psychological explanations for tempo changes are confirmed by the complex metrical scheme of the musical text. They all grow totally out of the actual music and the words.

One recalls that at his meeting with Olenina-d'Alheim in 1901, Lev Tolstoy was struck by the idea that music could convey motion. In her "classes" Olenina develops this idea. For, as she observes, we clearly sense how the irritated nanny sees the naughty little boy off into his corner. ("In the Corner") When she says: "Get-in-the-corner!" one can hear her shoving him there in the music. And recall the accents Mussorgsky places at this point: here the boy has taken offence, and this can be heard for quite some time in the music—Olenina points out the "moaning" intonations in the left hand of the piano accompaniment. All the shifts of tempo and mood in the song develop from the way in which the performer grasps these fine textual nuances; and these for Olenina are not only a source of the song's psychological development but also determine the dynamics and tempo changes. Hence the reason for Mishenka's gradual increase in volume towards the end of the song: because his nanny refuses to take any notice of the boy's complaints. The final page of the song with its successive shades of dynamic can only be understood, so Olenina maintains, if the singer is really familiar with the experiences of his little hero at every moment of the musical and psychological development. And this knowledge is essential in order to create a proper mood for the work as a whole.

Olenina-d'Alheim also finds a source of musical declamation in the text. Here her chief requirement is for simplicity. The performer should not invent. Everything is there in the text, and one must only know how to "read" it. And the main and essential point of the master classes was precisely this: Olenina demonstrated how she herself "read" the text. One cannot help noticing her unique attention to subtle details, which many singers bypass with total indifference. (In the song "Svetik Savvishna," for instance, Olenina, as we remember, observes that the heroine seems to have two different patronymics; there are numerous other such instances in these master classes.) It is impossible to summarise the master classes in words. If one had to characterise their overall substance with just one idea, one might choose the same expression that Olenina herself used to describe the music of Mussorgsky: "Just as we speak, so Mussorgsky wrote. Mussorgsky's speech is quite clearly taken from the speech of common humanity."

* * *

The greater part of Maria Olenina's artistic career passed by in the pre-gramophone era, or at least during a period when gramophone recording was so imperfect that it would be hard to form any proper idea of her performances. In some sense, therefore, the master classes she gave in the 1960s reflected her artistry more fully than anything inscribed on some rasping early gramophone disc or cylinder. One only regrets that these recordings of her classes were so few in number.

Olenina's lessons demonstrated how fruitful and productive this activity could have been despite her very advanced years. Yet none of the arbiters of Soviet musical culture—nobody even among the Moscow Conservatoire professoriate, and no major contemporary musicians—took up the idea of organising more such master classes. This despite the fact that her meetings with Pisarenko and Rybinsky and the content of these lessons were known to Soviet musicians from my article in Sovetskaya muzyka. After the Mussorgsky Competition Olenina was in extremely pessimistic mood. When she returned to Russia, she dreamed of handing on her ideas and musical philosophy to a new generation of singers. Once she realised this was impossible, she had the idea of leaving Russia again and returning to France by way of protest. Always quick to take decisions, within a month of the end of the Competition, in January 1965 she informed her friends that she was leaving for Paris. As usual, though, she had given no thought to the practical aspects and implications of her decision. Her friends of course took a very negative view of this new idea: where on earth was she heading for at the age of ninety-six? Elena Stasova was one of many who did their best to dissuade her.

Elena Stasova:
Dear Maria Alexeyevna,

It was a pleasure to get your letter, although, to tell the truth, your insistent wish to leave for Paris somewhat frightens me. In view of your state of health and the inevitable formal and material difficulties, is it worthwhile leaving Moscow—especially now, when the frosts seem to have ended and spring is coming? Of course, the will to do something is stronger than its opposite, but I fear that the scheme you have embarked on will entail a lot of energy and anxiety, which is not desirable for someone in your condition.

I understand your dissatisfaction with the fact that many people here do not understand Mussorgsky, and the Competition during the anniversary period took place in a way unworthy of the composer. However, recently I have completely lost touch with the musical world and would not presume to judge what is good about it and what is bad. [...]

I send you all my very best wishes. Please let me know how matters turn out with your plan to go to Paris. [...] (Letter of 19 January 1956, GMMC, fond 256, no. 4074.)

At the time when Stasova and others were warning her against travelling off into the blue, Olenina's rebellious soul was raring to get away from Moscow, no matter where. But where was she heading? Where did she envisage seeking refuge this time? Nothing could be more ironic. There was Olenina writing to the French Embassy and asking to be accommodated in that same Galignani institution for retired artists where Doda Conrad had once helped to place her and which she had complained was so stifling! The Embassy's answer came in June. It informed her that the Foreign Ministry had handed her letter to the Académie des Beaux Arts that dealt with admissions to the Galignani home, and that at the present moment there were no vacancies. But in the event of a vacancy arising, it was necessary that Madame Olénine's dossier should contain all the necessary documentation: birth certificate and medical certificates confirming absence of infectious diseases and her "general state of health." She was also required to confirm the seriousness of her intention to return to France.

On the reverse side of this official letter Olenina began drafting her reply in pencil, although her message remained uncompleted. She wrote that "My ambition and desire are to live beneath the sky of France." (Letter from the French Embassy of 1 June 1965 with note by Olenina on reverse, GMMC, fond 256, no. 4969, 3.) But the necessary medical reports were not obtained, no ticket was bought, and the train to Paris left without Olenina. And so the routine of Moscow life continued, but with a constantly narrowing circle of interests and acquaintances, and increasingly rarer thoughts about the future. Olenina now only came to life on the few infrequent occasions when guests appeared.

Just occasionally, she was visited by musicians and musicologists from various foreign countries. If only one could gather the evidence and records of these visits. In one instance I was fortunate. From correspondence with Arbie Orenstein,[14] an American musicologist with a special interest in Ravel and author of several books about him, I heard that during his visit to Moscow he had the good fortune to meet with Olenina several times. I asked him to recall these meetings.

Arbie Orenstein:
Your request to elaborate on my meetings with Marie Olénine d'Alheim brings back many memories. It was in the spring of 1966 that I made the trip to Moscow from Paris, where I had been studying on a Fulbright Grant from the United Sates government. I was told that she was still living in Moscow by Doda Conrad. [...] Madame Olénine d'Alheim was living with her niece at 36 Leninsky Prospekt in Moscow. [...]

I found her to be in excellent spirits (we spoke French), alert to my questions about the origins of the Maison du Lied, her relationship with Ravel, and I asked also about the manuscripts he had

sent to Russia of the *Chants populaires*. She did not remember
what happened to the manuscripts, but all the other questions
were answered fully and also with a fine sense of humor. When I
explained to her that I had come from the United States to France
to study the music of Ravel, she asked: "And who was the first
communist, do you know?" I replied, "Karl Marx." "No," she said
with a smile, "Jesus Christ. He wanted everyone to be equal."

Although I had tape recorded all of my Ravel conversations, I
did not bring my tape recorder to Russia. The essence of her replies
is contained in my book, *Ravel: Man and Musician*. [...] She
insisted —and it is certainly true—that she and her husband Pierre
d'Alheim were responsible for acquainting western European
musicians with the music of Mussorgsky. There can be little doubt
that Mussorgsky's influence on Debussy and Ravel, and indeed
the entire French school was considerable. Both Debussy and Ravel
copied out parts of Mussorgsky's *Nursery* for purposes of study.
Ravel's orchestration of *Pictures at an Exhibition* is not just a
brilliant orchestral transcription, but also an homage to a composer
he profoundly admired.

Although Madame Olénine d'Alheim was slightly hard of
hearing, she answered most of my questions without any repetition
on my part, holding a folded-up newspaper to her ear to amplify
the sound. [...] Madame Olénine d'Alheim easily recalled events
that had occurred some fifty years ago, and told me to verify them
by examining her diary, which was deposited at the Glinka
Museum of Musical Culture. I did so, and found two autograph
letters from Ravel at the museum, as well as her diary, which
indeed corroborated everything she had told me. However, about
five days later, when I came to say thank you and goodbye, as I
was returning to Paris, it took her several minutes until she
remembered who I was. [...]

Madame Olénine d'Alheim's work in western Europe was
largely devoted to recitals of Mussorgsky's music. [...] Her
secondary interest in folk song, specifically in artistically arranged
folksongs for the concert platform was the link between her career
and that of Ravel, who sent seven of his manuscripts to Russia in
1910, and won four of the prizes in the competition sponsored by

the Maison du Lied. [...] Claude Debussy summed up France's attitude and gratitude to Mussorgsky as follows: "Russian music interests me in the highest degree. Mussorgsky is admirable in his independence, sincerity, and charm. He is something of a god in music...The Russians will give us a new motivation to rid ourselves of ridiculous constraints. They will impel us to a better knowledge and more liberal hearing of ourselves." (Debussy in conversation with Henri Malherbe,[15] "La Musique Russe and les Compositeurs français," in *Excelsior*, March 9, 1911). (Letter to A. Tumanov of 29 July 1991)

Gradually, however, the number of visitors to the apartment on Leninsky Prospect became less and less. Olenina's defective hearing, which Orenstein mentioned so diplomatically, was in fact extremely bad. Nor was this the elderly singer's only ailment. Despite generally sound health, her age inevitably began to tell. But this was perhaps not the main factor. Every year that Olenina survived was marked by personal losses as more and more people from her circle died. The heaviest loss, or losses, occurred in 1966. The diary entry in her "Black Notebook" tells all.

Olenina-d'Alheim:
(ENTRY FOR 11 APRIL 1966)
I am committing some sad news to the pages of this book: on the 27 Jan[uary], my niece Tanya Turgeneva died. On the evening of the 25th (her nameday) she had very low blood pressure—that was the report of the doctors summoned by Tanya's daughter Lyolya [Olga Sergeyevna Solovyova, the daughter of Tatyana Alexeyevna from her first marriage to the poet Sergei Solovyov]. The doctors gave her an intravenous injection [...] and took her off to hospital No. 5 [the Gradskaya], where she seemed to be feeling better. Soon she began suffering terribly however. [...] Tanya died, so the doctors said, from infarction of the lung. [...]
   Tanya's death was a terrible blow to us all, and we still cannot recover from it. But then Gury contracted pneumonia and was taken to hospital where he spent a month and a half. He returned only on the 7 April and at the present time has become slightly odd. His doctor at the hospital said that he absolutely must have a

change of surroundings. Lyolya is concerning herself with this now
and has sent a telegram to summon Gury's sister from Donetsk (she
lives there with her family and is a doctor). [...]
(ENTRY FOR 12 APRIL)
[...] Yesterday Lyolya talked on the phone with Donetsk and
explained everything to them. [...] I was writing here and did not
know about their conversation [...] and even now I don't know
what was decided. I cannot help regretting that they do not tell me
—or forget to let me know—everything that goes on in the family.
(ENTRY FOR 13 APRIL)
They have called from the hospital to say that Gury died at 2.00
a.m. [...] All this is very hard to bear. My poor friend Gury! When
he returned [after his pneumonia], the two of us embraced and
were glad that at last he was home, but about a couple of hours
later he became quite strange. Their explanation is ambiguous:
when he looked in at the open door of Tanya's room, he immediately recalled that she had died, and he could not get over this.
[...] (BNB, 130–35.)

The deaths of Tatyana Turgeneva and her husband Gury were a
heavy blow to Olenina, and she now began feeling completely isolated
even in the family of her relatives. The atmosphere was sometimes
explosive. The great nieces and nephews sometimes found it hard to
get on with their old aunt who had an independent spirit and who
herself at times found life difficult. As she recorded in her notebook, a
lot of nervous tension was brought into their lives by the housekeeper,
who was "not a bad person, but totally unresponsible for her actions"
and "could be influenced for good or evil." (BNB, 159).

Olenina-d'Alheim:
(NOTE OF 1966)
Ever since the deaths of Tanya and Gury, I have found life hard.
[...] But I do not want to talk about it. It is too nasty, and one has
to say nothing and put up with it. But a year ago I had concussion
of the brain, and those who never had that cannot understand how
such a patient must feel, and whether they can behave like other
people. [...] Life is hard for me, oh how hard. (BNB, 160–62.)

The closest people to Olenina were the children of Tatyana Turgeneva, her daughters Lyolya and Natasha (by her marriage to Sergei Solovyov) and her son by her second marriage, Yury [Guryevich Ametirov-Turgenev], who Olenina was specially fond of and used to call "Yurka." She also made affectionate mention of "Murka"—Nikolai Muravyov, with whose family Olenina had been close back in her Paris days.

After the deaths of Tatyana and Gury, the question arose as to who Olenina should live with. After a family conference, it was decided that Olga Sergeyevna should move into the Leninsky Prospect apartment where Olenina was living. Soon however she exchanged this fairly comfortable apartment for another one. The new quarters were in a dilapidated old building in the Yamskaya area of Moscow, and it turned out to be a poky little flat, much worse than the previous one. Olenina's notebooks mentioned her "awful little room with a brick wall in front of the window and only a small chink of sky" (BNB, 162). In fact it was just like "Within Four Walls" from Mussorgsky's *Sunless*[16]—as time went on it seemed Olenina was increasingly haunted by characters and images from the composer's world.

After 1966, Olenina's health gradually declined, her hearing deteriorated catastrophically, her vision went almost completely, and it became more and more difficult for her to move about. On the 10 August 1966, the "Black Notebook" contained one final entry of just one phrase that tailed off incomplete: "In my right eye there has also appeared ..." (BNB, 206.)

The Centenary

During those final years, the Soviet press made no mention of Olenina at all. The only exception was in 1969, the year of her centenary, when a few superficial notices and comments appeared on the occasion of her hundredth birthday. In the weekly *Literaturnaya Rossiya* there was an interview with her entitled "The aim of my life was to introduce people to Russian music," and an article by Elena Alexeyeva in *Sovetskaya muzyka*, headed "Acknowledgement of a Great Artist." In her interview, published on the 19 September, her hundredth birthday, Olenina

The last photograph of Maria Olenina-d'Alheim, c. 1969–1970.

enunciated thoughts that harmonised perfectly with Soviet official statements on the flourishing state of the arts in the Soviet Union. There were words of gratitude to the Soviet government, and phrases about "art belonging to the people." One wonders who those words were uttered by—Olenina herself, or the editor of *Literaturnaya Rossiya*? And how did these pronouncements tie in with the elderly singer's attempts to leave the land of flourishing art as recently as 1965?

Olenina-d'Alheim:
How happy I am that I am home once more, and how infinitely grateful I am to our government. Only a person who has regained

his homeland is capable of understanding me. The meaning of that phrase to which everyone has got so accustomed: "Art belongs to the people" is something that I perceive in all its profundity and greatness. [...] Is it possible to live without art? People need it like they need food and air. A man can renounce everything, but to give up creating and hearkening to beautiful things is something that is beyond him. (*Literaturnaya Rossiya*, no. 38 (350), 19 September 1969, 21.)

There was no official celebration of Olenina's centenary. The only person who congratulated her—and even then only on his own initiative and on his own behalf—was F.A. Monakhov, a senior consultant at the All-Union Theatrical Organisation (VTO). He had learnt of her centennial from reading the interview in *Literaturnaya Rossiya*.

Natalya Solovyova:
[Monakhov] found out her telephone number and called up to make arrangements. He was told when to come. Maria Alexeyevna was very excited. He was struck by her noble face, grey hair, and her animation. She reminded him somehow of [the actress] Yablochkina. She was completely deaf. They poured out some red wine and clinked glasses. She drank and said, "Let's keep on living for a while." (UAA, No. 89–200.)

Not a single musicologist used Olenina's centenary as an occasion to evaluate her role in the history of Russian and western musical culture. Only in 1974 did some interesting material appeared about certain forgotten articles by Stasov dealing with Olenina's first concerts. In his introductory note to the publication, musicologist Iosif Kunin was the first to mention the scale of Olenina's achievement, explaining that she had "played a quite exclusive role not only in introducing the work of Mussorgsky to France," but also in "creating a Russian school of [vocal] chamber performance." (I. Kunin, "K izucheniyu naslediya V.V. Stasova," *Sovetskaya muzyka'* 7 (1974), 48.) Olenina did not live to read this assessment of her life's work however.

In early 1970 Olenina's health took a serious downturn. On the advice of doctors she was moved to an old people's home, where she survived for only a few months. She died on the 26 August 1970, just a

month short of her 101st birthday. Her death was passed over in the
same silence that accompanied much of her life. An announcement of
her death only occurred in the journal *Muzykalnaya zhizn'* in February
of 1971. She died as the heroes of Mussorgsky's songs died, and like the
composer himself, in total solitude, as though reliving the fate of those
she had once celebrated in song. As Camille Bellaigue once wrote:

> Tsar Boris is dead, dead too are the schismatics [...], beneath the
> snow the little *muzhik* sleeps the sleep of the tomb, the bones of
> warriors glisten white on the field of battle, and in a house without
> children a little bed stands empty. Dead at last is the sorrowful cre-
> ator of so many unhappy heroes, and it seems as though here within
> the walls of his room all these dead folk have gathered round his
> hospital bed to be present and pay tribute at his death.

Now, too, there had died a woman whose artistry once filled all
these human images with flesh and blood and a life of their own—a
life which, one hopes, will continue even after Olenina's death.

When I attempted in 1989 to find the tomb of Maria Olenina, it
proved impossible. Olga Solovyova gave me some vague directions: the
Vagankovo Cemetery, the first row to the left, following the sign "To
Esenin" (i.e., the poet Esenin's grave), in the area of the tenth pathway.
According to Solovyova, the urn containing Olenina's ashes was buried
in the tomb of her brother Alexander Olenin. Later on, at my request,
my friends attempted to find the burial site, but all in vain. In the area
of the tenth pathway there was no grave for Olenina-d'Alheim. And
none of the officials I consulted who were "responsible" for Soviet art
knew of its whereabouts. Was there indeed such a tomb? After her
death, just as during her life, her homeland largely ignored its great
daughter.

VIII

REFLECTIONS
ON A CENTURY
OF LIFE

aria Olenina d'Alheim lived a long life, full of creative activity, rich in events and encounters—a life that embraced many epochs and generations. Born only a few years after the emancipation of Russia's peasantry in 1861, Maria Olenina spent her youth in the latter years of the nineteenth century; the years of her prime coincided with the eventful early twentieth century, and her old age was rounded off in the latter half of this century. She was the witness of three revolutions, two world wars, the rise and fall of Nazism, and the birth, triumph and sunset of Soviet communism. She outlived three tsars of the Romanov dynasty and four of the communist one. Her hundred years of life she divided almost equally between France, which saw the dawn of her career, and Russia, which heard her in her best years. Born in 1869 on the provincial Russian estate of Istomino, she trod a strange path that led her from membership of the Russian nobility and intelligentsia to membership of the French communist party in 1946; from vegetating in a French home for elderly artists to her death in an old people's home in Moscow. She was famous in Russia and France, made a vast contribution to the art of both countries, and yet was forgotten by both of them—several times—and struck off the list of living artists. She outlived her daughter and her husband, almost all her relatives and friends, and probably all contemporary colleagues in her profession.

A fate such as that of Olenina, full of artistic achievements and yet at the same time a tragic one, is of inevitable interest to later generations. Olenina's life, though, is one that particularly intrigues, spent as it was in the thick of artistic and cultural events in both Russia and France in the late nineteenth and early twentieth centuries. Her life and work are important to us because they impinged on the main cultural, political and social events and processes of their time. Olga Solovyova, mother of the poet Sergei Solovyov, once waxed ecstatic about Olenina because she perceived in her the epitome of the "Russian peasant woman" (A. Bely, *Na rubezhe dvukh stoletii*, 1929), sensing her essential simplicity, disingenuousness and absolute honesty. Thus, the fate and artistry of this Russian peasant, singer, noblewoman, *intelligente*, propagandist, musical activist, writer and communist party member serve as a mirror that reflects the principal phenomena of culture and art, and the main political and social events of all those epochs spanned by her long life.

The singer's youth was bound up with the main musical movement of her time—the Russian National School. The greatest influences she underwent at the start of her career were the aesthetic ideas of the Mighty Handful, which shaped her destiny as a Russian Lieder singer who spanned and linked together the nineteenth and the twentieth centuries. Her personal ties to Stasov, Cui, Rimsky-Korsakov, and her long years of friendship and association with Balakirev were the foundation on which she grew as an executant and musical thinker.

Especially significant were Olenina's dealings with Mily Balakirev, which played an enormous role in her formation as an artist, and the correspondence between them as well as with Alexander Olenin is a valuable document of the era. Quite apart from advice and encouragement, Balakirev's letters contained important and often venomously critical revelations about the current musical life of St. Petersburg. Balakirev's obvious cherishment of her talent also provided exactly the moral sustenance that the young singer needed, and it gave her a specific knowledge of all that the Mighty Handful expected of her.

It was precisely these composers together with Mussorgsky who affected one decisive factor in Olenina's artistry—the link between music and the word. Of course, there were other singers before her who were aware of this. Petrov, Leonova, Lavrovskaya and Molas all collaborated with composers of the Russian National School, and for them too the word of the text was a vital expressive element. Olenina's particular distinction lay in having made the text the *absolute centre* of her art, from which she derived her entire understanding of artistic truth and directness. In this respect, closest of all to Olenina was the singer Alexandra Molas. But she hardly ever performed publicly, and Olenina-d'Alheim was thus the first in the history of the Russian vocal art to establish the centrality of the text as a vital source of interpretation. Assisted by the link between music and speech, Olenina established a tradition of expressivity that was the direct reverse of "pure technique" —the latter was something totally unacceptable to her, existing as a law unto itself and showing a mere superficial understanding of the poetic, and thus of the musical, text.

Olenina's directness of performance and expressiveness led her to follow Berlioz and others in campaigning against the use of large concert halls and against any conceptions too grandiose. A genuine contact between singer and audience could only arise in the intimacy of a small auditorium in which every word and every nuance could be heard. Olenina's views on this subject have not lost their relevance even today.

Olenina-d'Alheim was *the first Russian chamber, or Lieder, singer* in the strict sense of this expression. It was not merely that she performed only vocal chamber music. Prior to her appearance, a vocal recital had hitherto been a random collection of songs and arias designed to show off the voice and technique of the singer. Olenina laid the foundation of unified thematic programming that followed some central idea or stylistic principle. Thanks to her, vocal chamber music became established as an independent, complex and substantial musical genre, similar to opera and possibly requiring even more than opera in terms of subtle artistry. The development of this genre became a vital part of the Russian performing tradition, and many works of this type were remembered by contemporaries specifically in their interpretation by Olenina, who truly made these works "her own." This is true particularly perhaps of such works as Mussorgsky's *The Nursery*, in which her performance thrilled all who heard it, including the composers of the Mighty Handful, Lev Tolstoy, Alexandre Georges, Claude Debussy and many others.

In talking of Olenina's prominent role in introducing French and Belgian audiences to the work of Mussorgsky, it is often forgotten how important her promotion of Mussorgsky was specifically for composers and performing artists in these countries, who first heard these works and their inimitable intonations in Olenina's interpretations. When we read, for example, in the Penguin *New Dictionary of Music* (1973) that Debussy's opera *Pelléas et Mélisande* obviously owed its natural speech intonations to Mussorgsky, this is the direct achievement of Olenina-d'Alheim. So too is the profound interest of Ravel in Mussorgsky, as witnessed in his orchestral version of the *Pictures at an Exhibition*. It is no coincidence that the period of the d'Alheims' first *conférences* on Mussorgsky was the time when the French first became interested in his music. As in many other instances, it emerged that Olenina's activities simultaneously catalysed that interest and largely satisfied it with her own performances that placed her at the epicentre of important cultural changes in her time.

A typical instance of the "relevance" of Olenina's work was the link between her public musical activities and the Russian Symbolist movement in literature. When the d'Alheims first opened their House of Song in 1908, this event had a strong resonance among the Russian Symbolist poets, who at that time were formulating aesthetic principles that were markedly congruent. The younger, second generation of Symbolists—Andrei Bely and Vyacheslav Ivanov—actually met and discussed their ideas in the Moscow apartment of the d'Alheims. The Symbolists perceived the world as a manifestation of an all-embracing syncretic culture. In a letter to Alexander Blok of 1903, Bely wrote that "art must be multi-stringed" (i.e., it should manifest itself on many planes). Developing this idea, Ivanov talked about an art that would draw in and involve all people. Such ideas linked directly with those pursued in the House of Song, which was created in order to bring music and the sound of poetry to the masses. (T. Khmel'nitskaya, "Literaturnoe rozhdenie Andreya Belogo: Vtoraya dramaticheskaya simfoniya" in *Andrei Bely: Problemy tvorchestva* (Moscow, 1988).) The ideas of the younger generation of Symbolists and the House of Song in this respect were quite amazingly alike. Bely's own account is eloquent testimony.

Andrei Bely:
At that time [d'Alheim] dreamed of the birth of cells similar to the Moscow House of Song in every centre of the earth's five continents. Here he revealed in himself an obvious eccentric dreamer proclaiming his utopian ideas about the link between artists, poets and musicians of the entire world, inspired by the recitals of Maria his wife: "Quand Marie chantera..." (When Maria sings). From Moscow she was supposed to sing out to the whole world. [...] The House of Song supposedly would immediately spread from Moscow and set itself up in Berlin, Paris, Vienna, London, San Francisco, New York, and Bombay. In all these centres, poets, artists, male and female singers, whom he and Maria with our help would arm with the lightnings of artistic action, were to decapitate the thousand-headed hydra of slavery. (NV, 392.)

Bely at that time saw in Olenina a messiah: through her, art would penetrate life's deepest recesses. He described her as a "particular kind of spiritual guide" (A. Bely, "Pevitsa," *Mir iskusstva*, 11 (1902).) The Symbolists also perceived a correspondence between the music of Mussorgsky (and thus inevitably the influence of Olenina-d'Alheim) and poetry and the art of the so-called Itinerant painters (the Peredvizhniki, famous for their realistic content and travelling exhibitions). There was talk of the spread of Symbolism, which would embrace all the arts, and of the fact that music would come to occupy a supreme position in their hierarchy.

With the help of Pyotr d'Alheim, Olenina at an early stage in her career worked out her own artistic creed, involving the composite trinity of composer, performer and listener. In this conception, the role of the performer was quite unique; as we know, it involved a *renunciation of self* in order to execute the will and idea of the creative composer. The logical consequence of such a view of the performer's role was that he, or she, should retreat into a state of *internal silence*. The result of all the ideas in Olenina's creed was thus a conception of the singer who, as it were, bore the composer's music in front of him—as distinct from a singer who thrust himself, his own voice and his own technical virtuosity to the forefront. This was the expressive singer-performer, dedicated to the ideas and content of art—as opposed to the self-sufficient virtuoso singer, devoted merely to his own self-image.

In this respect too Olenina-d'Alheim emerged at the nexus of the aesthetic searchings of her age, which opened with the foundation of the Moscow Arts Theatre and elaboration of its methods following the "system" of Stanislavsky. Although it might at first sight seem that Maria Olenina rejected the principles of "artistic experience" required by the Stanislavsky system (*viz* her letter to Tanya Slonim), in fact her "renouncement of self" in favour of the composer's own artistic aims, and her "departure into an inner silence" were the vocal equivalent of Stanislavsky's notion of the "super-task" (the actor's prime artistic aim) and the "art of experiencing." One can also find several points in common in what Olenina and Stanislavsky had to say about the text as the principal semantic medium of artistic expression. "When he [the actor] colours with sound and delineates by intonation the thing *inside* him which he lives by," Stanislavsky wrote, "he makes me see with an *inner vision* those images recounted by the words of speech and which are fashioned by his creative imagination." (K.S. Stanislavsky, *Sobranie sochinenii* (Moscow, 1955), vol. 3, 322; emphasis added) Olenina's own plan of a performance, as evidenced by her own master classes, took account of psychological, social and historical factors in a way very reminiscent of Stanislavsky's definition of the "super-task."

The late nineteenth and early twentieth centuries were marked by a disappearance from the theatre of ideas typified by the "travelling showman" mentality and divorced from any aesthetic or ethical aim. There now began the age of the theatrical ensemble, the theatre of thought and artistic truth. It was for this reason that the appearance of the Moscow Arts Theatre played such a revolutionary role in the history of Russian drama. There also came to an end a period of meaningless singing that lacked any thought or idea and was conceived purely as a means of demonstrating the technique and vocal range of the singer. Thus the work of Olenina had a long-term effect and influence on the aesthetic and ethical aspect of vocal chamber performance. Her theoretical ideas on performance, however, were never recorded or analysed by musicologists, and they received only passing and laconic mention in the publications of the House of Song and in press reviews. But these ideas were present in Olenina's own singing and had a magical effect on public taste, which she changed and transformed totally from what it had been before. Her reflections on performance, expressed in her book *The Mussorgsky Legacy* and also in her reminiscences, letters and lessons have been collected in the present book and are thus now available to modern readers.

Inexplicably, by her art Olenina touched on something that excited all her contemporaries, ordinary listeners, writers, poets, and thinkers. Her encounter with Lev Tolstoy in 1901 aroused questions from him that inevitably bear witness to this. Her singing evidently prompted Tolstoy to think again about the problems he discussed in his book on *What Is Art?* (1897) and which were later modified and expanded in the article "On Shakespeare and the Drama" (1904). At the time when the d'Alheims visited Yasnaya Polyana, Tolstoy was evidently continuing to reflect on the nature of art. Without dealing in detail with the ideas in Tolstoy's tract, which many contemporaries regarded as symptomatic of his extreme religious dogmatism and reactionary attitude, one can see that in his conversations with the d'Alheims Tolstoy was still testing out what he had said with such pungency in *What Is Art?*

It was in this context that Tolstoy put to Olenina his question as to whether a totally deaf composer can create works of genius. The question was not a casual one. In Tolstoy's list of creators of "false art" Beethoven had figured alongside Shakespeare, Brahms, Richard Strauss, Wagner, Liszt, Berlioz, Dante, Sophocles and Eurypides. In his book Tolstoy had written:

> I know that musicians have a fairly vital ability to imagine and almost to hear what they read; but imagined sounds can never replace real ones, and any composer has to be able to hear his work in order to be in a condition to complete it. But Beethoven could not hear, could not complete, and he therefore brought forth works that were an artistic hallucination. (L. Tolstoy, *Chto takoe iskusstvo?* (Edinburgh, 1963), 150.)

This was written in 1897, and only four years later, when he quizzed Olenina, the writer seemed to be checking up whether he was right. Perhaps he had doubts?

Similarly there seems to be an element of doubt in Tolstoy's question as to how music was able to depict motion. He asked his question after Maria Olenina had just performed Mussorgsky's *Nursery*, in which the composer gave a very successful musical representation of movement and physical action. (See, for instance, Olenina's remarks about "In the Corner," in which the music lets us "hear" the nurse push the boy into the corner.) In the section of his tract devoted to Wagner, Tolstoy maintains the impossibility of syncretic art and mockingly talks about the failure of Wagner's attempt in *Der Ring des Nibelungen* to convey musically the movement taking place as the "wanderer strikes the ground with his spear, fire comes up from the earth, and in the orchestra one hears the sounds of the spear and of the fire." (Tolstoy, *Chto takoe iskusstvo?*, 163.) Or else in the scene of "the emergence of the monster, accompanied by notes in the bass [...] all these growlings, fire, and wavings of the sword [...]" (Tolstoy, *Chto takoe iskusstvo?*, 167.) We cannot know whether the author of *What Is Art?* later began to have doubts after hearing Olenina sing. Nevertheless, the very fact of his question possibly suggests that Olenina at very least gave him pause to reflect.

The only important coincidence of Tolstoy's thoughts on art with Olenina's own was in a definition of the link between the person perceiving a work of art and its author or creator. Art is "infectious," the writer maintained. It infects the perceiving agent with a feeling that unites him with the creator and with other human beings. This is an inner feeling. Tolstoy then goes on and virtually repeats Olenina's own belief in the trinity of composer, singer and listener:

> The main feature of this feeling lies in the fact that the perceiver of it to such an extent blends with the artist, that it seems to him that the object he perceives is made by none other than him himself, and that everything expressed by this object is the same thing as he himself so long wanted to express. In the mind of the perceiver, a real work of art causes the division between him and the artist to disappear, and not only between him and the artist, but between him and all people who perceive that same work of art. In this liberation of the personality from its isolation from other people, from its own loneliness, in this merging of the personality with others, lies the main attractive force and quality of art. (Tolstoy, *Chto takoe iskusstvo?*, 184.)

In Tolstoy there is stress on the socio-ethical aspect of the unity of creator and audience; Olenina emphasises the aesthetic, artistic aspect. Nevertheless, both of them are talking about similar phenomena.

A final feature in Maria Olenina's dealings with Tolstoy was in her revelation to him of Mussorgsky's "Field Marshal" and of the composer himself. This was not just the "discovery" of a new composer, but a discussion of the music itself. By her performance Olenina in effect refuted the author of *The Kreutzer Sonata* and his view of the corrupting influence of music. Tolstoy's hero in the story comes out with many of the writer's own ideas about music, the main one of which was that music evokes only an unhealthy excitement in people:

> Altogether music is a terrible thing. What exactly is it? I don't understand. What is music? What does it do? And why does it do what it does do? They say that music acts in a way that elevates the soul. Nonsense! It isn't true! It acts, and acts in a terrible way—I am talking about myself. [...] It acts in a way that irritates the soul. (L.N. Tolstoy, *Sobranie sochinenii* (12 vols.) (Moscow, 1975), Vol. 10, 235.)

Mussorgsky's song as performed by Olenina made an enormous impression and in effect "cancelled out" what the author had written earlier. "After all, what we have heard just now is more than splendid!" Tolstoy exclaimed after Olenina had finished singing. How significant that in 1901, when the Belgians and the French had already got to know and love Mussorgsky, the great Russian writer with Olenina's help was only discovering for himself the author of *Songs and Dances of Death* —and in French to boot!

All that Olenina-d'Alheim did during her career was of enormous relevance to her time. The singer met the aesthetic demands of various periods in the development of art that occurred during the long span of her life. One of the demands of the day was that of musical enlightenment and education and the attraction of listeners to an active role in music making. This explained the creation and the flourishment of the House of Song. Many contemporaries of course understood well the importance of this unusual institution. One of them was Andrei Bely.

Andrei Bely:
The role of the d'Alheim couple—the husband as organiser of the House of Song, and the wife as the sole and unique performer of songs cycles for the first decade of the new century—was enormous. They advanced the musical culture of Moscow. As one recalls, Olenina first appeared in 1902 and her concerts continued

till late 1916—fourteen years of immense labour that resulted in the raising not only of public taste, but of musical literacy. The Olenin [*sic*] couple broadened our familiarity with song literature. Starting in 190[8], the musical and artistic organisation headed by the d'Alheims, and with participation of the best musical critics, [...] translators, composers, [...] poets, engaged in promoting a series of pearls of song literature, hitherto unknown to the Russian public. One imagines that *nowhere in the capitals of Europe* [emphasis added] was the public offered such material—and with such taste and selectivity—as that presented to the Moscow public by the d'Alheims. The House of Song concerts for several years were both aesthetic gifts to Moscow, and educational courses. If in Italy they knew Scarlatti and Pergolesi, in England—song settings of Robert Burns, in Germany—the song cycles of Schumann and Schubert to words by Heine and the poet Müller, who is little known over here, in Moscow along with Glinka, Balakirev, Rimsky-Korsakov, Borodin and the song cycles of Mussorgsky (who before the d'Alheims was also little known) there were also presentations of Scarlatti, and Pergolesi, and Rameau and Grieg, and Schumann, and Schubert, and Liszt, and Hugo Wolf: in song. Year in year out, the House of Song taught Moscow the importance of these song cycles, and the role of artistic musical translation, and the history of music, not to mention that seven or eight annual concerts, carefully put together, amazingly performed, with programmes accompanied by articles and notes, noticeably raised the taste of those several thousand concert patrons, some of whom later collaborated with the d'Alheims when the House of Song concerts were restricted. (NV, 388–89.)

It is important to note that although plans to expand the House of Song around the globe did not succeed, its influence was not just limited to Moscow and St. Petersburg. The concerts were repeated in London and were regularly presented in Paris, forming an integral part of Paris musical life. At the same time Olenina introduced new French music into the House of Song programmes in Russia. Later, in Paris, after Pyotr d'Alheim's death, Olenina also continued her artistic links with the French composers of Les Six, appearing on the platform as the first performer of several of their works.

Nor were the traditions of the House of Song broken off with its own disappearance. During the Soviet period there was a proliferation of musical lecture-recitals along principles first established by the House of Song, which attracted an enormous public—from school-children for whom lecture-concerts were conducted on a regular basis, to serious music-lovers who attended the subscription concerts. The result of this was a purely Russian phenomenon, which probably owed its existence to the House of Song. If one compares the average age of the musical public in Russia with that of the West, it turns out that the audience in Russia is much younger than the western audience, especially that in North America. We live in an age when the public in our concert halls is noticeably aging, and in which the vanishing older generation is not being sufficiently replenished by the new one. Among North American chamber music and symphony concert audiences there is an absolute majority of elderly listeners. In Russia, by contrast, there are a lot of young people in concert audiences. Surely this is in part the legacy of the House of Song, still having a beneficial effect nearly ninety years after its first foundation?

However, even without its widespread effects on Russian musical life to which contemporaries testified so eloquently, the House of Song remains as a milestone in the history of Russian art, because of Olenina's own part in its concerts and recitals. Every performance by her was an event. Much of what she sang has never been excelled, despite the fact that in purely vocal terms she was not without her faults. As the faithful chronicler of Olenina's talent, Andrei Bely, wrote:

Even if people dispute what I say, even if her voice was disappearing in later years, I can state frankly that nobody so excited me as she did. I heard Figner[1] and Chaliapin, but Olenina-d'Alheim as she was in the period 1902–1908 I prefer to any Chaliapins. She captivated one not by the beauty of her voice, but by her *sole and unique expression.* I never heard the like of it later on.

With a shout of ecstasy we greeted a singer who we seemed to regard as a sword-bearer on behalf of the culture of the future, avidly following the consciously prepared sweep of her arms as she raised her black shawls in Mussorgsky in order then to utter a cry that flung apart her arms and forced out a gasp of "Death has triumphed!"

One was struck by her stature and the explosive glint of her sapphire eyes. In her intonations were the whirr of the spinning wheel, laughter, ravens' cawing, and tears. One song grew out of another, revealed in song. And significance and meaning grew. And for the first time we were caught unawares by a recognition that *Die Winterreise*, a cycle of songs, had a significance no less than that of Beethoven's Ninth Symphony. (NV, 390.)

The expressiveness of Olenina's singing also produced such an impact on contemporary listeners because of an intensity deriving from her profound tie with the Russian people. Olga Solovyova's observation of the Russian peasant-woman (*baba*) in Olenina was no casual remark. "Just like a holywoman. She chatters away into my ear, blinks like a bluebird; and she flutters her shawls; suddenly props herself up like a peasant *baba*; suddenly shrieks like a woman of the people!" Solovyova commented (NV, 391). Maria Olenina had a rare ability to get inside the national, popular *spirit* of a song, and—to judge by the reaction of those who heard her—not just of Russian song. Many have commented on her amazing understanding of German Lieder by Schubert and Schumann, Richard Strauss and Hugo Wolf. And even on the threshold of old age, when her voice was giving out, as Doda Conrad recalled, her performance of a Hebrew folk song in an arrangement by Ravel was quite extraordinary.

However, whatever the cosmopolitan variety in Olenina's interpretations, her most important quality was after all her *Russianness*, which was most manifest in the richness of her verbal expression. How much we have lost through the fact that no recordings were ever made of her singing. The only extant recording is of the master classes she gave in the 1960s. These at least record the amazing intonation of her voice, her speaking voice. They also demonstrate her rare gift and mastery of the music of the word, which takes us back to the early years of this century and in our day seems to have been lost or forgotten.

There was a certain contradiction in the way the singer thought of her own modest role, devoid of personal ambition, as an intermediary between the composer and the audience, and the enthusiasm of many of her listeners who hailed her as a medium or a high-priestess to be bowed down to. Olenina writes of her desire not to cancel out, but at least to restrain and delay the applause, in order that the inner silence should continue and turn into an outer physical silence after the work is finished. But the resulting ecstatic silence only reinforced the role of the priestess that Olenina renounced, preferring to refer to herself as "*yurodivaya*"—a holy fool.

Olenina's "holy-foolishness" was not just an empty phrase or a pose with her. This persona, a veritable incarnation of *idealism* and *impracticality*, was a manifestation of her character which was in fact full of contradictions. Olenina-d'Alheim suffered from her idealism, but much more than that she was proud of it; it was largely the philosophy that she lived by. And her loudly proclaimed, studied absence of practicality was a reflection of that self-awareness peculiar to a certain section of the Russian intelligentsia. We have seen on several occasions during her long life how Olenina refused to see the world as it really was. The idea for her was more important than the reality, and even after the year 1956 with its revelations about Stalin's crimes, and while still living in France where there was far more objective information to be had than in the USSR, she still clung to her sacred belief in the Soviet Union as a promised paradise ruled by a sense of social justice. And back in Moscow, after 1959, she discovered that many of her illusions were totally incompatible with the Soviet reality she observed around her. Particularly painful were the discoveries she made in the arts, and especially in the field of singing. Here there was a total decline of folk song, the domination of a popular culture impregnated by ideology and propaganda, and a purely formal—and in many instances, indifferent—attitude to the music of the past, and to Mussorgsky in particular. But none of this could shake Olenina's faith in the correctness of communism; in every instance it was not the system that was to blame, but merely individual officials.

Typical of the Russian intelligentsia, too, was Olenina's attitude to such a product of human civilisation as money. In her childhood reminiscences she could recall precisely the day when money became an absolute evil to her. The idea that money is dirty, that children should not touch money, the equation of money and profit-making (in reference to the normal earnings that justify engagement in any activity or enterprise)—all these terms of abuse, or the observation that a doctor takes money for his treatment as though committing some shameful act. How often are these words and expressions met in the converse of the Russian intelligentsia both before and after the Revolution!

In fact, not only did Olenina throughout her life curse money as the supreme evil and prime cause of all that is wrong in this world. It was on the basis of her supposed "campaign against profit" that she conducted all her dealings with friends (remember, for instance, her break with Cortot) and decided all her "business" problems connected with art (*viz* her correspondence with Balakirev à propos of the concerts in Germany). And ultimately, as a result of this, it was her own art that suffered. Noble, transparently honest, lacking any sense of practicality or money, Olenina in fact curtailed her own concert career and also limited it geographically by rejecting the notion of concert tours (which, alas, are based on the notion of making a profit). Her rejection of concert tours was a good example of the extremes to which her protest against profit-making in the arts drove her. Ultimately, her "total" protest against commercialisation of the arts in fact caused no less harm than their total commercialisation.

Olenina's ideology was driven by the most noble motives and a sense of equality and fairness. She also shared a fair measure of that "sense of guilt before the people," and was herself thus ultimately partly responsible for the revolutionary moods that led to the Revolution itself, a revolution which in the Soviet period ended up destroying its own children—the Russian intelligentsia. Yet today's post-Soviet Russian intelligentsia can often still be heard uttering the same curses against those who at present make fat profits through setting high prices. As an American acquaintance of mine recently commented: "Money viewed as something dirty and inherently corrupting is one of the most long-standing of Russian prejudices, for which the Russians are now having to pay very dearly." This Russian prejudice, like several others, was an important and unfortunate part of Olenina's philosophy of life.

Once she found herself living abroad, Olenina proceeded to condemn other émigrés and the whole notion of emigration. She was proud of the fact that her own brothers had not left their country and had "not gone against their own people." Here too was another feature of the Russian intelligentsia mind-set, which was and remains typical of people with a strong sense of subordination to authority, and this has been characteristic of Russia down the centuries. The idea is that people should not be able to exercise their own wishes in deciding where to live. If they are not with us, that means they are against us. Back in 1917, the poetess Anna Akhmatova wrote of emigration as an idea to be rejected, an inner voice to be suppressed, "so that my lamenting spirit not be defiled by this unworthy speech." Since time immemorial people who left Russia always left it forever. In the eyes of their motherland they became marked with the stigma of deserters and outcasts. And despite all her anti-émigré pronouncements, Olenina too became tarred with the same brush when it came to her wanting to return.

The saga of Olenina's return to Russia, like a reflection in a mirror with a thousand facets, was a repetition of many similar stories one could tell, the personal tragic tales of a host of nameless Russians who wanted to return to their own homeland. Olenina found herself in the position of those whom she herself had condemned when she first came to France—she was denied the right to choose freely for herself where she should live. It is typical that while writing her "Dream and Reminiscences" in 1948, and having already been several times refused permission to return, she still continued condemning others who left Russia.

Olenina was one of those Russian artists who at various times and for various reasons wanted to return to their native land. Among them were musicians such as Sergei Prokofiev, or poets and writers like Marina Tsvetaeva, Alexander Kuprin, Alexei Tolstoy, or Irina Odoevtseva.[2] All these returnees travelled their own Road to Calvary, making their way through the Kafka-esque labyrinth of Soviet bureaucracy. The obstacles that Olenina had to contend with were at the same time both extraordinarily difficult and absolutely typical. Extraordinary in her story was that her journey to Moscow took more than thirty years; all the rest was typical. Why was an elderly, sixty- and later seventy- and eighty-year-old singer not allowed back into the USSR? It is interesting to compare her story with the fairly easy return of Prokofiev. They shared in common the same motivation—neither could imagine a life for themselves outside Russia, a country of which they retained idealised memories from earlier years, and to which they desired to devote their whole creative lives.

One recalls the letters of Vladimir and Yulia Stepun sent to Olenina in the early 1930s and containing advice, warnings, and tales of their visits to various communist grandees and conservatoire professors. At the same time Prokofiev's friends Asafyev and Myaskovsky[3] were also weighing up the pros and contras of his returning permanently to the Soviet Union. (The essential difference between Olenina and Prokofiev was the latter's world fame and celebrity, and the fact that he had regularly made concert tours to Russia even during the Soviet period.) From his recently published diary of 1927, it is clear that the composer had an extensive though not total understanding of the political situation in Soviet Russia. (S. Prokofiev, *Soviet Diary 1927 and Other Writings*, ed. O. Prokofiev (London, 1991).) In January of 1935, soon after the murder of Kirov, in a letter to Prokofiev in Paris, Myaskovsky passed on Asafyev's opinion of the situation: "In the circles of the Leningrad Union of Composers (and everywhere where it can influence matters—in the Philharmonia and, most of all, in the theatres) people are terribly afraid of you and will do everything they can to stop you. [...] Therefore [Asafyev] considers that your production plans [for the ballet *Romeo and Juliet*] in the Mariinsky Theatre are built upon sand." (See R. Harlow, *Sergei Prokofiev. A Biography* (New York, 1987), 298–99.)

Prokofiev did everything in his power to prove that he was a part of Soviet music—by giving concerts in the Soviet Embassy in Paris, by publishing articles in the Soviet press about the need for simplicity in Soviet music, and by giving concerts in the farthest corners of Russia. In December 1936, he saw in the New Year in Moscow together with his wife, the singer Lina Ivanovna Prokofieva, and his two sons, having decided to remain permanently in the Soviet Union. The tragic reward for taking this step is well known: his wife was arrested and spent many years in the GULag, his sons were left at large but alone without their mother, and Prokofiev himself endured many years of Party criticism and official boycott. Returning to Russia, Olenina too endured another tragedy: she discovered she had returned too late to do any work in her own field of music.

It is difficult to determine exactly why Olenina-d'Alheim was not allowed back to Russia earlier. It is clear that Prokofiev's relatively easy return was explained by his celebrity and the political capital to be made out of this spectacle of a Prodigal Son returning to his homeland. These factors were absent in the case of Maria Olenina, who was elderly, forgotten, and of no obvious use to anyone.

Yet how many people were involved in the attempts to secure Olenina's return: Lunacharsky and Bubnov, Molotov and Krasin, Maxim Gorky and Romain Rolland. Statesmen, Party officials, and writers spent much time and trouble trying to do what any immigration official can do fairly quickly in any normal country. Olenina's long enforced exile was a reflection of certain features of the Stalin period, when arbitrariness was rampant, the whole country worked at night, blundering around in a lawless maze, and when even a routine matter was entrusted to nobody and had to be decided at high level. Even after her return Olenina continued to be officially ignored. Yet had she returned as she wished in the 1920s, there is no guarantee that in the Stalin period she would not have joined hosts of other former émigrés who were dispatched to the labour camps. And who is to say that she would have survived such an ordeal, when so many perished?

Contemplating the personality of Olenina, one inevitably returns again to her own self-confessed quality of the "*yurodivaya*." Her whole personality was riven with contradictions, and she was that "holy fool" in the same sense as Mussorgsky had been one: in a world dominated by conformism, both of them had spoken the truth, an *artistic truth* which was by no means to the taste of everyone. Throughout her life, Olenina staunchly defended her right to dissent, and she was a tireless propagandist of her own artistic ideas. Her eccentricity might be compared with that of the twentieth-century Russian pianist Maria Yudina,[4] who was a passionate propagandist of music by the Soviet avant-garde.

Richly gifted, contrary, totally consumed by her art, which was more important to her than her own daughter, Olenina was disinterested, intolerant, sincere, arrogant, modest, refined, plebeian, Russian, French, a writer, a *grande dame*, a *baba*; in the opinion of many a musical thinker, while in the opinion of others she was a puppet in the hands of Pierre d'Alheim. And she was also a great Russian singer whose memory deserves not· to be lost in the swiftly flowing stream of time.

Unjustly buried under the cultural accretions of many decades, almost erased from the cultural annals of her native land, Maria

Olenina-d'Alheim enters the confused scene of today, desperately in need of the same selfless artistic attention she herself once dispensed. And she enters as one of our own contemporaries without whom many vital pages of Russian cultural history, past, present, and future, could never otherwise be written.

Appendix

Открытые уроки Олениной-д'Альгейм (Расшифровка звукозаписей)
Olenina-d'Alheim's Master Classes (Russian Transcriptions)

Предваряя эту первуго публикацию Открытых уроков (ОУР), необходимо снабдить читателя рядом использующихся в их расшифровке условных обозначений, отражающих интонацию голоса Марии Алексеевны, которые помогут понять ее художественные идеи и то, как ее пение было связано с вербальным текстом, психологическим развитием и музыкальной структурой произведений Мусоргского. И хотя расшифровка магнитофонной записи не может дать полного представления о богатстве речи певицы, сохранившей особенности произношения и интонации русской интеллигенции начала века, она, тем не менее, поможет приближенно представить себе эту речь.

Условные обозначения, использующиеся в расшифровке "Уроков":

Значительная редукция гласного в конце слова
—"(ъ, ь, э)"

Ударение внутри фразы —"(é)"

Ударение внутри фразы и повышение интонации
—"(плАкали)"

Подчеркнутое разделение слов —"(V)"

Фрикативное "г" —"(ґ)"

Интонация вверх —"(↑)"

Интонация вниз —"(↓)"

Удлинение гласной —"(ааа)"

Обозначение темпа, относящееся к следующему слову
—"(*a tempo* →)"

Динамика, относящаяся к следующему слову
—"(*mf*→)"

* * *

Текст "уроков Олениной-д'Альгейм" публикуется без редакторских дополнений и с минимальной стилистической правкой и, таким образом, представлен с естественными для устной речи оговорками и повторениями.

РАСШИФРОВКА ЗАПИСЕЙ УРОКОВ ОЛЕНИНОЙ-Д'АЛЬГЕЙМ, МОСКВА, 1963

I. "Детская" Мусоргского в исполнии Г. Писаренко

Писаренко поет:

"Расскажи мне, нянюшка, расскажи мне, милая,
Про того, про буку страшного"

Оленина:

Там написано: "скоро". Да. И потом, почему таким тоном печальным? Девочке хочется знать. […] Тянет ее к разным сказкам страшным. Она хочет страшную сказку. (Напевает): "Расскажи мне, нянюшкъ, расскажи мне, милаэ, про тогó, про буку стрáшного. Как тот бука…" (показывает поспешность, сильно редуцируя концы слов) Быстро, быстро, быстро! (напевает): "Как тот бука в лес детéй носил, и как грыз он их белые кóсточки (последние два слова *accel.* и *cresc.*), и как дети те кричАли, (V) плАкали! (последние два слова разделяет экспрессивно, *accel.* и *cresc.*)" — Потом … начинает её разбирать страх: "Нянюшка, а ведь за тó их, детей-то, бука съел, что обидели няню старую, (ускоряя) папу с мамою не послУшали? Ведь за то их бука съел? Или вот что: расскажи мне лучше про княгИню с князем, (поет шире) что за мОрем жили в теремУ богатом. Ещё князь все нá ногу хромал. Как споткнется — так грыб (↑) вырастет! у княгини-то все нáсморк был. Как чихнё(↑)т — стЁ(↑)кла вдребезги! Знá(↑)ешь, нянюшка,

ты про буку-то уж не рассказывай, (говорком→) Бог с ним,
с букой! Расскажи мне лучше тУ(↑), смешнУ(↑)ю-то
(последнее слово — со смехом)".

Вот так, понимаете, быстро, быстро. Ей хочется, а потом
сразу [страшно] стало. Ей хочется думать, что, конечно, если
детей бука съел, так только потому что они сами виноваты.

Писаренко

поет всю песню.

Оленина:

Не удержалась и мимикой-то занялась. (Смеется) А этого-то
не полагается. (Все смеются.)

Писаренко:

Но ведь вы показывали тоже с мимикой.

Туманов:

Это само собой получается.

Оленина:

Да, само собой, но очень маленькой мимика должна быть.
Нельзя уж очень подчеркивать слова девочки. И потом, когда
она поет: "И за то их, детей-то бука съел", она себя сама
утешает, понимаете, она все же побаивается (смеется) буку-
то. А она не будет так [как дети] делать, она не будет: они
[дети] обидели няню старую, папу с мамою не послу(↑)шали!
Ведь за то их… понимаете, она сама себя утешает, сама себя
утешает. "Или вот что" — это уж она скорее гонит вон это
неприятное впечатление. "Или вот что: расскажи мне лучше
про княгиню с князем, (поёт) [что] за морем жили…" —
это уж она в радости поет, так ей приятно это. Такой терем
большой, бога́тый [Еще князь] все на́ ногу хромал. Как
споткнется — так грЫ↑б вырастет". Тут уж не приходится
ни очень улыбаться, ни очень [серьезной быть]: "так грЫ↑б
вырастет". "У княгини-то все (*ritenuto*→) нааа́сморк был: (*a
tempo*→) как чихнЁт — стЁкла вдребезги. Знаешь, нянюшка,
ты про буку-то уж не рассказывай (говорком *accel.*→). Бог с
ним, с букой. Расскажи мне лучше ту, смешную-то". Уж она
уехала в смешную сказку, а ту отстраняет. Потому что она
хоть и любительница таких страшных впечатлений, но она
все-таки побаивается (смеется), она не уверена, что над этим
можно… То же самое с мальчишкой.

Туманов:

Ну, давайте мальчишку.

Оленина:

Мальчишку с няней. Этот мальчишка с няней, ведь он потом говорит: "Я ничегО не сделал (растягивает ударный слог), (говорком, быстро→) нянюшка, я чулочек не трогал, (быстро→) нянюшка!" И знает, что он врет. "Клубочек размотал (быстро→)котеночек, и пруточки разбросал (быстро→)котеночек. А Мѝшенька был пáинька, Мѝшенька был ýмница. А няня (пауза) злая, старая. (Дальше говорит тише→): У няни носик-то запачканный. Миша чистенький, причЁсанный, а у няни чепчик на боку". (Смеется, дальше говорит громко→): "Няня Мѝшеньку обѝдела, напраАсно в угол поставила". Ему обидно, потому что нянюшка не обращает на него внимания никакого. (Говорит очень тихо→): "Миша больше не бýдет любить свою нянюшку. Вот что".

Туманов:

Ну что, споет Галя?

Оленина:

А он отлично знает, что котеночек… Он не может уверить нянюшку, что котеночек чернилами запачкал чулок. (Смеется) Про чулок он не рассказывает. Он только про пруточки, […] Пропускает. Но [это] значит, что он все-таки обижен. Ему все-таки очень неприятно было, что няня его поставила в угол, да еще никакого на него внимания не обращает.

Туманов:

Поэтому там у Мусоргского [стоит] *капризно*? Что он капризным тоном это все говорит?

Оленина:

Да, капризно. Немножко таким… (смеется) Он хочет доказать няне, что это не он, а доказать-то ему никак нельзя. Я знаю, что в Париже один композитор прослезился. Так ему было жалко Мишеньку, что он прослезился.

Туманов:

А кто пел? Вы, Мария Алексеевна?

Оленина:

Да.

Туманов:

Кто был этот композитор?

Оленина:

Александр Жорж. (Пауза) Ну-ка, "Ах, ты, проказник!"

Писаренко

поет целиком всю песню "В углу".

Оленина:

Когда нянюшка его [ругает] … "Ах, ты, проказник (напевает без слов) все петли спустил, чуло́к↔весь забрыз↔гал черни́лами, в у́гол, в у́гол, по-шел в у-гол". (Смеется) в музыке там толкает она его, толкает в угол.

Туманов:

Что, вот эти вот акценты: "по-шел в у-гол"? (На рояле звучат аккорды, имитирующие действия няни.)

Оленина:

(После последнего аккорда) "Про-каз-ник!" А тот [уж] обижен. Уж он обиделся заранее. (Смеется) "Я ничегО↑ не сделал, (*accel.*→) нянюшкъ". Он там довольно так долго [в углу стоит], пока он начнет плакать и жаловаться. Оправдываться! Он оправдывается. Ну-ка, спойте еще разок. Он оправдывается и одновременно невольно думает, как чернила-то [оправдать] (смеется). И котенок-то тут. И потом, когда он сразу выдумал, как он будет оправдываться — "Клубочек размотал котеночек, пруточки разбросал котеночек" — он на котеночка все валит.

Писаренко

поет еще раз всю песню.

Оленина:

Решил, да. А когда он говорит, что котеночек [все натворил], а "Мишенька был умница", [и потом] (говорит тихо→) — а "няня злая, старая", он понемножку начинает на нее нападать, не сразу. Он все-таки побаивается: в углу долго стоять придется тогда. [Он говорит] (чуть громче→): "А у няни носик-то запачканный" — понемножку. (Смеется) а потом: (скороговоркой→) "Миша чистенький, причесанный, (разделяя слова, громче→): А у няни — чепчик на боку". Он ей понемножку, а так как она не обращает внимания (значительно громче и шире→): "Няня Ми(↑)шеньку оби(↑)дела". Уж он тут обижен, совсем обижен [и] начинает уж понимать, что она ему не верит (смеется). (Говорит тихо и медленно→): "Миша бо↑льше не будет любить свою нянюшку. (Еще тише→): Вот что".

Туманов:

Ну что ж, давайте "Жука" послушаем?

Оленина:

Да. теперь, это самая такая уже, быстрая. Ну, как она будет ее [петь]?

Писаренко

поет всю песню.

Оленина:

Здесь в двух местах неверно. Во-первых, "Я играл там на песочке". Это слишком быстро. Вот, [он] хотя прибежал, запыхался, но все-таки не так быстро должно это идти (произносит говорком, быстро): "Я играл там за беседкой, на песочке, где березки…", как это там сказано, я уж не помню. (Показывает темп и ритм без слов, потом): "Строил дОмик (V) из лучиночек кленовых, тех, что мне мама…". Достаточно. Не надо напирать очень. (Возвращается к прежнему темпу): "Дóмик уж совсем построил. Домик с крЫ↑шей, настоящий домик". (Пауза) "Вдруг (V) (тихо) на самой крыше (*rit.*) жу́к (V) сидит (*poco accel.* и *cresc.*→) страшный, (*mf.*→) темный, (*f.*→) тО↑лстый такой, усами…" Вот это хорошо! (Опять взволнованно): "Чтó же, чтó же с жуком-то сталось? Меня удА↑рил, а сам свалИ↑лся! Чтó же-то с ним (V) сталось, (*dim.* и *rit.*→) с жуком-то?" А нянюшка (смеется) не обращает внимания. (Повторяет начальную фразу): "Я играл там на песочке, за беседкой, где березки" — так чтоб все слышно [было], а это слишком вы быстро [пели].

Недавно по радио передавали какую-то [программу], не помню, станция "Юность" или что-то такое. Чайковского играли концерт, это хорошо [было], а потом вдруг [какой-то певец] Варлаама песню запел. Ну, отвратительно ее пел. Быстро слишком. Какого-то Фигарó выдумал. Быстро! Пьяный монах так никогда бы не пел. Это нереально. Я помню, как

Шаляпин пел: Шаляпин пел прекрасно, Шаляпин необыкновенно хорошо пел эту роль. Лучше, чем Бориса, ей-богу, необыкновенно хорошо. Так он так не пел. Он так не торопился. И потом разные ха-ха-ха не приставлял. А этот и свои ха-ха-ха [выдумал]. Вот это не дай Бог. Да, и что меня еще поразило [в этой программе], что большая певица, которая претендует на Ленинскую премию, Архипова, в честь Мусоргского, что ли, такую пакость пела — песню Миньоны Амбруаза Тома. Это такая пошлятина, которую записали уже давно уличные певцы, и с шарманками ее поют. (Поет с издевкой песню Миньоны по-французски.) Меня заставили эту всю оперу учить. Я ее наизусть должна была знать. Когда мне пришлось в Опера Комик поступать, я должна была петь эту дрянь. А тогда как раз начинались [конференции о] Мусоргском, [и я сказала, что] я уже отклоняю Опера Комик к черту. Потом еще пошлость необыкновенная — это ария Пажа из "Гугенотов" Мейербера. Это же никто больше не поет во Франции. Это то, что надо выметать. А она поет это. Да что это такое за [репертуар]? Какая же это Ленинская премия? Ленин этого никогда [бы не одобрил]. Когда Долуханова приехала в Париж, на всех ее портретах [было]: Prix Staline. Эти премии Сталин выдумал, а не Ленин. А потом они взяли, переделали, теперь — Ленинская премия! Кому она нужна, эта ленинская премия? Это за деньгами, а? Ходить, просить милостыню. С шарманкой (смеется). Не дай Бог.

Писаренко:

Мария Алексеевна, я спою вам еще колыбельную?

Оленина:

Конечно. А это уж Тяпа. Девочка подражает так своей няне, что она уж…

Писаренко

поет песню "С куклой".

Оленина:

Я чувствую немножко более быстро, это слишком медленно. Более машинально. Ведь как няня ей делала, так и она. (Напевает быстрее, чем Писаренко→): "Тяпа, ба́-ай-ба́-ай, Тяпа, спи, усни́-и, угомон тебя возьми. (Говорком→): (второй слог выше первого) Тя(↑)па, спать (V) (↓)надо. Тяпа, спи, усни́-и". Вспомнила про волка-то (смеётся). "Тяпу бука съе́-ест, серый волк возьмё-от, в тёмный л↑ес снесё-от. (Более *legato*→) Тяпа, спи, усни́-и, что во сне увидишь, мне про то расскажешь, про остров чудный, где не жнут, не сеют, где цветут и зреют груши наливные, целый день пою́-ут птички золотые". А потом в конце — (говорит быстро→): "Баю, бай, (еще быстрее→) Тяпа". Она быстро [говорит], ее кладет и убегает. [Говорят], она сама заснула. Нет, ей надоело. "Баю, бай, Тяпа". (Все смеются тому, как М.А. естественно произносит последнюю фразу.) Ушла. Вот спойте ее более так… машинально.

Писаренко
поет более машинально, менее "выразительно", чем первый раз.

Оленина:
Это с маленьким криком (?) таким: (Говорит очень коротко→): "Баю, бай, Тяпа". Даже Репин нарисовал, что она [куклу] укладывает. Она ее укладывает, а сама убежала (смеется): не все же время мне куклу качать. Ну, давайте дальше — "на сон грядущий". Это необыкновенно. [Девочка] наполовину не понимает, что она поет. Молитву [не понимает]. Довольно скоро, — там сказано.

Писаренко
поет песню "На сон грядущий".

Оленина:
Тут много выдуманного, и этого нельзя. Как раз, когда она пересчитала всех тетушек: тетю Катю, тетю Парашу, дядей таких-то… потом Петю и Митю … и Дуняшу, она на них не сердится, а у вас получается, как будто она так уж [на них] обиделась, что ну их к черту. А она просто торопится кончить молитву, потому что она дальше не знает, что говорить. (Говорком, сильно редуцируя концы слов→): "Няня, а нянь̲, (неуверенно→) как (V) дальше, нянь? — (Нянины слова говорит просто и не очень громко, скорее устало→): Ишь ты, проказница какая. Уж сколько раз учила: (поучительным, спокойным голосом→) Господи, поми́луй и меня (↓→) грешную". А девочка не знает, что значит "грешная".

(Напевает→): "Господи, помилуй и меня (V) грешную".
(Робко спрашивает→): "Так, нянюшка?"

Я вам скажу: когда меня маленькую няня заставляла читать [молитвы], я никогда не понимала, что значит "отче наш, иже еси на небеси". [Это] для меня ничего не значило. Я не понимала, что это [значит] — "иже еси на небеси". Ничего не понимала. Единственное, что в этой молитве я понимала, это слова "прости нам долги наши, как мы прощаем" и что-то про хлеб, это я соображала. А потом [меня] заставляли [говорить] молитву Богородице: "Богородица, дева, радуйся". И какое это слово: "деварадуйся"? Я никак не могла понять, что это за слово, я решительно не понимала. Дети вообще очень часто не понимают тех слов, которыми их заставляют молиться. В церкви я, когда ходила, решительно ничего не понимала: по-славянски чего-то болтают там. "Господи, помилуй!", — вот только и знала, а другого ничего, никогда не [понимала]. Даже когда я большая была.

А маленькая, конечно, не понимает, что значит "грешная". А няня уж не так все серьезно ей говорит. У вас выходит, что няня как будто большому человеку говорит, а она маленькой девчонке говорит: (Спокойным, нравоучительным голосом, почти без интонации→) "Ишь ты, проказница какая. Сколько раз учила: Господи помилуй (разделяет слова, дидактически→) и меня грешную. (Повторяет за девочку, тихо и робко→): И меня грешную". Девочка может ошибиться словом, сказать "гешную". [Поэтому] она тщательно выговаривает: грешную. (Смеется) А про Митю, Петю, Дуняшу — не нужно так на них злиться. У вас выходит, будто она сердится, а она просто торопится.

Писаренко:

Она [у меня] не злится, она вспоминает.

Оленина:

Ну, а дальше что же? Гоп-гоп! Вы знаете, сегодня по радио [выступал] какой-то языковед, [советовал, как] поправлять наш язык и [говорил], откуда происходит [выражение] "поди, поди". Оказывается, в прежние [времена] всегда впереди бежали [гонцы], когда царь ехал, с криком "поди, поди"! А у Мусоргского-то тоже есть "гей поди".

Писаренко

поет "Поехал на палочке".

Оленина:

Хорошо все, кроме мамы. Мама нехорошо говорит. Мама
такая слишком важная. Она попроще, попроще. "Постой-
ко, встань на ножки прямо: вот так, дитя. (Мягко, тихим
говорком→): посмотри↑"... Она его хочет развлечь, не
чересчур [нажимая]. "Посмотри, какая (мягко повышая
интонацию к концу слова→) прЕ↑лесть... налево, видишь
— птичка". Более говорком.

Писаренко:

Не так напевно?

Оленина:

Да, не так выпевать. "Какие слезы! видишь? ну, что, прошло?"
А вот это уж ясно. "Прошло".

Писаренко

поет с meno allegro. *"Ой, боль-но, ой, ногу!"*

Оленина:

Это слишком быстро. Зачем так торопиться? (Писаренко
поет медленнее, но для Олениной и это слишком быстро.
Замедляет значительно, напевает со стоном, жалуясь→):
"Ой, больно! ой, ногу! ой, больно! ой, ногу!"

Писаренко

*поет текст матери. Во время пения Оленина вставляет слова
(из текста и свои), чтобы показать простоту интонации:
"пройдет, мой друг". Когда Писаренко доходит до слов "Вот так,
дитя", Оленина ее останавливает.*

Оленина:

Слишком сентиментально. (Проговаривает с интонацией,
понижающейся на каждом слоге→): "Вот так, дитя↓." Попроще.
*(Писаренко поет от слов "Посмотри, какая прелесть" до
"Прошло!" Оленина останавливает)*: Нет, нехорошо. "Ну, что
прошло?" — короче мать [говорит]. И потом (проговаривает
просто→): "Что за перышки! Смотри, какая пти́↑чка! какие
пёрышки!" Более говорком. Не надо так выпевать слишком
голосом. "Какая прелесть! В кустах, налево..." Она боится
[говорить громко], чтобы птичку не испугать. Она ему
тихонько говорит: "смотри налево: какая пти↑чка, какие

пё↑рышки". Потом: "Ну, что, прошло↑? — Про↑шло↓".
Гораздо более реально. Реально. Попроще, попроще. Ничего
задуманного заранее, а что приходится. Мать, она не станет
[говорить искусственно]: "Милый мой, мой мальчик, ну, что
за горе?.. Пройдет, мой друг." Как няня, [так и] и мама говорит
[просто]. Попросту. Очень просто. Гораздо проще мать
[говорит]. Не надо, чтобы она пела.

Писаренко:

А я себе другую мать представляю. Она такая благородная
дама, она вся в кружевах.

Оленина:

И моя мама такая была благородная дама, а со мной так не
разговаривала. (Смеется)

Писаренко:

Не простая такая дама прозаическая.

Оленина:

Так моя мама тоже дворянка была, но со мной говорила очень
просто. Никогда не говорила неестественно. (Смеется)

Писаренко:

Нет, просто бывает в голосе, в интонации благородство, а
бывает [простота?]. Я хочу ее такой... немножко дамой… она
ласково обращается [к мальчику], но она сама такая… она не
простая такая сама.

Оленина:

Она просто мама. (Обращаясь к своей племяннице Татьяне
Алексеевне): Ты как со своим сыном [разговаривала], Таня?
Спросите ее, как она говорила. (Татьяна Алексеевна: Да я
шлепака, может, дала бы кстати, если заслужил.) (Оленина
смеется.) "Милый мой, что за слезы?" Ну, что же что он упал.
Ну, упал, она его подняла. "Пройдет, мой друг, пройдет."
Она его уговаривает. Она вовсе не такая сентиментальная
аристократка была. Просто простая мама. Мама из семьи
таких детей, которые росли в своих детских.

Туманов:

Мария Алексеевна, а какое у Вас общее впечатление от
исполнения Гали?

Оленина:

Она хорошо все делает. Я как следует ее звук голоса не слышу.
[…]

Туманов:

Нет, я спрашиваю не о вокальной стороне, а об исполнении.
Как она Мусоргского исполняет.

Оленина:

Она почти все хорошо [делает], кроме тех мест, где она
задумала что-нибудь сделать.

Туманов:

Там, где есть что-то надуманное.

Оленина:

Да, да. А это не надо. Не надо подчеркивать особенно что-
нибудь, совсем не надо.

Туманов:

Мария Алексеевна, вы ведь слышали и других исполнителей
"Детской". Если сравнить, как пели раньше "Детскую" и как
ее поет Галя [Писаренко] сейчас, что изменилось?

Оленина:

А я не знаю, как пели раньше. Я никогда никого не слушала:
я всегда так боялась слушать какую-нибудь знаменитость —
как бы что-нибудь не поймать от нее плохое. Ведь плохое
всегда прилипает. А я всегда боялась: завязнет где-нибудь в
памяти. Вот так и бывает с этим. Вот отчего я не хотела даже
записи свои делать [на пластинки]. Потому что что-нибудь
захватят и имитируют. А зачем подражать? Все сказано у
композитора, все написано. Нужно петь просто то, что у
[него] написано. А вот [иногда] исполняют самые простые
романсы с каким-то "своим" подходом, разные там ферматы
делают. (В качестве примера приводит исполнение
Мясниковой арии Марфы из "Хованщины"): Чувствовалось,
как будто это не Мусоргский написал. (Рассказывает, хотя,
к сожалению часть рассказа не поддается расшифровке, о
том, как Барсова собиралась к ней прийти, чтобы обсудить
возможность возобновления "Дома песни", но так никогда и
не появилась.)

II. Запись урока В. Рыбинского:

Рыбинский
  поет песню "Козел".
Оленина:
  Надо, чтобы чувствовалось во всем рассказе какое-то
  критическое и насмешливое чувство самого автора. Вот
  особенно это подчеркивать. (Напевает): "Шла девица
  погулять." (Смеется) — Более певуче. [Затем]: "Вдруг
  навстречу ей козел" — более просто. (Говорит): "Вдруг
  навстречу ей козел". Ну, козел нам-то не страшен, а девица
  испугАлась и помчАлась и т. д. Козла не [нужно петь] чересчур
  тяжело. (Одну фразу невозможно расшифровать) Вторая
  [часть] очень хорошо. (Напевает): "Шла девица под венец", а
  [дальше] более говорком: "Знать, пришла пора ей замуж" (это
  говорит). Более насмешливо, иронически. Чтоб чувствовалась
  ирония самого Мусоргского. Ведь он этим высмеивал нравы.
  Все, что он политического написал — все так же. А "Раек"?
  (Смеется.) А потом этого поповича ("Семинариста")
  непременно надо выучить. Это необыкновенно хорошо
  сделано. (Вспоминает "Семинариста" и смеется.)
Рыбинский
  поет снова "Козла".
Оленина:
  "Пришла пора ей замуж — ну↑ (говорит это слово выше по
  интонации и раздельно) и вышла". Как сатира сразу. "Муж и
  старый, и горбатый…" — немножко менее грозно, чем козел.
  (напевает): "Что ж, девица испуга↑лась?" (Ответ говорком,
  значительно ниже→): "Как же." [Дальше] хорошо. Так же, как
  мы говорим, так Мусоргский и написал. У Мусоргского речь
  совершенно ясно взята из простой речи человеческой.
      Вот теперь будет монолог Бориса — это глубокое
  страдание, тут будет дело другое. И [это] все можно сказать,
  все продекламировать простым голосом. Оттого он так и
  правдив и (непонятное слово), поучает нас, артистов, так же
  относиться ко всем остальным авторам, которые того
  достойны. К художникам настоящим. Те песни петь и арии, в

которых в самом деле правда сказана, а не придумана. Когда придумано, то [это] чувствуется. Чем мы чувствуем? Внутренними чувствами. У нас ведь двойные чувства — духовные, душевные и — внешние. А внешние только рассудком вместе связаны. Можно выучить, можно продумать, можно подумать и т. д., но не прочувствовать глубоко, тогда как внутренние наши чувства нас учат именно проникнуть в самую душу человека, то, что Мусоргский хотел, и оттуда взять именно то, что есть, простым слухом и простым зрением невидимое.

Рыбинский

поет "Монолог" Бориса.

Оленина:

Про Русь, голодную, бедную — протяжно: "ГолО-о-дная, бЕ-е-дная…" А когда вы [поете о] мальчике, который просил пощады, тут (непонятное слово): "И нÉ-е было пощады." Он сам себя упрекает. Мусоргский Бориса строил по Пушкину, то есть он его считает убийцей, так что с этим надо считаться. [Мусоргский] из него делает настоящего убийцу. Он [Борис] хотел [убийства царевича]. Ход мысли по истории мы знаем. [Но] неизвестно, был ли он в самом деле [убийцей] или не был, или это Шуйский устроил. Шуйский подготовлял свое собственное царство. Ведь Шуйский поганый был человек. А этот татарин, у него особенная правдивость была. Он, может, хотел, старался как-нибудь, но это мы узнаем еще. Это он не знает. Мы знаем то, как быстро он закрепил крестьян и создал крепостное право. Он выдвинул этих хороших бояр, дав им возможность работы устраивать и все. Ну, а крамольных он боялся. Это даже у Пушкина [есть] тоже. Очень много крамольных бояр было, которые хотели власть захватить сами. Ведь бояре все-таки выдвигались среди своего народа, иностранцев у нас еще не было, немецких-то этих рыцарей. История нам показывает это. Марина Мнишек особенная девчонка была: полька, католичка убежденная, и все время вел ее иезуит. Когда первый самозванец погиб, она другого нашла. Она и с другим хотела то же самое проделать. Это по истории, которую мы не так давно знаем(?).

У Мусоргского Борис в сомнении: ведь он сам не знает, исполнено ли [было] его желание. Может, он желал, а Шуйский помог. Ему тяжело (говорит тихо, с придыханием→): "и не было пощады". Когда он говорит, что [вокруг] разлад, когда он страдает, — не так громко. Никогда не надо, чтоб певец шел за (непонятное слово, может быть — [за идеей]), что главное — фортиссимо своего голоса, потому что [пение] переходит в крик. А крик уже не имеет [ничего общего] с музыкой. Крик — это никуда не годно. Плач, крик, это есть в народе, я сама слышала. Во-первых, цыганку слышала, которая сидела около дверей тюрьмы, в которой ее мужа заперли за то, что он конокрадом был. Она сидела и причитала, плакала. Плакала, плакала, понемножку качалась, качалась, и ее причитания перешли в пение. Оттого я хотела, чтобы в программу (?) записан был для сопрано плач и причитание Ксении. Это нужно. И думка Параси. (Рыбинский: Думка Параси есть в программе. Оленина: А та есть или нет? Рыбинский: Нет.) А я слышала, как они здесь это воют, так это умопомрачение.

Я сама знаю, как это (причитание) [делается]. Я слышала невесту, которая была сирота наполовину. [Был] девишник перед самым венцом. Девушки все вокруг нее собрались. […]. Она закрылась таким платком большим и начала причитать, плакать и понемногу [начала] петь. Она и пела, и причитала: "Благослови ты меня, бá-а-тюшка. Осталась я сироткой без мá-а-тушки." Ну, как обыкновенно народ [причитает]. Она свои сочиняла слова — по тому, как она самá жила. А потом товарки говорят: "Молодец, Наташка, хорошо пела." (Смеется) Они ее, наверное, как артистку встречали.

Только никогда пересаливать нельзя. Потому что когда пересаливают, то тогда уж выходит не пение, не плач в пении, а наоборот, выходит, что пение переходит в крик. А кричать можно что хотите. И обыкновенно так и выходит. Они (певцы) начинают (имитирует крик в пении) [кричать]. Певцы из оперы даже когда они песни поют или романсы, [если] где-нибудь можно прицепиться, так уж они прицепятся. И они выбирают песни, например, у Чайковского, где Чайковский как-то помогает им — высокие ноты дает. (Смеется) Ну, они на этих нотах, конечно, задерживаются и поэтому меняют весь ри́тм самой его песни. А у Чайковского прекрасные есть песни. Например, "Не отходи от меня", ведь это очень хорошо сделано. Видно, что она у него из души вылилась. Потом еще "Ни слова, о друг мой" — прекрасная песня. А вот эту знаменитую "Средь шумного бала", тут он наврал здорово в ритме-то. Ее очень трудно петь, потому что она заикается все время. И слова там неважные: "Ночью люблю я, усталый, прилечь…" (Смеется) Как будто он [любит только] прилечь и никогда не спит. Вранья там много. Вот никогда не надо исполнять вещи, в которых есть вранье. (Смеется. Р ы б и н с к и й: Если бы это было возможно!)

(О начале "Монолога" Бориса. Говорит о том, что нельзя петь грубо.) Он это сам с собой говорит: "Скорбит душа…", прежде чем начать свое обращение. Он начинает: "О, праведник, о мой отец…" тогда [уже] громко. А вначале он говорит вполголоса, совершенно как Сусанин. Сусанин ведь себе говорит: "Чуют правду", а у нас он в опере воет так, что можно слышать в Замоскворечье. Разве можно это делать? Ведь если бы Сусанин так пел, не себе пел, а во всеуслышание, все бы [поляки] его сразу поймали (смеется). Вообще надо считаться с [одним] — единственный для нас проводник хороший — это правда. Правда, правда и правда! Конечно, если это неправда в жизни, так ее надо вон. А вся эта итальянщина, все эти вариации… Я все учила итальянские арии, но всегда избегала всяких там скачков, стаккато разных, задержания на одной ноте. Какой это смысл имеет? Никакого.

Р ы б и н с к и й

поет "Монолог" Пимена.

О л е н и н а:

Понимает, что поет. Это очень много значит. Очень хорошо! Все хорошо спел, все. Никаких замечаний. [Пимен говорит:] мой труд безымянный. Я вот к тому стараюсь молодежь привести, что в будущем театре все артисты будут анонимы. Для того, чтобы они об себе не думали. А ведь это главное, что необходимо настоящему исполнителю — забыть об себе.

А это почти никогда не случается. Себя надо совершенно забыть — это первое правило. [...]

Рыбинский

поет "Классика".

Оленина:

Вот что бы я сказала. Хорошо. Но только когда он негодует, тут не надо таким воинственным [голосом], а более таким злым. "Я личный вра́г" (последнее слово произносит открыто, каркающим голосом). Более резко, пафоса не нужно здесь.

Рыбинский

поет песню "Светик Саввишна".

Оленина:

Хорошо. Хорошо, что он все время одним темпом [поет]. Все время, все время говорком, говорком. Он все-таки не может говорить, как другие. И, между прочим, я всегда, когда пела это, думала о самом Мусоргском. Ведь он тоже такой же юродивый перед жизнью и красотой жизни был. Так что тут надо совсем... Когда Мусоргский сам исполнял [эту песню], он говорил одному исполнителю (генерал такой был, который любил очень их всю "Могучую кучку", и вот этот генерал [жаловался Мусоргскому]: "Задохся, задохся, не могу передохнуть нигде".) С начала до конца — говорком, не подчеркивая ни в каком случае чувства. [Нужно петь] все время одинаково, одинаково.

А вот хотела [бы] узнать как-нибудь, я все хочу найти, нет ли здесь сестры Павла Ламма, потому что она, вероятно, видела разные записи самого Мусоргского. Что у него сказано: Светик Саввишна, свет Ивановна или свет Ива́нова? Это огромное бы имело значение. (Туманов: "Почему, Мария Алексеевнав?") (Напевает): "Светик Саввишна, свет Ивановна" — это уж [он] совершенно юродивый какой-то. (Оленина объясняет, что и Саввишна, и Ивановна — это отчества, так что логично было бы, чтобы Ива́нова была фамилия.) А он все-таки проснулся. У него чувства проснулись, так что тут надо узнать: если "Ива́нова", то у него, значит, какой-то проблеск, чем если он говорит "Ивановна". Он похож был на полусознательного, на бедного этого

юродивого [из "Бориса"], потому что он то же самое все
говорил. Ему толковали, а он все свое.

Рыбинский:

Для меня очень важно, что Вы сказали, что тут чувства не
надо вкладывать.

Оленина:

Таким шопотом [он говорит] все время, все время, до конца.
Он набрал таких слов, которые сами по себе показывают
проснувшиеся в нем чувства человеческие, рассудочные
(сознательные?). Он привык говорить таким шопотком, без
конца, без конца, как юродивый в "Борисе Годунове". Я не
могу слышать, как его [юродивого из "Бориса"] исполняют.
Это такой ужас! Я не знаю, что они из него делают. Какого-то
кретина. Ведь если бы он у Мусоргского кретином был,
Мусоргский бы не поставил его в конце своей драмы. Это
был такой свидетель, собственно, из народа. Ужас! В 1887 году
в Париже то же самое было. И здесь я слышала то же самое.

(ОУР, текст публикуется полностью)

Notes

I— **CHILDHOOD AND YOUTH: Russia—1869–1893**

1. Kasimov—a town in Ryazan Province on the banks of the river Oka, founded
    1152; until 1471 known as Gorodets-Meshchersky; from the mid-fifteenth-
    century centre of a realm ruled over by Kasim-Khan; by late nineteenth
    century a typical central Russian provincial town; its present population is
    around forty thousand.

2. Alexei Nikolayevich Olenin (1763–1843), Russian archeologist, historian, and
    artist, director of St. Petersburg Public Library (from 1811), and president of the
    St. Petersburg Academy of Fine Arts (from 1817). Elected member of the
    Academy of Sciences (1786); contributed to the first Russian Slavonic dictionary.
    Scholarly reputation based mainly on decipherment of the Tmutarakan Stone
    (*Ryazanskie russkie drevnosti*, 1831), which laid the foundations for Russian
    palaeography. As an artist he followed classical models.

    Anna Alexeyevna Olenina (1808–1888)—youngest daughter of the Alexei
    Nikolayevich Olenin. Linked with several poems written in 1828 by Pushkin,
    who heard her sing at the house of composer Mikhail Glinka. She was dedicatee
    of the poems "Ya vas lyubil…," "Ty i vy," "Predchuvstvie," etc. Pushkin's "Ne
    poi, krasavitsa, pri mne…" which was dedicated to Olenina, was set to music
    by Glinka using a Georgian song melody brought from the Caucasus by
    Alexander Griboyedov.

3. Anna Petrovna Kern (1800–1879)—close friend of the Olenins. Pushkin made
    her acquaintance in 1819 at one of their soirées. According to Maria Olenina,
    she was even buried in the Olenin family vault: "In that same year [1883] Varya
    was engaged to Sergei Nilus […] and travelled with him to his grandmother
    […] at Torzhok, and from there to Mitino. […] Mitino is on the river Tverets.
    The whole family's tomb is there. I recently heard that Pushkin's 'fleeting

vision' and 'genius of pure beauty' in his poem 'Ya pomnyu chudnoe mgnoven'e' was buried in this Olenin family vault." (BNB, 181–82.)

4. Ivan Andreyevich Krylov (1769–1844)—Russian journalist and playwright, most famed for his fables.

5. Maria Olenina's family consisted of the following:

Alexei Petrovich Olenin (d.1910)—father, amateur artist, director of the Stroganov Institute of Painting and Sculpture, Moscow (1888).

Varvara Alexandrovna Olenina (1841–1893), née Bakunina—mother.

Ekaterina Alexandrovna Bakunina (1836–1893)—maternal aunt, lived with the Olenins and looked after Maria's daughter Marianna d'Alheim (1891–1910) who died of tuberculosis in her youth.

Pëtr (Pyotr) Alexeyevich Olenin (1864–1926)—brother, writer, published under the pen name Olenin-Volgar.

Alexander Alexeyevich Olenin (1865–1944) (Sasha)—brother, composer and collector of Russian folk song, studied with Pavel Pabst, P. and M. Erdmansdoerfer, later with A.A. Petrov. Befriended and maintained lifelong friendship with Balakirev in St. Petersburg. Composer of opera *Kudeyar* (1915), symphonic poem *After the Battle* (*Posle bitvy*), cycles *The Street* (*Ulitsa*), *The Peasant Son* (*Krest'yansky syn*), *Autumn* (*Osen'*), *The Home* (*Dom*), etc.). Frequent accompanist of Maria Olenina, active in the House of Song, from 1922 member of the Musical Ethnographical Commission, Moscow.

Varvara Alexeyevna Olenina (1867–1915)—sister, artist, lived with her sister in France and Belgium where she studied painting.

Pëtr (Pyotr) Ivanovich d'Al'geim (Pierre d'Alheim) (1862– 1922)—husband, writer, music critic and spokesman, author of books on François Villon and Mussorgsky; translated Mussorgsky's songs into French. Collaborated with his wife in propagating Mussorgsky's music in the West and directed activities of the "Dom pesni" (House of Song) in Russia, known as "Maison du Lied" in France and Belgium. Died in France.

6. Kurland—part of the Russian Empire's Baltic provinces, acquired in 1795, forming part of present-day Latvia and Estonia.

7. Pavel Avgustovich Pabst (1845–1919)—Russian pianist, teacher and composer. Studied in Vienna, and from 1878 taught at Moscow Conservatoire; professor at Moscow Conservatoire 1881–1897.

8. "À livre ouvert"—i.e., simultaneous reading of text in one language and spoken translation in another.

9. *Night on Bald Mountain* (*Noch' na Lysoi gore*), Mussorgsky's orchestral piece (1867), depicting a witches' sabbath, underwent several authorial revisions; its final version was arbitrarily reworked by Rimsky-Korsakov, and it is now performed in this version. The work's large number of dissonances repelled many contemporaries (including Olenina's father) who regarded the work as ultra-avant garde.

10. Alexander Lvovich Gurilyov (1803–1858)—Russian composer of piano music

and songs; piano pupil of John Field; *inter alia*, he left some outstanding settings of Lermontov's verse, folksong settings and song arrangements with elegant, virtuosic piano parts.

11. "Close by the city of Slavyansk" ("Blizko goroda Slavyanska")—an aria from the romantic opera *Askold's Tomb* (*Askol'dova mogila*) by A.N. Verstovsky (1799–1862), founder of Russian operatic vaudeville, one of Glinka's predecessors in Russian musical theatre.

12. *Igrushechka*—illustrated journal for children of pre-school age, published in St. Petersburg in the 1880s. It had two sections catering for various age groups.

13. Camille Flammarion (1842–1925)—French astronomer, well-known author of popular scientific books.

14. Elizaveta Andreyevna Lavrovskaya (1845–1919)—Russian contralto, studied at St. Petersburg Conservatoire; début in 1867 at Mariinsky Theatre, St. Petersburg; in 1890 at Moscow's Bolshoi Theatre; gave Tchaikovsky the idea for an opera on the subject of *Evgeny Onegin*; enjoyed worldwide celebrity and performed in Germany, Italy, Austria, and Great Britain; Tchaikovsky regarded her as one of Russia's finest vocalists and dedicated to her his *Six Songs*, opus 27 (1875), and the vocal quartet *Night* (1893).

15. Stroganov Institute—School for training in decorative and applied art, founded in 1825 by Count S.G. Stroganov as a "school of draftsmanship in relation to the arts and crafts."

16. *Woe from Wit* (*Gore ot uma*)—well-known verse drama of social satire by Alexander Griboyedov (1795–1829).

17. Alexander Sergeyevich Dargomyzhsky (1813–1869)—Russian composer of operas, songs and orchestral fantasias; his finest opera, *The Stone Guest* (*Kamennyi gost'*), was completed by Cui and orchestrated by Rimsky-Korsakov; early encouraged by Glinka (see note 19), he considerably influenced the development of a recognisably Russian national school; his observance of a close link between words and music became a vital principle for composers of the Mighty Handful (see note 22).

18. Marie van Zandt (1861–1916)—soprano of American origin who enjoyed great success in Europe and the USA in the late nineteenth century, often visiting Russia; she was coached by Delibes for the title role of his *Lakme*.

19. *A Life for the Tsar* (*Zhizn' za tsarya*)—first opera by Mikhail Glinka (1804–1857), also known as *Ivan Susanin*. Glinka studied privately in St. Petersburg and travelled widely in Western Europe, becoming celebrated as composer of operas, songs, chamber and piano music; his first opera, using Russian local colour, eschewed the currently popular ornate Italian operatic manner; his second opera *Ruslan and Lyudmila* (*Ruslan i Lyudmila*) (1842) first established an authentically Russian opera style.

20. Emilia Karlovna Pavlovskaya (née Bergman) (1854–1935)—Russian soprano and voice teacher; had a voice of broad range and a strong dramatic talent, appearing in varied roles, including Tatyana (*Eugene Onegin*), Natasha

(*Rusalka*), Violetta (*La Traviata*), Carmen, etc.; from 1895 taught in opera class of the Bolshoi Theatre; among her pupils were Antonina Nezhdanova and Leonid Sobinov who later became the leading singers of the Bolshoi Theatre.

21. "Protocols of the Elders of Zion," a faked document that was used to justify anti-Semitism in Russia in the early twentieth century; it purported to have been written in 1897 during the first Congress of Zionists and to reveal a conspiracy to achieve world rule by Jews and Freemasons; the first (abbreviated) edition appeared in Russia in 1903, supposedly translated from the French; later published in full as a preface to Sergei Nilus's book *The Great Within the Small and Antichrist: an imminent political prospect (Velikoye v malom i Antikhrist, kak blizkaya politicheskaya vozmozhnost')*; in 1921 "Protocols of the Elders of Zion" was revealed as a fake, based on a satirical work by Maurice Joly, "Dialogue in Hell between Machiavelli and Montesquieu," and the novel *Biarritz-Rome* by John Ratcliff.

22. "The Mighty Handful" ("Moguchaya kuchka"—a name coined by their promoter Vladimir Stasov, see note 24), sometimes also known as "The Five" —were the composers Balakirev, Borodin, Cui, Mussorgsky, and Rimsky-Korsakov. Together they formed a recognisably Russian "national" school, using Russian historical, folkloric, and literary subject matter and texts in operas, songs, and other titles, as well as exploiting popular Russian melodism and harmonic progression, etc.; all this contrasted with the obvious Western European leanings of such as Tchaikovsky and Rubinstein. The rise of the Mighty Handful corresponded and coincided with the flourishing of the Russian "realist" novel and a similar school of pictorial artists, the "Itinerants" ("Peredvizhniki").

23. Mily Alexeyevich Balakirev (1837–1910)—leader of the Mighty Handful (see note 22), although a difficult temper sometimes aggravated relations and eventually led to a rift with other members; first prominent as a pianist, but later devoted himself to teaching; ran the first Free School of Music in St. Petersburg, later director of the Court Chapel; his musical style, a blend of Russian folk elements with western Romantic features, was embodied in two symphonies, symphonic poems, songs, a sonata, concerto and concert pieces for piano.

24. Vladimir Vasilyevich Stasov (1824–1906)—critic and writer on music, friend and promoter of the Mighty Handful (see note 22).

25. Barbizon—French village near Paris, which provided the title and location for a group of landscape painters centred there; they included Théodore Rousseau, Jules Dupré, Narcisse-Virgile Diaz de la Peña, Jean-Baptiste Corot, Charles-François Daubigny, Constant Troyon, and Jean-François Millet (see note 26); their reaction against classical painting, and stress on air and light paved the way towards French impressionist painting.

26. Jean-François Millet (1814–1875)—painter of the Barbizon school (see note 25); famed especially for landscapes and depictions of French peasant life.

27. Léon Gambetta (1832–1882)—politician, Prime Minister, and Foreign Minister of France in 1881–82.

28. Georges Clemenceau (1841–1929)—politician and several times Minister and Prime Minister of France in 1906–9 and 1917–20; radical leader in the 1880s and 1890s.

29. Yulia Fyodorovna Platonova (1841–1892)—Russian singer who made her début at the Mariinsky Theatre in 1863; promoter of music of the New Russian School; left the theatre in 1876 and appeared in concerts of the Russian Musical Society, the Free Music School, and also taught.

30. Alexandra Nikolayevna Molas (*née* Purgold) (1845–1929)—Russian singer and voice teacher; studied under Dargomyzhsky; deeply engaged in the activities of the Mighty Handful; at their evenings, she performed almost all the songs of Mussorgsky, Dargomyzhsky, Rimsky-Korsakov, Balakirev, and Cui, but hardly ever performed in public; organised house concerts for promotion of composers of the New Russian School; active as teacher from the early 1890s; her pianist sister Nadezhda was the wife of Rimsky-Korsakov.

31. César (Tsezar) Antonovich Cui (1835–1918)—Russian composer of French and Lithuanian origins; loyal member of the Mighty Handful (see note 22), although his bland lyricism lacked any strong Russian national features; best represented in songs and piano music, he was a prolific opera composer; *inter alia* completed Dargomyzhsky's *The Stone Guest* and Mussorgsky's *Sorochintsy Fair*.

32. *The Marriage* (*Zhenit'ba*)—unfinished work by Mussorgsky, written in 1868 to a text by Gogol as a "dialogue opera" on the pattern of Dargomyzhsky's *The Stone Guest*; it related to the Mighty Handful idea of exploiting melodic recitative without any truly musical dramatic development.

33. Alexander Konstantinovich Glazunov (1865–1936)—composer, pupil of Rimsky-Korsakov; professor and later director of St. Petersburg Conservatoire; emigrated after the 1917 revolution and died in France; though associated with Mighty Handful nationalists, he wrote in mainly "cosmopolitan" style and lacked authentic originality; his massive output included choral and instrumental work, songs, seven string quartets, eight symphonies, six orchestral suites, serenades, and several instrumental concerti; he also assisted Rimsky-Korsakov in completing Borodin's unfinished opera *Prince Igor* (*Knyaz' Igor'*).

34. Anatoly Konstantinovich Lyadov (1855–1914)—composer, conductor, and teacher; pupil of Rimsky-Korsakov, subsequently professor at St. Petersburg Conservatoire; well-known collector of Russian folk-songs; composed songs, piano, choral and orchestral music; best famed for his symphonic poems *Baba Yaga*, *The Enchanted Lake*, *Kikimora*.

35. Georgy Ottonovich Dyutsh (1857–1891)—Russian conductor, teacher, and collector of folk song; conducted the Russian Symphony Concerts and Russian Music Society open concerts, also led the student orchestra of Petersburg University; taught piano and headed the orchestra class of Petersburg Conservatoire.

36. Nikolai Vladimirovich Shcherbachev (1853–?)—pianist and composer, student of Franz Liszt, composed works for orchestra, piano, and songs; close to the Mighty Handful in the 1870s.

37. See also *M.A. Balakirev, Vospominaniya i pis'ma* (Leningrad, 1962), 320–21. There are slight variations between the two sources.

38. Alexander Porfiryevich Borodin (1833–1887)—prominent as composer and organic chemist (Professor at St. Petersburg Academy of Medicine); early stimulated by meeting Balakirev who directed the premiere of his first symphony in 1869; one of the most markedly national composers, drew on Russian folksong and Oriental sources; works included three symphonies, two quartets, songs; the second of two operas, *Prince Igor*, was completed by Rimsky-Korsakov and Glazunov.

39. Felix Mikhailovich Blumenfeld (1863–1931)—pianist, conductor, and composer; 1895–1911—conductor of Mariinsky Theatre; gave first performances of works by Lyadov, Glazunov, Rimsky-Korsakov, et al.; successively professor at conservatories of St. Petersburg, Kiev, and Moscow.

40. Vladimir Nikanorovich Ilyinsky—doctor and friend of Mussorgsky; possessed a pleasant though not powerful baritone voice; first performer of many male operatic roles and songs by Rimsky-Korsakov, Borodin, Mussorgsky, and Cui at concerts in the Mighty Handful circle; invariably accompanied by Mussorgsky, later by Ippolitov-Ivanov.

41. Pierre Lalo (1866–1943)—music critic, son of French composer Édouard Lalo; in 1898 founded musical section of the newspaper *Le Temps*; publisher of collected musical articles, *La Musique* and a book *De Rameau à Ravel: Portraits et Souvenirs* (1947).

II— THE BEGINNING OF A CAREER: Paris 1893–1901

1. Nadezhda Alexeyevna Nevedomskaya-Dyunor (Dunord) (1832–1905)—Russian soprano; studied in Paris with Pauline Viardot, in London with Garcia (fils) and Milan with Lamperti; active as operatic and concert singer in many European capitals, often sang in Moscow and St. Petersburg; much admired by Turgenev, Fyodor Glinka and Apukhtin (who dedicated verse to her).

2. Édouard Colonne (1838–1919)—French violinist and conductor; founder of Concerts Colonne, originally known as "Concerts Nationaux," specialising in French music, particularly Berlioz; conductor of the Paris Opera (1891–1903) and performed in many European countries.

3. Lycée Condorcet—French school based on a five-level system of education devised by the Marquis de Condorcet in 1729; aimed at increasing the range and accessibility of education, the system involved primary and middle school, followed by institut and lycée, leading to the National Society of Arts and Sciences.

4. Bobrishchev-Pushkins—Russian noble family going back to the twelfth century; family members were involved in the Decembrist uprising of 1825;

Nikolai Sergeyevich B-P (1800– 1871) spent the period 1827–56 in exile; Pavel Sergeyevich B-P (1802–1865) spent 1827–56 in hard labour and exile.

5. Louis XII (1462–1515)—King of France from 1498 to 1515.

6. François Villon (1431–?)—great French poet, whose works are filled with realism, vitality and celebration of earthly pleasures; a university graduate, he was also involved with a criminal "Brotherhood of the Coquille" in whose jargon some of his ballades were written.

7. "Coquillards"—mediaeval French brigands, recognised by their neckbands of seashells (*coquilles*), with whom Villon was associated.

8. For example, the sons of participants in the Paris Commune.

9. Henri Clémence von der Welde (1863–1957)—Belgian artist, architect, and leading Art Nouveau designer.

10. Menard d'Orian—music-loving wife of French industrialist who ran a well-known salon in Paris.

11. Julie Vieuxtemps (*née* de la Blanchette)—French voice teacher, pupil of Labord; teacher of Olenina-d'Alheim 1892–96.

12. Gilbert-Louis Dupré (1806–1896)—celebrated French tenor, and composer of eight operas, oratorios, masses, chamber and vocal works; Paris Opera soloist 1837–45; Paris Conservatoire professor 1842–50; author of two books on method: *L'art du chant* and *La mélodie;* founded own singing school 1853.

13. Emma Calvé (1858–1942)—celebrated French dramatic soprano; début in 1882 at Brussels Opera; first major success at La Scala 1890; 1890–1904 performed at Metropolitan Opera and Covent Garden; also worked at Opéra Comique.

14. Opéra Comique—second major opera theatre of Paris after the Grand Opéra, first founded 1714; specialised in production of "opéra comique" with dialogue in addition to music (the original versions of Gounod's *Faust* and Bizet's *Carmen* also combined dialogue and music); in the twentieth century produced Debussy's *Pelléas et Mélisande* and Ravel's *L'heure espagnole* after their rejection by the Grand Opéra.

15. Pessard and Chaminade—French composers best known for their salon pieces. Émile-Louis-Fortune Pessard (1843–1917)—pre-Impressionist author of popular piano and vocal pieces; professor at Paris Conservatoire from 1881. Cécile Chaminade (1857–1944)—composer and pianist, pupil of Godard; frequent performer in Britain; composer of salon pieces with evocative titles that have recently enjoyed a certain revival.

16. Olenina continuously uses the word *konferentsiya* in Russian. An obvious Gallicism, it renders the French word *conférence*, in the sense of "lecture, talk." We have retained the original French word *conférence* in our own text and in translations from Olenina.

17. Ignacy Jan Paderewski (1860–1941)—Polish pianist, composer and statesman; one of most celebrated pianists of his time; studied in Warsaw; Warsaw Conservatoire professor 1878–84; 1909 director of Warsaw Conservatoire; 1919 nominated Prime Minister of Poland.

18. Pyotr Petrovich Suvchinsky (Pierre Souvchinsky) (1892–1986) —Russo-French litterateur and musicologist; pupil of Felix Blumenfeld and associated with Diaghilev's Paris presentation of *Boris Godunov* in 1908 with Chaliapin in the title role; from 1927 permanent resident of Paris; friend and collaborator with Stravinsky who entrusted him in 1967 with publishing his archives (a project halted by the composer's heirs); co-founder with the linguist Trubetskoi of the "Eurasian" movement (prominent in Russian émigré circles in the 1920s, the movement envisaged Russia's post-revolutionary fate as tragically linked to a general historical mission that combined European and Asian modes of economic and spiritual development; Suvchinsky assisted in production of the journal *Evraziya* [Eurasia]); cultivated contacts with Gorky, Mayakovsky, Roman Jakobson and others in the 1920s; after World War II collaborated with Pierre Boulez in the "Domaine Musical" society; publisher of journal *Russkaya muzyka* and involved in the *Encyclopédie de la musique*; extensive correspondence with musicians including Messaien, Ansermet, Asafyev, Igor Markevich, Olenina-d'Alheim, and writers Michel Butor, Nabokov, Ungaretti, Pasternak, Ehrenburg, et al.

19. Robert Godet and Jules de Brayer, friends of Pyotr d'Alheim and close associates of Debussy; the latter lent Debussy the score of *Boris Godunov* when the work was totally unknown in France.

20. Petrograd—i.e., St. Petersburg, renamed and replacing Germanic forms with Russian following the outbreak of the First World War; it was renamed Leningrad in 1924 in honour of the deceased Bolshevik leader. After the break-up of the Soviet Union in 1991, the original name of St. Petersburg was restored.

21. Pierre d'Alheim, *Moussorgski* (Paris: Mercure de France, 1896) —the first complete biography of Mussorgsky in French.

22. Mercure de France—still extant Paris publishing house, established 1886; producer of monthly journal bearing the same title.

23. Stéphane Mallarmé (1842–1898)—French Symbolist poet.

24. Louise Merci d'Argenteau (1837–1890)—ardent French propagandist of the music of the Mighty Handful; author of a book *César Cui, Étude critique* (1888); spent the last several years of her life in Petersburg as Cui's resident guest. Repin's portrait of her hangs in the Tretyakov Gallery.

25. Anton Grigoryevich Rubinstein (1821–1894)—Russian composer-pianist, studied in Berlin; founded and directed the St. Petersburg Conservatoire; as composer and teacher he followed traditional Western Romantic models, eschewing Russian national tendencies; produced operas, orchestral works, songs, piano solos and concerti, still occasionally performed but lacking strong personal individuality.

26. Mitrofan Petrovich Belyaev (Beliaeff) (1836–1903/04)—propagandist of Russian music; founded the Glinka Prize (1884), Russian Symphony Concerts (1885), Russian Quartet Evenings (1891); established music publishing house in Leipzig (1885); the Belyaev Circle, with close links to the Mighty Handful and headed by Rimsky-Korsakov, met at his house in the 1880s and 1890s.

27. Jean Noté (1859–1922)—Belgian operatic baritone.
28. Dosifei—hero of Mussorgsky's uncompleted opera *Khovanshchina*; in the religious conflicts in Russia of the 1680s, just prior to Peter the Great's reign, Dosifei leads those adhering to the old faith and persuades them to accept death by self-immolation. *Khovanshchina* was first produced in 1886 in Petersburg, edited by Rimsky-Korsakov; a later version, closer to Mussorgsky's conception, was prepared by Shostakovich.
29. Irina Andreyevna Fedosova (1831–1899)—Russian peasant tale-teller and performer of lamentations and epic sagas; achieved some celebrity and performed in major towns of Russia.
30. Les Sables d'Olonne—coastal resort area in the Vendée, on the Bay of Biscay.
31. Ivan Trofimovich Ryabinin (1844–1909)—peasant fisherman, performer of epic songs, who worked with and learned from the peasant artiste Ilya Elustafyev; knew six thousand verses by heart; brought to Petersburg to perform in 1892.
32. Khodynka—site of a catastrophe on 18 May 1896, just outside Moscow, at a gathering of half a million population celebrating the coronation of Nicholas II; inadequate preparation of the site and provisions for crowd control resulted in about two thousand deaths and several thousand injured. The name Khodynka is frequently used to refer to the event, and not just the site of the tragedy.
33. Pinyin Li Hong-Zhang (1823–1901)—Chinese statesman, who did much to assist modernisation of China.
34. Raoul-François-Charles Le Mouton de Boisdefferre (1839–1919) —French major general, chief of staff in 1893; removed from duty as a consequence of the Dreyfus affair (see note 48).
35. The score of *Boris Godunov*—Olenina has in mind Rimsky-Korsakov's 1896 redaction of this, which took many liberties with the work and was later widely condemned for its distortions. Mussorgsky wrote two versions of his opera, one in 1869 and another in 1874. The similarities and differences between the two became a source of much discussion and confusion. Numerous misleadingly "corrected" redactions by several composers and musicologists (by Rimsky in 1896 and 1906–7, Shostakovich in 1940, and David Lloyd-Jones in 1975) randomly combined various scenes from both of Mussorgsky's versions. As a result, audiences worldwide have always seen and heard an altered *Boris Godunov*— never the one conceived by Mussorgsky, who clearly wanted to see his second version used. On this, see: Caryl Emerson and Robert Oldani, *Modest Mussorgsky and Boris Godunov: Myths, Realities, Reconsideration* (Cambridge: Cambridge University Press, 1994).
36. In his later career, Mussorgsky was criticised by other members of the Mighty Handful for ignoring basic compositional canons; Stasov and Balakirev spoke disparagingly of him in correspondence in 1863, and particularly condemned *Boris Godunov*; his personal friend Cui also criticised him; the hostility of the "Handful" led eventually to Mussorgsky's total break with them. See *M.P.*

Musorgsky: K pyatidesyatiletiyu so dnya smerti: 1881–1931. Stat'i i materialy, ed. Yu. Keldysh and V. Yakovlev (Moscow, 1932).

37. Mishenka in the corner—reference to "In the Corner" from Mussorgsky's *The Nursery,* in which the boy Mishenka, placed in the corner as punishment for his pranks, blames it all on the cat.

38. Lev Alexandrovich Tarasevich (1868–1927)—microbiologist, pupil of Pasteur, worked at the Pasteur Institute in Paris 1900–1902; later, in Moscow, he played an important part in serum and vaccine development; the Moscow Institute of Serums and Vaccine Control was later named after him.

   Anna Vasilyevna Tarasevich (*née* Stenbok-Fermor)—singer and close friend of Maria Olenina, actively involved in creation of the House of Song.

39. Louis Welden Hawkins—landscape artist, of English parentage born in Stuttgart, naturalised French citizen. His daughter Jacqueline was a friend of the d'Alheims' daughter Marianna.

40. Charles Henusse—Belgian pianist, professor of Brussels Conservatoire; accompanied Olenina in Belgium, and in Russia in 1910.

41. Pyotr Sergeyevich Olenin (1874–1922)—Russian baritone, cousin of Maria Olenina, sang in Moscow private opera, the Bolshoi Theatre, and Zimin's Opera Theatre; also operatic producer 1915–18 at Bolshoi Theatre, and from 1918 at State Academic Theatre of Opera and Ballet, Petrograd.

42. Émile Verhaeren (1855–1916)—Belgian poet, dramatist and critic, connected with the Symbolist movement.

43. Octave Clauze—music critic of the newspaper *L'art moderne.*

44. Joseph Lambeaux (1852–1908)—Belgian sculptor, creator of the monumental relief "Les Passions humaines" (1889–94).

45. Leopold II (1835–1909)—King of Belgium from 1865.

46. Georges Soudry—French composer of the turn of the century, creator of instrumental chamber music, works for voice and piano; mainly active 1897–1935.

47. Vasily Vasilyevich Bessel (1843–1907)—Russian music publisher; formed firm Bessel and Co. with his brother Ivan in 1869; publisher of almost all the front-ranking Russian composers of the nineteenth and early twentieth century.

48. The Dreyfus affair started in 1894 following the accusation of French army officer Alfred Dreyfus, who was of Jewish origins, of treasonable revelation of military secrets; although an investigation proved the evidence was falsified, two retrials confirmed the verdict against Dreyfus; a national scandal erupted over the corruption of justice and anti-Semitic aspect of the affair, in which Zola's open letter to the President "J'accuse!" was followed by his own imprisonment; Dreyfus was released in 1899 under pressure of public opinion, but only acquitted by appeal court in 1906.

49. Léon Daudet (1868–1942)—son of author Alphonse Daudet, right-wing journalist and publicist.

50. Octave Mirbeau (1850–1917)—French satirical prose writer and dramatist.

51. Henri DeGroux (1867–1930)—Belgian sculptor and lithographer, friend of Verlaine and connected with the symbolistes; made a bust of Debussy in 1909; lived for long periods in France.

52. Semyon Nikolayevich Kruglikov (1851–1910)—Moscow music critic and friend of Rimsky-Korsakov, active promoter of works by the Mighty Handful; contributor to the papers *Sovremennye izvestiya* and *Novosti dnya*.

III— **THE TIME HAS COME TO SING FOR RUSSIA: Russia—1901–1902**

1. Maria Semyonovna Kerzina (c. 1876–1926)—pianist and accompanist, and Arkady Mikhailovich Kerzin (1857–1914)—Moscow lawyer; founders of the Russian Music Lovers' Circle in 1896, whose members included several remarkable Russian singers and pianists, as well as music lovers; rehearsals were usually held in the Kerzins' apartment, and concerts by the Circle normally took place in the hall of the Slavyansky Bazaar; programmes consisted mainly of Russian music, with special attention to Mussorgsky.

2. *Novoe vremya*, a major Russian newspaper published in St. Petersburg, 1868–1917. Initially liberal, under A.S. Suvorin's management in 1876 it became more conservative, and in 1905 became an organ of the extremist right-wing Black Hundreds; in the period in question the music section was headed by the mediocre composer M.M. Ivanov.

3. Mikhail Evgrafovich Saltykov-Shchedrin (1826–1889)—Russia's most celebrated satirical author of the nineteenth century.

4. Evgeny Vasilyevich Bogoslovsky (1874–1941)—pianist and musicologist; graduated from Moscow Conservatoire under N.E. Shishkin and S.I. Taneyev; involved in organising the Moscow Popular Conservatoire (1906), and performed with the Kerzin Circle and House of Song.

5. Paul and Sophie Clemenceau—friends of Olenina, frequented the salon of Menard D'Orian.

6. Felia Vasilyevna Litvin (1861–1936)—world-famous Russian soprano; in the 1890s sang in Moscow, Petersburg, and other European capitals; famed Wagnerian soprano.

7. Presumably Doctor D.P. Makovitsky, Tolstoy's house doctor; his diaries were published in *Literaturnoe nasledstvo* 90 (1979).

8. Alexander Borisovich Goldenweiser (1875–1961)—Russian pianist, composer, teacher; graduated from Moscow Conservatoire under Pabst and Ippolitov-Ivanov (see note 17 in chapter V); for many years director and Rector of Moscow Conservatoire.

9. Wanda Landowska (1877–1959)—Polish harpsichordist and pianist; studied in Warsaw and Berlin; opened school and concert centre near Paris, 1919; lived in New York from 1940; played key role in modern revival of the harpsichord and its repertoire; dedicatee of concerti by de Falla and Poulenc.

10. Nikolai Kazanli (1869–1916)—Russian composer and conductor; pupil of

Rimsky-Korsakov, graduate of Petersburg Conservatoire 1894; from 1897 directed concerts in Munich.

11. Camille Chevillard (1859–1923)—French composer and conductor; assistant conductor (from 1897) and chief conductor (from 1899) of the Concerts Lamoureux; conductor of the Grand Opéra from 1914.

12. Balakirev refers to the modern Western, or Gregorian, calendar, as distinct from the Julian calendar used in Russia till 1918; the Julian calendar ran 12 days behind the Gregorian in the nineteenth century, and 13 days behind in the twentieth.

13. Yuly Genrikh Tsimmerman (Zimmermann) (1851–1923)—music publisher and owner of wind instrument factory; founded a music publishing house in Petersburg (1876) with branches later opened in Moscow, Leipzig, London, and Riga; publisher of Balakirev from 1899.

14. Balakirev presumably refers to Sergei Mikhailovich Lyapunov (1859–1924) whose composing, conducting and pianistic activity was closely linked with the ideas and traditions of the Mighty Handful; professor at Petersburg Conservatoire from 1910.

IV— INTERNATIONAL CAREER: Russia, France, Belgium, England & Switzerland—1903–1908, 1912

1. Camille Bellaigue (1858–1930)—French music critic; from 1885 contributed to *Revue des deux mondes* and *Le Temps*; his article "Un grand musicien réaliste" reprinted in *Dom pesni* was first published in *Revue des deux mondes*, 15 April 1901, 858–89.

2. Michael Calvocoressi (1877–1944)—English music critic and historian, of Greek origins; specialist in Russian music, author of general histories and surveys, and of two monographs on Mussorgsky.

3. Alfred Cortot (1877–1962)—French pianist, conductor, music critic and teacher; born in Switzerland, studied at Paris Conservatoire; founded Société des Festivals Lyriques (1902), Association des Concerts Cortot (1903); from 1905 formed world-famous trio with Thibaud (violin) and Casals (cello); close friend of the d'Alheims, he accompanied Olenina and also invited her participation in his concerts.

4. Darius Milhaud (1892–1974)—French composer of Jewish ancestry, conductor, critic and teacher; studied at Paris Conservatoire under Widor, d'Indy and later Dukas, 1945–62 professor at Paris Conservatoire; member of Les Six; long-term collaborator with poet Paul Claudel, some of which settings were first performed by Olenina; collaboration with Olenina from 1910 to late 1920s; 1940–47 lived in USA.

5. Nadia (Juliette) Boulanger (1887–1977)—French composer and teacher; studied at Paris Conservatoire, where she was later professor; teacher of many prominent musicians; lived in USA during World War Two; prominent in revival of ancient music, esp. Monteverdi.

6. Pablo Casals (1876–1974)—Catalan cellist, conductor, composer; concert soloist since 1898; in trio with Cortot (see note 3) and violinist Thibaud; left Spain 1940 in protest at Franco regime, living in France where he founded a Casals Festival at Prades (French Pyrenees), then (from 1956) in Puerto Rico; famed especially for Bach interpretations, raised status of cello as solo instrument.

7. Emelyan Pugachev (c.1744–1775)—Russian Cossack soldier who in 1773 proclaimed himself as Peter III, Catherine the Great's dead husband, and organized widespread rebellion in the south of Russia, promising his followers freedom and property; eventually defeated near Tsaritsyn, he was brought in a cage to Moscow and executed.

8. *Kadet*—the Kadet, or Constitutional Democrat (i.e., liberal) Party in pre-Revolutionary Russia.

9. Pavel Alexandrovich Lamm (1882–1951)—Russian musicologist and pianist; graduated from Moscow Conservatoire as pianist (1912); famed for his work on Mussorgsky's legacy, Mussorgsky scholar and biographer; edited the (unfinished) complete collec-tion of Mussorgsky's compositions; worked on reconstructing the original score of *Boris Godunov*; accompanist of Olenina in House of Song concerts; close friend of Prokofiev and Shostakovich.

10. Osip Afanasyevich Petrov (1807–1878)—Russian bass; from 1830 sang in Petersburg (later Mariinsky) Opera Theatre; first interpreter of many roles: Ivan Susanin, Ruslan, Varlaam, etc.

11. Ivan Alexandrovich Melnikov (1832–1906)—Russian baritone, soloist and producer at Mariinsky Theatre; first interpreter of roles of Boris, Igor, the Demon, etc.

12. Fyodor Ignatyevich Stravinsky (1843–1902)—Russian bass, father of composer Igor Stravinsky; worked at Mariinsky Theatre from 1876; memorable performer of many Russian and Western operatic roles.

13. Fyodor Avgustovich Stepun (1884–1965)—Russian author, philosopher and literary critic; emigrated 1922, residing in USA and Germany, where he held a personal professorship at Munich University; one of last surviving main figures of Russian Silver Age culture.

14. Fyodor Ivanovich Chaliapin (1873–1938)—the Russian bass made his début in Moscow in 1896; successful in Italian opera and recital, but best known for his Russian operatic roles, especially Boris Godunov; apart from his vocal qualities he was famed for his superb sense of the stage.

15. Yury Sergeyevich Sakhnovsky (1886–1930)—Russian composer and critic; studied in Moscow under Arensky, Taneyev, and Ippolitov-Ivanov; music critic with newspaper *Kur'er* 1900–1903, and *Russkaya pravda* from 1904. Compiler of Musical Dictionary with Engel, Riemann, et al.

16. Yuly Dmitrievich Engel (1868–1927)—Russian Jewish musicologist, very active in Russian musical life as a music reviewer and critic; collector of Jewish folk music; 1922–24 resided in Berlin where he opened a Jewish music publishing concern and brought out a three-volume edition of songs; emigrated to Palestine in 1924.

17. Sergei Mikhailovich Solovyov (1885–1942)—Russian Symbolist poet, translator and philologist; nephew of philosopher Vladimir Solovyov; second cousin of poet Alexander Blok, and also related to the Olenin family; on returning to Russia Olenina lived with her niece Tatyana Alexeyevna who was first wife of S.M.S.

18. Doda Conrad (1905–1998)—French chamber singer (baritone) and artist of Polish origin; his mother Maria Freund was a long-term friend of the d'Alheims; he himself knew Olenina closely in his youth.

19. Alexander Tikhonovich Grechaninov (1864–1956)—Russian composer, pupil of Rimsky-Korsakov; works include five symphonies, orchestral and choral (including liturgical) music, quartets, chamber works, songs, piano music; emigrated after the Revolution, lived first in Paris and settled in New York in 1941.

20. Andrei Bely (real name Boris Nikolayevich Bugaev) (1880–1934) —poet, novelist, critic, theoretician, and leading exponent of Russian Symbolism; influenced by Vladimir Solovyov (see note 21), he viewed contemporary art, culture and history with apocalyptic forebodings as part of a prelude to a new spiritual apotheosis that would unite all conflicting principles; deeply involved in personal and sectarian disputes that split the Symbolist movement, he left and spent several years in Western Europe as a follower of Rudolf Steiner (see note 23); his apocalyptic euphoria after the 1917 Revolution was short-lived and, although still productive, he found himself increasingly marginalised from Soviet literature.

21. Vladimir Sergeyevich Solovyov (1853–1900)—poet, author, teacher and religious eschatological philosopher who had a profound influence on the thought and literary culture of his time, especially the Russian Symbolist writers such as Bely, Blok, Vyacheslav Ivanov and Merezhkovsky.

22. Artur Nikisch (1855–1922)—German-Hungarian conductor; at various times chief conductor of Boston Symphony Orchestra, Budapest Royal Opera, Leipzig Gewandhaus and Berlin Philharmonic Orchestra; one of the finest conductors of his day, particularly of works by Tchaikovsky, Bruckner and German Romantics.

23. Rudolf Steiner (1861–1925)—German philosopher and anthroposophist founder, established centre in Dornach (Switzerland) for study and propagation of anthroposophy; exercised influence on many artists and writers, including Andrei Bely and Mikhail Chekhov (see note 24)

24. Mikhail Alexandrovich Chekhov (1891–1955)—Russian actor and producer, nephew of Anton Chekhov; from 1913 worked in Moscow Arts Theatre, and was artistic director 1924–27; emigrated to the West in 1928. On Steiner's influence on M. Chekhov see: *Vospominaniya i pis'ma* (Moscow, 1986).

25. Zoya Petrovna Lody (1886–1957)—Russian chamber singer (soprano) and teacher; studied at Petersburg Conservatoire, later in Milan; appearances in Moscow and Petersburg from 1912; her initiative established chamber singing classes in all Soviet conservatoires.

Anatoly Leonidovich Dolivo (1893–1965)—Russian chamber singer (bass) and voice teacher.

Georgy Pavlovich Vinogradov (1908–1980)—Russian chamber singer (tenor), pupil of N.G. Raisky; many radio performances.

Nina Lvovna Dorliak (1908–1998)—Russian chamber singer (soprano) and teacher; studied at Moscow Conservatoire with her mother X.N. Dorliak; Moscow Conservatoire professor from 1947, produced many famous pupils; wife of pianist Svyatoslav Richter.

Viktoria Nikolayevna Ivanova (born 1924)—Russian chamber singer (soprano), soloist of Moscow Philharmonic Society.

Zara Alexandrovna Dolukhanova (born 1918)—Russo-Armenian soprano; from 1939 worked at Erevan Opera Theatre; from 1959 soloist with Moscow Philharmonic Society.

Boris Romanovich Gmyrya (1903–69)—Ukrainian opera and chamber singer (bass); worked at Kiev Opera and Ballet Theatre; frequent chamber concert performances.

26. Re: Gmyrya's performance of *Die Winterreise*, see A. Tumanov, "Zimnii put," *Sovetskaya muzyka* 5 (1965), 73.

27. A phrase from letter of 8 December 1857 from A. Dargomyzhsky to L. Karmalina; see O. Levashova, Yu. Keldysh, A. Kandinsky, *Istoriya russkoi muzyki* (Moscow, 1980), Vol. 1, 533.

28. Galina Alexeyevna Pisarenko (born 1934)—Russian soprano and voice teacher; studied with Nina Dorliak (see note 25); soloist with Moscow Stanislavsky and Nemirovich-Danchenko Musical Theatre, Moscow Conservatoire professor; frequent performances as chamber singer.

Viktor Panteleimonovich Rybinsky (born 1930)—Russian bass; soloist with Moscow Philharmonic Society in 1960s and 1970s; attended master classes with Olenina along with Galina Pisarenko.

V— THE HOUSE OF SONG: Russia & France—1908–1918

1. Grigory Alexeyevich Rachinsky (1859–1939)—literary scholar, translator and philosopher; president of the Moscow Religious and Philosophical Society.

2. Semyon Vladimirovich Lurye (1867–1927)—writer and journalist, contributor to the journal *Russkaya mysl'* 1908–11.

3. T. Khmelnitskaya, "Literaturnoe rozhdenie Andreya Belogo: Vtoraya Dramaticheskaya Simfoniya," *Andrei Bely. Problemy tvorchestva: stat'i, vospominaniya, publikatsii* (Moscow, 1988), 104.

4. Vyacheslav Ivanovich Ivanov (1866–1949)—scholar, critic and poet of the Symbolist movement; believed in the continuity of human culture, ruled over by divine principle; envisaged art as an expression of human striving towards universal community and unification with the divine cosmos; advocated revival of public religious drama, with audience involvement, as a means to this end.

5. Anna Vasilyevna Stenbok—see note 38 to Chapter 2.

6. Maria Freund (1876–1966)—French soprano of Polish extraction; début in Berlin 1903; resident in Paris from 1912; celebrated interpreter of Classical and Romantic music; also associated with first performances of Schoenberg's *Pierrot Lunaire* in Paris and other works by Ravel, Stravinsky, Bloch, Milhaud et al.

7. Davos—popular Swiss mountain health and sports resort.

8. M. Olénine-d'Alheim, *Le legs de Moussorgski* [The Mussorgsky Legacy] (Paris, 1908); Russian edition: *Zavety M.P. Musorgskogo* (transl. V.I. Grechaninova) (1910).

9. *Mimiambi*—oratorio-like work by Greek poet Herodas (fl.3rd century B.C.), translated for the House of Song by Vladimir Nilender; the same concert included scenes from *The Ladies of Syracuse* by Theocritus, and from Shakespeare. The *commedia del arte* Harlequin was a central protagonist in French popular pantomime of the eighteenth and early nineteenth century, and was adapted for the Comédie Française and *comédie bourgeoise* theatre by such authors as Jean-Pierre de Florian (1755–1794), Pierre Marivaux (1688–1763) and Alexis Piron (1689–1773). In the farce *The Corsair-Harlequin* the central character appears in the guise of a buccaneer.

10. Oskar von Riesemann (1880–1934)—German musicologist, studied in Russia 1899–1904 and resided in Russia after 1913.

11. Johann Eccard (1553–1611)—German composer principally of church music, pupil of Lassus.

12. Johann Hermann Schein (1586–1630)—German composer, mainly of choral works in various styles, and of instrumental suites.

13. Albert Soubies (1846–1918)—French music critic, contributed to *Le Soir* and *Revue de l'Art Dramatique*.

14. The opening lines of "Within Four Walls" ("V chetyryokh stenax"), the first item of Mussorgsky's cycle *Sunless*, to words by A. Golenishchev-Kutuzov (1874).

15. *Intermezzo*, composed 1867.

16. Sergei Ivanovich Taneyev (1856–1915)—Russian pianist and composer, studied with Tchaikovsky and Anton Rubinstein; Moscow Conservatoire professor 1880–1906, and director 1885–89; works include symphonies, operas, quartets, chamber music, choral music and songs.

17. Mikhail Mikhailovich Ippolitov-Ivanov (1859–1935)—Russian composer, pupil of Rimsky-Korsakov, professor of Tiflis Conservatoire and later Moscow Conservatoire director; works include operas, orchestral pieces, choral music and songs.

18. Paul Vidal (1863–1938)—French composer and teacher, studied and later taught at Paris Conservatoire; one-time chief conductor of the Paris Opera.

19. Music publishers founded in 1861 by Pyotr Ivanovich Jurgenson (1836–1904).

20. Alexandre Georges (1850–1938)—French composer, studied and later taught at the Paris École Niedermeyer; known mainly for his songs.

21. Durand, now known as Durand & Cie; important French music publishers, established by Marie-August Durand (1830–1909).

22. The folk songs by Ravel were later found and included in his collected works; also published separately as "Four Folk Songs."

23. Gabriel Pierné (1863–1937)—French composer, organist and conductor; studied in Paris under Franck and Massenet; composer of ballets, operas, oratorios, suites, piano and chamber music, and songs.

VI— FORTY YEARS IN EXILE: Paris—1918–1959

1. Platon Mikhailovich Kerzhentsev (1881–1940)—Soviet government and Party official and diplomat; for several years in charge of Soviet media and arts.

2. Joseph Canteloube (1877–1957)—French composer.

3. Florent Schmitt (1870–1958)—French composer, pianist, critic and teacher; pupil of Massenet, Fauré and others; cultivated a French impressionistic style with modernist elements.

4. André Caplet (1878–1925)—French composer and conductor, friend of Debussy, some of whose works he orchestrated.

5. Emma Claude Debussy—wife of composer Debussy; played an important role in the work of Fauré, whose cycle *La bonne chanson* was written under her influence; her son by her first marriage Raoul Barzac was Debussy's pupil; she continued active in musical life after Debussy's death.

6. *Le Ménestrel* (the Minstrel)—musical paper and publishing house; headed in 1883–1916 by Henri-Georges Heugel.

7. Clair Croiza (1882–1946)—French concert and operatic mezzo-soprano; premiered several works, including Debussy's *La demoiselle élue* (1919); dedicatee of songs by Milhaud, Poulenc, Debussy, Fauré and Honegger; taught from 1934 at Paris Conservatoire; her pupils included Gérard Souzay.

8. Paul Claudel (1868–1955)—French poet, dramatist and essayist; his plays served as the basis of Milhaud's opera *Christoph Colombus* and Honegger's *Jeanne d'Arc au bûcher.*

9. Jane Bathori (née Jeanne-Marie Berthier) (1877–1970)—French mezzo-soprano important in promoting Les Six; premiered several works by Debussy, Ravel, Fauré, Roussel, Satie, Milhaud, and others; concert organiser and author of *Sur l'interpretation des mélodies de C. Debussy* (1953).

10. Blair Fairchild (1877–1933)—American composer; studied at Harvard and in Florence (with Giuseppe Buonamici), and Paris (with Widor); author of orchestral, piano and vocal music in pseudo-oriental style.

11. Nikolai Karlovich Medtner (1880–1951)—Russian composer and pianist, emigrated in 1921, and lived in England after 1936; wrote in romantic idiom, mainly works for piano, including three concertos.

12. Anatoly Vasilyevich Lunacharsky (1875–1933)—Soviet state and Party official, author and critic; headed the Commissariat of Education 1917–29.

13. Vladimir Stepun (18 ?–1960)—brother of F.A. Stepun (see note 13 in chapter IV), actor at Moscow Arts Theatre; prison and camp sentence under Stalin.

Yulia Lvovna Stepun—daughter of Lev Tarasevich (see note 38 in chapter II) and Anna Stenbok; lifelong friend of Maria Olenina.

14. Konstantin Nikolayevich Igumnov (1873–1948)—Russian pianist and teacher; student and later professor (from 1899) and Rector (1924–29) of Moscow Conservatoire.

15. Vyacheslav Mikhailovich Molotov (1890–1986)—perennial leading member of the Soviet Communist Party and government. During the 1930s he was Prime Minister and one of Stalin's closest entourage.

16. Leonid Borisovich Krasin (1870–1926)—Soviet Party and government official.

17. Andrei Sergeyevich Bubnov (1884–1940)—Soviet Party and government official, succeeded Lunacharsky as Commissar for Education in 1929; arrested and sentenced in 1938.

18. Maya (Maria) Pavlovna Rolland (née Cuivilliers) (in first marriage: Kudasheva) (1895–1985)—Russian poetess of half-French origins; worked in Gosizdat publishing house in 1920s; secretary (from 1929) and second wife (from 1931) of Romain Rolland; worked as Rolland's assistant, translator, and promoter of his contacts with the USSR.

19. Heinrich Neuhaus (known in Russian as Genrikh Gustavovich Neigauz) (1888–1964)—Russian pianist and teacher of German origins, one of the finest of his age; Moscow Conservatoire professor from 1922.

20. Vladimir Petrovich Potyomkin (1874–1946)—Soviet diplomat, Party and government official; long-term appointment at Soviet Embassy in Paris.

21. Boris Savelyevich Yagolim (1888–1969)—Soviet musicologist and bibliographer; worked in library of Moscow Conservatoire and RSFSR Union of Composers; author of bibliographies and musical calendars.

22. Boris Vasilyevich Asafyev (real name: Igor Glebov) (1884–1949) —leading Russian musicologist and composer, member of the USSR Academy of Sciences; one of founders of modern Russian musicology, his main theoretical work was *Muzykal'naya forma kak protsess* [Musical Form as a Process]; musical works include ballets *The Fountain of Bakhchisarai* and *The Flame of Paris*.

23. Claude Delvincourt (1888–1954)—French composer and director of Paris Conservatoire.

24. In 1946 Olenina visited Asya Turgeneva at Dornach in Switzerland.

25. Ilya Grigoryevich Ehrenburg (1891–1967)—journalist, novelist, poet and memoirist; as *Izvestiya* news correspondent spent long periods in Western Europe in 1920s and 1930s; a doyen of Soviet letters, during the 1950s and 1960s he was known as one of Russia's most enlightened, European-oriented and open-minded litterateurs.

26. Nicolas (Nikolai Leonidovich) Slonimsky (born 1894)—Russo-American musicologist, composer, conductor, pianist and teacher; studied with I. Vengerova, V. Kalafati and M. Shteinberg in Petersburg, and with R. Glière in Kiev; emigrated in 1920 and resident in USA since 1923; founded Boston Chamber Orchestra (1927); editor and compiler of various musical reference

works, including *Baker's Biographical Dictionary of Musicians*, and most recently *Lexicon of Musical Terms* (1989).

27. André Schaeffner (1895–19??)—French musicologist; headed ethnological section of Musée de l'Homme, Paris, 1929–65; president of Société Française de Musicologie 1958–67; author of several monographs ranging from jazz to Stravinsky; French editor of Riemann's Musical Lexicon (1931).

28. Boris de Schloezer (1881–1969)—Russo-French writer and specialist in music; born Vitebsk, studied in Brussels and Paris; known as philosopher and aesthetic theoretician in pre-revolutionary Russia; close friend of Scriabin, whose second wife was Schloezer's sister; emigrated to France (1920); author of monographs on Scriabin, Bach, Stravinsky, et al.

29. Regarding Cortot's collaboration with the Nazis during the occupation of France, Doda Conrad in interview recounted an interesting episode involving his own mother Maria Freund:

> Cortot was the most despicable human being. And he was a Secretary of Fine Arts in the government of Pétain. Yes, officially. But here it is, my mother (we are Jews) [...] was deported—she was living in Paris—and as a Jew she was taken to d'Arcy before being taken to Auschwitz. But she was not taken to Auschwitz, thanks to Cortot. Cortot was making a lot of music with my mother. And when friends of mine went out of their way [trying to save my mother], I was in the American Army in those days. I knew nothing about that. These friends of mine said to me afterwards, "We would not have been able to look at you, if we hadn't done everything to get your mother out of there. And so Cortot and Germain Lubin, a singer who was a pupil of my mother and also a collaborator, they got her out of there and brought her into a Jewish hospital or an old age home, mother was 67 in those days, when she was taken to d'Arcy, and Cortot decided that she was sick. And Cortot swore in front of the Germans that my mother had done more for Germany than anyone because she sang the first after the war in 1920 in German, Schubert and Schumann in German with Cortot. Cortot said that my mother was the greatest propagandist of Germany. So she was put into an old age home of Rothschild. These people taken were still arrested. My mother is the only person whom I heard of who escaped. And she escaped in a way which Marie d'Alheim could have done. My mother was a comedian. I mean she could play. And she decided that she would play as if she were like that. She simply walked out of the place without anything. She had a ... twenty-franc note and an old subway ticket. She walked out of that place in her own clothes at noon when people were having their lunch. She had a letter, an envelope with a name, and she walked out as if she [went with permission]. She said [later] that if somebody had asked me something I would have said that I am putting that into the mail box, which was of course forbidden—to go out in the street. She walked very calmly out and when she reached the first street to the right,

she turned around and started to run. She ran without knowing where, because Paris is a huge city, and she didn't know where she was. She came to a graveyard, to the cemetery. In front of the cemetery there is always a flowershop. She bought a huge bunch of flowers because she thought that one would not suspect somebody who is carrying flowers ran out of prison. She went with her subway ticket and her flowers and she only remembered one address. Of course, she didn't want to go to friends [...] so she went to an accompanist of mine called Irene Aitoff of Russian origin. She had never been there, she knew by chance that address. She rang at the door. [When the door was opened], she said "Happy birthday!" And that girl said, "How did you come here?" She did not know that my mother was arrested. And so my mother settled for the afternoon there and they started telephoning to friends who came there. And that's how my mother has gotten money and clothes. [...] And my mother lived a whole year under an assumed name, she was called Mademoiselle Fournier. And that's why [...] I remember having a discussion with Marie d'Alheim [when she said], "Ce cochon de Cortot." And I said, "Don't speak with me against Cortot." She understood perfectly well because I had a coup de nerf completely for Cortot. (DC, 4–5.)

30. Clo—i.e., Clothilde Bréal (d. 1947), daughter of celebrated linguist Michel Bréal; wife of Romain Rolland until 1901; divorced and became first wife of Cortot in 1902; divorced in 1931.
31. *Ogonyok*—a popular weekly illustrated journal in Soviet Russia.
32. Elena Dmitrievna Stasova (1873–1966)—niece of V.V. Stasov (see note 24 in chapter I), took part in October Revolution 1917, Soviet Party activist.

VII— THE LAST DECADE: Russia—1959–1970

1. Natalya Sergeyevna Solovyova (1915–1995)—theatrical producer and writer, daughter of T.A. Turgeneva and S.M. Solovyov (see note 3 below and note 17 in chapter IV).
2. Olga Sergeyevna Solovyova (born 1916)—actress, younger daughter of T.A. Turgeneva and S.M. Solovyov.
3. Tatyana Alexeyevna Turgeneva (1890–1966)—first married to S.M. Solovyov (see note 17 in chapter IV), niece of Olenina-d'Alheim; second marriage to Gury Gesplovich Ametirov. The Turgenev sisters, Natalya, Anna and Tatyana had been friends of the d'Alheims in Russia and during their residence abroad. Tatyana and artist Anna (Asya) Turgeneva and her husband Andrei Bely visited the d'Alheims near Fontainebleau in 1912, while Bely was at work on the novel *Peterburg*.
4. Ekaterina Alexeyevna Furtseva (1910–1974)—Soviet Minister of Culture during Khrushchev's rule.
5. Harvey Lavan (Van) Cliburn (born 1924)—American pianist, first prize winner in the First International Tchaikovsky Competition, Moscow, 1958.

6. Yma Sumac—American singer, famed for her alleged six-octave range, popular in the 1950s and 1960s, performed pseudo-folkloric Peruvian repertoire; toured the USSR in the 1960s, where a technical fault during one concert demonstrated that she was inaudible without microphone and amplifying equipment!

7. Svyatoslav Teofilovich Richter (1914–1997)—Russian pianist, a leading artist of his age, studied with Neuhaus (see note 19 in chapter VI).

8. The Mussorgsky Competition was first held in the USSR in 1964, and has been held regularly since then.

9. The action of Glinka's *Ivan Susanin* is set in 1612 during the occupation of Russia by Polish forces. In act 4, scene 2, after the Poles try to force Susanin to show them the way to Minin's encampment and then to Moscow, he deliberately leads them astray into dense woodland, where they finally decide to camp for the night. Realising the Poles suspect his deception, Susanin expects to be punished, contemplates his fate and awaits death. When the Poles awake, he defiantly reveals what he has done: "For Russia's sake I went to meet my death!" whereupon he is killed by the infuriated Poles.

10. St. Sophia's Cathedral, Kiev, built in the mid-eleventh century, the main centre of the Orthodox faith in Kievan Rus; famed also for its splendid acoustics created by voice-reflecting niches (*golosniki*) in each of which were placed resonant earthenware vessels.

11. The Gnesin Musical Pedagogical Institute, Moscow (known since 1990 as the Moscow Gnesin Musical Academy) founded by the Gnesin sisters as a music school in 1895; became an institute of musical higher education in 1944; along with Moscow Conservatoire, one of the leading institutions of its type.

12. A. Tumanov, "V gostyakh u sovremennitsy Stasova," *Sovetskaya muzyka* 7 (1964).

13. Vera Yakovlevna Shubina (1909–1989)—pianist and accompanist with the vocal faculty of Moscow Conservatoire and Gnesin Institute in the period 1950–80; regular accompanist of Nina Dorliak.

14. Arbie Orenstein (born 1937)—American musicologist, professor of Queens College, New York State, specialist in the work of Ravel, author of *Maurice Ravel: the Man and the Musician* (1975); *Ravel: lettres, écrits, entretiens* (1978), et al.

15. Edmond-Henri Malherbe (1870–?)—French composer and teacher; his works include several operas and oratorios.

16. The first song of the cycle *Sunless*, "Within four walls" was written by Mussorgsky when he was sharing quarters with the Russian poet Golenishchev-Kutuzov; each of them had his own small room; the image of a "cramped room" in which the hero of the cycle is confined was evidently close to Mussorgsky's musical thought, and it appeared in several of his compositions.

VIII— REFLECTIONS ON A CENTURY OF LIFE

1. Nikolai Nikolayevich Figner (1857–1918)—Russian lyric and dramatic tenor; studied in Russia and Italy; début in Naples 1882; soloist with Mariinsky

Theatre, St. Petersburg 1887–1907, where he was admired by Tchaikovsky; soloist and director of People's House opera company, St. Petersburg 1910–15.

2. Irina Vladimirovna Odoevtseva (1901–1990)—poet, novelist and memoirist; she emigrated in 1923 and lived in France, returning to Russia only in 1987.

3. Nikolai Yakovlevich Myaskovsky (1881–1950)—Russian composer, pupil of Glière, Rimsky-Korsakov and Lyadov; taught at Moscow Conservatoire after 1921; works include 27 symphonies, quartets, songs and piano music; in 1948 he was severely rebuked by Party critics along with Prokofiev, Shostakovich and others for propagating ideologically harmful "unharmonious" music.

4. Maria Veniaminovna Yudina (1899–1970)—one the finest pianists of her generation; in addition to promoting avant-garde compositions, she was also well known for her impromptu "lectures" from the platform during her recitals, which often alluded to religious and other ideologically taboo subjects and frequently caused problems with the Soviet authorities.

Index

About the Author

DR. ALEXANDER N. TUMANOV is Professor Emeritus of Russian with the Department of Modern Languages and Cultural Studies at the University of Alberta. His career has been one of an educator, scholar, and musical performer. He received his Master's of Music in Voice at the Moscow Gnessiny Institute of Music and Ph.D. on comparative studies of language, literature, and music from the University of Toronto. Dr. Tumanov has written extensively on the linguistic and literary aspects of music and text. At present he is Artistic Director of *Cantilena Consort*, a vocal chamber ensemble in Edmonton, Alberta.

About the Translator

DR. CHRISTOPHER BARNES is Professor of Russian and Chairman of the Department of Slavic Languages and Literatures at the University of Toronto. Educated at Cambridge and Moscow State University, he taught for many years at St. Andrews University in Scotland and also worked in the Research Department of Radio Liberty, Munich, before coming to Toronto in 1989. A specialist in modern Russian literature, he has made a particular study of the life and work of Boris Pasternak, and his translations and two-volume biography of this author have become standard works. Known also as broadcaster and lecture-recitalist with a deep interest in Russian musical culture, he is at present working on a monograph on the composer-philosopher-poet Alexander Scriabin.